PRESBYTERIAN WOMEN
IN AMERICA

Contributions to the Study of Religion
Series Editor: Henry W. Bowden

Private Churches and Public Money: Church-Government Fiscal Relations
Paul J. Weber and Dennis A. Gilbert

A Cultural History of Religion in America
James G. Moseley   ◉

Religious Mythology and the Art of War: Comparative Religious Symbolisms of
Military Violence
James A. Aho

Saints, Slaves, and Blacks: The Changing Place of Black People Within
Mormonism
Newell G. Bringhurst

Southern Anglicanism: The Church of England in Colonial South Carolina
S. Charles Bolton

The Cult Experience
Andrew J. Pavlos

Southern Enterprize: The Work of National Evangelical Societies in the
Antebellum South
John W. Kuykendall

Facing the Enlightenment and Pietism: Archibald Alexander and the Founding of
Princeton Theological Seminary
Lefferts A. Loetscher

PRESBYTERIAN WOMEN IN AMERICA

Two Centuries of a Quest for Status

**Lois A. Boyd and
R. Douglas Brackenridge**

A PUBLICATION OF
THE PRESBYTERIAN HISTORICAL SOCIETY
Contributions to the Study of Religion, Number 9

GREENWOOD PRESS
Westport, Connecticut . London, England

Library of Congress Cataloging in Publication Data

Boyd, Lois A.
  Presbyterian women in America.

  (Contributions to the study of religion, ISSN 0196-
7053 ; no. 9. A Publication of the Presbyterian His-
torical Society)
  Bibliography: p.
  Includes index.
  1. Women in the Presbyterian Church—United States
—History. 2. Ordination of women—Presbyterian
Church—History. 3. Presbyterian Church—United States
—History. I. Brackenridge, R. Douglas. II. Title.
III. Series: Contributions to the study of religion ;
no. 9. IV. Series: Contributions to the study of
religion. Publication of the Presbyterian Historical
Society.
BX8935.B68   1983   285'.1'088042   82-15845
ISBN 0-313-23678-X (lib. bdg.)

Copyright © 1983 by The Presbyterian Historical Society

Library of Congress Catalog Card Number: 82-15845
ISBN: 0-313-23678-X
ISSN: 0196-7053

First published in 1983

Greenwood Press
A division of Congressional Information Service, Inc.
88 Post Road West
Westport, Connecticut 06881

Printed in the United States of America

10 9 8 7 6 5 4 3 2 1

The Presbyterian Historical Society in Philadelphia, Pa. has
graciously given permission for the use of material from the
following articles that were originally published in the JOURNAL
OF PRESBYTERIAN HISTORY:

R. Douglas Brackenridge, "Equality for Women? A Case Study in Presbyterian
Polity, 1926-1930," 58:2 (Summer 1980), 142-65.

Lois A. Boyd, "Shall Women Speak? Confrontation in the Church, 1876," 56:4
(Winter 1978), 281-95.

Lois A. Boyd, "Presbyterian Ministers' Wives—A Nineteenth-Century Portrait," 59:1
(Spring 1981), 3-17.

Grateful acknowledgment is given also to the Office of Women, Mission
Board, Presbyterian Church in the United States for the use of a chart
by Janie McGaughey, *On the Crest of the Present*, Board of Women's
Work, Presbyterian Church in the United States, Atlanta, 1961, p. 200.

CONTENTS

SERIES FOREWORD

A prominent theme today in many large denominations is the attempt to achieve greater racial and sexual equality among members. Presbyterians have only recently displayed much sensitivity to equal rights for women in their ranks, and even now this differs in the church's three main branches called northern, southern, and Cumberland for convenient reference. The authors of this volume have investigated every major aspect of Presbyterian denominationalism to uncover the roots of sexual discrimination. They articulate the traditional position, holding sway virtually unchallenged for so many decades, that women should not speak or pray aloud in mixed assemblies. Using materials relevant to both ecclesiastical and cultural contexts, they show how discriminatory prohibitions found supporting arguments in the Bible, in nature, and in a historically conditioned sense of propriety. So women were systematically subordinated in policy as well as excluded from the pulpit, and that standard formed the backdrop against which reformers had to struggle.

In the period between roughly 1870 and 1920 American society was more amenable to reform in women's rights, and Presbyterians reflected that interest too. This was the time when Presbyterian women developed an independent base of power in their own boards founded to support missions and Christian education. Boyd and Brackenridge have utilized masses of archival and documentary material to depict this initial stage of female leadership in the churches. They show how women's groups were eventually incorporated into other boards for administrative efficiency, gaining a symbolically inclusive role but losing a base for autonomous operations. Even after American women could vote in national politics, they were still second-class citizens in Presbyterian churches. Although women constituted fully half of the membership, they could not sit in their church Sessions and could not vote in their church courts. They could send no women to a meeting of the General Assembly, and no women could receive ordination as a minister, although many performed clerical functions as evangelists.

After a period of disinterest, the reform movement rose to new heights by the middle of this century. Boyd and Brackenridge keep us aware of the general cultural milieu related to this question, as well as to specific events in Presbyterian circles that furthered the quest for status. The authors use oral history sources wherever possible to flesh out the contributions of important figures along the way. This massive research provides readers with a balanced account of the stages through which church constitutions evolved to permit ordination of women. By the

1980s women were admitted to Presbyterian courts and pulpits, and the authors show how a century of prior activity made this possible.

However, ordination by itself is not the only objective under study. Boyd and Brackenridge go on to explore the question of full sexual equality as women seek to serve their churches at every level. The authors draw upon the same meticulous research in recent decades as evidenced in earlier chapters. Within the last ten years they note that sexual discrimination is still present in ecclesiastical thought and practice. Indeed, women have made great strides in serving the causes of world mission, church extension, Christian education, and annuities and relief work. But they still face sexist attitudes in theological perspectives, liturgical symbols, and interpretations of biblical teachings. Now that they have been encouraged by some intelligent advances, women want to work in more areas and dedicate themselves fully. They do not want to be relegated tasks like taking committee notes or serving coffee.

As late as 1981 there were only 621 female clergy in a total of 14,502 clergy. This imbalance has held despite the fact that women constitute 57 percent of the membership. Taking the long view, it is clear that Presbyterian women have raised their status considerably, but they are not yet full partners in religious work. Boyd and Brackenridge suggest that the present trend raises questions about the nature of the ministry and the roles different people play to meet church members' needs. Boyd and Brackenridge also suggest further inquiry into the church's educational functions and its continuing outreach in this country and beyond. This thoroughgoing study accomplishes much in a historical context and then points ahead to questions that need thoughtful investigation. For its information about the past, balanced assessment of the present, and realistic anticipation of future developments this volume may well endure as a landmark publication.

PREFACE

This study traces the relation of American Presbyterian women to their denominations for almost two centuries—from 1789 to 1981. Although it focuses on the United Presbyterian Church in the U.S.A. (formerly the Presbyterian Church in the U.S.A.), it attempts to draw in and compare events in the other Presbyterian denominations that share common heritages: the United Presbyterian Church in North America; the Cumberland Presbyterian Church; the Presbyterian Church in the U.S. (southern). That such a history should be compiled indicates a special character to a relationship in which the woman's role has been defined largely by the institution, based on biblical, theological, and cultural interpretations.

During the first century after the General Assembly was established, churchmen relied on traditional interpretations of Scripture that required them to prohibit women from speaking, teaching, and praying aloud in mixed assemblies. From the pulpit and from the courts of the church, leaders acknowledged that they saw women as "religiously inclined" but insisted that the Bible, nature, and propriety demanded that a female be silent, subordinate to the male, and submissive. Suggesting that women use only quiet influence, the church fathers banned them from any elected policy-making or ministerial positions.

Churchmen in the northern and Cumberland denominations relaxed their stance somewhat in the latter part of the nineteenth century. By this time, women throughout the country had formed church-related organizations and were successfully raising money over and beyond regular benevolences. Their programs were directed toward "women's work for women and children," but, especially after the rise of the women's Boards in the 1870s, their influence went far beyond any limited area. Women of the southern denomination (the Presbyterian Church in the U.S.), although active on a local level, were slower to develop a denomination-wide organization. Nevertheless, they too joined their northern sisters in having a great impact on mission and Christian education endeavors. This prompted an adjustment of policies in order to utilize the skills and interests of women.

In attempting to define a role for women during the nineteenth and into the twentieth centuries, church leaders dealt with anomalous situations: Females could not sit on a Session, yet they constituted more than half of the membership of the church; they could not be commissioners to the General Assembly, yet they wielded influence on the national and foreign mission policies of the church through their organizations; they could not be ministers, yet a number taught, preached, and served as evangelists in the mission fields; they had no representation on male governing boards, yet for fifty years they operated national boards of home and foreign missions that surpassed denominational boards in efficiency and economic stability; they were subordinate to males, yet they worked alongside their minister husbands or fellow missionaries in a team ministry; they had no political base in church or society, yet they demonstrated a profound political energy in lobbying at national levels for reform and social justice; they were applauded by the General Assembly for their financial and administrative talents, yet they suffered periodic charges that they were setting up a "parallel church."

Such ambiguities often created a tense relationship, one of competitiveness and even suspicion, although Presbyterian women prided themselves on their loyalty to church policies. Especially in the Presbyterian Church in the U.S.A., this loyalty was put to the test when the denomination reorganized its administrative structure in the 1920s and co-opted women's work into a system projected to work more efficiently for the good of the whole church. For the first time, women had a more inclusive role in the denomination but in the process lost what they realized was a power base without equal. They saw programs and institutions they had formerly controlled moving into a new bureaucracy in which they had limited representation on policy-making councils and no vote in church courts.

Out of this grew a concerted effort by both men and women sympathetic to a concept of equal status for the sexes to get the denomination to change the constitution to allow women's ordination as elders and ministers. Although occurring at different times, this effort was successfully carried through in all Presbyterian churches. After opening the courts and the pulpit to women, the church of the 1960s, 1970s, and 1980s continued its study of the "woman question" in terms of full sexual equality in the church.

One cannot separate women's history from the broader view of Presbyterian history: The role of the minister's wife related directly to the definition of the role of the minister; the acceptance of a national committee of women for home missions related to the struggle to establish an educational system of national mission work as an evangelical necessity; the uncovering of unrest among Presbyterian women related to the more general study of unrest among all members of the church; and the call for ordination of women related directly to the broader question of the nature of the ministry. It is not within the scope of this book to set out this broader context in detail, but our comments are written with such a context in mind.

What also was not possible within our treatment but still needs exploration are interpretive questions concerning the influence of women on particular historical occurrences. For instance, one might analyze the impact of the feminine majority on the character and theology of the mission policies; on the relation of women to the Old School–New School division; on the involvement of women Sabbath school teachers and inspirational writers in curriculum development; and on the effect of women on the social programs of the church. Moreover, because of their unique relationships to denominational history, the contributions of minority women deserve thorough research and documentation. Although ground has been broken in such studies as *The Rise and Decline of the Program of Education for Black Presbyterians of the United Presbyterian Church U.S.A., 1865–1970* by Inez Moore Parker and *Iglesia Presbiteriana: A History of Presbyterians and Mexican Americans in the Southwest* by R. Douglas Brackenridge and Francisco Garcia-Treto, and in articles in journals and periodicals, much remains to be done.

In reconstructing this history, the authors examined primary materials from the Presbyterian Historical Society, the Historical Foundation of the Presbyterian and Reformed Churches at Montreat, the Library of Congress, the libraries of Princeton Theological Seminary and Austin Presbyterian Theological Seminary, and other collections. We took oral histories from women across the country and from men involved in key policy decisions. We have carefully considered secondary sources, including not only the religious women's study materials but also the work being done by secular historians and women's study scholars. We have conscientiously studied this material in our attempt to relate Presbyterian women both to their denomination and to the life-styles and influences surrounding them.

Despite the abundance of primary and secondary sources available to scholars, the study of the role of women in the earlier period is limited by the availability of interpretive materials written by women themselves. Presbyterian women, especially in the nineteenth century, have not left an easily identifiable body of literature. In many instances, we have had to rely on official records, documents, and periodical accounts, which usually reflect either male thought or what women perceived to be the official stance of the church.

Finally, from our research, we took a model of a white, adult, middle-class female active in the life of the church as a unifying identification necessary in such a general overview. That the wealthy and the poor, the minorities, the young, were also vitally important in the development of women's role in the American Presbyterian church is clear; nevertheless, for the purposes of this work, we chose to write within the framework of what seemed to be an "average" churchwoman. We have also chosen not to include specific biographies of the many interesting persons who contributed to the events described here for two reasons: A good deal of such material has been printed in a variety of sources such as denominational histories, women's periodicals, journals, and in privately published documents and is readily available in the collections of the Presbyterian historical archives; and the nature of this work as a topical survey covering two centuries allowed neither the space nor format to include individual life stories of the many important figures who would have needed attention.

What we have attempted to do is to examine the growth of organized work of women, the quest for women's ordination, the development of professional and lay participation of women in church careers, an overview of the role of the Presbyterian women in the southern denomination, and a summary of the contemporary scene.

ACKNOWLEDGMENTS

The authors would like to express their gratitude to the following people:

William B. Miller, manager of the Presbyterian Historical Society, for his unswerving support during this project, and to Jean Miller for her warm hospitality.

Gerald W. Gillette, archivist of the Presbyterian Historical Society, for his advice, assistance, and availability in all phases of our work, and to Louise Gillette for her warm hospitality.

James H. Smylie, editor of the *Presbyterian Journal of History*, for reading parts of the manuscript at various times and for sharing his own vast knowledge of Presbyterian history.

Jerrold L. Brooks, executive director of the Historical Foundation of the Presbyterian and Reformed Churches, Montreat, North Carolina, and Mary G. Lane, librarian, for providing information from this important collection.

The Editorial Committee of the Board of the Presbyterian Historical Society for its consideration of our text.

The support staff of the Presbyterian Historical Society in Philadelphia, every one of whom made the years of research pleasant and rewarding. These staff members are Dorothy Kurtz, Mary Plummer, Jane Ramsay, Nora Robinson, Barbara Roy, Sarah Gangemi, Ed Starzi, Max Kofsky, and various others who over the years aided in our searches.

The librarians of the collections we visited: the Library of Congress, Princeton Theological Seminary Library, Austin Presbyterian Theological Seminary Library, Union Theological Seminary in New York Library, and Trinity University Library.

The Women's Opportunity Giving Fund Committee, who supplied research funds to enable the authors to study as many sources as possible.

Trinity University, who over the years assisted the authors with research funds and released time.

The various individuals who consented to oral interviews and many others who spent a good deal of time gathering information, answering questions, and writing their reminiscences: Lilian Hurt Alexander, Eugene Carson Blake, Barbara Campbell, Lynda Carver, Sarah Cunningham, Eleanor Gregory, Beverly Harrison, Katherine Hawthorne, Rachel Henderlite, Alfreda Hinn, Margaret E. Kuhn, Birdie Lytle, William P. Lytle, Elizabeth McConnell, Mrs. John Milholland, Margaret Shannon Meyers, Margaret Murdoch, Katherine McAfee Parker,

Wilmina Rowland Smith, Sarah Sondstrom, Emily Stickney, Virginia Stieb-Hales, William P. Thompson, Margaret Towner, Kathy Treviño, Elizabeth Verdesi, and various retired missionaries at Westminister Gardens, Duarte, California.

Our colleagues at Trinity University, who advised us on research potentialities and who discussed issues within their areas of expertise: George N. Boyd, Philip Detweiler, Donald E. Everett, and Linda B. Hall.

We are especially thankful for the support and friendship we received from Virginia Olmo Cabello, office manager of Trinity University Press.

A special acknowledgment should go to each of our family members, who participated patiently in this project.

PART ONE
The Organization of Women

1

PIOUS FEMALES:
Ornamental and Useful in the House of God, 1789-1870

As the eighteenth century turned into the nineteenth, some American Protestant women began to concern themselves with activities outside the home related to the program of institutional Christianity. The country's developing cultural, political, and ecclesiastical structures provoked new patterns of social behavior in the young society, including a movement toward organizations devoted to various causes. Females, although limited by disenfranchisement and a prevailing view that they should be subordinate to males, nevertheless shared in the altering life-styles. Many became interested in mission and educational projects and thus made themselves, as one observer noted, "ornamental and useful in the House of God."

Although official documents of the Presbyterian church do not mention women for two decades after the formation of its General Assembly in 1789, clearly some female members were noticeably engaged in promoting various interests. In 1811, the General Assembly first publicly recognized the work of "pious females" in voluntary mission, benevolent, and reform organizations, and in 1817, the commissioners said, "It is among the distinguished glories of the commencement of the nineteenth century, that PIOUS FEMALES are more extensively associated and more actively useful in promoting evangelical and benevolent objects, than in any former period of the world."[1] Such a pronouncement recorded the influence that the religious voluntary association movement in America had on women in the early nineteenth century and foreshadowed the resulting status the female societies would acquire in the denomination.

In the early 1800s, an aggressive evangelic fervor and a modification of the Calvinistic theology of colonial and post-Revolutionary America led Protestant men to band together in associations, usually nonsectarian, devoted to education, publication, missions, colportage, and societal reform. Historians have viewed the establishment of these benevolent, mission, and reform organizations from different perspectives. Some have claimed that it represented a means of social control of society, perpetuated by prominent laymen and clergy who sought to assert their interpretation of proper moral behavior; others have seen it as a religiously motivated drive among this same group toward sharing salvation, spreading the gospel, ministering to the heathen and the needy, all undergirded by the spirit of revivalism and millennialism.[2] Various scholars have seen the Americans as consciously emulating the English, who had formed many organizations.[3] Some have claimed that the post-Revolutionary passion for independence and individualism extended to support for voluntary action that avoided granting powers to the central government, while others have emphasized the interrelationship of voluntary, nonsectarian societies and the rise of American denominationalism.[4]

These suggestions, one or in a combination, pertained directly to the world of the American male—a world in which he controlled public decision making in the church, in the government, and in society in general. Nevertheless, indirectly they were relevant to the motivation for women to organize, for, as men developed their policies and programs, their wives, mothers, and sisters observed and even participated without voice, or vote, in the privacy of their homes. Within a very short time, many women found this supportive activity to be not enough and began female groups in which they could promote projects of their own, initially to aid the poor, the orphaned, and the needy seminarians.

Nineteenth-century feminist Margaret Fuller saw such gatherings as the women's hope for "an animation for her existence commensurate with what she sees enjoyed by men."[5] Others would expand on this view and argue that women's being shut out from participation in major social structures led them to build organizations they themselves could control. Some, however, ignored such interpretations and suggested that women saw great needs in society that they could meet. A female participant in the nineteenth-century mission movement disputed the notion that women organized primarily because they wished to minister to the immigrants or that they shared in national remorse over the treatment of the Indians. She even discounted that it was in response to the command of Jesus to "disciple all nations." Instead she claimed emotional susceptibility to "a *human cry* appealing expressly to woman's tenderness, and it pierced her heart."[6]

The literature of the early societies, limited as it is, revealed such personal motivation. At the same time, Presbyterian women, as well as women of other denominations, apparently felt a compelling responsibility to participate in good deeds so that when Christ returned, they would not be found lax in their obligations and in their obedience. With a decided millennial flavor, they feared that their time for doing good might be short. In 1806, a Presbyterian woman of Guilford, Connecticut, in a letter of frustration to a woman friend about a pastor's opposition to female missionary societies, discussed the need for contributions toward "civilizing and Christianizing the Heathen World." She then ended her letter with this impassioned hope, "O! when shall the happy period arrive when the Lord shall appear in His Glory to build and move in His Church."[7] An observer in 1842, surveying the effect of female societies, claimed that "every reason for undertaking any good work should excite those engaged in it to go forward unto perfection." The observer argued that by growing in grace persons should recognize their obligation to Christ and the worth of immortal souls that demand saving them from the bondage of sin. "Besides," the writer continued, "our time of labouring is fast diminishing; what we do must be done quickly. And our reward, too, is nearer."[8]

Along with religious motivation, the organizations operated within cultural and ecclesiastical influences. Social and political changes in American life demanded a response; urbanization, industrialization, immigration, and the westward movement provided a climate of need; the rise of denominational activities supplied the context. American women saw dramatic alterations occurring in their own life-styles. Although generally limited to the running of the home, they nevertheless were alert to exercise influence. Furthermore, they were on the threshold of opportunities for higher education and professional careers, with such an early work as Mary Wollstonecraft's *The Vindication of the Rights of Women* (1792) foreshadowing the demands for women's rights that would erupt in mid-century. The social changes, along with the "influence of a popular 'romanticist' spirit that stressed feeling," and particularly the resurgence of religious revivals that promoted perfect sanctification, universalism, and millennialism resulted in energetic action.[9]

Those who concentrated attention solely in regular church activities, rather than in revivals, were encouraged by spokesmen of the Presbyterian church, who defined the essential nature of the church as an agency for missions. "The Presbyterian church has, in fact, been always a Missionary Church," wrote Ashbel Green.[10] A woman's mission magazine later in the century indicated the lasting effect of this definition, titling an article, "The Church Fundamentally a Missionary Society and the Individual Christian Essentially a Missionary."[11] This missionary obligation was not optional, and it had to be administered. Since women made up a majority of most congregations, according to commentators of the time, they heard this obligatory duty preached, and since that religious activity provided an appropriate arena outside the home, they responded to the call for action. They gathered to sew and quilt and gather boxes of useful items not only for the missionaries but also for the poor and needy; they walked two by two in immigrant neighborhoods to distribute Bibles and religious tracts; they held bake sales and craft sales to supplement their often meager personal donations for benevolences; they began instructing the "poor and ignorant" in Sunday schools.

These associations fit the image of women's place in society and their duty to God, and gave "comfort to themselves, and light, and direction for others."[12] When Isabella Graham, a pioneer in women's societies, organized the Orphans Society in 1806, she said that women could not bear to see the plight of the homeless in New York, "no melting heart to feel, no redeeming hand to rescue them from a situation so unpromising for mental and moral improvement."[13] This was woman's sphere—the feeling heart, the redeeming hand, the guiding spirit—proffered within the context of Christianity.

In 1811, the same year the General Assembly commented on women's work, Matthew La Rue Perrine, in an address entitled "Women Have a Work to Do in the House of God," supported women's joining together in organizations. Arguing that women ought to receive the approval, encouragement, and assistance of ministers so long as their activity was consistent with female characteristics, he asked, "Who will not delight in the sweet and heavenly work of honouring the weaker vessels, and of endeavouring to make them ornamental and useful in the house of God?"[14] Although Perrine supported a larger role for women, like others he framed it within their culturally defined sphere—that of wife and mother. As the spokesmen addressed this issue, they articulated a role that endured for more than a century: Women's work in any organization should be an extension of their maternal and subordinate nature.

Documents from some female groups indicated that all men did not agree even with this limited involvement. One minister called the societies "ostentatious" and "not serviceable."[15] Isabella Graham described an early association of ladies for the relief of destitute widows and orphans as "feeble in its origin; the jest of most, the ridicule of many, and it met the opposition of not a few. The men could not allow our sex the steadiness and perseverance necessary to establish such an undertaking. But God put *his* seal upon it."[16] Believing despite male reservations that God approved, Protestant women went on to form numerous associations, both large and small, devoted to missions, education, humanitarianism, and reform within a Christian context. In this manner, the "pious females" moved from silent partners to active participants.

The story is told of a dinner party at the home of Deacon John Simpkins and his wife, in Boston in 1802. As guests discussed the importance of providing Bibles and religious books to the poor, someone suggested that it could be done if the "well disposed" would contribute only a cent a week to that goal. One of the guests raised a newly poured glass of wine and said, "I can now forebear drinking this glass of wine, and devote my cent to this good purpose," and they all set their wine aside and gave their cents. The person relating the story added, "If I have been rightly informed, the good woman of the house was appointed to take charge of the money, and to receive what might be sent to her, for this benevolent purpose."[17]

This Boston dinner is said to have inaugurated the Cent Society, one of the early nineteenth-century institutions that came to be identified as a strictly female endeavor. Similar groups carried such names as Female Charitable Society, Female Praying Society, Female Mite Society, and Female Harmony Society. Although many Presbyterian women joined such societies, church historians have had few documents with which to reconstruct particulars on how the various organizations began. Some have assumed that the groups "sprang up spontaneously on the initiative of the women themselves";[18] others have suggested that they were closely related to the male organizations and "conformed to patterns set by men." The "constitutions" of some of the earliest groups strongly support this second theory.[19]

A specific reference in 1817 by the Trustee's Committee of the New Hampshire Missionary Society reminded the "pious females of New Hampshire" that the Cent Societies were instituted to aid the funds of male missionary societies.[20] Even so, the General Assembly of the Presbyterian Church in the U.S.A. recorded in its Minutes that "the Cent Societies are peculiarly their [women's] own."[21] Origination of the cent and mission societies may have been as diverse as their purposes. There is no question, however, that the societies began multiplying in the first few years of the new century and that Presbyterian women in the North and the South became actively engaged early in associational work.

Women's societies reflected a characteristic of the male groups—that members of various denominations would "pool their efforts to meet particular needs."[22] Some female societies organized within a congregation, although even these might invite acquaintances from other churches to join. Some opened their membership to men and some did not. Some even specified membership as open to both married and single women. Various ones met monthly, bimonthly, semiannually, and annually.

A few groups grew out of previously instituted informal and often irregular gatherings in which the women sewed or prayed together. The Female Domestic Missionary Society (1816), Second Presbyterian Church, Philadelphia, for instance, originated from "a few females who were in the habit of meeting at the house of a widow for social prayer."[23] The Foreign Missionary Society of Third Presbyterian Church (ca. 1854), Richmond, Virginia, grew out of a prayer meeting of a band of "elect ladies."[24] Others formally constituted themselves after working on specific projects, as did the Female Harmony Society (1814), Second

Presbyterian Church, Wilmington, Delaware, which became an official group after it opened a Sabbath school and raised funds to provide a day school.[25] Some served societal crises, such as Graham's "Society for the Relief of Poor Widows with Small Children" (1797) that was instituted just before the onset of yellow fever epidemics in 1798 and 1799.[26]

Some groups had the support of their pastors. For instance, one of the first such organizations in Virginia and one of the first in the South, the Female Bible Society of Richmond and Manchester (1817), was organized because of the pastor's interest. Various ministers preached sermons, many of which were published, on behalf of the women's societies. On the other hand, some groups dealt with ministers' and elders' attempts to block the organizations. Defending the associations, Perrine, for one, chastised "wise and good men" who condemned female projects "which have in view the glory of God, the good of souls, the welfare of society and the prosperity of the Church."[27] Those Presbyterian clergymen and elders who encouraged women's benevolence still demanded that females conduct themselves decorously. Church newspapers and journals were by and large supportive. Intermittently the General Assembly of the Presbyterian Church in the U.S.A. praised the women for their benevolent work. Reference to the work of "pious females in communion" who were still devoting themselves to the promotion of all the charities of the day specifically named women's exertions as the most efficient the church enjoyed in 1824.[28]

Nevertheless, many people—men and women—remained skeptical. A Female Cent Society member wrote in a missionary magazine in 1816 that "even some characters of influence, speak against it." She further reported that some women members themselves questioned whether it was right for females to meet together for prayer. The editor tried to assure her that a few females could assemble in private and suggested, "By consulting the ministers of the Presbyterian Church in the United States of America, you will find such societies spoken of with most decided approbation, and even encouraged by the strongest motives."[29] Not all ministers would be so encouraging. Frequently recounted are words attributed to different pastors. Insisting on a minister's presence at the women's meetings, one account says, "No one knows what those women would pray for if left alone."[30] A similar story comes from the Presbyterian Ladies' Missionary Society, Oxford, Pennsylvania, where it was said that Dr. Dickey, the pastor, was advised by his session to be present at every meeting.[31] A third minister allegedly added an adjective when he said, "There's no telling what these *misguided* females would ask for in their prayers."[32]

The women in some societies chose to invite a minister or elder to open and close each meeting with prayer. The Presbyterian Female Benevolent Society of Princeton, New Jersey (1816), went a step further and by its constitution required the society to have a patron, "some respectable gentleman chosen by the society at their annual meetings" to attend meetings and counsel the institution in the execution of its benevolences, while minutes of the Female Domestic Missionary Society of Richmond and Manchester, Virginia (1829), recorded that all meetings were conducted by the pastor.[33]

That the women would act prudently and discreetly was not at all surprising, for clearly Presbyterian women and those of other denominations did not step out of their "sphere" when they joined the societies. Not only were they often timid about assuming leadership, but also the wives and mothers as well as single women seemed generally to defer to the males, accepting responsibility only as educators of the children and guardians of personal morals. This context provided the framework for the societies. Yet, beyond such a passive role, women's maternal and feminine characteristics also led to the development of a professionally oriented group of females who preached, taught, and aided women and children among the increasing population of an expanding country and of the non-Protestant abroad. Women's societies, supportive but unassertive in the denominational hierarchies, thus exemplified one nineteenth-century view of a woman's position: "Let man then, exercise power; woman exert influence."[34]

Activities of these groups—gathering, mending, and boxing useful items for missionaries; sewing collars and "false fronts" for seminarians and helping support these students financially; making quilts for sale; aiding widows and orphans; focusing on the Christian education of children—reflected much about the women's interests. An early Presbyterian women's group, begun in 1803, originally called itself the "Female Society for the Relief of the Poor and Distressed Persons in the Village of Newark"; later its name was changed to the "Female Charitable Society, for the Relief of Poor and Distressed Widows and the Instruction of Poor Children" and then came to be known simply as the "Female Charitable Society." The *Thirteenth Annual Report of the Free Home for Destitute Young Girls*, sponsored by the Woman's Aid Society of New York (Reformed and Presbyterian), used on its cover the quote: "Inasmuch as ye have done it unto the least of these my brethren, ye have done it unto me."[35]

The Presbyterian General Assembly in 1815 requested the females' aid for "indigent students in Theological Seminary,"[36] and in 1818 and 1819 specifically approved woman's work in organizing Sunday schools. As Arthur T. Pierson wrote, "In all education women are God's ordained pioneers as wife, mother, sister, daughter, she holds in the home the sceptre. . . .The plastic clay is in her hands, she sits at the potter's wheel."[37]

Although the early groups emphasized "womanly" interests, little by little they ventured into more aggressive and public interests such as sponsoring missionary preaching tours. The Female Missionary Society of the Western District in Utica, New York (1813), for one, began employing home missionaries and sent the recently converted Charles Finney on a county-wide missionary tour in 1824.[38] As women demonstrated their capacity to raise and handle money efficiently, the cents that the dinner guests at Deacon Simpkins' home thought "would soon amount to a great sum, and do extensive good," did just that.[39] Records show substantial sums being disseminated, not only by the cent societies, but also by all the women's groups. As denominational missionary and educational enterprises broadened, and as the Presbyterian women's groups aligned themselves directly with denominational projects, the boards and agencies became heavily dependent on their financial assistance.

Members raised money by dues, fines, initiation fees, and contributions. For example, the Presbyterian Female Cent Society, Hopewell Presbyterian Church, Bullville, New York (1814), had an initiation fee of 6 cents; dues of 1 cent per week; life membership of $5.00.[40] Being tardy to a meeting or absent without excuse led to a fine. Women in the various groups accepted donations from persons not in the organization and arranged sales of handmade goods. The Presbyterian Female Missionary Society of Alexandria, Pennsylvania, in 1823 reported that "arriving just after a 12 o'clock dinner, they worked until bedtime, making gentlemen's socks, needle books, and pin cushions for sale."[41] The Female Education Society of the Tabb Street Church, Petersburg, Virginia (1822), whose objective was to aid seminarians, raised money originally through the sale of a little silk bag, then pincushions, then works in wax.[42] The Female Bible Association of Ballstown, New York, (1828), directed that the neighborhood be divided into districts for the purpose of soliciting subscriptions and donations.[43] The women of Spencer Presbyterian Church, Spencer, New York, financed extensive repairs to the church, with "chicken pies, suppers, dinners, and fairs—the usual things."[44]

The number of societies increased during the first four decades. An observer writing near the half-century mark about female missionary societies in general, and one Philadelphia group in particular, speculated on the benefits of the associations. The writer claimed not to know what influence the organizations had on women's knowledge of missions nor whether they had affected their piety. "All this may have been exemplified in their Church relations, in the Sabbath School, in the house of mourning, in the obscure lanes, and the neglected garrets of poverty." Even the duties and charms of domestic life may have received a new life, but certainly "the financial benefits could be determined."[45]

As the women sewed together, prayed together, and raised money together, they learned by experience how to administer and finance associations. Speaking of their mission work, a woman commented, "It is sometimes claimed that we (women) are much disposed to talk and not always to talk wisely. We have not always had very great things to talk about; but now we have something worthy our time and trouble."[46]

During the first two decades of the nineteenth century, Presbyterian women formed cent, sewing, praying, or charitable societies. Although the purpose of a majority of the groups touched on "missions" of one sort or another, only a few put the word "missionary" in their associations' names. Widespread use of the term did not begin until the late 1820s, when a rash of missionary societies organized. This probably was in response to the reorganization of the General Assembly's Board of Missions in 1828 that led it to form auxiliaries and to increase subscriptions for the support of the growing number of Presbyterian missionaries.[47] Women, although little considered in the administration of anything other than the home, became a willing group to whom the church turned.

Churchmen had seen what women had done in their cent and mite groups, and by the 1830s openly solicited women's support for denominational projects. For instance, in 1833, the executive committee of the Western Foreign Missionary Society (which in 1837 would become the Old School Board of Foreign Missions) asked Presbyterians, "In our extended connection are there not thousands of *pious females* to whom the moral and social degradation of the heathen (so painfully attested by the condition of wives and mothers and orphan children in those lands) must make a strong appeal?"[48] The Board of Missions' report in 1834 gave in detail a plan and constitution for auxiliary societies, designed either for the entire church or the male part, although it could also be suitable for females.[49]

As the century progressed, Presbyterian ministers supported the administrators' appeals. The ministers themselves were moving through a role change that emerged with the separation of church and state. Their concerns in the nineteenth century were to build churches, increase membership, and develop sources of financial and moral support. With so many females, powerless but not ineffective, on the church membership rolls, the clergy perceived that women could indeed assist in various projects. In fact, the ministers suggested, women had a responsibility to participate because Christianity had given them an "appropriate and noble sphere" that freed them to use their influence in the home and in religion.[50] The clergy particularly suggested that the effort should be "woman's work for woman," a phrase that became the keynote for the Presbyterian women's mission endeavors. According to E. P. Rogers, Presbyterian pastor, "Is she not under peculiar obligations to that Christianity, which has furnished for her such a sphere, and made it possible for her to secure so noble a destiny?"[51]

The need to establish schools and hospitals, seen as crucial in home and foreign missions, was identified as a particularly appropriate field for women's support. Influential board members, ministers, and missionaries sought women's financial aid by appealing to their concern for the educational and medical needs of women and children. One declaimer asked women to decide "whether we shall be a nation of refined and high minded Christians, or whether, rejecting the civilities of life, and throwing off the restraints of morality and piety, we shall become a fierce race of semi-barbarians, before whom neither order, nor honor, nor chastity can stand."[52] Hearing their responsibility put in such terms, and listening to visiting missionaries or their agents speak about the needs of the "heathen" and the "savages" and the "ungodly," many Presbyterian women enthusiastically and willingly put their energies into the mission cause.

Initially the mission-oriented women responded by providing funds and goods for use by specific missionaries and missionary wives whom each group sponsored. They packed boxes—the famous boxes and barrels of the nineteenth century—that clothed and provided supplies for the field workers and their families. By mid-century, the Board of Missions asked that the women send all boxes to a central receiving office so that they could be distributed systematically and fairly among the missionaries.[53] When denominational officers reminded the women that the missionaries also needed money, some groups raised funds particularly designated for distribution of Bibles and tracts. Other associations guaranteed a certain sum each year to a particular missionary. The boxes, however, consistently provided the largest contribution. Through good and bad years, through affluence and depressions, through war and peace, women filled the boxes with shirts, gloves, stockings, nightclothes, seeds, needles, candles, rugs, quilts, and other such items. Some carefully made sure the boxes should not reflect "charity." For instance, the Female Praying Society members of the Presbyterian Church in Catskill, New York, refused to wash the nightshirts and unbleached muslin as was the custom, "so the missionary might not feel he was getting second-hand things."[54] Letters from missionaries indicated gratitude and dependence on the boxes and asked for the continuation of such gifts.[55]

Churchwomen gained recognition from time to time for their efforts, although appreciation was not unanimous. Elizabeth Cady Stanton, raised in the Presbyterian faith, recalled how she headed an association of young women in her family's church to raise money to send a man to seminary. Their beneficiary later preached a sermon in the Johnstown, New York, church on woman's inferiority. "As he began his discourse, his patrons, dressed in their Sunday best and seated in the first row of the church, silently rose and marched from the church in protest, with

Elizabeth Cady leading them out."[56] Other groups found that the theological students they supported voted against females' speaking and wrote tracts on the biblical passages involved, reflecting the training they received in the denomination's teaching institutions.

On the other hand, a few novels and articles hinted at competitiveness and pridefulness among some of the women themselves. A particularly caustic description of a Ladies' Aid Society appeared in Eleanor Porter's novel *Pollyanna,* the story of a little girl who spent her young years depending on articles from missionary barrels. She had devised a "glad game" to mask her disappointment when the barrels' contents did not match her needs or desires. The orphaned Pollyanna was taken in by her aunt, and soon thereafter the girl attempted to get some aid for a poor boy in town from the churchwomen's group. They voted instead to send all their money to educate boys in India on the grounds they would get no credit for local donations. "It sounded almost if they did not care at all what their money *did,*" thought Pollyanna, "so long as the sum opposite the name of their society in a certain 'report' 'headed the list.' "[57]

Perhaps one of the most candid and explicit criticisms came from an anonymous minister's wife writing in the *Atlantic Monthly*. She admitted that, having been connected with many women's organizations, she felt that most of the societies "exist in order to hold meetings." "Finger occupations," such as sewing and packing missionary boxes, dominated activities, but "any effort to remove the causes of poverty and suffering,—like temperance work or sociological reform—this kind of 'Ladies Aid' I have never seen." The aims of benevolences of churches, she argued, was "palliative, not curative."

Speaking of the work for missions, she believed that the enormous contributions represented the intense interest of a few individuals who were always women. She suggested that the well-organized Boards where a woman may hold office "and even speak at its public meetings, without danger of social ostracism, as in temperance work" fostered denominationalism, and that "I often think that our officers enjoy their little arena."[58] Prohibited from taking part in the leadership or ministry of the church, Presbyterian women clearly built groups that they themselves could control. As they became more sophisticated in their administration and handling of large sums of money, the officers assumed substantial power. The abolition cause, the women's rights movement, and the temperance movement influenced women's life-views;[59] certainly the Civil War was pivotal in their performing traditional male roles.

Frank Ellinwood, Secretary of the Board of Foreign Missions, for one, considered that Christian women of America learned their power of organization and effective effort in "the hospital and sanitary operations of our Civil War."[60] An unnamed writer in *The Presbyterian* of 1863 recognized women's work during the war to be something the church would reckon with in the future. Acknowledging that some men "have sneered or scolded," he or she claimed that honorable men had commended "the care, kindness, and constancy with which the necessary tasks had been accomplished." The writer argued for allowing women to work for the church. "We know that it already exists, and that its influence is felt in every department of the Church's operations." But this person wanted to see more participation by women and called for "the effective ministry of woman, guided by the authorities of the Church, and consecrated to the relief of the wretched, and the succour of the fallen."[61]

A book on pastoral theology written by a Presbyterian minister confirmed the usefulness of women to the minister. He suggested women join in prayer meetings; form pastors' aid associations to encourage membership and attendance; visit the aged, sick, and poor; and join together in benevolent work. "Women have the piety, they have the feeling, they have the tact, they more generally have the time, to do such work, and hence they can do it more efficiently than men."[62] A Presbyterian woman in 1883 admitted that American church women were firm in the belief that "silence is woman's part in meetings where there is a mixture of sexes." Nevertheless, she saw some relaxation of this view, because of those ministers who were "willing, as Paul was, to accept and acknowledge their pious women as helpers."[63]

Such views envisioned a somewhat more open attitude to women's potential participation in "ministry," although the terminology still emphasized a limitation based on "the character and position of women." The war, coming as it did in the early years of the women's rights movement and amid the proliferation of reform, humanitarian, and benevolent associations, provided another set of opportunities for females to perform in new and different ways. Experiences in the societies earlier in the century helped prepare them to step in when conditions called for their help. In turn, women's activities during the war would have far-reaching ramifications for their groups in the second half of the century; women gained administrative and technical knowledge, confidence in their stamina and abilities, security in working outside the home, and respect for one another. Consequently, Presbyterian women in the postwar decade developed their own powerful agencies, staffed by women, for the benefit of home and foreign missions. Intertwined with such professionalization of women's organizations would come a move for status in the courts and ministry of the church.[64]

2

CHURCH WOMAN'S DECADE:
Carrying on this Great Work,
1870-1880

Katharine Bennett, the Presbyterian executive whose career began in one century and ended in another, called the years 1870–80 the "Church Woman's Decade."[1] She was referring to an extraordinary commitment by women in postwar America toward the establishment of national and regional denominational societies that supplied funds, supplies, and leadership for the mission fields. Juxtaposed to this effort in the Presbyterian Church in the U.S.A. was controversy over the structure that women's work should take, particularly as it pertained to a division of resources between foreign and home missions. The way this issue was handled during the decade influenced the profile of women's groups in the Presbyterian Church in the U.S.A. and would affect the United Presbyterian Church in North America and the Cumberland churches after they united with the Presbyterian Church in the U.S.A.

The 1870s brought relief from the responsibilities of the war years, allowing Presbyterian women in the North and South to expand their cent, mission, and benevolent societies. Some of the churchwomen undoubtedly participated in secular reform movements of the time, such as temperance and women's suffrage, but those who chose to work within denominational groups dealt primarily with missions. This emphasis led one observer in 1871 to note that the promoters of equal rights talked of the downtrodden position of American women, while the participants in church societies directed their attention to "their less-favored sisters in heathen lands."[2] This observation was not wholly accurate since churchwomen also were concerned with American women and children in need, such as prostitutes, widows, orphans, paupers, and the unchurched of the frontier. What was accurately implied in the statement was that American churchwomen believed that Christianity had awarded them favor and freedom compared to women of other lands and to the non-Christian of America, and they felt a responsibility to share this with others.

Although relaxation of restrictions on women's participation in activities outside the home was not universal among all women by the 1870s, the changes in life-styles because of "modern inventions and improvements" provided empty hours that churchwomen thought needed to be filled with worthwhile endeavors. Annie Wittenmyer, making a plea for women's organizations in the Presbyterian Church, wrote that the devil had set women "to hemming ruffles, and frilling their garments, and frizzing their hair," instead of going out "to overcome sin, and conquer the world to Christ." Claiming women to have superior ability and fitness for benevolent and Christian work, Wittenmyer pointed out that when "the Christian Church, heeding the providential indications of the times, shall recognize them as a part of her working force, and provide ways and means for their employment, and give full scope to their spiritual powers, then, and not until then, may we hope to see the dawn of the millennial glory."[3]

Many similar comments indicated that Presbyterian women of the final decades of the nineteenth century still operated within the heritage of millennial expectations and revivalistic rhetoric, placed continually in the context of "woman's sphere." Breaking away from the pattern of females keeping silent in public, however, the women themselves proclaimed their incentives to be "laborers for God." Reacting to the increasing immigration, Mary E. James, a prominent Presbyterian, said, "What a heritage is given us, Christ is to be King of kings. His people (the Church) are the laborers who are to go forth to battle for Him, and as two-thirds of the church are women, what a large part of the work belongs to us . . . woman is the lever to lift up the nations of the earth."[4]

Officers of the newly organizing groups called the Presbyterian women to action with fervor: "So let woman walk that not one only but thousands and millions may feel the power of a pure womanhood to carry the Lord's purpose of deliverance to our race from eternal death."[5] Leaders assured individuals who gave their time for mission work that "the gracious master holds a crown for all who, by hand, or purse, or pen, or tongue, or prayer help to usher in the day of his glorious appearing."[6] An early leader saw the systematic organization of churchwomen to be a "wonderful revolution, such as history, not romance, can furnish."[7]

Given such rationales, the key issue of the "Church Woman's Decade" rested, then, not on whether women should or should not work through groups; this issue essentially had been settled even though the Presbyterian church formally still took the traditional stand that women should have no voice in church affairs. Rather, the question dealt with the emphasis and organizational structure that women's work should take. Women themselves defined three areas in which they appropriately could serve: foreign missions, home missions, and freedmen's work. They systematically studied the needs of these areas, leading to the establishment early in the 1870s of fairly large boards located in various regions of the country, each with auxiliaries among local churches and judicatories. These boards supported both home and foreign projects, or foreign missions exclusively, with emphasis on foreign work. Later in the decade, as home mission efforts gained prominence and especially when the goals promoted the education of the young, the needs of western America so captured the interest of some Presbyterian women that the focus turned toward the attempt to form a national organization for home missions. Out of this grew the volatile issues of how such an organization would relate to women's work for foreign missions, how it would go about raising additional money for home missions without taking it away from foreign missions, and how it would avoid fostering competition among churchwomen for their allegiance to either foreign or home missions.

The roots of the large denominational women's organizations of the 1870s came from the nonsectarian women's regional societies established during and right after the Civil War. These earlier groups by and large had responded to emotional and impassioned pleas by individual home or foreign missionaries or by those who observed the needs of the missionaries. The best-known group was the Woman's Union Missionary Society of America for Heathen Lands (1861), founded by Sarah R. Doremus, a Presbyterian. Presbyterian women also were instrumental in instituting the Santa Fe Missionary Association in Auburn, New York (1867), and the New Mexico, Arizona, and Colorado Missionary Association in New York (1868), both of which were directed toward educating the "exceptional populations" of western America. Presbyterian and Congregational women began the Woman's Board of Missions of the Interior in Chicago in 1869. Upon the Old School–New School reunion, the Presbyterian women withdrew from this board and organized the Woman's Presbyterian Board of Missions of the Northwest (Chicago) in 1870, originally involved with both home and foreign missions. That same year, the Woman's Foreign Missionary Society of the Presbyterian Church of Philadelphia was founded.

As Presbyterians became more denominationally minded, women broke away from the New Mexico, Arizona, and Colorado Missionary Association in 1870 to form the Ladies' Board of Missions of the Presbyterian Church of New York, auxiliary to the PCUSA General Assembly's Board of Home and Foreign Missions. Led by Julia Graham, in whose home the women had offices until her death and for a time afterward, this Board developed considerable influence and prestige in the denomination. Other PCUSA regional groups that organized in the 1870s included the Woman's Presbyterian Board of Foreign Missions of the Synod of Albany (1871), changed in 1883 to the Woman's Presbyterian Foreign Missionary Society of Northern New York; the Occidental Branch of the Philadelphia Society (1873); and the Woman's Board of Missions of the Southwest (St. Louis, 1877).[8]

These boards were not constituted exactly alike, but their goals and aspirations were the same, matching the stated purpose of the Ladies' Board of New York: supporting female missionaries, teachers, Bible readers; educating scholars in missionary schools; supplying the needs of families of inadequately supported ministers; supplementing the work of the "more formally constituted Boards of our church."[9] The emphasis on support of women and children in the mission field indicated what would be a primary theme in woman's work—woman's work for women and children. This suited the denominational leaders, although any kind of banding together of females still bothered some. The women made little of such opposition. The minutes of the monthly meeting of the Ladies' Board of December 16, 1879, had the cryptic comment: "The frequently expressed opinion of outsiders that our Board had not the sympathy of the New York pastors was spoken of but after some discussion it was decided to take no further action in the matter."[10]

The General Assembly encouraged women to support both foreign and home missions so long as they directed their activities only toward women and children. In 1874, in fact, the Assembly adopted a straightforward resolution that recommended to pastors and elders the formation in all churches "of Women's Mission Circles, in connection with our Home and Foreign Mission Boards, that thus all the Christian women of our Church may be actually interested in the great Missionary cause, to the deepening of their own piety, as well as the enlargement of our evangelistic work."[11] Although a welcome sign of denominational approval for the women, this and other such recommendations kindled a smoldering issue of the "Church Woman's Decade": the competition for support between home and foreign missions.

Since foreign missions had been emphasized in most of the early large groups such as the Ladies' Board of New York and the Woman's Foreign Missionary Society of Philadelphia, the competing claims led to bitter arguments centering on the possible diversion of women's giving from foreign missions. Furthermore, the women working with foreign missions feared that their members would lose zeal if other emphases were introduced, that the women could not handle more demands with enough energy, and that the distinctive character of the groups would be imperiled. The issues got so emotional that women even quibbled over whether the work for foreign missions was responsible for encouraging those trying to organize similar groups for home missions, or whether the work of foreign missions had grown out of the example of the sewing and cent societies devoted to the needs of "domestic missionaries."[12]

The *Annual Report* of the Board of Home Missions in 1874 chastised the women, saying the "same want of harmony which characterized the work among the women last year, has prevailed this year." Charging that the problem was that some wanted to restrict contributions to foreign missions while others wanted to embrace both, the board pointed out, "More men have made up their minds and more women are beginning to perceive, than [sic] an exclusive policy that shuts out Home Missions, is a policy neither wise nor Christian." Women who wanted their groups to support home missions, or even both areas, threatened to leave existing local church societies that donated exclusively to foreign work.

The Committee on Home Missions recommended to the General Assembly of 1875 that each church organize distinct auxiliaries with the work designated for either home or foreign missions. "Such recommendation, without restricting the liberty of the women of each congregation, will express the clear judgment of the Assembly, that home evangelization and the conversion of the heathen are one and the same work of the Lord."[13] The assembly reopened an earlier discussion that Henry Kendall, secretary of the Home Board, and others had had prior to the reunion of the Old School–New School of organizing a denomination-wide Woman's Home Mission Society with auxiliaries in local churches. This Assembly commended such an organization to exist under the advice and counsel of the Board of Home Missions and its officers.[14]

Just after 1875, numerous synods and presbyteries supported the establishment of women's organizations in their judicatories.[15] Because of the diversity and growing number of these groups, the deliverances from the Assembly in 1876 emphasized the need for effective channels of communication between the Boards of Foreign and Home Missions and the various women's organizations, recommending a committee of women in each synod for this purpose.[16] The next year, the Assembly specified that the organizations should find their connection to the Board through the systems of the church—session, presbytery, synod, and General Assembly.[17]

Although aggressively promoting its interests, mainly from dire financial need, the Home Board appeared wary of causing friction between those women organized for or sympathetic toward foreign missions and those interested in home missions. Cornelia W. Martin, founder of the Santa Fe Association and active in organizing Presbyterian auxiliaries to the Ladies' Board, wrote Sheldon Jackson, superintendent of Presbyterian missions in Wyoming, Colorado, New Mexico, Arizona, Montana, Utah, and Alaska, that a committee of five gentlemen were conferring with the Ladies' Board and other associations already organized in connection with the Home Board, on the question of organizing women's home mission societies. "I see that the secretaries [of the Board of Home Missions] wish to avoid any clashing and they proceed with caution which is the part of wisdom."[18]

Many of the societies instituted primarily for home missions became part of a drama being played out by those attempting to effect a basic change in Home Board policy: a change that would recognize the necessity of schools on the frontier and empower the Board to take the already existing mission schools under its care.[19] Principal actors in this drama included Sheldon Jackson and Henry Kendall. Kendall recognized that women had displayed a vital interest in all types of mission work, especially through their missionary boxes, and that a few Presbyterian groups of women, independent of the Home Board, had already organized to establish schools in New Mexico.

One group in particular was the Santa Fe Association, begun at the instigation of Cornelia Martin. Her daughter, who accompanied her military officer husband to New Mexico, wrote to her mother of the need for education and evangelization of the population. Martin organized a group of local women in Auburn, New York, in the summer of 1867, with the group's first project the establishment of a mission school in Santa Fe. The next year, Martin's good friend, Julia Graham, organized a larger group in New York called the New Mexico, Arizona, and Colorado Missionary Association, whose objectives were to learn of the needs, disseminate such information to female members of the churches, and awaken interest in the Home Board's work. This group paid salaries for teachers, sent out reading materials, and purchased property for schools and buildings.[20]

Since the work among the Indians and foreign-speaking populations in the West was placed under foreign missions, this left only the English-speaking communities as "home" territories, although the Board in fact overlapped the Foreign Board in work among the Indians and exceptional populations.[21] Home mission policy was directed primarily toward evangelism and starting churches in the frontier areas, but Jackson for one felt that this was not enough; he saw education to be imperative. Because of a high rate of illiteracy and a large non-English-speaking population, Jackson, with Kendall in agreement, charged that schools were needed as much as churches. Since the Foreign Mission Board chose not to expend funds for such a project, Jackson began a personal promotion among church members. One of the women who became a leader in home mission work described the appeal: "The missionaries sent out by the Home Board, being convinced that multitudes of our exceptional populations would never be reached, except through their children, called loudly for missionary schools."[22]

Jackson himself confirmed this motivation in beginning the entire movement for women's support. "I was sent to the frontier as a young missionary to do missionary work among the Indians, but as I looked over the field I could do little without the aid of a missionary teacher. I wrote Dr. Kendall, then secretary of the Board, that we must have a teacher to go into the homes of the Indians, to gather the children, and to open the way for the minister." He found later that he needed the same when working among the Spanish-speaking population. Kendall was unable to help him, replying that the Board did not have the financial resources to employ missionary teachers, only preachers. Jackson wrote back, "They won't come to hear preachers; send us a teacher." To help supply the teachers, Jackson suggested, "We must have a 'Woman's Society for Home Missions.' "[23]

Jackson hoped that an appeal to help educate children would attract the attention of the women of the church. A biographer of Jackson suggested also that this type of request for assistance elicited support among those who, for the most part, had seen home missions as the work of ordained ministers (i.e., men) "whose independence of female controls and support was to be taken for granted."[24] (Foreign missions were not seen in such terms, for women had been involved for years in the fields abroad as teachers, Bible readers, and medical workers.) Women in home mission groups could thus not only justify their work on behalf of non-Christian women and children but could also support one or more of their sex in professional roles as mission teachers. When Jackson began promoting educational interests through the columns of the *Rocky Mountain Presbyterian* and contacting prominent Presbyterian women by letter and visits, he discovered that his ideas on education indeed were meaningful to them. Furthermore, since he pointed out the needs of the home missionary wives who worked alongside their husbands, Jackson encouraged women to recognize such support to be as important as aid to women workers abroad.[25]

The need for assistance and the general goals of home missions were discussed in letters from Jackson to the interested women and from the women to Jackson. Jackson gave public addresses, wrote articles, persuaded privately, and toured presbyteries. Some women in the eastern and midwestern areas began to organize to aid the work. They raised money and collected items such as hymnbooks, communion services, and furnishings, in addition to packing the missionary boxes. The Ladies' Board of Missions of the Presbyterian Church, New York, carrying on its work in both the home and foreign fields, appropriated a portion of its annual receipts to projects under Jackson's supervision, but not without complications.[26] Julia Graham wrote to Jackson that Cyrus Dickson, co-executive with Kendall of the Home Mission Board, thought the Ladies' Board had not done much for the home work. She thought differently: "At all events, we have done all we could. It is perhaps unfortunate for us that we did not turn our attention exclusively to foreign missions. If we had done so, we should have a much larger receipt to show." With a note of irritation, she continued, "Now when we have lost so much by our adhesion to the HW [home work], that board don't give us any credit for it."[27]

Perhaps because of this type of reaction and because of his own overriding interest in the home field, Jackson inevitably supported the groups who were interested solely in home missions and did not encourage them to become auxiliary to the Ladies' Board, which Jackson saw as turning its interest more toward foreign missions.[28] Jackson not only actively promoted and helped organize local groups but, despite acrimonious and influential opposition, argued for the need of a central organization devoted entirely to the work of home missions. Those antagonistic to such a plan charged that Jackson was attempting to divide and weaken the strength of women's work. A corollary, of course, was that he was seeking to attract funds away from foreign missions. Actually, Jackson encouraged cooperation, not a division of gifts.[29] Nevertheless, the climate was so hostile that one of Jackson's biographers could write, "It is safe to say that in no other undertaking in which he was engaged was he subject to so much misapprehension, reproach, and determined opposition."[30]

Women figured prominently among his most outspoken foes. Emily J. Paxton, who claimed to be the first woman to invite Jackson to come to Pittsburgh and Allegheny to address the women on work in home missions, said that after she had sent notices of his talk to the Presbyterian pastors in those two cities, a committee of Presbyterian women "visited the several pastors and pleaded with them not to make the announcement, claiming that the meeting would injure the woman's foreign mission work."[31]

Evidently many women were concerned that the women's work would be split asunder. One woman wrote to Paxton that the women in New York City "would regret much to have any effort made" to form the proposed organization. "We have so many different Societies connected with our churches that we feel that our Mission work is done more effectually by uniting the two."[32] Another woman disagreed: "Any jealousy between two departments of Christian work seems to me absurd, and wicked."[33] Julia Wright, a popular Christian fiction writer, tried to counter the argument that since the women had begun their work in foreign missions, they had primary responsibilities there. "They tell me, 'The women have a great work on their hands in foreign missions.' Very good; never abate one jot of it; it has taught you how to work unitedly and effectively, and exactly fitted you for this home work."[34] One woman wrote Jackson that it took all her time and strength to work in one organization. "Our Christian working women, I believe they would almost unanimously echo my words when I say 'From more societies and meetings, and organizations and machinery, Good Lord deliver us.' " This woman confided further, "I *know* that we women are not made to carry these loads, and we are out of our sphere when we attempt it."[35]

Various church leaders suggested that the already existing Ladies' Board oversee separate organizations for home and foreign missions. That Board announced in 1874, however, that "there was not enough effective material to make up successful and separate organizations for both Home and Foreign Missions without clashing."[36] Their proposal, instead, was that two months in the fall be set aside by the women of the local churches especially to raise money for home missions, with the money to be sent to the treasury of the Home Board, an idea with which the Assembly agreed and thus designated October and November to be those months.

Kendall and Jackson still were determined to see an organized program for the home work. Support came from women of Iowa, who overtured the General Assembly in 1873 and 1875, and from the Presbyteries of Utah and Colorado, who overtured at various times. Recognizing that many others did not agree and adamant that they did not want to antagonize any of the women's groups already functioning, Kendall and Jackson had to come up with a rationale that would not disturb the definition of woman's sphere and that would not compete with those women dedicated to foreign missions. Particularly sensitive were relations with the influential Ladies' Board. Proud of their record of giving to both the Boards of Home and Foreign Missions, the women of that Board were anxious not to lose their standing in the church nor to disturb their successful organizational structure. Obviously the denominational Boards did not want to alienate these women who had so generously and loyally supported their programs.

At the same time, Kendall and Jackson, seeing women's support as imperative to their program, kept corresponding about their ideas for a central organization. One proposal, unsigned but kept in Jackson's materials, recommended a structure that would set up a Ladies' Board of Secretaries in New York—"say five ladies of good executive ability (not already prominent in other works, if possible) that they may consecrate sufficient time and effort to this special field." These women would be officers under the Home Board and would not constitute a sub-Board. One would be the presiding secretary to work with the Home Board, while others would work with the synods. Each synod would then set up its own board of secretaries, accountable to the Synodical Board. The author specified, "For the successful working of this plan all will depend upon the executive ability and personal consecration of the ladies acting upon the Synodical Boards. They should be prominent ladies, enthusiastic in the work and with means enough to meet the necessary expenses of postage and traveling out of their own pockets."[37]

Kendall invited Jackson to visit synods in major eastern cities in the fall of 1875, not to make a general missionary appeal but to discuss the women's work, the Sabbath-school work, and also to "press home on them this one feature—woman's and children's work for women and children on Home Mission fields." He emphasized that "we must move among the masses, stirring up the women in the city and country in this great work. If we cannot organize as we would we must work as we did last year, only more extensively and more vigorously."[38]

Probably the strongest impetus toward the organization of a central board came in 1877 when the General Assembly officially authorized the Home Board to take charge of school work. Several schools by then had been established and staffed, and the Assembly, in fact, was being asked formally to acknowledge their existence. Overtures from the Presbyteries of Utah and Colorado that year requested that the Board assume direction of the mission schools in those states. Furthermore, Utah urged the Assembly to authorize the commissioning of women teachers and Bible readers for mission schools among exceptional populations.[39] The commissioners, although aware that schools were already operating, were reluctant to approve this policy. After an impassioned plea on the floor of the Assembly from Kendall, however, the commissioners agreed. The General Assembly acknowledged that in the Territories of Utah and New Mexico circumstances necessitated the establishment of secular and religious instruction. "These schools should not be left uncontrolled; and it seems eminently desirable that the [Home] Board control them."[40] Specifying that the teachers be "recommended by the Presbyteries in which they are" and commissioned by the Home Board, the Assembly recommended that "the Board be allowed to sustain such schools by payment of the teachers needed." The final comment was blunt and indicative of the direction that the entire movement for developing mission schools had taken: "It is expected that the funds for such schools will be raised by ladies mainly."[41]

Although the Assembly of 1875 had recommended "the organization of a Woman's Home Missionary Society, with auxiliary societies, under the advice and counsel of the Board of Home Missions, or its officers,"[42] the Assembly of 1877 specified its hesitation to encourage the forming of distinct organizations in each church for the purpose of raising funds for the Home Board, as this would tend to "the undue multiplication of such organizations." However, it encouraged that benevolences be used for the whole world at home as well as abroad.[43] Despite this statement, a group of women meeting concurrently with the General Assembly were "deeply impressed with the urgent necessity of greater activity on the part of the ladies in behalf of Home Missions." With Kendall presiding and Jackson and other missionaries speaking to the women, the theme was expressive of the mood of the project: "woman's work for women in this land."[44]

Despite this display of interest, heavy opposition among churchwomen continued. Probably the most detailed description of the kind of disagreements was contained in a leaflet published by the Woman's Board of Missions of the Interior. Even though that group was aligned with the Congregational Church, the editor of the Presbyterian magazine *Woman's Work for Woman* printed it in its entirety, with a note that it "so well expresses our views on this subject, that we give it to our readers."[45] Questioning whether woman's boards and their auxiliaries, *as organizations*, should undertake the threefold work for freedmen, foreign missions, and home missions, the writer summarized arguments on both sides. To combine these activities into one group would simplify operations, save expenses in office management, broaden the intelligence of the members, increase the number of workers and thus contributions, and "do away with the injustice of concentrating the zeal and efficiency of the female members of the church upon a single object, when other causes have an equal, if not superior, claim."

On the other hand, the joining of pursuits would change the character of the groups and divert the boards from the "one object through which came their existence." The culminating argument, however, declared that woman's work for foreign missions was a work specifically fitted to women, *"and one which they only can do."* Arguing that the women of the so-called heathen world could be reached only by missionaries of their own sex, the writer could not see that women in the United States or the blacks of the South were cut off from hearing the gospel. Granting that there was much that women could do for home missions, she would not agree that *only* women could do it. The practical argument with which the writer ended was that it appeared from experience that by combining two interests the contributions would not increase but would remain approximately the same. Thus, funding would have to be divided three ways, and foreign missions would suffer.[46]

These arguments and others were discussed throughout the Presbyterian Church. Jackson himself put replies to objections that he had heard in a letter to F. E. H. Haines. To the complaint about too many societies, he countered that in the Presbyterian Church women had four auxiliaries for foreign work and three for both foreign and home work and none for just home missions. To the argument that it could cause friction, he suggested that all boards could be of mutual assistance to one another. His justifications for the national society were that its usefulness would be greater with central and national leadership; that the General Assembly had recommended it; that local organizations needed guidance; and that many women wanted it.[47]

Believing so firmly in his ideas, Jackson entreated women leaders in the synodical societies to call a general convention for the formation of a central organization. The women, arguing partially in terms of propriety, were reluctant to assume this responsibility. No doubt they were also wary of stepping forward in the face of the continuing bitter debate over this move. When the women declined, Jackson decided to take the responsibility and, with the assistance of some sympathetic women leaders, managed to get a Women's Home Missionary Convention staged in conjunction with the meeting of the General Assembly at Pittsburgh in 1878.[48]

With Jackson and Kendall in attendance, the interested women met at First Presbyterian Church on May 24, 1878, and selected Mrs. W. A. Herron of Pittsburgh, Pennsylvania, as chairwoman and Emily J. Paxton of Allegheny as secretary. Delegates presented communications and papers that discussed the role of the Ladies' Board of New York, the desires of various synodical groups to have a national organization, and the importance of a central organization to aid home missions. The two questions the women studied were: "1st. Are we ready for Organization? 2nd. Will such an organization conflict with the Woman's Foreign Mission Work?"[49]

The first question indicated anew the context within which many nineteenth-century women viewed themselves. Anxious to participate yet fearful of their abilities and posture, the women expressed throughout the meeting "the prevailing sentiment . . . that it was a great responsibility to organize a 'Home Mission Board.' " Furthermore, it showed the effect that the public debate was having, even on those who wished to do something for home missions. The second question reflected the concern over the appropriateness of competing with the Ladies' Board that had so effectively serviced both home and foreign missions and with other regional organizations devoted to foreign missions.

The question put to vote, "Shall we organize now" was answered in the negative. Choosing a slower and politically more tactful path, the women resolved to appoint a committee to confer with the Ladies' Board and to see if they would agree to devote their organization exclusively to home missions. If that Board did not comply, only then would the same committee be empowered to call a meeting of delegates from different churches to organize a new Board. The committee selected was composed of prominent leaders in church work, including F. E. H. Haines of Elizabeth, New Jersey. Haines, a philanthropic leader in Christian causes, was at that time vice-president of both the Ladies' Board and Woman's Missionary Society of Philadelphia and was president of the Woman's Synodical Society for Foreign Missions in New Jersey.

Haines took an active role, studying the Assembly minutes and preparing for a meeting with representatives of the Ladies' Board on July 11, 1878. After securing proofs of the Report on Home Missions adopted by the 1878 Assembly, she asked Jackson why the Ladies' Board report was appended to it, as if it were an auxiliary of the Home Board.[50] Jackson replied that his impression was that the Home Board recognized the group as a synodical or local board that raised money for home missions. Anxious to keep the interest keen toward a central organization, he reiterated that friction need not occur and emphasized the value of a central organization for existing societies.[51]

Haines' committee met with representatives from the Ladies' Board as scheduled at the Presbyterian Mission House, 23 Centre Street, New York City. Myra Scovel, one of the participants, recalled the meeting in detail. Because of the importance of the occasion, the evening before the meeting several committee members "retired apart to pray for help in a felt time of need." When the group arrived at Mission House the next day, they ". . . entered a large room on the main floor, whose wide open windows admitted not only the glare and heat of a July sun, but such a rumble and clatter as only the meeting of two New York Broadways can possibly produce. . . . The place was so noisy, so public, so utterly undevotional, that one just in from the country involuntarily exclaimed, 'Do you pray here?' "[52]

The group moved to a quieter room in which they met the representatives of the Ladies' Board, one of whom was Julia Graham. The committee proposed that the Ladies' Board become exclusively a Home Mission Board, arguing that this group's experience, reputation among church leaders, and history would make such a concentration effective. To this resolution and petition, "a most tender and appreciative response was made by the President of the Ladies' Board."[53] Graham announced, however, the impossibility of such a radical change in their organization. Instead she proposed that those interested in home work join the Ladies' Board and form branches in states not then connected to the Board. Each synodical group for home missions would be headed by a president, who would become a vice-president of the Ladies' Board. Scovel recalled that the conference was "free and cordial" even though it did not result in the desired organization.[54]

Committee members at this point realized that negotiations or plans of organization could not be drawn up by correspondence or convention of all women interested, but should be pursued by the committee itself. Foreseeing that the proposal was unlikely to be acceptable, this group discussed strategies for a new organization. They knew that any plan would have to go before the churches with the sanction of the General Assembly, the Home Secretaries, and the Board of Home Missions; thus, they decided to submit the matter to the Board of Home Missions before entering upon a final organization.[55] At the same time, they sent Graham's proposition to members of the committee not present. With the situation causing concern and divided loyalties, one woman on the committee wrote Jackson: "As far as I can see the Ladies [Board] consider the proposal made as 'Providential' and whereas they prayed for wisdom, and know that many others prayed, they conclude that what they did must be right. Perhaps it is. However, I think we have in this age got in the habit of talking a great deal of religious balderdash without knowing it."[56]

Reaction to Graham's plan came back negative; thus, the committee sent a brief history of the movement and all formal resolutions to the Board of Home Missions. The Board appointed a committee of seven, of whom the President of the Board was chairman, to consider the subject and soon afterward an "appreciative" response indicated that the Board welcomed the movement. The Board recommended the appointment of a general executive committee that would communicate with the Board of Home Missions. They further recommended that arrangements for a meeting of synodical committees be handled by the Pittsburgh committee with the purpose of organizing a Woman's Executive Committee of Home Missions.[57]

The committee set the meeting for December 12, 1878, at the Bible House in New York. Difficult as it always was to assemble a group of women from various parts of the country, the attendance was chiefly from the Synods of New York and New Jersey. The spirit of the meeting, as Scovel remembered it, "was at once frank and determined, as well as cordial and hopeful. . . . The absorbing thought of the day was not so much who shall have the honored place in carrying on this great work, as how can it best be done."[58] The object of the meeting was accomplished, and the first national Presbyterian woman's organization, the "Woman's Executive Committee of Home Missions" (WEC) came into being that day.

The plans for operation of the committee, drawn up by Haines but influenced by Jackson, specified that the committee should cooperate with the Board of Home Missions and undertake no work without its approval. Its objectives were "to diffuse information, to unify, stipulate and superintend the work of the women throughout the Church for Home Missions in all its branches, including the raising of money for Teachers' salaries, the distribution of 'boxes' and aiding such other objects as may be suggested or approved by the Board of Home Missions."[59]

Serving as an organ of communication between the synodical committees and the Board, the committee would consist of the presidents and secretaries of the synodical committees. Officers would include a president, four vice-presidents, two or more corresponding secretaries, a recording secretary, and treasurer, annually elected. Headquarters would be in New York City. The committee would meet once a month from October 1 to May 31 and would submit an annual report to the Board of Home Missions. Synodical committees had the freedom to carry on their work as approved by their synod. The first set of officers included Mrs. Ashbel Green, president; Julia E. Graham and Mrs. J. B.

Dunn, vice-presidents; F. E. H. Haines, Mrs. A. R. Walsh, corresponding secretaries; Mrs. J. D. Bedle, recording secretary; Mrs. O. E. Boyd, treasurer. Graham, after consultation with the officers of the Ladies' Board, declined the appointment, and Scovel was elected in her place.[60]

A week later, the WEC began its work in a small, dark room that had previously been a storage area in the Board of Home Missions' building. Despite the cramped space, the women immediately began to set plans. One of their first actions was to reiterate that their purpose was not to divert money from foreign missions but to double the giving, and that they did not wish to disturb any boards, societies, or groups already working for home missions. At the first General Assembly meeting after the formation of the Women's Executive Committee, the *Minutes* extolled women's work in both fields, emphatically stating in theory: "There is no conflict. Women loves her own sex, and she is willing to work for her sister, whether on the foreign shore or in the home field, because redemption has been purchased for both, and her work cannot be done, or her responsibility ended, nor her heart-throbbings stilled, till the dark mind of the women on the heathen shore is enlightened, and the careless or neglected one in her own land is made alive, by the grace which brings salvation."[61]

Despite this hopeful note, conflict persisted. This was particularly evident in some of the many letters from women to Sheldon Jackson declining appointment as vice-president or synodical representative to the Women's Executive Committee, citing as reasons "multiplying machinery" and infringement upon giving for foreign work.[62] Furthermore, various regional groups kept home missions as one of their projects. At the Ninth Annual Meeting of the Ladies' Board, held April 21, 1879, the president of the Foreign Board spoke, indicating that he was particularly pleased with the joint work of the Society, that the work of missions was *one*, whether at home or abroad. Approval of the union of home and foreign work from such a source was "particularly gratifying to the Ladies' Board," reads the report.[63]

In 1880, some women in the West, with support from R. W. Patterson, pleaded for the continuance of autonomous organizations, with funds being designated for one or the other of the fields.[64] These persons saw value in the way women's work for foreign missions had been organized, with no ecclesiastical connection or control, and were skeptical of the WEC's connection to the Board of Home Missions, their relationship to the synods, and their endorsement by the General Assembly. They did not share the opinion of the editor of the *St. Louis Evangelist*, who felt that appointed women "go forth with more courage, because not self-elected, but acting by the direction and endorsement of the synod."[65] Those who loved the former voluntary and independent style felt that the WEC would have to prove the efficiency of their method. This the WEC attempted in the period from 1800 to 1923.

During the 1870s, even with the attention given to the conflict between the home and foreign missions work and the establishment of a national organization of women, regional groups expanded their activities at an astounding rate. In foreign missions, PCUSA women continued to work within seven regional societies (six when two Boards in New York united in 1908) until the consolidation of the woman's boards into one united Board in 1920.[66]

The Ladies' Board in 1870 had forty-five auxiliaries in New York City, in New York state, and in Pennsylvania and Ohio. In their first year, they raised some $1,200, which they used to support Bible readers, educate a child, purchase a boat for mission posts in Africa, build a chapel in Persia, help buy property and build a church in Las Vegas, buy a horse and buggy for a missionary in Missouri, and put a new roof on a church.[67] By 1883, when the Ladies' Board voted to support foreign missions exclusively, and took the name the Woman's Board of Foreign Missions of the Presbyterian Church, New York, they represented nineteen presbyterial societies and 497 local societies, with cash receipts over the thirteen years of $296,317.57. The Board was supporting twenty-five missionaries and eighteen schools in the United States and thirty-two foreign missionaries, thirty-eight native teachers and evangelists, and thirty schools in eight foreign fields. A second woman's board in New York State was the Woman's Presbyterian Board of Foreign Missions of the Synod of Albany, begun in 1872. In 1883, its name was changed to the Woman's Presbyterian Foreign Missionary Society of Northern New York. It merged with the Woman's Board of Foreign Missions in New York in 1908.[68]

Another major foreign missionary group was the Woman's Foreign Missionary Society in Philadelphia that served Pennsylvania and adjacent states. Begun in 1870, it was the first such organization to be founded solely for foreign missions. During the first month of its existence, members assumed support of two missionaries in India. Six months later, the number was increased to a dozen.[69] In twelve years, the society raised just over $900,000, with forty-eight presbyterial societies, 1,189 local societies, and 758 children's bands. At its twenty-fifth annual meeting in 1895, receipts for the period totaled more than $2,500,000 and at its fortieth meeting, the sum was more than $5,000,000.[70]

This Society was particularly anxious to take on varied projects, not merely to "support a few women and schools on mission ground."[71] They not only began mission stations and built schools, homes, and hospitals, but they also helped in seeing that printing was done in native languages and aided in type-making for the Bible in the Laotian language. Interested in utilizing the printed word, this society began the popular periodicals, *Woman's Work for Woman* in 1871 and *Children's Work for Children* in 1875, and published a series of *Historical Sketches of Presbyterian Foreign Missions* in 1881. One of the presidents of this society, Margaret E. Hodge, was selected as Executive Secretary of the merged six woman's boards in 1920.

Women were also forming into groups in other parts of the country. In 1870, Chicago Presbyterian women organized the Woman's Presbyterian Board of the Northwest. Originally cooperating with Congregational women in the Woman's Board of the Interior, this group came into being with some organizational functions intact. Beginning with an interest in both home and foreign missions, after one year the group chose to support only the foreign field. By their seventh year, the group had raised nearly $250,000. In 1875, the General Assembly voted to authorize this board to carry on the work of foreign missions in the western part of the country, "using its own methods, independent of other control." By its fortieth anniversary, total receipts had reached nearly $3,000,000.[72]

In the far West, eight women organized in San Francisco as the California Branch of the Philadelphia Woman's Foreign Missionary Society in 1873. The name was later changed to the Occidental Branch and in 1889 to the Woman's Occidental Board of Foreign Missions. This group of women apparently met special problems, with one minister declaring in 1876 that he would not "countenance women doing such things."[73] They also met severe opposition when they attempted to help young Chinese girls brought into California for immoral purposes. Gradually they overcame the hostility and indifference and by their twenty-fifth anniversary had raised considerable money, established the Rescue Home for Chinese Girls, begun schools in major west coast cities and supported fifteen missionaries on the foreign field.

The women in St. Louis, Missouri, encountered no problems from the ministers of their presbytery. Instead, one of them said, "We urge our sisters in the churches, to come together and in every church organize a missionary society and a Sabbath School Band. Let these associations open correspondence with the woman's committee in St. Louis."[74] On April 20, 1877, the Woman's Presbyterian Board of Missions of the Southwest was officially organized, with the intention to work for both home and foreign missions. In ten years, the women more than quadrupled their contributions. In 1882, they relinquished their home work to the WEC and concentrated on foreign missions.

In the Pacific Northwest, the women did not organize until the 1880s. In 1881, a woman's synodical society was formed as the North Pacific Branch of the Woman's Foreign Missionary Society, Philadelphia. A separate group was established to support home missions. In 1887, these two groups united into one, taking the name The North Pacific Woman's Board of Missions of the Presbyterian Church. They, too, were concerned with Chinese women and girls in Portland brought to America for immoral purposes, and they opened a home for these women in addition to sponsoring a missionary in Japan. All of these boards continued to function until the 1920 merger.

Women members of other Presbyterian denominations also became interested in organizing for missions during the 1870s. In the United Presbyterian Church of North America (UPNA), the Women's General Missionary Society (WGMS) became one of the most efficient and best-known women's groups of the nineteenth and twentieth centuries.[75]

Although the UPNA women had formed a few isolated societies, in 1872 the General Assembly asked the women to "exert themselves" and take a greater interest in missions. As a result, interested women met several times to devise a constitution describing women's organizations.[76] In 1875, a formal request for the Assembly's assistance to set up a central organization was made. Sarah F. Hanna, a minister's wife from Washington, Pennsylvania, presented in person a memorial to the 1875 General Assembly requesting that the Assembly sanction the organization of presbyterials and the founding of a General Women's Missionary Society for the support of foreign missions. In these extraordinary circumstances, the first time that a woman had addressed any Presbyterian Assembly, the commissioners answered affirmatively. The Assembly appointed a general committee to organize auxiliaries in all congregations of the church.

The women on the planning committee met in November with some sense of concern over their tasks. Hanna took the lead and recommended that congregational societies be formed first and then presbyterials; ultimately the whole would be united.[77]

The local groups were organized. Since many of the groups were also interested in home missions, the officers decided to broaden the scope to include home as well as foreign missions. Presbyterial societies began to be organized in 1877; by the end of the decade, there were 168 such groups. In May of 1883, James M. Fulton of the Fourth Church of Allegheny brought together some of the women leaders from Pennsylvania churches to discuss the need of a coordinating group. A general meeting of representatives from all of the societies met in the First United Presbyterian Church, Allegheny, and organized a national women's organization. At the first delegated convention, held in Sparta, Illinois, in 1884, the name "The Women's General Missionary Society" was chosen, and a constitution was adopted. Within two years, the WGMS decided to establish a continuing central agency to direct the work. Amid some concern about the propriety of ladies administering a board, the women established the Women's Auxiliary Board. In 1889, a woman participant claimed that the organization had proved its right to exist, and the fears of some who thought it might conflict with the work already done were happily dispelled.[78]

The Board's stated policy was "that this Society take up only such work as relates to women and children. When all the women and children of the world are brought under the transforming power of the Gospel, our work, and the work of all other instrumentalities will be done, for this world will be won for Christ."

This extremely active Board supported numerous projects and promoted membership among groups of women of all ages. Their magazine, *Women's Missionary Magazine,* was founded in 1887. The famous "Thank Offering," suggested by a minister's wife from Springfield, Ohio, brought in much money for missions. The women supported work among the blacks in the South, among American Indians, among mountain people in the southern Appalachian highlands, among the immigrants, and they carried on an extensive foreign mission program. By 1889, the women supported two-thirds of the unmarried foreign missionaries and managed a hospital in India.[79] It continued as a separate board until the merger of the United Church with the Presbyterian Church in the U.S.A. in 1958.

The Cumberland churchwomen formed their Woman's Board in 1880.[80] A missionary and his wife suggested in a letter to W. J. Darby of Evansville, Indiana, that women should be more actively involved in foreign missions. Darby presented the idea to the women in his church, who took it upon themselves to call a convention of women to meet at Evansville on May 25, 1880, at the same time that the General Assembly was meeting. The three-day meeting resulted in the drafting and adoption of a constitution and the selection of members of a Woman's Board of Missions. The women worked fast enough to be able to present the plan to the General Assembly before it adjourned. The Assembly gave it a unanimous vote of approval. Its headquarters were located in Evansville.

The Board was constituted to serve both home and foreign missions. The women found in the first year some conflict, however, for the first annual report to the Assembly said, "The principal objection we meet is a claim for the paramount importance of the home work. This home work, we acknowledge, is essential, and should be accomplished; but it does not follow that the other should be neglected."[81] Consequently, this board generally gave its primary support to foreign missions, although it gave some aid to home missions. Its annual contributions grew from about $2,000 in the first year to about $18,000 at the end of the century. The Board merged into the Presbyterian Church in the U.S.A. organizations when the Cumberland–PCUSA union occurred in 1906.

3

WOMAN'S BOARDS:
A Vital Asset in Nation-Building,
1878-1923

Although Presbyterian women of the late nineteenth and early twentieth centuries were barred from the pulpit and the ruling bodies of the church, they exerted considerable influence through their highly efficient boards for home and foreign missions. Banded together in local, presbyterial, synodical, and national coordinating groups, the women not only promoted expansion of the church's missions but also raised large sums of money apart from their regular contributions to the budgets of the denomination to accomplish it. Reminiscing on fifty years' work for home missions alone, Katharine Bennett defined women's gifts of buildings and services as a "vital asset in nation-building"[1] and certainly "woman's work for women and children" abroad represented a substantial contribution to the missionary endeavor.

Auxiliary to the Assembly's Boards of Home Missions (BHM) and Foreign Missions (BFM), and subject to their direction, the woman's boards influenced major decisions, especially relating to education, health services, and literature distribution in the mission fields, and they administered operations at the stations they supported.[2] As responsibilities increased year by year, so did criticism from some church leaders, who openly suggested that women were seeking to establish a power base separate from the general work of the church.[3] Ironically, the church had by its interpretation of Scripture and dogma forced women into activities segregated by their sex, but some now criticized this very blending. Especially touchy were questions as to whether the woman's boards were encouraging women to contribute a majority of their money to the women's organizations rather than through regular channels to the budget of the church.

Evidence does not substantiate such charges, at least in the general operating principles of the various organizations. Instead, the by-laws and instructions encouraged cooperation with the Assembly's boards and over-and-above giving to women's work. In an "Appreciation" to the Board of Home Missions on May 11, 1915, the officers of the Woman's Board of Home Missions claimed that "Mrs. James brought us up with deference and obedience to the Assembly's Board. 'Loyalty to the Board' was one of her re-iterated maxims, and when her mantle fell upon her associate Mrs. Bennett, the same policy was pursued."

A strongly worded article in *Woman's Work for Woman* in 1883 illustrated such loyalty in financial terms: "Ever since the organization of our woman's society we have declared, both in public and private, that we did not and do not wish our contributions from the women of the Church to interfere in any way with, or take the place of, the regular collections which should be taken in every church for the Foreign Board. In some instances where the fact of this being done has come to our knowledge we have remonstrated, and are ready to do so always." The writer directed the women to decline gifts that should be sent through the regular channels of the church.[4] Women's double-giving had begun with the earliest "cent" societies in which a basic tenet was the sacrifice of a luxury for the spread of the Gospel. Even as the groups grew more sophisticated and much larger, this idea remained intact.

Other criticisms seemed less serious. Frank Ellinwood, in an address to the general meeting of Woman's Missionary Boards in 1885, alluded to some that he had heard: that women's interest was a "fad," that the women were likely to run away with the work and not remain true to the Boards, that the women would forsake their homes, and that the women would become exhausted.[5] All of these were disputed, and women's literature emphasized loyalty to the purposes of the Assembly's boards.

Events of the "Church Woman's Decade" established that the local Presbyterian women's societies chose to support the work either of foreign missions or of home missions. The seven boards for foreign missions (reduced to six in 1908) and the single central organization for home missions were responsible to their respective Assembly boards. To facilitate their projects, in like manner each developed judicatorial and local auxiliaries. These auxiliaries reported to the women's boards through a presbyterial and synodical scheme, and their leaders, in turn, communicated with the parent boards.

Presbyterian women concentrated home missions efforts through the Women's Executive Committee (WEC), the first national women's organization, whose coordinating office was in the same building with the Assembly's Board of Home Missions. The boards for foreign missions chose to maintain their autonomous regionally based groups, identified by the geographical connotations of New York, Philadelphia, Northern New York (Albany), Northwest (Chicago), Southwest (St. Louis), Occidental (San Francisco), and North Pacific (Portland, Oregon). By the early 1880s, these women realized they needed some central office for the exchange of information among themselves and for liaison with the Assembly's Board of Foreign Missions. In 1885, they organized the

Central Committee of Presbyterian Women for Foreign Missions, composed of representatives from each of the boards. Mrs. H. H. Fry of Chicago was elected General Secretary and Treasurer, a salaried position with her headquarters in New York.[6]

Although the Central Committee was only advisory, the women combined the publications of each board into one organ, *Woman's Work for Woman*, with the editor located at Central Committee headquarters. Some women raised the question of uniting the scattered boards into one agency as early as 1894, and others continued to raise the issue periodically, but the leaders decided to strengthen the Central Committee while keeping the autonomy of the various boards. This position was maintained until 1920 when consolidation of the six boards occurred.

Since the agencies for home and foreign missions operated in different forms, this chapter will deal separately with the Woman's Executive Committee for Home Missions, renamed the Woman's Board of Home Missions in 1897, and with women's work for foreign missions. More space is assigned to the WEC simply because it operated as the first national women's organization.

From its inception, the WEC displayed extraordinary organizational skill in promoting contributions, disseminating information on schools, producing new programs, and recruiting missionary personnel. The volunteer officers traveled to the mission stations; wrote letters to missionaries, teachers, and society members; organized auxiliary societies and annual meetings; supplied articles to the *Rocky Mountain Presbyterian (RMP)* and later began their own periodical, the *Home Mission Monthly (HMM)*; coordinated requests and assigned support; recruited and placed teachers; and prompted the building of schools, hospitals, and churches. A female writer in 1890 claimed that *"the genius for organization"* that developed among women had been "a surprise to themselves."[7] The program began in Utah and among the American Indians and expanded to include work among Alaskans, Puerto Ricans, the Spanish-speaking people of the Southwest, the mountain people of the South, the freedmen, and the immigrants in American cities.[8]

That the WEC immediately functioned so efficiently could be attributed to two things. First, the committee had a sizable number of Presbyterian women who were anxious to support home missions and who needed only a central agency with administrative leadership. Second, even though the first sets of officers of the WEC were volunteer and had no professional assistants, they were neither naive about office procedures nor unacquainted with fund-raising and business practices. Furthermore, they were given and accepted advice from Sheldon Jackson, Henry Kendall, and others experienced in home mission work. Spending countless hours working on budgets, communications, and bookkeeping in their attic office at 23 Centre Street in New York, they worked out practical lines of authority that they disseminated to the societies. Contradicting the nineteenth-century idea that women could neither physically nor emotionally handle pressure or physical exertion, they not only kept regular office hours but also traveled throughout the West to visit the mission stations. A president, vice-presidents from the different synods, secretaries, and a treasurer were elected annually by synodical representatives. Advisory committees provided working groups for the transaction of business and preparation of materials.

The early officers continued the philosophy of the local groups that served with sewing and cents. Mrs. Ashbel Green, the first president, and F. E. H. Haines, the corresponding secretary, died within the first decade; nevertheless, they had established a pattern of strong leadership and had considerable influence. This leadership continued with Mary E. (Mrs. Darwin R.) James, who led the WEC throughout the remainder of the nineteenth century and into the twentieth, resigning in 1909.[9] The next president, Katharine Bennett, presided until the dissolution of the Board in 1923.

James, wife of a member of the U.S. House of Representatives, combined devotion to missions with a keen political sense and a sizable number of prominent contacts. Whether dealing with the issue of polygamy or attempting to free Sheldon Jackson after a questionable arrest, James and her officers intervened at the highest levels. In her fight against polygamy, James called on four presidents of the United States.[10] She marshaled women to petition the government on behalf of the starving and poverty-stricken Indians of the West. Other issues in which she was involved were the respect of the Sabbath, the war on alcoholism, and the dissemination of impure literature.[11] James, an assertive and proud leader, turned down an office near the headquarters of the male board members at the 1900 General Assembly, insisting that she stay with her office force. Reporting that she did not care in the least for being where the men were, the secretary wrote, "She does not need any prestige higher than the place she has made for herself, and I fancy the 'big guns' will seek her even if she is not quartered in their midst."[12]

In later years, James reminisced about the early days of unpaid workers, overwork, and financial fears: "I am glad it is all over, and I shall not have the work to do over again." Noting the current Board with its twenty-two paid employees, she wrote, "None but an omniscient one can sum all the labor and care that has been necessary to the present development."[13]

With only the barest of equipment, seven volunteer officers,[14] no salaried staff, and poor office facilities, the WEC collected more than $11,000 and organized twenty-two synodical committees during the first fiscal year, March 1879 to March 1880. The volunteers distributed 30,000 informational circulars and held approximately fifty public meetings, which resulted in more than doubling their receipts during the second year and, in the third year, reaching nearly six times the first year's gifts. By the last decade of the century, the receipts were $345,857.53, and the estimated value of the property administered by women was $750,000. In 1890, the General Assembly noted that the women outcontributed all the Presbyterian churches by $40,000 or more "by the multiplication of small offerings, together with pledged, stated amounts."[15] Observers attributed this financial success to two things: The women's tenacity in securing and collecting pledges; and their encouragement of small gifts, an inheritance from the early philosophy that only 1 cent a week would multiply into sufficient sums to do good.[16]

Equally successful was stress on aiming the program at the individual Presbyterian woman. Using this method, leaders personalized the giving so that local societies knew for what specific purpose their dollars were being used. In the early years, Haines would write, "Would you like to have your $50 spent to benefit the Girls Home at Fort Wrangel, Alaska? We should be glad to apply it to payment for the building, upon which there is quite a debt. It would also pay the scholarship for one year of a girl there."[17] or "Where a society or band cannot raise $75.00 to keep a boy in school a whole year we propose to cut a boy in pieces, and to give parts of him to several bands. . . . Of course, you will explain that we shall 'cut up' only the money to feed, clothe and teach a boy for a full year."[18] The groups could choose projects with names, locations, photographs, and promises of personal visits from teachers and missionaries.

Almost immediately after the WEC's inauguration, societies began asking for assignments. This interest encouraged the WEC to buy school properties, erect new buildings, and repair old edifices, all of which led to increased enrollment and demands for more teachers, books, supplies, and equipment.[19] Within a short time, the WEC was managing ongoing and growing responsibilities. To implement projects, the officers wrote hundreds of letters annually to teachers, missionaries, and local society members. At first, the principal letter writer was Haines, the corresponding secretary. Laboriously writing by hand, she never skimped on words despite the hours it took to compose the letters. Within the decade, the women boldly experimented with "electric pens" and a typewriter some years before the Board of Home Missions did so.[20]

The incoming letters were not always cordial, often containing complaints over delays in financial assistance, discomforts in living conditions, restrictions on the teachers' independence, and general problems of the mission endeavor. Haines tried to soothe the irritable and often exhausted missionaries and teachers, patiently suggesting reasonable solutions. By reading such letters, however pessimistic, and by traveling to the locations themselves, Haines gained a comprehensive view of the needs of the home fields and presented plans and reports to the executive committee for attention.[21]

The centralization of the work for home missions encouraged growth, and by 1883 the WEC reported to the Board of Home Missions that women and children of the Presbyterian church seemed ready to support as many schools as were needed. The Committee at the time employed fifty-seven teachers in Utah, Idaho, Alaska, New Mexico, Indian Territory, Arizona, and Colorado, with five more commissioned. By this same year, the regional boards which combined home and foreign work, including the Ladies' Board of New York, had given up their home work to the WEC.[22] Just three years later, the WEC reported nearly four times the number of teachers: 221 teachers in 110 schools among Indians, Mexicans, Mormons, freedmen, and southern whites.[23]

Along with the other boards and agencies, the WEC's financial situation year to year depended on economic conditions in the country. Panics and depressions forced the leaders in bad years to borrow money or to plan ingenious campaigns for more contributions. Some of these included a centennial fund, decennial fund, memorial fund, self-denial fund, contingent fund, and building fund. Although the WEC tried to plan programs as funds were pledged, it had ongoing and inflexible commitments once teachers were hired and schools built.

The WEC ended the 1884–85 fiscal year with its first deficit of $29,000. Despite this, it responded favorably to the General Assembly's recommendation that the work include a Woman's Department of Work for Freedmen. The secretary of the new department wrote to presbyterial societies setting forth the needs, asking that an explanatory paper or address be given at local programs, and suggesting that each society have a representative to oversee the work. The objectives were to organize schools of secular and religious instruction for the children and to visit women in their houses to teach care for families and how to "make attractive Christian homes." In order to send women missionaries two by two into the area, the WEC solicited funds for their salaries and for the erection of schools.[24]

To insure expanding funds, the officers encouraged new societies and aided existing ones to function efficiently. In a document that educated the women in parliamentary and practical matters, Haines wrote in longhand the details of "How to Organize a Home Missionary Society," even instructing where the presiding officer should sit: "She must take a chair in front, not too far away, and facing the others—The one elected secretary had better have a seat at a table near by—so as to do her writing conveniently"; how to take votes, "ask those present to say 'aye' if they approve of what is proposed: and afterwards asking those opposed to say 'no.' Sometimes a vote is taken by rising and counting the names"; and discouraging more than one person speaking at a time or whispering during the meeting.[25] She then followed up with "How to hold a Home Missionary Meeting," again precisely ordering what the women should do."[26] In 1882 and 1883, she submitted similar advice to synod committees for home missions, this time written in longhand but using the "electric pencil." Haines appended a note saying, "The above is merely suggested as a guide, as regards the organization of a Syn–Society—as approved by the W's Exc. Com[tee] of Home Missions January 1883."[27]

Disseminating such information to local women concerned the officers of the WEC. Although the women had space in the *Rocky Mountain Presbyterian*, by 1886 they began their own publication. The *Home Mission Monthly*, with Mrs. Delos E. Finks as editor, was self-supporting through subscriptions after the first year. During some years, it even had an excess of funds that was turned over to the general treasury. This magazine relieved some letter writing (but not all) and became important to the proliferating societies and growing number of teachers and missionaries.[28] The women used the pages of the *Home Mission Monthly* for suggestions for organizing and conducting mission groups. In the first volume, a woman successful in organizing small groups encouraged members to hold meetings in the home so as to include younger members of the household. At the meeting, the participants were to sing hymns, pray, recite scripture, sew on mission projects, and hear chairmen report on mission boxes, mission papers, and business matters. Refreshments could be a cup of tea or coffee, a piece of bread and butter, a slice of cold meat, a pickle, and a piece of fruit.[29]

Letters from local members contained ideas, questions, and often quips. One writer claimed that her group would do good work, "not pack a box of obsolete styled plug hats, 78 for one poor, alone, worn missionary man who would have astonished the natives if he had appeared in any one of them (a fact of past experience)" if they had a particular project. "An unknown destination does not include quite so much romance as when you furnish cabinet photographs of the destined recipients. I beg your pardon if I tred upon the *serious* toes of anyone in that dread New York office; but people are so *funny*, and some of them do find such cute excuses; probably your human nature around missionary headquarters is properly proper and duly sanctified."[30]

Aside from the personal communications, the strength of the organization resided in the synodical committees. In 1882, the General Assembly reiterated that synods should appoint "Ladies' Synodical Committees" to cooperate with the WEC. The president of the Ohio synodical society pointed out in this same year: "The time was when a few boxes of clothing to a missionary on the frontier, or to a school, was all that was expected of the women of the church. But there is a rapidly increasing demand upon them now for schools and teachers, for places of worship and means of furnishing boarding schools, where Mormon mothers and Indian women and children can learn the truth as it is in Jesus."[31] In each synod, all funds were to be reported to the synodical treasurer and all names of members and methods of work to the president. The synodical society was to make a full report to the synod at its annual meeting, transmit pledges and gifts to the national office, and act as a medium of communication between the presbyterial societies and the WEC.

Presbyterial and synodical meetings constituted an important part of women's home missions work, but not all members could attend because of distance, expense, or family responsibilities. Within a few years "district meetings" were devised for representatives from nearby churches. These more modest gatherings provided a setting in which women got acquainted and shared information on home missions.[32]

Although women of the WEC operated in a pragmatic style, they tried to adhere to Presbyterian order in their meetings. The large formal gatherings combined business matters with inspirational speakers. Some of the meetings ran so long that they lost their effect. Never reticent in pointing out problems, the writers in the first issues of *Home Mission Monthly* gave advice for shortening meetings, posing the situation with humor. After one long-winded address, a writer said, the final hymn was announced, "Hallelujah tis done."[33] The same item reported that the final hymn after a two-hour speech was "The Morning Light is Breaking."[34]

Despite travel inconveniences, active members faithfully attended meetings. The WEC scheduled its annual meeting in conjunction with the General Assembly since many of the members and officers were ministers' or elders' wives who regularly accompanied their husbands. Unescorted females also traveled freely on public transportation, so these meetings were a time of reunion, sociability, and good times. On one such trip to Omaha, Nebraska, a group of women left New York by train from Grand Central Station, picking up more women in Chicago. "What a company was that which filled the car. Bright, social, genial, voices blending in lovely tones as greetings are exchanged and plans eagerly discussed."[35] The organizers attempted to secure prestigious speakers, and they did not neglect aesthetics, with the platform usually decorated with plants and flowers. These stated meetings contained full reports, election of officers, devotional exercises, and inspirational speeches.[36] Because a representative of the WEC was requested to be present at the annual synodical meetings, two secretaries split the duties, one responsible for the western and northwestern states and the other for the eastern states, west to Illinois.[37]

Within the first decade, pure numbers of affiliate societies necessitated a diagramed reporting system with precise lines of authority. To reach all 450,000 Presbyterian women and to delineate proper routes of communication with the local and regional societies, the WEC effected an orderly plan that would make the New York office accessible to the remotest church group, but only through the channels of the synodical and presbyterial officers. Assignment of sums to be raised for scholarships and salaries, names of missionaries to whom to send boxes, securing of applications for work in the mission schools, and requests for printed matter still involved direct correspondence with the WEC. All monies were to be transmitted to the WEC treasurer through the presbyterial treasurers.[38]

In systemizing the work, the WEC set up procedures for dealing with the teachers in its mission schools. Teachers complained about various new practices during the first years of the women's taking over the support of the work, although many problems could be attributed to delays in payments from the BHM. The WEC could not disburse funds nor approve disbursements without the concurrence of the school committee of the BHM, which met monthly. The BHM treasurer was sometimes slow in sending salaries, scholarships, and sums for necessities. Even so, the women felt obligated to respond to the complaints.

The teachers questioned other new practices. Some of the teachers had been operating in their stations on the basis of private judgment and independent actions. Specifically, many solicited and secured financial aid outside the channels of the Board and WEC, which elicited a reprimand from the Board. To ease hard feelings over the reprimand and to clarify the relations between the WEC and the teachers, Mrs. William M. Ferry of Park City, Utah, represented the WEC before the Presbyterian Teachers Convention at Monti, Utah, August 26, 1887.[39]

The primary area of conflict dealt with money. Many of the teachers apparently resented the new centralized accounting, wanting the freedom not only to contact their own sources but also to receive the money directly. With the new organizational system, many times the persons whom the teachers contacted would rightly send the money to the WEC instead of to the teacher. The money then fell under the routine procedure involving approval by the WEC, the BHM's school committee, and then disbursement by the Board's treasurer, which involved delay in processing and payment. Ferry carefully and at length explained the policies and reiterated that the difficulties could be resolved by the teachers' making orderly applications to the WEC. The WEC clearly allowed the teachers to make personal solicitations but only after presenting the need to the national organization. "It is a mistake that the

Board forbids the teacher making effort to secure aid—they do not," she explained, but first the appeal should be sent to the secretary of the WEC to be placed before the executive committee. After approval, Ferry assured them, "You are fully authorized to make personal solici-tations. . . . Will not your personal friends as willingly give for the same object when they understand that your appeal is approved by the organization under which you are at work?"[40]

A later rough draft of a manual for teachers specified that the mission school work was under the direct control of the BHM, with the WEC committed to raise money and to care for details. Since the teachers were principally women, "between them and the women employed as Secs of the WEC, there should be free exchange of opinion and of course more intelligent sympathy, than if these teachers in their far off and sometimes isolated fields had merely official correspondence with the BHM." The manual set forth regulations, including qualifications of teachers, application procedures, reporting systems, financial arrange-ments, and general rules and regulations.[41]

The teachers' complaints uncovered problems in the national offices. Prime among these were the cumbersome decision-making policies and payment requirements, caused by the tight control the BHM officials kept over the women's work. Eleven years to the day after organization, the WEC boldly submitted some suggestions to "the gentlemen of the School Committee [BHM] in view of the disatisfaction [sic] of some that seems to exist with our present methods of work."[42]

Attributing problems to the increase of programs and operating funds, the women pointed out that methods effective when receipts were only $5,000 "are not satisfactory in the disbursement of such a sum as $300,000." The officers asked for a salaried treasurer in their office who would receive daily a statement of BHM disbursements for the WEC. They wished to approve all bills except for teachers' salaries, which were to be paid when they came due. For the approval of small expenditures, they requested the approval of only one member of the school committee. They supported the need of a field superintendent, a suggestion made by the General Assembly in 1887. They asked that no plans for school buildings be accepted without the approval of the WEC. They requested the addition of a secretary of the BHM responsible only for the school work. In the midst of these strong comments was an even more revolutionary request: The women asked that the WEC be repre-sented at the school committee meetings either by their senior secretary or by a woman appointed in her place.[43]

The BHM on December 24, 1889, approved the school committee's reaction to the WEC's letter. Not willing to open the school committee meeting to women entirely, they agreed to have the senior secretary present for conferences during a portion of the meetings; also, the chairman would be instructed to consult with the women prior to the committee's meetings. They turned down the idea of a field superintendent. More importantly, however, they insisted that all disbursements be controlled by the BHM. One reason given was that money often had to be borrowed to meet school expenses, and the banks would not give credit to the treasurer of the WEC. Instead of a treasurer, they recommended a cashier to receive, acknowledge, and deposit contributions to the WEC and to keep books on each school, using records from the Board's treasurer. In conclusion, the committee warned the WEC against undertaking any new work between meetings of the school committee and without close consultation with the BHM.[44]

Two months later, the WEC and the school committee reached agreement on operating principles that somewhat followed the women's suggestions. They reiterated that a representative could be present at a portion of the monthly meeting of the school committee. More dramatically, they agreed that no educational or structural work could be approved by the school committee unless it was also approved by the WEC on each matter. The WEC was empowered to take prompt action in case of emergencies in school work with the approval of the corresponding secretary of the Board and one member of the school committee. Finally, they recommended a salaried treasurer be employed to credit contributions and receipts and deposit them with the treasurer of the BHM, who would pay all bills. On warrant of the finance committee of the WEC, office and incidental expenses would be paid, but all other expenses would need the approval of the school committee. The WEC treasurer would keep all records of receipts and disbursements of the entire school work of the Board.[45]

These rules represented a measure of success for the women. Although still limited in accountability, they gained a significant amount of autonomy in dealing with the teachers and at least paper control over money spent. A particularly important precedent was established with a woman being allowed at least some representation on a board committee. The women were rewarded in 1890 when the General Assembly stated, "The annual Report of the WEC is a marvel of business clearness but the success of their work is of chief interest."[46]

While the women were redefining their relationships with the BHM, they were also dealing with the practical aspects of reporting procedures for the presbyterial and synodical societies. Printed report forms requested information on officers, number of members, meetings held, money raised, value of "boxes" and where sent, and other such details.[47] Also distributed were manuals and lists of requirements for teachers in the mission schools with meticulous suggestions for behavior and teaching methods as well as detailed explanations of reporting and request rules.

To instill a habit of contributing among children and young people, the WEC and local societies encouraged such an interest in the children and young people in the Sabbath schools. In 1892, the General Assembly, at the request of the WEC, confirmed an annual action begun in 1889 that set aside the Sunday preceding Thanksgiving as a day in which children in the Sabbath schools might direct their giving to the mission school work.[48] In 1893, the WEC set up a Department of Young People's Work with a paid staff person as secretary. The BHM also had such a department, but in 1896, by Assembly action, the BHM and WEC consolidated their young people's work, with management of the department falling to the WEC, "subject to the counsel and supervision of the Secretaries of the Board."[49] Receipts of the gifts from young people were divided equally between the BHM and the WEC. This department primarily attempted to enlist the cooperation of the Christian Endeavor Missionary Committees, to develop societies and bands of young people and children dedicated to home mission interests, and to supply evangelistic and educational information to the groups. When the Westminster Guild was originated in 1906, the department cooperated when the bands decided to divide their gifts equally between home and foreign missions. In 1911, the joint secretaries of both the women's home and foreign Boards visited schools and colleges to interest young people in missions and recruit workers.[50]

By 1900, Endeavor Societies were supporting seventeen full salaries for ministers, missionaries, and superintendents of mission schools. Junior Christian Endeavor Societies were underwriting seven salaries and contributing toward a training school. Some groups "adopted" special workers in the field, but also increased contributions to the general fund, which was used by the BHM and WEC at their discretion. By 1901, Sunday schools figured prominently in the sending of funds.[51] The department worked through presbyterial young people's secretaries, supplying literature and suggesting methods of work. The report of the year asserted that "the Young People's Department is not a separate organization, but an integral part of the home mission work of the Presbyterian Church." As was women's work, young people's work was grounded on the "power of the littles," for the average contributions to home missions from a young people's society was about $5.00.[52] Nevertheless, the combined contributions each year were in the tens of thousands of dollars. In 1915, the officers of the Home Board and Woman's Board met to work out a plan for separately promoting missionary interests in the youth groups and Sunday schools. In effect, they agreed to divide the two areas, with the Home Board taking the Sunday schools and the Woman's Board working with the young people's organizations.

In the same year that the Young People's Department was begun,

1893, overtures by the Presbyteries of Lehigh and Chicago asked for an "enlargement of the scope of the work of the Woman's Executive Committee to include the educational work among the exceptional populations of large cities."[53] The officers were reluctant to engage in systematic work among the immigrant populations, primarily because they felt that they were regularly being asked to overextend their program. At the same time, they acknowledged the need of schools among the foreign-speaking. Consequently, the WEC compromised on the request by allowing such work on the local level.

The issue did not end with that decision. In 1895, the General Assembly recommended to the WEC that they assume work among the immigrants in the cities, in the mining regions of Pennsylvania, and in the West.[54] The women again did not agree to do so, citing financial problems owing to their decision to discontinue accepting government aid for the Indian schools, thus increasing the women's monetary commitments, and to a general economic downturn in the country. The matter stayed before the women, however, leading to a charge by the corresponding secretary of the Woman's Board in 1900 that the church was expecting too much of the women. "Our women's Home Missionary Societies, called into being by General Assembly, for specific, well-defined work, and *made the only agency* of the Presbyterian Church *for such a necessary work,* are besieged on all sides for kindred work of the church, synodical sustentation, temperance work, local presbyterial and church obligations, city benevolent work and the like, to the distraction of conscientious workers who wish to be loyal to the trust committed to them and who find it hard to avoid positive diversion of their Home Mission funds—technically so called."[55]

Continuing discussion led to a resolution from the 1902 annual meeting of the Woman's Board that called for attention to the needs of the immigrants and again emphasized that "the Woman's Board should assume no financial responsibility beyond the amount designated for this work."[56] Year after year, the question was debated, and finally in 1907 the women gave in and supported such work officially.

When the Board made this decision, they also set into motion policies that would monitor the work of the various presbyterial and synodical societies in this area. In 1913, the Board set forth a set of rules: The Board would be a direct agent in the training of women for service in immigrant communities; in the establishment of large centers of entry and industrial localities; and in the institution of work in smaller settlements, Christian social settlements, and vocational boarding schools. The Board took upon itself to commission workers and put them under the direction and supervision of the School Department. Furthermore, it specified that funds spent would be equal to 5 percent of the total annual receipts from women's auxiliaries for current work but that any funds raised for local projects over and above the regular expenditures, although sent to the national treasurer to be recorded, would immediately be returned to the treasurer of the local organization for disbursement. These special gifts would not be included in the 5 percent. In 1920, the Woman's Board articulated a policy of Christian service for the foreign-speaking and called on all their organizations to study congestion, housing, and the immigrants' social, educational, and religious opportunities. The Board urged a detailed reporting system, the appointment of secretaries for the work (to be paid by the Board), and the promotion of scholarships for the training of young foreign-speaking women. It also encouraged participation in interdenominational enterprises for immigrant work.[57]

By the end of the nineteenth century, the women recognized that their multiplying responsibilities had established their usefulness. To make their organization's name more compatible with its stature, the women decided to retitle the WEC. From 1897 on, it was known as the Woman's Board of Home Missions, a fact noted in the General Assembly *Minutes* in 1898. It was a Board in name only, however, for it was not incorporated and was auxiliary to the BHM. The report of that year summarized the twenty-year history of the women's work, mentioning its separate treasury, "the funds of which are gathered by the women and children of the Church and administered by the Assembly's Board. These funds are applied to the special work of evangelization which the Board could not otherwise prosecute."[58] The General Assembly pointed out that, despite the women's main responsibility for the schools, more than seventy churches had been established as a result of the school work. "The teachers are missionaries, preaching often in the most effective and economic way," it declared.[59] Because of the Woman's Board, the General Assembly noted that property in the amount of $750,000 dollars was held by the BHM in trust for the Woman's Board or had been turned over to the several presbyteries covering the bounds of the field.

In the last year of the nineteenth century, the General Assembly announced to the church, "During the year which has just closed the Woman's Board have carried on the work assigned them in the same earnest spirit of helpfulness to the Board of Home Missions, and with the same hearty loyalty to the General Assembly, which have characterized their efforts in the past. The Board of Home Missions can do nothing wiser than to . . . emphasize the duty of pastors, Sessions and the Church at large, to encourage the Woman's Board in order that their work may be made even far more successful in the future."[60]

By 1902, the Standing Committee on Home Missions declared, "The policy of the Woman's Board has been to enter the field to stay." Any doubt about the ongoing and self-sustaining nature of the women's enterprises had been dispelled by the more than two decades of estab-lishing schools and missions, a solid basis for the growth of churches, presbyteries, and synods.[61] As the twenty-fifth anniversary of the work approached, the BHM reported that ninety-eight church organizations had resulted from the work of the Woman's Board, "an average of one every three months."[62] In its silver anniversary year, the Board reported 130,000 members in auxiliary societies. In 1905-1906, the Board for the first time passed the half-million-dollar mark in contributions during a one-year period, collecting $505,830.97.

In 1907, the Woman's Board of the Cumberland Church and the Woman's Board of the PCUSA agreed on a plan of union. In the local societies, the two groups either reorganized and joined together or, where only one or the other society existed, went on as formerly. How-ever, all reporting and contributing after July 1907 was to the Woman's Board of the PCUSA. The merger expanded the work by adding three new synodical societies and many presbyterial and local auxiliaries "tested by years of service in the Cumberland Woman's Board."[63]

As did the early societies in the nineteenth century, the twentieth-century groups participated in nondenominational activities. An edu-cational movement, the Missionary Education Movement that jointly sponsored mission study and publications, organized in 1902. The Council of Women for Home Missions (1908) coordinated work among the immigrants and among migrant workers.[64] The Interdenominational Council of Women for Home Missions organized in 1910. Nine members of each of the national women's boards of home missions of various denominations composed this Council.[65]

Such evidence of stability and growth was counterpointed by the passing of an era, for in 1909 Mary James resigned as president because of ill health, and Sheldon Jackson died. At this point, a new set of leaders emerged. Katharine Bennett became president and David R. Boyd, founder and president of the State University of Oklahoma, as-sumed the superintendency of school work. Julia Fraser moved into the position of secretary of the Board.[66] The addition of these new staff members coincided with the publication of printed standing rules that succinctly set forth the purpose and organizational structure. The pre-amble restated the Board's responsibility to collect and apportion funds for work approved by the General Assembly, delineating the limitation that the BHM had authority over all work and expenditures. The work of the Board was listed as:

The support of missionary teachers, Bible readers, evangelists and medical mis-sionaries; the erection, equipment and maintenance of necessary buildings; the diffusion of information regarding Home Missions.[67]

The pamphlet listed the seventeen committees that handled the Board's affairs, including a committee for each mission field area and for publication, finance, building, membership, periodicals, youth adjuncts, devotions, and hospitality. This statement derived from the pattern set by the earlier volunteer officers. Katharine Bennett set the tone for a more direct communication between the General Assembly and the Woman's Board. Because the constituency considered the Board a powerful and influential agency, some members raised the possibility of its becoming an incorporated body in 1910.[68]

Incorporation could be argued on practical as well as prestigious grounds. Members of the law profession already had raised questions about the legality of the Woman's Board receiving financial gifts and legacies while not incorporated. Because of its auxiliary nature, legacies designated for women's work potentially could have been in jeopardy if challenged by heirs. A second impetus toward discussing incorporation arose when the General Assembly began to decentralize the work of the Board of Home Missions. Bennett pointed out that she doubted that the medical and pedagogical work supported by the women could be adequately administered by some of the weaker presbyteries. She cited an instance where the Woman's Board had approximately $500,000 of property and an annual expenditure of $100,000 in a presbytery composed of one pastor, one associate pastor, and ten stated supplies.[69]

The Woman's Board appointed Mrs. S. P. Harbison of Pittsburgh, Mrs. L. B. Brownell of New York, and Mrs. M. V. Richards of Baltimore, to pursue the issue.[70] They consulted a lawyer who studied the Board's property holdings and bequests and prepared a statement on the operations of the men's and women's boards, the system of bequests, the criticism of the system as it existed, and the law relating to such.[71] They conferred with the officers of the BHM, but the meetings apparently raised more problems than they solved. After more research, the committee sent a letter to Charles L. Thompson of the Board of Home Missions, with questions and their lawyer's report. This letter was referred to the lawyer of the Board of Home Missions, John E. Parsons, who objected strenuously to the points made in the lawyer's statement to the Woman's Board, and to suggestions of the value of incorporating as set forth by the committee. He particularly disagreed with their statement: "In addition we would say that the fact that the Woman's Board is incorporated would encourage our women to leave bequests to the Woman's Board." He felt that it might possibly operate the other way, arguing, "But when it comes to a question of serious amounts, involving investments possibly, is it not pretty universal experience that for the administration of the trust involved, men have been and are treated as possessing greater business experience, and as being more conversant with business matters?" As a lawyer, he stated,

"It once in a while happens that a man by Will may appoint a woman as executrix or trustee; never, however, save in a few exceptional cases . . . unless joined with men. But we have rarely known of a case of the Will of a woman which left the administration of an estate to women."[72]

Nothing was settled before the General Assembly met in May, so the Woman's Board formed a new committee and asked it to work with the Committee of Conference and Co-operation of the Board of Home Mission. The committee, chaired by Mrs. D. E. Waid, was to study whether incorporation was desirable; if so, what form it should take; if not, what alternative action should be taken. Waid, in writing to those on the committee, set forth the situation it faced in blunt terms: "From the view point of the Board of Home Missions incorporation of the Woman's Board may mean the removal of large property interests and responsibilities, the great lessening of duties for Secretary and Treasurer and those members who serve on School and Building Committees for the Woman's Board, and a diminishing of the office force necessary in various departments, likewise a largely decreased budget. It also means the strict reservation of all endowments and funds—notably the Kennedy fund—for the definite purposes of the Board of Home Missions, and separation of work on the field in some instances."[73] For the women, however, Waid suggested that the incorporation may mean "entire legal freedom and responsibility, holding of legacies, endowments and properties, and administering the same, financial responsibility for all work under its care, and the increased expense in officers' salaries, travelling expenses and office hire necessary to administer so large a fund."[74] The letter evoked an immediate reply from the chairman of the former committee, who felt that "one is tempted (?) [sic] to think that added responsibility and freedom of action will not mar but make for better service." Harbison warned: "It is very difficult perhaps to divest oneself wholy [sic] of personal prejudice, but this is just what must be done, and to take one's view from the vantage points of all interested will require a large amount of Christian tact, and I say it reverently, Divine illumination."[75]

That the women and men were judging the same situation from two different viewpoints was clear. While the men were convinced that women would not provide funds in their wills to be used by other women, the women felt they would. The women saw themselves as bearing the brunt of the work for home missions. One woman committee member from Michigan wrote to Waid:

I sometimes wonder what the men would accomplish if it were not for the women keeping everlastingly at it. I think they all need education along these lines (men of Mich. not excepted) but they are coming on all right it needs time and good hard work by a few persistent women. We must be very decided and yet just in all of our dealings with the Men's Board but they must be made to realize that we are earnest about having our business on a more solid basis and in a first class business style.[76]

This committee gathered many pertinent facts and conferred closely with the Home Board. Waid's report to the annual meeting was inconclusive because of the committee's view of the import of the action and its evaluation of the attitude of the constituency.[77] In the meantime, Charles Thompson, secretary of the BHM, had submitted a plan for a united board, which clearly left the control in the hands of the men.[78]

The process of negotiations brought to the surface what appeared to have been continuing difficulties in the relationship between the two Boards. The women wanted more control over their funds and projects, feeling a readjustment of relations was imperative for efficiency and effectiveness, and wanted lines of authority clarified. Katharine Bennett discussed the relation of the Board to the Board of Home Missions. One of her primary points of contention was that the Woman's Board should not be considered a department of the BHM. Claiming that a department was for information or planning, she pointed out that the Woman's Board was self-supporting; "it is responsible for expenditures incurred for the administration of its office and field work, and for all expenses incidental to said field work—it has no claim on the General Treasury of the Board, has but seldom profited by gifts therefrom, and in past emergencies of the Board has aided it."[79]

Quoting the treasurer of the Home Board, H. C. Olin, as saying that "it was not contemplated that its functions should be administrative, but money raising only" and that the Woman's Board "has become a competitor of the parent Board," Bennett pointed out that the methods of the Woman's Board had developed over long years with the sanction of the Board of Home Missions and that *"the situation must be dealt with as it has developed, not as it should in any opinion have developed."*[80] She maintained that its constituency and the Church at large saw it as a distinct, responsible entity; thus, the Woman's Board should have more responsibility and autonomy. She proposed three alternatives, including incorporation. The others involved different plans of reorganization that would keep the Woman's Board auxiliary to the Assembly's Board but would give it far more control over its money and administration.

That same month in 1912, the Executive Commission of the General Assembly took action on the incorporation of the Woman's Board. As Bennett recounted the history, she surmised that it had been raised again because of the question of the legality of an unincorporated Board holding gifts.[81] She heard of this action as she was passing by some members of the Executive Commission after having met with them concerning the Board's budget. A man whom she did not know made a remark to her which she understood to be "We are going to incorporate the Woman's Board."[82] Because of the casual nature of the remark, she told no one of it, expecting to hear something official. No communication came. In the spring, one of the members wrote to ask if it would be satisfactory to have the Board incorporated in New Jersey, to which she replied she could not answer since her Board had not met.[83] To this reply, she heard nothing. At the Assembly meeting, the Executive Commission recommended and the Assembly ratified favorable action on the matter of the incorporation, with the provision that it be auxiliary to the Board of Home Missions, and appointed the Executive Commission to confer with the Board of Home Missions and the Woman's Board to clear the way for the incorporation. No meetings were ever held. Between themselves, the officers of the Board of Home Missions and the Woman's Board agreed to postpone any considerations until February 1915. Nevertheless, the Board of Home Missions, meeting on September 17, 1914, agreed "that in the judgment of this Board the incorporation of the Woman's Board at this time is not advisable."[84]

Bennett and other leaders of the Woman's Board received news of this action with great consternation. Edith Grier Long, Secretary of the WB, after a meeting with officers of the Home Board, wrote Bennett that it appeared that all agreed "that it was a grief that the Board of Home Missions has gone on record as it had."[85] Long reported to these officers that the Woman's Board had, in response, taken unilateral action by appointing representatives to meet the committee of the Executive Commission who were handling the incorporation issue and by instructing those representatives to ask for incorporation. The emotions of this episode were evident in Long's parting paragraph to Bennett, "I do not need to tell you how earnestly some of us are bearing you on our hearts to the end that you may not be overborne by this time of stress, and that the outcome may be in accordance with the Divine plan for our work."[86]

Misunderstandings, charges, accusations, and omissions abounded throughout the three years this issue was before the church. Foremost as a problem seemed to be a curious lack of official communications among interested parties, from Assembly on down. In this instance, for example, neither the Woman's Board nor the Board of Home Missions had been officially informed that a subcommittee of the Commission had been formed to meet on September 29, 1914, to work out incorporation plans. Bennett found this out, although she did not make it clear how, and she and Annie Hyatt, first vice-president, attended. Neither was called before the group. The Commission appointed yet another committee consisting of three members from each of the Boards and three from the Commission to work out details and present an Act of Incorporation to the Executive Commission in February 1915. Despite the

death of two committee members during subsequent months, the subcommittee finally agreed upon a charter, which was approved.[87] Thus,
after thirty-seven years, the Woman's Board was able to receive and
administer its own money and receive legacies in its own name. Although the incorporating charter made the woman's work "auxiliary" to
the Assembly's Board, the Woman's Board reported to the General Assembly directly.

The fact of the incorporation concerned the men of the Foreign Board
as well as the Home Board. In August 1915, with some restraint, A. W.
Halsey, secretary of the Foreign Board, wrote to the Board's Executive
Council that "there are some indications" that the women representing
home missions in joint local groups for home and foreign work were
urging the representatives of the Foreign Mission Societies to ask for an
independent Woman's Board of Foreign Missions. Claiming not to be
judging such a move, Halsey reported that the Home Department
Council he represented felt the Board should "exercise great care" in
dealing with the women's societies.[88]

In 1916, Katharine Bennett became the first woman ever to make a
Board report to the General Assembly.[89]

Just as the Woman's Home Mission Board achieved incorporation
about the time the church began to consider abolishing the women's
boards, so the woman's foreign mission boards merged their regional
societies into one central Board during the same period. For fifty years,
the separate boards for foreign missions had resisted any efforts by men
or women to unite their groups into one national organization. Their
philosophy was to keep intact the self-sacrificial, personal element of the
mission enterprise. A few of the Foreign Board's leaders and many
males in the synods and boards recognized that the ever-growing
numbers of projects and the increasing amount of money under the
women's control demanded more coordination. Nevertheless, the influential women continued to believe "the time had not come" to give
up their independent groups.[90]

In New York, where the Ladies' Board of Missions, the Woman's
Presbyterian Foreign Missionary Society (Albany), the Woman's Foreign
Missionary Society of Long Island, and the Woman's Foreign Missionary Society of the Presbyterian Church (Philadelphia) all had auxiliaries, the work was somewhat unified in 1883. At the request of the
Woman's Executive Committee of Home Missions and the Ladies'
Board, but instigated by male members of the judiciary, the Synod of
New York appointed a committee to meet with the various organizations and draw up some agreement. The synod wished to get the
foreign work under one group, and the WEC wanted home mission
work given to them. The whole matter was resolved even before the
committee reported, when the synod appointed a Woman's Synodical

Committee of Home Missions, consisting of presbyterial committees, and thus arranged for the "unifying of the Home Work and its systematic management."[91]

Resignedly, the Ladies' Board voted to work exclusively for foreign missions in the future, although with evident distaste. "With great reluctance we have come to the conclusion that it will be necessary at our annual meeting in April to make a change in our mode of work. . . . This action has been taken in the desire to promote harmony and in the hope that all the societies working for foreign missions in our Synod will also unite. These few words seemed necessary to make the matter clear to any who had not been before informed in regard to it."[92] Although the committee recommended that all the foreign work in New York come under one group renamed the Woman's Board of Foreign Missions of New York, the Albany society voted against it. Nevertheless, the name change occurred, and most of the auxiliaries from the other groups became part of this one organization.[93]

In 1884, at a conference at Saratoga, New York, Frank F. Ellinwood, secretary of the Board of Foreign Missions, recommended a further coordination of efforts. He wanted the women's groups to combine their various missionary publications into one and also suggested a salaried person as a liaison between the woman's boards and the Foreign Board. As a result of this conference, the women again reluctantly merged their periodicals into one, *Woman's Work for Woman*, and formed the Central Committee of Presbyterian Women for Foreign Missions, a compromise solution to the demand for unity.[94]

The Central Committee became responsible in great part for increased efficiency among the various boards. Made up of representatives of each one, it coordinated points of common interest and avoided duplication of efforts. Out of the Central Committee came a plan for training schools for missionary candidates and the standardization of application blanks.[95] As the years went by, the growth of the work necessitated more frequent meetings for the Committee. When Margaret E. Hodge was elected executive secretary in 1917, she visited each board annually and represented them on the Executive Council of the Board of Foreign Missions, where she served on the candidate committee to consider applications of all women candidates.[96]

The productiveness of women's work for foreign missions was perhaps best summarized as early as the twenty-fifth anniversary of the Ladies' Board of New York by the then president, Mrs. Henry N. Beers, who said, "In earlier days, little was recognized as distinctly foreign mission work, except the direct preaching of the Word. Now, with no less preaching, we have everywhere schools for the children, house-to-house visitation, wayside teaching, evangelistic tours far from the mission centre, and last, as the consummate flower of Christian sympathy, we have medical missions."[97] The latter was a particularly important contribution of the women's work—not only for the mission of the church but also for the professionalization of women in society. Aware of the need for "educated consecrated women with medical training," the New York Board instigated a "Medical Missionary Fund" in 1887.[98] Contributions to this fund were outside the regular gifts for the Board's work, and $500 a year was awarded to a woman to go to medical school. By 1895, Beers could announce, "The Presbyterian Church is in the front rank . . . with its twenty-two trained women doctors."[99]

These boards were no less successful than was the Home Board in raising money. The principal means used were similar: the envelope system, pledges, voluntary contributions, life memberships, curio sales, and other socials. Their copious communications with individual missionaries demanded the institution of a Bureau of Exchange for Missionary Letters, to receive letters and reports and to send copies or extracts to auxiliaries contributing to their support. By 1921, the Boards had moved from "friendly correspondence" to a more official relationship whereby each mission was to designate a woman correspondent to present the woman's work.[100]

In the second decade of the twentieth century, despite good results, concern pervaded the reports and minutes, indicating that many churchwomen were not interested or active. In the report of the New York Board in 1909, the secretary chided the women who "in the search for something new and attractive . . ." lost sight of "the right value of things." Hence, she wrote, "Political Activity Club meetings and Dante lectures at five dollars a ticket kill attendance at the missionary meetings."[101] Of particular concern was the lack of participation by young women. This drop in interest, probably attributable in great measure to women's increased freedom to move into spheres other than those relating to women, children, and religion, must have been influential in the women's decision to consolidate their individual groups' efforts in 1920. Official records are free of such a statement, but the hints are frequent in earlier reports.

As the foreign mission groups moved toward unification, their contact with the Woman's Board of Home Missions became closer. Even with the early problems between the home and foreign missions groups, and even though the two still competed for participation and donations, the leaders worked closely on administrative policies and especially on dealing with young people and college-age students. With Hodge and Bennett leading these boards, the two groups effectively presented the work of Presbyterian women.

In 1920, the women marked the fiftieth anniversary of their work for foreign missions with a Golden Jubilee celebration and the merger of the six autonomous groups. During the year, 2,000 new societies were formed and nearly 200 new missionaries sent to the field. The Jubilee goal of raising $500,000 was surpassed by $100,000.[102] An advertisement in 1920 listed their accomplishments of fifty years: more than $13,000,000 donated; missionaries all over the world; native leaders developed; hospitals and schools created; one-third of women and children in the church enlisted.[103] The new organizational structure, with Margaret Hodge as general secretary, expected to continue and even expand this record.

Details of the merger were included in the 51st annual report, the number of years the New York Board had existed, and in bits of correspondence intact. Although the idea for union emanated from the Northwest Board, not all the women were happy with the union; although every board voted in favor of it, a minority wished to keep the separate groups. With some trepidation, Hodge, en route to the decisive meeting of the Woman's Committee on Unification, November 12–14, 1919, wrote "I am hoping and praying that from these various suggestions [from the six Boards] the committee may work out a plan that will win women of many shades of opinion."[104] Apparently it did, for the changeover seemed to go smoothly. The summary of the year indicated that a new style of operation was emerging, especially with a closer relationship with the Assembly's Board of Foreign Missions. There was, for example, a joint executive council of the secretaries of the Assembly's Board and the Woman's Board and the united departments for candidates, education, and home base work. The two Boards had a joint literature showroom in New York. In former years, the woman's boards had published in their annual reports a summary of the work of women missionaries; now the report of the Assembly's Board would cover women as well as men. "It is hoped that this will tend to a fuller realization of the unity of the whole work," read the women's report.[105]

The scope of the women's responsibilities and the organizational hierarchy was indicated in the summary of the general secretary's role in 1922: to relate to the constituency of the Woman's Board, to the district committees through the executive secretaries, to the Board of Foreign Missions through the executive council, to the missionaries through letters from official correspondents, and to interdenominational movements.[106] This would be the next to the last report of the Board, however, for in 1923 the final report would disclose the end of the two Woman's Boards.

4

REORGANIZATION CONTROVERSIES:
Ongoing Processes,
1923-1933

The network of women's missionary societies, an integral part of the mission program, by the early 1920s encompassed some 6,000 local societies. These groups channeled about $3,000,000 annually to a variety of missionary endeavors. Through their policy of "double-giving" (contributing separately to individual societies and to regular church benevolence budgets) the boards set higher and higher fiscal goals. According to Katharine Bennett, Presbyterian women were thinking of "larger plans, new forms of service, and a new emphasis that would embrace more of the activities of the church and enlist more women actively in the service of the church."[1]

Despite these positive reports, two issues loomed: There were indications that the future of traditional missionary organizations was less secure than a superficial reading of annual statistics might suggest, and there was evidence that the question of women's equality in the church would affect the future of the groups.

Following World War I, financial receipts declined, so a considerable percentage of the societies' income actually was derived from endowments from a previous generation.[2] Furthermore, the traditional missionary societies failed to interest Presbyterian women not aligned with any church organization. Bennett admitted that in many churches, less than 25 percent of female church members belonged to a missionary group.[3] Even more serious was the recognition that few young women participated in presbyterial and synodical programs. Leaders saw this as a sign of a new generation questioning old values. "How to interest the young women is the universal problem of missionary society presidents," reported Board of National Missions (formerly Board of Home Missions) executive Ellen Louderbaugh. This spokeswoman attributed much of the dissatisfaction to the denomination's unwillingness to treat men and women as equals in areas of ordination and representation.[4]

Bennett noted that the young women of the 1920s belonged to a completely different world from that of their parents. They were "a generation looking with unafraid eyes at all institutions, even ecclesiastical—and asking 'why?' of many accepted customs."[5]

Criticisms of the traditional missionary societies went deeper than those suggested by Louderbaugh and Bennett. College-educated women in this period tended to suspect the validity of the entire missionary enterprise, alleging its lack of sensitivity to non-Western cultures.[6] On a more personal level, the term "missionary woman" had negative connotations to younger women, conjuring up a dominating "do it my way" person with little patience for innovation or a rising generation of "liberated women." Katherine McAfee Parker, an active young churchwoman, with many of her friends, recalled that they did not want to be associated with "stuffy missionary societies" and preferred rather to work for the creation of more broadly based organizations involved in all phases of church activity. "The missionary societies," Parker said, "had really become so well organized that unless you knew the exact language and followed the rules, it wasn't very interesting. They needed a whole big new look."[7]

By the mid-1920s there was a notable increase in the number of inclusive women's organizations that united women's work in one body. Under the title of Women's Associations and Federations, they brought together such diverse groups as ladies' aid, missionary societies, sewing circles, and various community service organizations. According to the program of one such group, the Woman's Society of the First Presbyterian Church of Berkeley, California, their women would be involved in service in the local church, community, nation, and the world. Every woman in the congregation was automatically considered to be a member of the society. Although the society's budget indicated a strong commitment to denominational missionary enterprises, funds also supported local orphanages and charities and local church improvements.[8]

In addition to internal problems, missionary societies faced mounting pressure from churchmen who feared that the establishment of separate boards for women had been predicated on fallacious theological principles and who were wary of fostering a "church within the church" divided artificially on the basis of "men's work" and "women's work." Even such a zealous supporter of foreign missions as Robert E. Speer acknowledged that ultimately there should be no place in the church for organizations designed specifically for one sex. Speer asked: "If we have in our churches women's organizations, what have we got? Haven't we got two churches? We have one church made up of men and women, with a social program, an educational program, and a religious program. Then we have a separation of women, with identical programs except worship. We do not want to divide what is spoken of as 'the church' and 'the women.' The great danger is that the women will think that their society is the only thing they have to work over."[9]

Reinforcing these sentiments was friction that resulted from competition between men and women, especially on the home field. In some synods in which the Woman's Board had a number of schools and hospitals, women controlled budgets far greater than the total budget granted to the synod by the Board of Home Missions. This engendered disputes over which projects should be given priority in the synod, and who should have the say. Extensive correspondence between synod committees and the national board indicates that many men resented the power women exerted to designate funds to special projects when synod committees thought the money could be put to another use. In the Synod of New Mexico, for example, local committees concluded that many of the small schools supported by women's giving were anachronistic and should be closed, but were rebuffed by women who did not want to give up schools with which they had such a long and personal attachment.[10]

At the same time that this tension was growing, the General Assembly had been considering ways to simplify the ad hoc administrative structure forged in the hectic years of rapid expansion in the latter part of the nineteenth century. By 1919, the denomination had twenty boards in addition to a number of permanent committees all of which reported annually to the General Assembly. After several abortive efforts to modify what many church leaders considered to be an unnecessarily complicated and frustratingly ineffective administrative structure, the General Assembly in 1920 appointed a committee chaired by John Timothy Stone (referred to popularly as "the Stone Committee") to consider possible ways in which boards and agencies could be consolidated. Following three years of study, the Assembly approved a sweeping reorganization plan that combined existing groups into four major boards—National Missions, Foreign Missions, Christian Education, and Ministerial Relief and Sustentation (later known as Pensions).[11]

As a result of reorganization, the women's boards were dissolved and their work subsumed under the Boards of Foreign and National Missions. Although Stone's committee would have preferred to recommend also the dissolution of synodical, presbyterial, and local societies, it yielded to pleas from women who feared that such a drastic action would alienate a large segment of Presbyterian women and undercut the financial resources of established missionary programs.[12] In its final report, the reorganization committee noted the "spirit of cooperation, and indeed, of sacrifice," with which the women had entered consolidation and emphasized "the importance of conserving in every way the invaluable and specific work of the Woman's Missionary Societies in the local churches and in Synods and Presbyteries." The committee emphasized that local societies should continue to have the privilege of selecting what projects they would support and recommended that boards, synods, and presbyteries be discouraged "from making appeals to Women's Missionary organizations for the support of work in the homeland outside of the field as above defined." This did not mean, however, that the interests of individual women in the wider work of the church would be restricted.[13]

In its desire to reach an acceptable compromise, the Stone Committee left questions about the future of women's work unresolved. While removing the national boards, it left all local and regional missionary structures intact, somewhat analogous to severing the head but not disposing of the body. Presbyterials and synodicals were unclear about their relationships to the new boards, creating difficulty in maintaining previously well-established lines of communication with New York offices. Nor did the Stone Committee precisely define the financial relationship of missionary societies to the new Board structure. While other boards and agencies were "discouraged" from making financial appeals to women's organizations, it did not go unnoticed that the word *prohibited* had not been utilized. In particular, the Board of Christian Education interpreted this language as sufficient justification to promote its own program among existing missionary groups. Finally, the tentativeness of the committee's thinking about the exact status of women's work is reflected in its statement regarding the Division of Schools and Hospitals of the Board of National Missions. Prefaced to its provision that women should be free to designate their giving to long-established projects are the significant words, *"Until otherwise determined by the General Assembly."*[14] At no other point in its lengthy report did the Stone Committee leave such a vital relationship unsettled. In this case, failure to do so paved the way for an extended period of uncertainty and unrest.

The men who developed the new denominational structure tried, in their words, "to be generous to the ladies." As noted above, they left the local and regional missionary society structure virtually intact and permitted women to continue their designated project-giving. They also provided for female representation on each of the four boards and stipulated that the vice-presidents of the Boards of Foreign and National Missions, Margaret Hodge and Katharine Bennett, should have a seat on the General Council as ex officio members. Moreover, each mission board had a Women's Committee that provided continuity for existing programs and a forum where women could discuss matters of special interest apart from the larger board responsibilities.[15]

When the General Assembly approved the reorganization program in

1923, the initial outward reaction of Presbyterian women to the sudden demise of their national boards was a combination of disbelief and reserved acceptance. Loyal churchwomen felt compelled to acquiesce even though they had no representation on the decision-making body. Katharine Bennett told commissioners to the Assembly that once women had recovered "from the shock and astonishment" of reorganization they would no doubt "fall in line." She admitted, however, that the allegiance of Presbyterian women to the General Assembly had been sorely tested by its approval of a plan that meant the end of the cherished and respected women's boards.[16] Nevertheless, Bennett wrote a small pamphlet entitled, "Hold Steady," in which she encouraged women to continue their sacrificial giving and to accept the will of the church as expressed in the General Assembly's action. In a similar vein, Margaret Hodge stressed the opportunity for participation by women in board decisions and urged them to "look forward with faith and courage" in the new organizational structure.[17]

The anger and resentment that women suppressed in public they vented privately in letters to Bennett, Hodge, and other female board members. "Why should the women of the church who are the loyal faithful supporters of our Woman's Work have this taken from our hands, and given to the management of men who can't begin to do it well?" queried a woman from Indiana. Another complained of the "high-handed measures" and "ruthless actions" of insensitive General Assembly commissioners in dissolving the women's boards and proposed that women do something to reverse the decision. A synodical president reported her "distinct and disappointing shock that after so many years of faithful cooperation" the women's boards should be "swallowed whole without even Fletcherizing" (a reference to a well-known laxative). Conscious of their responsibilities as board representatives and reticent to air publicly ecclesiastical controversy, Bennett, Hodge, and other women leaders pleaded for patience and restraint during the transitional years of reorganization.[18]

The letters received indicated that churchwomen's anger centered around three areas: consultation, representation, and finances. Many women pointed out that they had virtually no input into the proposed reorganization plan that was conceived, debated, and voted on entirely by men. Lacking ordination rights, women were ineligible to speak or vote on the issue. Scattered correspondence from the period 1920–23 indicates justification for this complaint, showing that the Stone Committee consulted with officers of the Woman's Board of Home Missions and the Woman's Board of Foreign Missions only *after* major decisions had been made. Moreover, the average churchwoman had access to none of these deliberations and learned of the radical changes only when she read about them in denominational papers. Since the women's boards had always sought to communicate with each individual member, this was not only considered high-handed but also contrary to women's experience.[19]

A second source of irritation concerned women's representation on the new Boards. The Assembly allotted women fifteen seats on the Boards of National and Foreign Missions (forty members), twelve seats on the Board of Christian Education (thirty-six members), and three places on the Board of Ministerial Relief. Appointments on the latter two boards resulted from amendments to the reorganization plan made on the floor of the General Assembly and were not even included in the final version of the Stone Committee report. Although these figures were later modified to accommodate increases in committee size, the ratio of men and women remained essentially the same.[20] As one woman caustically observed, " 'God bless the efforts of these good women' can be uttered with fervor, since in a ratio of one to three their opinion can never change anything!"[21]

Third, financial considerations loomed large in the women's discontent. Through the long-established program of double-giving, missionary societies had established themselves as a valuable source of benevolence income. Despite the Stone Committee's recommendation that outside groups should be "discouraged" from approaching women for funds, the new structure allowed individual ministers and judicatory committees to tap these resources for their own local projects and to assume control over the societies' goals. Letters from presbyterial and synodical officers to the Board of National Missions gave specific examples of financial tampering. The president of the Rio Grande Presbyterial in New Mexico reported in 1926 that area ministers were discouraging the formation of new missionary societies because they believed that women were "so energetic in reaching their quota that they drain funds of other departments of the church." One minister, she related, told churchwomen that the best way to use their missionary money was to remodel their church sanctuary.[22] In the Detroit Presbyterial, one society "under pressure" gave $1,500 for a church organ and consequently was not able to meet its missionary pledge.[23] A New Jersey correspondent reported that her pastor had informed the missionary society that it should consult with the session before taking on any financial commitment to the presbyterial because "no woman had a pocketbook of her own." Discouraged, these women disbanded their society.[24]

In a presentation to the General Council, Katharine Bennett recounted what she termed "absolutely typical" examples of how local pastors and committees rode roughshod over local missionary societies. In one instance, a chairman of a presbytery church extension committee sent out a letter over his signature and that of the synodical president to missionary societies requesting gifts over and above their apportionment to build new churches. Despite women's protests that this was contrary to denominational policy and was an unfair burden on their financial resources, they ultimately contributed to the local project. On another occasion, Bennett reported, a synod unilaterally ruled that 50 percent of all money raised by the Woman's Missionary Society of the synod should be given to church extension work in that particular judicatory.[25]

Such problems were minuscule when compared to the extended conflict that developed between the missionary societies and the Board of Christian Education (BCE) over the relationship of organized women to that new Board. In its new portfolio, the BCE had responsibility for missionary education, young people's work, stewardship, and social education and action, all of which had at one time or another been a major interest of the women's boards. Not unexpectedly, the BCE assumed it had a right to share in the largesse of the women's double-giving, especially when it reported a deficit of $250,000 after its first year of operation. Noting that the missionary societies had the available machinery to promote certain aspects of Christian education, Harold McAfee Robinson, administrative secretary of the BCE, reportedly told his staff, "We want to use that machinery."[26]

In its first formal report to the General Assembly in 1924, the BCE openly expressed its desire for a "more definite and vital connection with the willing and capable womanhood of the Church." Resurrecting the "woman's sphere" arguments, the report stressed the Board's intimate connection with children and youth and their relationship to home and church and concluded that "the motherhood of the Church holds the destiny of organized Christianity in its hands. . . . To arrest the attention, capitalize the personality, and enlist the devoted cooperation of the total group of Presbyterian women must be the undeviating purpose of this Board."[27] The Board followed this initial announcement of its intentions with a series of advertisements in various church papers. A typical advertisement began with a question in bold type: "WHERE WILL OUR CHURCH GET ITS MINISTERS, HOME MISSIONARIES, AND FOREIGN MISSIONARIES if the future of the work of our Presbyterian Board of Christian Education is curtailed?" Identifying the questioner as president of a woman's missionary society in an eastern city, the text pointed out that although women were represented on all four boards, only the mission boards had women's organizations to support their work. The advertisement concluded with a suggestion that a woman's group could "adopt" a college or seminary student for $150 per year.[28]

Amid these confusing developments following reorganization, Bennett, Hodge, and other female board and staff members continued to assure women that their best course of action was to be cooperative, patient, and optimistic regarding the restructuring process. Behind the scenes, however, Bennett and Hodge demonstrated considerable anxiety about mounting pressure on missionary societies to include Christian education and other projects in their programs and budgets. Characteristically, they moved cautiously, fearing that unnecessary aggravation would be counterproductive. Bennett suggested a conference of women representing the four boards and selected presbyterials and synodicals. She proposed to Hodge that preparations for such a conference be kept from the attention of the General Council as long as possible because "someone may forestall us with a plan that would make our situation difficult. I feel that we need to go to them with a well-worked out statement for which we are prepared to fight if need be."[29] To Lucy Dawson, Bennett confided, "Personally, I am more and more convinced that it is useless to let General Council know that we are confused, until we have a solution."[30]

While Bennett and Hodge worked behind the scenes to find a viable solution, one Presbyterian woman decided to confront the General Assembly directly with the widespread unrest and dissatisfaction among churchwomen. Louise Blinn, an officer of the Cincinnati presbyterial, told local reporters that Presbyterian women were subscribing large quantities of money but had no voice in its expenditure. They had become "tired of acting as a collection agency," she said, and were "drifting into other work and will continue to do so unless they are accorded equal suffrage privileges."[31] Largely on her own initiative, but supported by some members of her presbyterial executive committee, Blinn drew up a petition, which she circulated widely for endorsement and forwarded to the General Assembly in May, 1924. The petition asked for the removal of all sexual discrimination in ordination standards, for the organization of a Woman's Missionary Society that would have power to appoint women to sit on General Assembly boards, and for the right of such an organization to receive and disburse funds from women's organizations designated for the work of the boards.[32]

The General Assembly, embroiled in a prolonged fundamentalist/liberal power struggle, did not give much attention to Blinn's proposal. It simply referred the petition to the General Council with instructions to report the following year.[33] After consideration, the General Council opposed the formation of a new woman's organization on the grounds that consolidation had not been given sufficient time to prove its adequacy. It rejected the request for full representation on judicatories because the issue of ordination had been voted down by presbyteries as recently as 1921. In his personal reply to Blinn, Clarence Macartney, chairman of the General Council, indicated that she and her supporters had no recourse but to resubmit their request to a future Assembly. As an acknowledged opponent of equality for women, Macartney's concluding remarks provided Blinn no consolation: "We are proud of our women—their intelligence, their industry, their great achievements for the Kingdom of God, and their loyalty to the faith of the New Testament."[34]

Blinn received little support from the women serving on the new mission boards because of her tactic of head-on confrontation with the General Assembly. When Blinn requested the names and addresses of missionary officers, Bennett and Hodge refused to cooperate because they considered such lists confidential. In addition, Bennett and Hodge issued a statement disclaiming any responsibility for the petition and systematically refuting most of its arguments.[35] Gertrude Schultz of the Board of Foreign Missions sent a personal and confidential memo to staff members in which she warned that any formal association with Blinn's petition could "put us in a rather bad light" and expressed her hope that "things would quiet down in Ohio instead of being stirred up again."[36]

In the meantime, the Woman's Committees of the Boards of National and Foreign Missions had worked out details in preparation for a conference to discuss "The Future of the Women's Organizations in the Church," to be held in April 1925 in New York. Female members of each of the four boards attended as did a group of women from the church at large, one of whom was Louise Blinn. Chaired by Bennett and Hodge, the conference produced two resolutions that represented a compromise solution to the confused status of women's organizations. First, the conference agreed that women should be related to all four General Assembly boards rather than to only the two mission boards; second, that there should be in each local church one inclusive organization, its program uniting educational, service, social, and financial interests. In the crucial matter of finances, participants, after considerable debate, agreed that "the financial program shall be *primarily* the support of work committed to the organized women by the General Assembly," i.e., the traditional home and foreign missionary projects.[37]

Stenographic notes taken at the 1925 conference indicate that women were still confused and angry at what was happening to their organizational structures. A number had heard rumors that the Board of Christian Education was about to form its own women's organization if missionary societies were not willing to cooperate. One woman expressed her frustration with an apparent decline in missionary giving: "We've got to reach the women because the men aren't going to do anything." Another gave this candid appraisal of recent developments: "This whole question seems to be about church dollars and politics. Until the women get in our whole church organization a much more representative organization, the men must willingly and by right give women their place. We are still in a position where if we cannot be loved, we must be respected." She concluded her remarks with this conviction: "I think the men are absolutely puzzled to death to know what to do with us, but I do believe that holding your own budget simply as a symbol of ability to carry a big task lovingly, prayerfully, and successfully has done more for the women of the Presbyterian Church than anything else has done."[38]

While some conference members differed on matters of timing and method, most agreed that the trend demanded unifying and integrating women's work into the life of the total church. "The four boards should be on a uniform basis," said Mrs. Robert W. Freeman of Pasadena, California. "It is not fair for the organized women to be disorganized in such a way."[39] Nevertheless, Bennett expressed a consensus that the work of fifty years by women's missionary organizations should be preserved. In a rhetorical question to which all apparently responded affirmatively, Bennett said, "Is not our first interest to conserve all of that work and to see the way that we can adjust ourselves to a new program?" She concluded with a hope that the new plan "not revolutionary, not very strange, be blessed."[40]

Responses from the boards to the resolutions were slow in coming. The Board of Ministerial Relief never formally replied because it anticipated becoming self-supporting through a proposed pension plan. The BCE accepted the resolutions in principle but declined to make a final decision until financial relationships were clarified. It countered with a suggestion that "each of the four Boards of the Church have a definite percentage of the budget in the new inclusive organizations for women in church, presbytery, and synod."[41] The Boards of Foreign and National Missions issued a joint response that rejected the feasibility of organizing women's work on a national level and deemed it unwise to enlarge the financial responsibility of the organized women of the church.[42] Clearly, those Boards did not want to share any of the women's $3,000,000 budget with the Board of Christian Education. As one minister observed privately, "We men better let alone the goose that lays the golden egg."[43]

Thwarted in their efforts to clarify the relationship of women's organizations to the four boards, Bennett and Hodge urged the General Council to effect some resolution in the deteriorating situation. Distracted by other pressing denominational problems and of divided opinion about the future of women's organizations, the Council requested Bennett and Hodge to prepare an analysis of "Causes of Unrest Among the Women of the Church" to provide a framework for discussion and possible action. This report, given to the General Council on November 30, 1927, presented a direct and comprehensive statement of women's concerns. It chronicled the rise and development of women's organizations, including the traumatic effects of the 1923 reorganization, and made a strong plea for ecclesiastical equality for women (see chapter 8). It also warned that unresolved questions regarding the nature of women's organizations and their relationships to the four boards should be dealt with immediately through consultations involving both men and women. "Until this is done," the report concluded, "there will be unrest with potentialities of loss to the church."[44]

Impressed with the clarity and directness of Bennett's presentation, the General Council appointed a Committee of Four (Bennett, Hodge, Mudge, Speer) to study ways in which recommendations contained in the report could be implemented. The committee decided to call a conference between fifteen representative women and the General Council on November 22, 1928, in Chicago as an initial step. It hoped that a frank and open exchange of ideas would provide a basis for formulating specific recommendations to the General Assembly so that the status of women as individuals and the place of women's organizations in the Presbyterian Church could be settled.[45]

As the conversation between the churchwomen and General Council members developed, it soon became evident that neither group could articulate a simple course of action regarding the future of women's organizations. In fact, although the question of women's organizations had a prominent place on the agenda, discussion repeatedly focused on the more general question of equality for women in terms of ordination rights and equitable representation on church boards. Speer, who played a prominent role in the conference, was convinced that the theoretical question of equality should have priority over the more practical matters of organizational structure. He preferred a hands-off policy vis-à-vis women's organizations, letting them decide their own future without direct interference by the General Assembly. As a result, the Committee of Four, with Speer as chairman, recommended to the General Council a series of overtures to change the *Constitution* to permit women to be ordained as ministers, elders, and evangelists.[46]

Both Katharine Bennett (who was unable to attend due to family illness) and Margaret Hodge were troubled that the General Council had elected to deal with the ecclesiastical status of women rather than with the specific question of the relationship of women's organizations to the BCE, which continued to press the General Council for the right to be included in missionary society budgets. Bennett and Hodge both wrote to Speer, urging him not to underestimate the importance of settling this long-standing problem. Aware of Speer's deep interest in foreign missions, Hodge pointed out that with missionary societies under tremendous financial pressures, the trend to siphon off funds for local causes was "widespread and of alarming proportions." Supported by a request from the Council of Woman's Committees of the Mission Boards, Hodge asked Speer to recommend that the General Council call yet another conference of women who would survey the whole field of women's service to the church and suggest the type of organization needed to fit changing conditions in church life.[47]

Speer agreed to this and asked the General Council to call a Conference on Women's Status and Service in the Church to meet in St. Paul, Minnesota, just prior to the opening session of the General Assembly. Membership of the conference, which met on May 20–21, 1929, included female board representatives, members of traditional missionary societies and the inclusive federations and associations, and churchwomen unaffiliated with any local organization. This diverse group agreed upon some far-reaching changes in the nature of women's organizations. Reiterating the decision made in 1925, the women proposed that local organizations should relate their educational and service programs to all four church boards, although local societies should have freedom to adopt structures best suited to their individual needs and preferences. After prolonged discussion, participants agreed to undertake the new financial responsibility of Christian education provided that missionary programs already in effect would not be cut back. The exact basis of financial cooperation was to be worked out by a representative committee of men and women from the three boards, General Council, and synodical and presbyterial societies.[48]

Moving quickly, the General Council appointed a "Committee on Basis of Financial Cooperation," chaired by William Hiram Foulkes, pastor of the First Presbyterian Church of Newark, New Jersey. The committee met in the fall of 1929 and adopted several significant resolutions: First, that the mission boards add to their budget for 1931–32 "a suitable financial objective for the Board of Christian Education based on specific objects." Second, that the exact amount of this financial objective be determined by the committee after an "adequate educational program" had been completed. Third, that a syllabus be prepared to be used in local missionary groups as a basis for discussion of the whole question. These resolutions, along with an appeal for cooperation, appeared in *The Presbyterian* and other church papers early in October prior to the meeting of the General Council and precipitated another series of confrontations between women and the denominational hierarchy.[49]

The Committee on Financial Cooperation made a tactical error in distributing its report to church papers before it had been approved by the General Council. Missionary society leaders felt that the denomination was moving too far and too fast. Gertrude Schultz warned Speer that "the women of our church are up in arms against again being legislated without consultation."[50] Letters and calls poured into the mission board offices, opposing the proposals of the Committee on Financial Cooperation. One woman said that she and her friends were fed up with "the coercion from the 'higher-ups.' We are ceasing to be Presbyterian," she complained. Another wrote, "It is just too bad that the great General Council of the Presbyterian Church in the U.S.A. has not, and cannot have, an approach to the large body of our women who sit silent and timid in a Synodical meeting but have plenty to say when they get home."[51]

Apparently both the General Council and the "representative women" who met in St. Paul underestimated the discontent among the "missionary women" that had built up since the 1923 reorganization. Reacting to the opposition, the General Council modified the Committee on Financial Cooperation's report so that no final action about the future of women's organizations would be taken until women had time to study the syllabus and express their opinions. Moreover, the sensitive issue of financial support of Christian education was deferred and the vote limited to the question of including Christian education only in the program of missionary societies.[52] In a letter to "The Organized Women of the Presbyterian Church," Cleland B. McAfee, chairman of the General Council, assured women that "the selection of objects toward which these societies will contribute will be under their own direction, as hitherto." McAfee asked women to study the syllabus that presented the work of all three boards without prejudgment and to take a vote in the spring of 1931 on what work their societies wanted to include. This and similar attempts did not pacify angry churchwomen and failed to end the syllabus controversy. Strained relationships between the General Council and missionary societies existed for a number of years.[53]

While women were studying the "Syllabus on Women's Service in the Church," the General Council imposed a policy of strict neutrality on the mission boards and Christian education. Mission board files indicate that officials made every effort to implement the policy. When presbyterial and synodical presidents solicited opinions from staff members about the pros and cons of the syllabus, they received nothing but noncommittal replies. One frustrated synodical president complained to Stated Clerk Mudge that "the silence of our missionary leaders has proved very bewildering" especially when women were so accustomed to receiving guidance from the New York offices on important issues.[54] Katharine Bennett declined invitations to address local societies because she observed that her neutrality apparently convinced women that she was actually supporting the inclusion of Christian education.[55]

The Board of Christian Education, perhaps sensing its "underdog" status, adopted a less restrained interpretation of neutrality. Although its newsletters warned representatives of the BCE not to solicit invitations to speak to missionary societies, the Board took other partisan actions. In 1929, it appointed Mary Amelia Steer as a staff member whose responsibility was to "cultivate the interest of the women of the church in the nation-wide work of the Board of Christian Education."[56] The Board also issued a small pamphlet entitled, "Helps to the Study of the Syllabus," which presented Christian education as a logical extension of missionary endeavor. Vociferous protests from the mission boards caused the General Council to order the "Helps" withdrawn from circulation but not before the mission boards had written a letter to synodical and presbyterial presidents proclaiming that the "Helps" contained "unfair and inaccurate statements."[57] Caught in the crossfire of feuding boards, Hiram Foulkes wired mission headquarters in New York that he was "greatly distressed" to learn that the letter was already causing unfavorable repercussions at BCE headquarters in Philadelphia. His patience wearing thin, Foulkes confided to Mudge, "I feel it would be wonderful if these dear brethren and equally dear women who work with them, could just get together and be frank and talk things over in the presence of each other, instead of talking and writing separately."[58]

Resentment over aggressive BCE tactics accelerated dramatically when an article written by Mary Amelia Steer appeared in the December 1930 issue of *The Presbyterian Magazine*. Entitled, "All of Us Together," the article had as its thesis that Christian education should be included in the total life of the church, including women's missionary societies. The mission boards notified the General Council of their intention to issue their own statement of the implications of the syllabus and were dissuaded from doing so only when Mudge promised to reprimand the Board of Christian Education for not using better judgment and his influence to have another Steer article, "Christian Education Looks to Women," scheduled for 1931 publication, withdrawn by the editor.[59]

In local congregations, syllabus discussion engendered tension and resentment just as it did among board executives and staff members. "Missionary women" registered their disapproval that the General Council planned to tally votes on the syllabus by individual societies rather than by presbyterials. This apparent repudiation of traditional Presbyterian government suggested to them that the General Council did not take women's organizations seriously and perhaps wanted to influence the outcome of the vote in favor of inclusive groups.[60] From Christian education advocates came complaints that some missionary societies were circulating distorted representations of the possible impact of inclusive federations and associations. A California woman reported how "missionary women" at the Immanuel Church in Los Angeles had convinced that congregation to vote against including Christian education in its annual program. According to the informant, the "missionary women" argued that including Christian education would inevitably involve financial responsibility. That would necessitate closing schools and hospitals and sending missionaries home. Moreover, this would be the first in a long line of budget-draining additions: Red Cross, P.T.A., Community Chest, and other civic interest would surely follow. As a clinching point they alleged (incorrectly) that Christian education already had more money than it could spend, so funds diverted from missionary projects would only add to an already large surplus.[61]

When the vote was taken in the spring of 1931, it was evident that there was considerable opposition to the inclusion of Christian education. In response to the question, "Does your organization favor the inclusion among your yearly programs on Foreign and National Missions of one or more programs of the work of the Board of Christian Education?," the vote was 2,001 societies no, and 1,669 societies yes. Another 3,000 societies did not vote, an act that some interpreted either as disinterest or as a silent protest to the entire procedure. In terms of individual votes, 34,094 women voted no, and 29,337 voted yes. Therefore, a negative majority of 333 societies and 4,577 individuals did not wish at that time to include Christian education in their programs.[62]

Having expressed their opinion, Presbyterian women assumed that the syllabus controversy was over and that they could retain their traditional societies at least for the immediate future. Some members of the Committee on Financial Cooperation, however, dissatisfied with the small percentage of societies participating in the balloting, were convinced that the figures indicated ambivalence rather than conviction.[63] In particular, Lewis Mudge, who had indicated privately on a number of occasions that he favored the inclusion of Christian education, thought that a representative committee of men and women should be appointed to analyze the enormous amount of correspondence that had accumulated during the syllabus controversy. Such information, he thought, would give the General Council a clearer picture of what the majority of churchwomen were thinking. At Mudge's urging, the Committee on Financial Cooperation recommended this action to the General Council in May 1931.[64]

Women reacted to this as a rejection of their expressed will, and their outpouring of resentment culminated in a public confrontation with Mudge at their third biennial meeting in May 1931. With every seat in the auditorium filled and with women standing along the walls and in the aisles, Mudge responded to questions concerning why the General Council did not accept the syllabus vote as the will of organized churchwomen. The full account of the meeting in *Women and Missions,* while factually accurate, does not convey the hostility that Mudge faced at the meeting.[65] Notes taken by an eyewitness indicate that women were uninhibited in expressing their displeasure with the "heavy-handed" tactics of the General Council. When a woman asked Mudge if he thought that a committee could objectively interpret the significance of the vote, there were loud shouts of "No!" before Mudge could formulate a reply. Another questioner asked Mudge if he thought that the General Council or the General Assembly really took the votes of women seriously. Mudge assured her that both bodies "represent all of us, men and women," to which again there were "loud No's." The questioner retorted, "In the words of the little boy, cite your proofs!"[66]

After Mudge left the auditorium, the women debated what action, if any, they as a biennial would take. By an overwhelming vote, the biennial went on record as registering "our earnest protest" against the creation of a committee to study the significance of the syllabus vote because it would "continue and exaggerate the confusion and unrest which have hampered our work during the past year."[67] The General Council continued its plans, but as a concession to the irate women, it reduced the size of the proposed committee, eliminated the male members, and made Katharine Bennett chairman. This action mollified a large number of churchwomen who had confidence that Bennett and the two other committee members, Margaret Hodge and Mary Marcell, would represent their interests fairly.[68]

Katharine Bennett gave the final word on the extended syllabus controversy in her report to the General Council in the spring of 1932. After soliciting additional responses from synodical and presbyterial officers and pastors, the committee concluded that the evidence indicated that there was a "general prejudice against and lack of sympathy with the agencies of the Church" and a fear that additional financial burdens at the present time would jeopardize the established missionary program. It also thought that the negative vote of the missionary societies did not necessarily reflect the wishes of all women in the denomination. The committee agreed that there was "a growing desire for unification of program and for the study by all of the church of the whole work of the church." While not suggesting financial relationships, the committee recommended that the mission boards and Christian education continue to cooperate wherever possible and that local missionary societies wishing to incorporate Christian education into their programs should be encouraged to do so.[69]

This report reflected what Bennett, Hodge, and other leaders of the former Woman's Mission Boards were saying privately. Missionary societies as constituted in the nineteenth and early twentieth centuries could no longer maintain a separate existence and had to be related to the denomination to avoid unilateral action from the General Council and the General Assembly, which might radically alter their status. Following the syllabus debate, Bennett openly supported a move to encourage the formation of inclusive societies while at the same time preserving some of the best features of missionary programs. Writing for *Women and Missions,* Bennett described efforts to incorporate Christian education into the program and budget of missionary societies as an "on-going process" in the life of the church. "This process had not been approved by some," she admitted, "but it is necessary to accept facts and to make an impartial study apart from personal preferences." Recalling the negative syllabus vote, Bennett concluded, "One would not minimize the influence nor result of the Syllabus, but one faces facts—that on-going processes are making necessary open-minded consideration by the women of the church and of any and all matters that affect their organizations."[70]

The General Council subsequently facilitated this "on-going process" of unification discreetly by making changes in the structures of women's relationship to the three boards. Warned by Hodge that "there would be a real uprising on the part of women" if the General Council continued to force the Christian education issue on women, Mudge followed what he termed "a tactful and patient approach."[71] In its report to the General Assembly in 1934, the General Council recommended that the women's meetings held in conjunction with Assembly sessions should be directed jointly by all three boards "on an equal basis of influence and action." This gave Christian education an opportunity to share the limelight previously reserved solely for the mission boards. The General Council also authorized a *Handbook for Women's Societies,* prepared cooperatively by the three boards, that emphasized the values of inclusive local organizations. At the same time, the General Council created the Women's Joint Committee consisting of four women from each of the three boards to interpret structural changes to women through the country and to minimize within the boards themselves clashes over territorial rights and prerogatives.[72]

By the mid-1930s, the trend regarding the relationship of organized Presbyterian women to denominational structures clearly pointed to an inclusive organization. Although moving cautiously, the General Council appeared determined to integrate Christian education into the mainstream of women's concerns. During Mudge's tenure as stated clerk, he used his influence to support policies and procedures that promoted inclusive societies. Many women recognized that if local societies adopted this style, they would inevitably need to create an inclusive national organization to unite the diverse interests of Presbyterian women throughout the country. To develop and secure Assembly approval would take a decade; nevertheless, the "on-going processes" so evident to Katharine Bennett in the 1930s were leading the women into a new era.

5

NATIONAL ORGANIZATION:
Simple, Flexible, and Capable
of Development,
1933-1958

Controversy engendered by reactions to denominational reorganization
and the continuing question of Christian education and its relationship
to women's work rallied "missionary women" together in their efforts to
preserve their societies. Leaders such as Bennett, Hodge, and Schultz,
while supporting the right of women to determine their own future,
became convinced that Presbyterian women would fare better if they
followed sister denominations and adopted the principle of inclusive
local societies. With such a structure, a variety of programs and causes
would merge into one congregational organization. Moreover, aware of
the pain women had experienced over their loss of a national identity
with the demise of the Woman's Boards in 1923, the leading churchwomen explored ways in which the fragmented unity could be restored.
To do so was difficult, however, in terms of convincing both the General
Council and Presbyterian women throughout the country of the desir-
ability of a representative national organization of women to complete
the existing local, presbyterial, and synodical structure.

Impetus for such an inclusive national organization stemmed in part
from the positive experience of Presbyterian women who had participated in interdenominational missionary and church associations
since the early 1900s. In these groups, women experienced the importance of cooperation on specific projects, the value of exchanging ideas
and insights, and the increased power and influence that accrued when
women united to support worthy causes. The Central Committee of the
United Study of Foreign Missions (1901), The Federation of the
Women's Boards of Foreign Missions (1908), and the Council of Women
For Home Missions (1915) were some of the notable pioneering interdenominational groups. Katharine Bennett served the Council of
Women for Home Missions as president from 1916–23, and Margaret
Hodge, Gertrude Schultz, Florence Tyler, and other Presbyterian

women held important offices in various foreign missionary organizations. Along with the missionary-oriented groups were local interdenominational councils of churchwomen whose programmatic interests included but was not limited to home and foreign missions. By 1924, there were approximately 1,200 such local councils in the United States. They subsequently organized into the National Council of Federated Church Women and merged with two other groups to form the United Council of Church Women in 1941. In 1950, the United Council of Church Women became the General Department of United Church Women of the National Council of Churches and in 1966 was called Church Women United under the Division of Christian Unity of the National Council of Churches.[1]

Presbyterian women had also been active ecumenically within their own Reformed tradition through what is now known as the World Alliance of Reformed Churches. In 1892, a group of women formed the International Women's Union (IWU), which met in conjunction with the World Alliance meetings but had no official relationship with that group. In 1933, the IWU requested formal recognition and asked for the right to elect a number of women to sit as corresponding members of the World Alliance with the right to speak but not to vote. With the strong support of William B. Pugh, who became stated clerk of the PCUSA church in 1938, the World Alliance approved the request. In 1954, a Department of Women's Work was established in order to integrate women more fully into the life and work of the World Alliance.[2] Contacts with women in other churches in the Reformed tradition made American women aware of opportunities for service open in other denominations but denied them in their own. Discussions conducted by the World Alliance on the place of women in church life, for example, sparked renewed interest in the ordination of women to the gospel ministry in the 1950s.[3]

A more specific factor in creating interest in a national organization of Presbyterian women was the proposed merger of the Boards of National Missions and Christian Education, a move that was under serious consideration by the General Assembly in 1934–35. Although the committee appointed to study unification of the two boards ultimately recommended maintenance of the status quo, many women were deeply concerned that such a merger would drastically curtail longstanding home missionary programs and negate their symbolic victory in the syllabus controversy. Consequently, during 1934–35 Katharine Bennett and Margaret Hodge talked informally with the General Council and mission board members to ascertain their feelings about creating a national organization of Presbyterian women that would provide continuity no matter what was decided about board mergers.[4]

At this point, Louise Blinn intervened with a proposal to confront the General Assembly in 1935 with a petition for the creation of a "National Association of Women's Missionary Societies." In her inimitable free-wheeling style, which went around and over rather than through formal channels, Blinn informed Bennett and Hodge of her decision to circulate the petition only after she had contacted presbyterial and synodical presidents and, through the Executive Board of the Women's Missionary Society of Cincinnati Presbytery, had sent a copy to Stated Clerk Mudge. "We need a national organization," the petition concluded. "We must have a single instrument through which we can voice the opinion of the women of the church."[5]

Blinn's unilateral action upset the strategy of Bennett, who had suggested a similar plan to the Council of Woman's Committees for its consideration. Bennett's proposal, however, envisaged an inclusive organization that would incorporate the concerns of Christian education under its canopy, while Blinn's petition specifically referred to "missionary societies." When Blinn's action became public knowledge, Bennett and Hodge wrote McAfee and Speer to disassociate themselves from the petition. Acknowledging that Blinn was "an able woman and one whom we wish to consider, but a trifle difficult to work with," the women urged the men to use their influence on the General Council to have the petition referred to the Boards where they were confident it would not receive a sympathetic hearing. The General Council followed this course of action, and the request for a national organization was not raised at the General Assembly in 1935.[6]

Bennett and Hodge's opposition to Blinn's proposal was both philosophical and practical. They opposed the idea of a limited missionary organization because, through their interdenominational experience, they had become convinced that only inclusive organizations would appeal to the diverse interests of Presbyterian women, particularly those in the younger age group. They also wished to bury the Blinn petition because it had stirred up considerable resentment in the General Council and among leading churchmen in the denomination, with the argument reemerging that the women were trying to "go their own way" and were seeking to form a "church within the church." Mark Matthews, who had been so influential in diverting the General Council's recommendation of full ordination for women in 1929, was incensed at the Blinn petition and announced his intention to organize opposition at the General Assembly, where he was a perennial commissioner.[7] Speer concurred with Matthews on this point. Speer told Hodge, "There would seem to be no reason why women should feel that they need a special separate church organization. As a matter of fact, they are in the majority and if they are not adequately represented in Presbytery and Synod and the General Assembly, it is simply because they do not exercise their full constitutional rights."[8]

When Blinn's hopes of stirring the General Assembly into immediate action did not materialize and the General Assembly decided in 1935 not to merge National Missions and Christian Education, the issue of a national organization for women receded into the background. Although Blinn made another abortive attempt five years later, Bennett and Hodge worked through the Woman's Committees of the Boards and the national meetings to lay the groundwork for a national organization. At the 1935 national gathering in Asheville, North Carolina, which Bennett chaired, the 300 participants agreed that social education and action, at that time a division of the Board of Christian Education, should be an essential, ongoing concern for women's groups. The Asheville assembly endorsed the statement that "any area of life not occupied by the Spirit of Christ is a 'mission field.' "[9]

At the national gathering of Presbyterian women at Buck Hill Falls, Pennsylvania, in 1938, delegates took another step toward a national organization. Affirming that "a broad program is required to meet the needs of the age in which we live," the women delineated a wide range of concerns including race relations, international relations, temperance, and industrial relations, and projects in Bible study, mission education, stewardship, and social education and action. They also recommended that the Woman's Joint Committee of the Boards of National Missions, Foreign Missions, and Christian Education assume the responsibility for working out a viable method of cooperation in the prescribed areas. As the result of actions taken at Buck Hill Falls, a single *Handbook for Leaders of Women's Organizations* was produced to replace the publication formerly issued by the mission boards. In addition, in the spring of 1939 the Woman's Joint Committee published a brief statement of "Cooperative Relationships in Women's Work," which was distributed to presbyterial and synodical organizations throughout the country.[10]

These decisions did not arbitrarily change the emphasis of women's groups but rather reflected developments at the local level, where Presbyterian women already were establishing inclusive societies. The number of restricted local societies gradually declined so that by 1941 there were approximately 4,500 as compared to a high of more than 6,000 in 1930. The growth of inclusive associations and federations was significant. Between 1932 and 1941, their number grew from 378 to 1,953.[11] These changes also affected presbyterial structures. By 1943, 138 of the 258 presbyterial societies had voted to become inclusive rather than strictly missionary organizations, and by the 1950s all presbyterial and synodical societies had accepted the inclusive philosophy.[12]

All that remained following the action at Buck Hill Falls in 1938 was to include Christian education in the annual women's budget. Although resistance to this step persisted into the 1940s, a new generation of women evidently was ready to change former practices. A survey of younger women conducted at the request of the 1938 quadrennial concluded that in order to enlist their interest and support there should be a much broader and varied program of women's work. One woman summed up her feelings of frustration, which were shared by many of her friends: "Isn't it beneath the dignity of a great church such as ours that groups of women, either in committees or in National Meetings, should haggle for seventeen years over the question of who should give to what and why and when?"[13] At their national meeting in 1942, women approved a recommendation that set up an annual goal of $50,000 for Christian education to be attained by voluntary offerings from local societies. By 1947, two out of every three presbyterials were supporting Christian education financially and a decade later the portion of the budget designated for Christian education had grown to over $500,000.[14]

Meanwhile, the quadrennial committee appointed at Buck Hill Falls to plan the next national meeting in 1942 had also been instructed to include among its deliberations some course of action that might result in the formation of a national organization of women. With the retirement of Mudge in 1938 and the election of Pugh as stated clerk, the General Council appeared more open to discuss impassionately the future of women's work in the denomination. Pugh apparently did not share Mudge's misgivings about a national organization, and leaders such as Speer and Matthews were no longer powerful forces in church politics.[15]

While the quadrennial committee chaired by Katharine R. Strock discussed strategy and conferred with Pugh about forming a national organization of women, an incident occurred at a meeting of the Indiana Synodical in 1941 that provided a catalyst for immediate action. It involved a conversation between Peter Marshall, the nationally known Presbyterian clergyman and chaplain of the senate, and several leading Presbyterian women, including Katherine McAfee Parker and Marian Clements. During a luncheon at the Parker home, discussion centered on the question of organizing women into some new type of national organization. Some guests favored such a step, and others were hesitant about changing the status quo. Suddenly Marshall, who had been listening quietly to the extended discussion, offered his opinion. "These women shouldn't be squabbling over what kind of organization they should have," he said. "I think the General Assembly should simply tell them what kind of organization they should have." No one responded directly to Marshall, but after lunch Marian Clements and Katherine Parker decided that they preferred to control their own destiny rather than to be directed by churchmen who held the same views as Peter Marshall. From their hands came the first draft of a petition from the Indiana Synodical requesting the immediate creation of a national organization of Presbyterian women.[16]

In response to requests from the quadrennial committee for assistance, Pugh suggested that the *Form of Government* under the provisions of Chapter XXIII gave women and other groups freedom to unite in national organizations provided only that they secure approval from the General Assembly and report annually to that body. Although women had long been aware of the provisions of Chapter XXIII, they wanted some indication from the General Council that their petition would be favorably received and would not result in further interference of that body with their internal organization. Assured by Pugh, they proceeded to present their request.[17]

The petition to the General Council cited three major reasons for creating a national organization of Presbyterian women. First, it would provide national representatives for interdenominational groups such as the recently formed United Council of Church Women and would enable Presbyterian women to plan interdenominational projects such as the World Day of Prayer and the May Luncheons in the interest of missions. Under existing arrangements, women were officially represented by women board members and secretaries of the mission boards who did not have sufficient time to devote to interdenominational activities. Second, the proposed group would provide a continuity of leadership to plan the quadrennial meetings and other national gatherings and would enlist the support of women outside the traditional missionary society structures. Third, it would keep as its stated primary purpose the deepening of the spiritual life of women by providing materials for intensive Bible study, opportunities for corporate prayer, and updated information on denominational policies and projects.[18]

Even with Pugh's endorsement and the enthusiastic support of the women members of the General Council, the petition did not pass routinely. Only after several extended discussions, during which some Council members expressed the oft-repeated concern that the request might be the beginning of an effort to launch a "women's church," did the Council approve the recommendation. Final ratification was the responsibility of the General Assembly, meeting in the spring of 1943.[19]

The women selected Helen Weber, an articulate and highly respected member of the General Council, to present their recommendations to the 155th General Assembly. In her speech, Weber assured commissioners that the new organization would represent all churchwomen, "not just the missionary-minded who form our present set-up and who constitute less than half of all Presbyterian women." While chiding her audience that of the 464 commissioners that year only eight were women, Weber nevertheless assured them, "Do not be anxious. The women have no desire to separate from you, taking their contributions with them. . . . You know that the women have never failed in loyalty and service."[20] By a unanimous vote, the General Assembly approved the creation of The National Council of Women's Organizations of the Presbyterian Church in the United States of America and, just as it had done for well over a century, applauded the significant contribution of women to the life and work of the denomination.[21]

The National Council of Women's Organizations, later referred to simply as Presbyterian Women's Organization (PWO), was designed by its founders to be "simple, flexible, and capable of development," and one that relied essentially on volunteer staff. At the local level, where there was still division between "missionary" and "inclusive" societies, the PWO gave women an option of either, depending on individual preferences. At the same time, however, it defined the national organization as "a fellowship which accepts new responsibilities for new adventures, and sees as part of its whole work everything Presbyterian women do in their own churches, committees, the nation and the world which is related to them as church women."[22]

Inez Moser, chairman of the executive committee charged with working out organizational procedures, became the first president of the PWO and presided over the initial plenary session in 1946 when for the first time sessions opened to nondelegates. In attendance were some 1,500 women, guests from national and foreign mission fields, and young people from the recently organized Westminster Fellowship. The program featured the introduction of a new magazine for women, *Outreach*, and of new program planning materials that stressed missions, Christian education, and social and political issues. It also highlighted the appearance of Rev. Tamaki Uemura, the first Japanese civilian to visit the United States following World War II, whose presence precipitated a controversy over the ordination of women. (See chapter 9.)[23]

As it came to be recognized and accepted by Presbyterian women as "their organization," PWO replaced the mission boards as the focal point of women's work in the denomination. Writing to a friend shortly after her retirement in 1942, Katharine Bennett acknowledged that the creation of PWO had "closed one period of women's organizations in the church" and that power now resided in the national organization rather than in the women's committees of the three boards.[24] Yet progress was slow. During the first five years of its existence, for example, the General Assembly *Minutes* recorded only that the PWO president had made a report, which "was received." Not until 1949 did a full report of PWO activities appear in the *Minutes* and from then on became standard procedure. This report increased the visibility of the PWO at

General Assembly meetings and to the entire denomination, thereby helping secure and maintain status during its formative years.

On one occasion, observers credited PWO president Moser with making the pivotal speech that influenced the General Assembly to make one of the largest financial commitments in the history of the denomination. At the end of World War II, the Presbyterian Church initiated the Restoration Fund, a program to raise $25,000,000 over and above regular benevolence giving to help alleviate the suffering and starvation caused by the war and to assist struggling Christian congregations and missions in Europe and Asia. At the General Assembly in 1947, the commissioners, reflecting some ambivalent feeling from the church-at-large, wavered on approving a $17,000,000 budget and adding to that a 62 percent increase in benevolence giving to implement the Restoration Fund.[25]

In this context, Moser gave her report to the General Assembly as president of PWO. She described her visit to Leyte in the Philippines where with a Filipino pastor she had viewed a military cemetery containing 12,000 crosses. "We paid a heavy price, didn't we?" Moser inquired of her host. The pastor expressed his hope that the Filipino Church might be worthy of that sacrifice. In retelling the incident, Moser made a dramatic appeal to the commissioners. "I prayed that the American Churches would make themselves as expendable as our boys made themselves. I came here to ask you to do that. We can have one world if we care enough. . . . We can have it only if we are ready to expend ourselves utterly in sending out men of good will to preach the gospel. If we fail, if we do not build one world, it will be because the church in America is too complacent to be able to see the opportunity God is putting into our hands today." According to Harold E. Fey, correspondent covering the Assembly for the *Christian Century*, "That speech decided the issue." The Assembly approved the Restoration Fund without a dissenting vote, and the commissioners, caught up in the emotion of the moment, rose spontaneously to sing the doxology.[26]

Moser's appeal for the Restoration Fund reflected the long-standing concern of Presbyterian women for the missionary enterprise and ecumenical witness of the Christian church. The PWO continued to stress these interests. On a regular basis, the president of the PWO and members of the executive committee went on fellowship missions to Europe, South America, Mexico, Alaska, and most of the mission areas of the United States. The trips were undertaken as expressions of "the loving concern of women from our churches to those women in other lands, and to our neighbors in our own country," and usually resulted in some significant monetary support or leadership assistance.[27]

The PWO continued the traditional support of the mission and education programs of the church through its "second-mile giving." In the first ten years of its existence, the PWO annually contributed between $2,000,000 and $3,000,000 to benevolence projects supported by the three boards. In 1954, the PWO report listed its projects in the areas of National Missions, Overseas Work, and Christian Education, among which were the erection of buildings and chapels, training of nurses, health projects, and financial assistance to forty-four Presbyterian colleges.[28]

From the outset of its existence, the PWO also took a position on contemporary social issues. At its initial meeting, delegates passed a resolution urging the prohibition of the sale of alcoholic beverages near military bases and asked the government to consider imposing a ban on the manufacture and sale of intoxicating beverages for the duration of the war. Another resolution expressed a message of sympathy for displaced Japanese-Americans "assuring them of continued fraternal interest and prayer and eagerness to be of help."[29] The PWO later supported the work of the United Nations, endorsed the "Letter to Presbyterians" condemning the tactics of Senator Joseph McCarthy, and championed the Supreme Court decision to render segregation in public schools unconstitutional.[30]

The PWO frequently raised the question of the status of women regarding representation and ordination before the General Assembly. In her first address to the General Assembly, Moser reminded the commissioners that women had not yet attained full equality in opportunities for service in a church where theoretically there should not be "male or female but all one in Christ."[31] In 1954, PWO president Elizabeth Buchanan noted that women had a very small representation on the General Council (three of twenty-six voting members) and that these women represented the boards rather than the women of the church. She asked the General Assembly to consider doubling the female representation and adding the PWO president as a continuing member of the General Council, a request which the General Assembly subsequently approved.[32] The role of the PWO in promoting an overture to change the Constitution so that women could be ordained as ministers is described in chapter 9.

The PWO supported its social pronouncements with concrete actions. In the field of race relations, for example, Presbyterian women had a longstanding policy of integrating its national meetings. As early as 1931, Presbyterian women resolved that there was "a need for better adjustments among all races to promote economic justice and friendly understanding, and to eliminate the color line."[33] Whenever national convocations were held, those responsible for hotel arrangements insisted on written confirmation that facilities would be open equally to all races. In preparation for the meeting in Ocean Grove, New Jersey, in 1950, Marian Clements, chairman of the committee on arrangements, could not secure clear assurance from the Ocean Grove Camp Meeting Association (Methodist affiliated) that "colored women" would be given equal treatment with Caucasian delegates. After warning officials that the PWO would cancel all its reservations unless she received written confirmation of compliance, Clements enlisted the support of Stated Clerk Pugh and Methodist Bishop G. Bromley Oxnam. Through their offices, the PWO received written assurances of open accommodation. In terms of such active demands on racial equality, the PWO was in advance of the General Assembly itself, which did not put such a policy in force until the 1950s.[34]

In addition to its benevolence program and social concern, the PWO developed informed leadership at virtually every level where women were permitted to serve. By encouraging Bible study and prayer groups as an integral part of the service programs and by providing scholarly study aids, the PWO balanced its activities with intellectual growth. At the national meetings and through a variety of leadership training schools at presbytery and synod levels, PWO women received the tools and information necessary to participate responsibly in church life. What became evident was that through such preparation PWO women became more knowledgeable about the denomination's programs, policies, and theology than did most members of an average session except for the pastor.[35]

The PWO maintained a continuing interest in interdenominational and ecumenical cooperation, primarily through the World and National Councils of Churches. Within the Reformed tradition, PWO initiated conversations with women in the PCUS in 1948 to discuss areas of common interest and to explore possible cooperative ventures in Christian service. Women of both denominations held a meeting in Knoxville, Tennessee, with leaders from both traditions sharing in the planning and presentation of the program. Gertrude Irvine, PWO president, subsequently sent a letter to the presbyterial and synodical presidents of the PCUS inviting them to participate in the PWOs annual Prayer Advent Tryst. Through such contacts and cooperative programs, the leadership hoped they could speed "the ultimate reunion of these two branches of the Presbyterian Church."[36]

Although union negotiations broke down between the PCUS and PCUSA in 1955, a merger with the United Presbyterian Church of North America occurred in 1958. As a result, the PWO combined forces with the Women's General Missionary Society (WGMS) to form United Presbyterian Women (UPW). In bringing together two distinct traditions of women's service to the church, UPW hoped to enable women to "share more fully and more effectively in the life and work of our Church."[37] As approved by the 170th General Assembly, the UPW had as its purpose: "to proclaim the Gospel of Jesus Christ, to demonstrate His love in all areas of life, to declare our oneness with fellow Christians everywhere, to grow in Christian faith and responsibility."[38]

Despite its many accomplishments and evidences of growth and stature in the denomination, the PWO continued to face several unresolved tensions. Many churchmen remained unconvinced that women should have a separate organization both on theoretical and practical grounds. According to some churchwomen, it was not uncommon to hear comments from respected leaders, such as "When are you women going to join the church?" When a major reorganization of denominational structures took place in the early 1970s, the women once again had to defend their existence. Moreover, even though the PWO claimed some 500,000 members by 1958, more than three times that number of women on church rolls did not participate in local societies. The problem of attracting and keeping the interest of younger women continued to plague PWO leaders. Finally, the missionary versus inclusive society dichotomy of the 1930s and 1940s had not completely died. The union with the UPNA church brought in a number of women whose orientation was primarily missionary-centered. Although there were no overt controversies as there had been in the 1930s, the newly formed UPW had to go through a period of readjustment and transition during its initial years of organization.

Nevertheless, the creation of the UPW pointed up how women's organizations had developed since their humble origins as Female Cent Societies and sewing circles in the early nineteenth century. In that era when women were denied official status in church courts, their organizations afforded them identification in denominational life. With ordination no longer an issue, the function of the UPW would be to combine the strengths of the UPNA and PCUSA traditions and lead women in service to the Church. Paradoxically, this period would immediately be marked by major social and ecclesiastical developments that would have an impact on Presbyterian women. In particular, ecumenical currents, secularization, and the issue of feminism in American society would again cause women's organizations to reconsider their role and future in Presbyterian church life.

PART TWO
The Ordination of Women

6

QUESTIONING WOMEN'S ROLE:
Shall Women Speak?
1789-1880

Shall women speak in the church? This question had engaged the attention of Protestants long before the nineteenth century. It was, in fact, the reformer John Calvin's understanding of biblical teaching regarding women in church and society that provided an authoritative undergirding of Presbyterian exegesis for more than four centuries.

Presbyterian doctrine posited the subordination of women and the supremacy of man in the structure of human relationships as ordained and established by God. Calvin had argued that from the beginning of human existence, man was given the prerogative of the exercise of authority and leadership, while woman was assigned to be an aide and helpmeet to man. In his commentary on Genesis, Calvin concluded that since the order of nature implies such a role, "women should study to keep this divinely appointed order." Although insisting that female subordination was not degrading, Calvin nevertheless defined the female *imago dei* as being "in the second degree," that is, under the dominion of males by God's creational ordinance.[1]

Such a mandate toward role definition was so firmly instilled in the doctrine of the church that early fathers of the Presbyterian Church in the U.S.A., Old School, New School, or United, never approved an explicit restriction concerning women speaking in the *Constitution* of the church. Earlier in the century, they probably felt that their interpretation of the biblical basis for keeping women from speaking was so generally accepted that no polity issue needed to be raised. In his commentary on First Corinthians, Professor Albert Barnes of Princeton Theological Seminary noted in passing that Paul's injunction that women be silent in church was a "positive, explicit, and universal rule. There is no ambiguity in the expressions and there can be no difference of opinion in regard to their meaning."[2] Confirming such, a writer in *The Presbyterian* claimed in 1872, "Our Confession of Faith and Form of Government say nothing on the subject [of the speaking and praying of women in mixed assemblies] simply because it never entered the head of any man in the Westminster Assembly that such a thing would ever be attempted in our denomination."[3]

In the early years of the establishment of the General Assembly in America, few women attempted to speak in the church, and the subject only intermittently appeared in print. By the 1870s, however, some men and women supported a more lenient interpretation of Scripture regarding women, influenced by the obvious: Women constituted a majority of most Presbyterian congregations, worked diligently for missions and education, participated in a substantial way in fund-raising and donations, and indeed were speaking in front of mixed groups. Pragmatically the commissioners to the General Assemblies and the Board executives walked a line between the need to accept and even broaden women's position and the theological pressure to maintain the traditional biblical teachings on the female role.

Besides the churchmen's ambivalence based on practice versus policy, they seemed confused by what it meant for women to "speak." Usually the term included preaching, teaching, lecturing, and praying in the social gatherings, the Sunday worship, and the special prayer meetings. In some cases, "speak" and "preach" were used interchangeably, but for those careful about language, preach had a more specific connotation. In one instance in 1876, a minister attempted to get a Presbyterian court to define "public speaking and preaching of women in the churches" to mean one or all of three things: as persons ordained to the ministry in the three offices of preacher, pastor, and bishop; as lay persons who take part in the social meetings of the church; and as lay persons invited into the pulpit to preach as an ordained minister preaches. The moderator ruled the point out of order, thereby leaving the question unresolved.[4] Also unresolved was the ambiguity concerning whether there might be a time or place appropriate to a woman speaking. Some thought it permissible for a woman to speak or pray aloud in all-female groups, while more liberal spokesmen even stretched this permission to the "social gatherings" (mixed) of the church. Very few clergymen condoned women's participation in the formal services.

These more practical considerations were joined by basic inquiries about what the scriptural prohibition against women speaking actually entailed. Influenced by new hermeneutical and theological approaches, some clergy began openly to suggest a modification of biblical assumptions evident in earlier discussions.

Presbyterian women generally were silent on the issue. Their forum was limited, of course, since they had no voice in church courts and rarely published in denominational journals. There is some support for the suggestion that women themselves were strongly opposed to a female's participation in public speaking in the church. Evidence suggests that Presbyterian women tended to stay in a culturally defined sphere of domesticity, maternalism, and political, social, and ecclesiastical subordination and were sensitive to any accusations of impropriety.

Indirectly, however, and perhaps inadvertently, many of these same women forced the issue of a female's right to speak in the church when they modestly and without publicity began to join in benevolent, humanitarian, missionary, and praying associations. As demonstrated in Part One, the impact of the societies on the churches' outreach led to increasing occasions for the women members to be invited to lecture and pray. Although admitting to timidity and fear of appearing before others, the women reported on the needs of missionaries, the evils of alcoholism, the observance of the Sabbath, or the responsibilities of the congregation members to further the work of the church at home and abroad.

Motivated by the increasing participation of women and by the evident benefit of it to the church, ministers began to address such activity early in the century. In 1837, a Presbyterian pastor, J. F. Stearns, lectured a group of Presbyterian women concerning "Female Influence, and the True Christian Mode of Its Exercise." In discussing women's spheres of influence, benevolence, and religion, Stearns went so far as to acknowledge that there were women undoubtedly capable of public debate, "who could make their voices heard from end to end of the church and the senate house." He even suggested that some might be better orators or more intelligent than men holding offices. Nevertheless, he admonished, "The question is not in regard to *ability*, but to *decency*, to order, to christian *propriety*."[5]

A Presbyterian judicatory spoke out against women speaking at least as early as 1826. Because a so-called "itinerant female" had been admitted as a public preacher into two churches under the care of presbytery, the Presbytery of Philadelphia enjoined ministers and elders to be "watchful for the future, and guard against such innovations."[6] The phrase "itinerant female" and the temper of the time suggest her relationship to the new surge of revivalism in America during the early nineteenth century. The Presbyterian clergy's opposition to the revivalists' support of itinerant and lay preachers and leniency in allowing women to actively participate in worship was no secret.

In fact, this opposition erupted into a public encounter in 1827 between Asahel Nettleton and Charles Finney, two well-known evangelists, when Nettleton criticized Finney's revival practices, particularly his support of women praying in public. Some ministers, including Lyman Beecher, agreed with Nettleton, while others aligned themselves with Finney. At a meeting termed the New Lebanon Convention, held on July 18, 1827, eighteen Presbyterian ministers attempted to resolve the conflict, but split evenly in their vote. The argument continued until a truce was called on May 27, 1828, when twelve of the main participants agreed to cease all public discussion of the subject.[7] Such a stalemate foreshadowed the intransigent attitudes that would color future discussions. Ambivalence, another sidebar, was evident as Finney himself was quoted as believing women's sphere to be in the home and as cautioning women to be silent if their speaking might cause problems.[8] Without question, however, the style of revivalism encouraged women to ever-increasing commitment and participation.

Certainly revivalism was the specific catalyst for the General Assembly's first and oft-quoted statement in 1832 on women speaking and praying in public. During the "dispute and debate" regarding revivals at the Assembly, it was suggested that a decisive letter be circulated to warn churches against practices in contention, one of which was females praying in public assemblies. The commissioners were divided on whether to send the letter with only four votes deciding the issue—126 yeas and 122 nays approved the pastoral letter. The three sentences pertaining to women, to be faithfully relied upon for most of the rest of the century, were contained in the "Pastoral Letter to Ministers and Churches" concerning revivals:

Meetings of pious women by themselves, for conversation and prayer, whenever they can conveniently be held, we entirely approve. But let not the inspired prohibitions of the great apostle to the Gentiles, as found in his epistles to the Corinthians and to Timothy, be violated. To teach and exhort, or to lead in prayer, in public and promiscuous assemblies, is clearly forbidden to women in the Holy Oracles.[9]

Exceptions to this sentiment still occurred. In 1836, the Presbytery of North River (New York) heard allegations of "a Female preaching in the Congregaton of Pittsburgh, with the consent & authority of the Session." The investigating committee found this to be true and recommended that the Session be censured for allowing not only such an irregular but also an unacceptable thing to happen.[10] Apparently such incidents were isolated but the subject was not put aside.

As the debate evolved over the years, the arguments based on the biblically inspired relegation of females to silence and subordination grew to include a substantive definition of what women were meant by "nature" to do. Admitting the woman's inherent affinity for religion, the writers suggested that this attribute should be used for influence only, giving her an exalted status. In popular literature, for one example, Cortland van Rensselaer's *The Presbyterian Magazine*, begun in

1851, printed "Household Thoughts." In the first volume, a woman writer claimed, "Women seem sometimes to forget in their complaints of the inferiority of their position to that of man, the honour, the glory, God has shed upon their sex."[11] In the second volume, "In religion is the crowning excellence of the female character . . . and . . . the woman who lacks it . . . fails of the dignity and destiny of her nature."[12]

In a more scholarly journal, the publishers of the influential *Biblical Repertory and Princeton Review*, Princeton Theological Seminary professors Charles Hodge, Archibald Alexander, and Samuel Miller, wrote of "ornamental womanhood." The *Review* readers, clergy and laymen who looked to it for guidance on theological and social issues, found that the editors believed women's activities should be limited to piety, sobriety, and righteousness in the wedded and maternal state, and that no female should attempt to assume any authority. Through the pages of this journal, these Old School, orthodox spokesmen defended their concepts about women's place for some years.[13]

Woman's culturally acceptable role—to make the home happy, to raise and educate the children (particularly in religious matters), to soften man's materialistic and political inclinations, to regulate social manners and morals, and to exemplify Christian piety—fit the model of "quiet influence." Churchmen pointed to Paul's injunction in 1 Cor. 14:35, "And if they will learn anything, let them ask their husbands at home; for it is a shame for women to speak in the church."[14] Any changes in social and religious patterns obviously would affect the workability of such a limitation. That was why the revivalists' practices of encouraging women's prayer meetings early in the century alarmed the clergy. "Set women to pray?" they argued. "Why, the next thing, I suppose, will be to set them to preach!"[15]

Despite the pervasive reinforcement of such role definition, many women toward mid-century began to change their patterns not only in supporting voluntary associations but also by moving into higher education and by assuming professional positions. Some of those who became active outside the home apparently saw no conflict between their maternal and domestic role and their other interests. Others seemed to recognize their breaking of stereotypical restrictions. Both inevitably found themselves engaging in a public sphere. Those who joined the antislavery movement, for instance, were discussing a political as well as a moral question, "an arena of controversy," that would have repercussions both on national concerns and on women's activities.[16] In fact, the exclusion of women from participation in the 1840 World's Anti-Slavery Convention in London led Americans to organize the famous 1848 meeting at Seneca Falls, New York, the first public demand by women for equal rights, including ecclesiastical rights. At this meeting, convened to "discuss the social, civil, and religious conditions and rights of woman,"[17] one resolution indicated the restlessness of these women over the churches' restrictions on speaking:

Resolved, therefore, That being invested by the Creator with the same capabilities, and the same consciousness of responsibility for their exercise, it is demonstrably the right and duty of women, equally with men, to promote every righteous cause by every righteous means; and especially in regard to the great subjects of morals and religion, it is self-evidently her right to participate with her brother in teaching them, both in private and in public, by writing and by speaking, by any instrumentalities proper to be used, and in any assemblies proper to be held.[18]

The issue that seemed to stir Presbyterians' concern over women speaking was female involvement in the temperance cause. The forum American Christianity provided for the temperance crusade meant that women active in the cause would be addressing congregations as well as secular gatherings. Nevertheless, Presbyterian women chose a fairly retiring role. Maintaining their "sphere" served as a means of self-identity, garnered social and ecclesiastical approval, and actually provided an opportunity for women to function in some areas without criticism. One Presbyterian, an active and involved individual influential in establishing church-related mission schools, wrote to her mother, "The only 'Women's Rights' I believe in is the right to do good, and I don't think we quire any legislating to avail ourselves of that."[19] Others openly criticized women who spoke in public. One woman who attended the American Board of Commissioners for Foreign Missions complained that she found it "decidedly tiresome to stand in the aisle for two hours to listen to feminine oratory," preferring that the speaker be a man if she had to stand for anyone.[20]

Writers in popular church journals invariably reinforced a subordinate role for women. The Presbyterian admonished its readers in 1849, "A Don Quixote fighting with windmills, may afford us amusement, but a Donna Quixote so occupied is quite a different affair. In a word, we give the supremacy to women, until she so far forgets herself as to declaim in public on woman's rights."[21] One clergyman opened with prayer a mixed meeting to be addressed by a woman, but "went out immediately after finishing, declaring that he would as soon rob a hen-roost as remain there and hear a woman speak in public."[22]

Clearly some women were ably functioning within the church. In the Cumberland Presbyterian Church, which also maintained a scriptural prohibition against women speaking, some women broke silence during church services. This might have stemmed from the Cumberland church's evangelical posture, from its location in frontier country, or from its "practical adaptableness, democracy in the form of government, and liberty in the choice of ministers."[23] One woman was said to have been a better preacher than her husband. As other women preached, one observer said, "We witnessed without offense those outpourings of earnest hearts which, we were satisfied from other sources, were right in the sight of God."[24]

Other such reports indicated that however strong the biblical and cultural standards, practice did not always match a denomination's utterances. The times when women spoke, though, did not represent a rebellion against the church but were isolated incidents, based on expediency, different beliefs, and, in many cases, ignorance of the church's stance.

A significant change in women's life-styles in the home, community, and church occurred after the Civil War. During the war, in addition to their war efforts, Presbyterian women continued their normal church activities, particularly in supporting home and foreign missionaries. Their work provoked an unprecedented article in *The Presbyterian,* which commended them for their many contributions during the conflict. Furthermore, it called for increased female participation in the church in peacetime.[25] After 1865, opportunities for Presbyterian females to work in the church appeared broader. Women themselves began to initiate responsibilities for various aspects of the church's program. The Bible, Cent, and Praying societies turned toward support of denominational missionary enterprises, and the local groups organized into regional and national associations in the 1870s. Women took a predominant role in teaching in the church schools and serving on home and foreign mission fields. Some ministers raised the issue of creating an order of deaconesses to utilize the women's skills of nurture demonstrated so ably during the war. The temperance movement, now largely composed of women, recruited women to speak on the subject in churches.

Consequently, in the last three decades of the nineteenth century, women began speaking, not only in the sense of addressing an audience but also in having a voice in church affairs. As a result, the arguments against such a thing took on a pragmatic character: First, if they were allowed to preach, the extensive training they would undergo might be forsaken for marriage and thus the education rendered useless and, second, men might forsake the work of religion more than they had already done. Even the liberal Unitarians were concerned. S. G. Bulfinch, in the *Monthly Religious Magazine,* pointed out that in most denominations women already controlled the charity work and dominated church attendance. "If we look at the condition of our churches . . . we find some ground for alarm lest religion should come to be regarded as woman's exclusive privilege. . . . Man may be willing to yield his place in the pulpit; will he long continue to occupy his place in the pew?"[26]

Traditional views indeed were being challenged, and attitudes began to waver in the face of expediency. In the postwar period, women from the sects and denominations that allowed women preachers began to gain a following, even in the Presbyterian church.[27] One such woman was the Quaker preacher Sarah F. Smiley. Smiley was described in *Harper's Weekly* as being a "woman of maturity, of sweet Christian character, and gifted with extraordinary powers as a preacher."[28] Smiley was respected by many clergymen and was in demand as a speaker in various churches including Presbyterian congregations. In 1872, Smiley was invited by Theodore L. Cuyler, prominent Presbyterian clergyman and author, to preach from the pulpit of the Lafayette Presbyterian Church in Brooklyn, whose membership was more than 1,400. Although a magazine article reported that the congregation took no offense at the unusual spectacle of a woman in the pulpit, the Presbytery of Brooklyn immediately called a meeting to consider what action should be taken in regard to Cuyler. [29]

At the meeting, Cuyler explained the circumstances of Smiley's address. He spoke of his cordial relations with the Society of Friends. He had spoken at a Friends meeting and in return had invited Smiley to his pulpit. Having announced this to his congregation in advance, he had received no objections. At the Sunday evening service, Cuyler reported, "her address, or discourse, was weighty, solemn, Scriptural, orthodox, tender, and melted some men to tears whom I have never seen so much moved before."[30] The members of the presbytery were moved not to tears but to rebuke Cuyler.[31] Although the presbytery took no direct action, it enjoined the member churches to abide by the 1832 deliverance of the General Assembly.

Women were speaking and praying in other Presbyterian churches. In that same month, a writer in *The Presbyterian* reported that he had received a letter from a friend who said: "Our younger Presbyterian ministers advocate, with all their might, females praying in mixed assemblies, and do not hesitate to declare, publicly and loudly, that there is not a word within the lids of the Bible against it. They seem to think there can be no revivals of religion without it. They are not satisfied with female prayer-meetings." The friend went on to describe how one minister attempted to get women to pray and expressed pity at the spectacle of a "modest and unassuming woman, who, contrary to her own wishes, was constrained by her husband's importunities to attempt praying in public."[32]

Concerned because of the Cuyler incident, the Presbytery of Brooklyn overtured the General Assembly of 1872 to make the 1832 deliverance binding by adopting and transmitting to the presbyteries rules forbidding women's licensing, ordaining, teaching, and preaching.[33] The Assembly replied that there was no need for a change in the *Constitution* of the church touching the question and called the previous deliverance "the judgment of this Assembly."[34]

Right after this meeting, the session of another Presbyterian church, the Second Church in Geneva, New York, invited Smiley to preach in the church on two Sundays in June 1872. According to *The Presbyterian*, Smiley preached on the first Sunday, but, because of so much opposition, "chiefly from the ladies of the church," the session reconsidered the invitation. The newspaper claimed that "Some persons have also left the Second church, and the excitement in the place is great. The only excuse given by the session for so troubling the waters is that Miss Smiley is a good woman, and that the expressions of the General Assembly in its late deliverance were only 'advisory.' "[35]

Two years later, Smiley was again in the Presbyterian papers, once more connected with the Lafayette Avenue Church in Brooklyn. Cuyler again invited Smiley to speak, but this time church members erected a special platform in front of the pulpit to avoid opposition to her use of the pulpit. She herself claimed that her visit was primarily "one of instruction to her Christian sisters and not that of a disturber of the peace."[36] Nevertheless, the presbytery chastised the church again, sending representatives to exhort the session to avoid such offenses in the future.

By this time, ministers and editors sympathetic to women participating in the church began to justify limited actions by the women. Social gatherings, midweek meetings, prayer groups, and women's societies were acceptable; the pulpit and the Sunday service were not. The editor of the *Herald and Presbyter*, published in Cincinnati, approved of Smiley's talks, claiming that she was not an ordained minister but only a teacher, and stating, "Those who have heard her and have expressed their gratification with her teachings are not to be understood as holding to the propriety of ordaining females to the office of the ministry."[37] The editor of the *Occident*, published on the west coast, however, found it difficult to draw the line between what a woman could and could not do. "She may teach in the Sunday-school, hold her Bible classes, composed perhaps of hundreds or even thousands of both sexes, lead the congregation in the service of song, etc.; in these things we all are agreed. She may not be a bishop; in that we are nearly or quite unanimous. But where the 'lecturing' ends . . . and the sermon begins, is not so plain."[38] The editor of *The Presbyterian* could not accept Smiley's appearances and wrote, "Just why the lady about whom so much of the discussion has centered, should be impelled, by a relentless destiny or some other cause, to exercise her gifts within the bounds of this particular ecclesiastical body, while there are so many liberal churches open to her, without any danger of bigoted opposition or notoriety, is an inscrutable mystery."[39]

In June 1874, another judicatory, the Presbytery of Rock River, Illinois, overtured the General Assembly to explain its 1872 judgment. "Does the Assembly mean to enjoin that in the regular weekly prayer-meeting of the Church no woman shall speak or lead in prayer?" The Committee on Bills and Overtures first recommended that the Assembly answer "Yes, except in emergencies, to be decided by the pastor or session." That recommendation was turned down, and a commissioner, Robert Aikman, substituted a resolution, stating that he hoped that "we shall make no authoritative utterance upon this subject, but leave it where it belongs; and thus permit every man to abide under the shadow of his own 'catalpa' or other tree, in peace." His resolution would say, "The Assembly expresses no opinion as to the scriptural view of woman's right to speak or pray in the social prayer-meeting, but commits the whole subject to the discretion of the pastors and elders of the churches."[40]

One minister at the Assembly called on his mother's memory in rebuttal, saying he must "resist this endeavor to place woman where God had not allowed her to come." Pointing out that he had a sister active in the temperance cause and another the originator of the Woman's Foreign Missionary Society, he claimed not to be one to put chains on women. "If there be chains, then they are golden ones, which intelligent Christian women wear with willing minds and cheerful hearts." The other side was supported by a self-described old-stager. "I am not at all given to new measures . . . but I hope we shall yield to the wishes of the Western brethren, and lift woman up to the level of speaking for the Lord Jesus and of working for Him."[41]

Clapping, even stamping, by Assembly commissioners broke out during the debate on the "woman question." A report in *The Presbyterian* disclosed shock and disgust over such unbecoming behavior that "came in with the war." The reporter could not understand "why Christian men and ministers should get so uproarious about women praying and exhorting in meetings for social prayer." Maybe the men were tired of doing all the praying, he concluded, or perhaps they wanted to shift responsibility to women.[42]

The final vote was 211 for the substitute resolution, 84 against. An observer's comment reflected much of the controversy that would emerge in following years on this resolution. He bemoaned the prospect of "a class of masculine women talking against time and endurance, because they have the right by overture of the Assembly, or the pastor and session must interfere, and some of these will have a delightful time in suppressing a fluent woman who thinks she has the right from the Assembly."[43]

Many in the church felt that the resolution was ambiguous, confusing, even evasive. A little more than a month later, *The Presbyterian* was declining articles that criticized a Philadelphia church session's action declaring against the speaking of women because, "We are of the opinion that the Assembly dodged a question which it was its place to answer; but when it authorized the churches to pass such rules as they saw fit on the subject, we think that members and ministers of other churches have no call to sit in judgment on them publicly, and condemn them."[44] Nevertheless, the Assembly's action also produced thoughtfulness and discussion that prompted some to reconsider the church's position. Even *The Presbyterian*, reporting that fifty more women than men were on the mission field, wrote, "Who knows? Perhaps even the question of lay-preaching by women may have to be remanded to the 'sanctified common sense' of the Foreign Board, after the manner of the famous decision of the Assembly of '74."[45]

Unquestionably the women's activities in missionary organizations and on the fields of service led to female speakers. Missionaries addressed groups to gain support for their projects. The very definition of the societies—to educate, promote, study, and pray for missions—demanded that the members assume a speaking posture. Many women had to be encouraged to do so. Mrs. S. M. Henderson in 1876 read a paper before the Pittsburgh and Allegheny Committee on Woman's Foreign Missions in which she charged that the church's sentiment against female prayer meetings put Christian women "at a great disadvantage from a consequent lack of training." She found women avoiding public praying because of want of talent, fright at the sound of their own voices, and loss of control of thoughts. Challenging her audience to try, she said, "We must be willing even to blunder for Christ."[46]

With the "woman question" openly an issue, the scene was set for what became the major confrontation in 1876 over two women speaking at a Newark Presbyterian church. This incident led to an ecclesiastical trial that involved all three judicatories of the Presbyterian Church, U.S.A., received national attention from church leaders and journals, and was placed in the record of the struggle for women's rights.[47]

In October of the centennial year, the Woman's Christian Temperance Union's (WCTU) national convention met in Newark. During the conference, Isaac M. See invited two women attending the meeting to speak at the Wickliffe Presbyterian Church. Upon learning that women had spoken from See's pulpit at the Sunday morning and evening services, Elijah R. Craven, pastor of the Third Presbyterian Church of Newark, instituted proceedings in the Presbytery of Newark. He formally charged See with "disobedience to the divinely enacted ordinance in reference to the public speaking and teaching of women in the churches, as recorded in 1 Corinthians xiv, 33–37, and 1 Timothy ii, 11–13."[48]

Craven did not explain why he singled out See as the sole target of his charge, since women from the WCTU delivered addresses from at least two other Presbyterian pulpits. A minister from one of the other churches tried to make a distinction between women speaking and preaching in explaining why See was charged. He wrote that "two women, licensed if not ordained, preachers were invited, as such preachers, to occupy brother See's pulpit morning and evening of the Sabbath, and they both *preached,* presenting themselves before the congregation which they addressed, not as mere temperance talkers but as duly authorized preachers of the gospel."[49] Whatever the reason, Craven chose personally to prosecute a charge, asserting that he was doing so because he felt that "there should be a judicial decision on this important case."[50]

The presbytery trial was long, opening on November 1 and ending on January 3, with the sessions held nearly weekly. Colorful and passionate speeches by the principals and attending presbyters appeared in both secular and religious newspapers, and spectators crowded the hearing room. If there was any question about women's interest in this subject, it was dispelled by the numbers of female attendees, including leaders from the suffrage movement.[51]

Craven spoke initially for some four hours in support of his charge, defending at one point more his view of a divinely arranged subordination than his charge of See's disobedience to Scripture. Craven put the matter this way:

I believe the subject involves the honor of my God. I believe the subject involves the headship and crown of Jesus. Woman was made for man and became first in the transgression. My argument is subordination of sex. Dr. See has admitted marital subordination, but this is not enough, there exists a created subordination; a divinely arranged and appointed subordination of woman as woman to man as man. Woman was made for man and became first in the transgression. The proper condition of the adult female is marriage; the general rule for ladies is marriage. Women without children, it might be said, could preach, but they are under the general rule of subordination. It is not allowed woman to speak in the church. Man's place is on the platform. It is positively base for a woman to speak in the pulpit; it is base in the sight of Jehovah. The whole question is one of subordination.[52]

See spoke to the presbytery the next day. If Craven was passionate in his oratory, See was inflammatory. He jolted the presbyters: What Paul may have said to the Corinthians did not necessarily concern the Newarkians. He further asserted that in the Corinthian church "there was a variety of women, not extinct, who were addicted to 'babbling' and 'gossiping.' This naturally failed to meet the views of St. Paul, and he therefore directed that Corinthian women should neither babble nor gossip, or, in other words, that they should keep silent in the churches." See's argument, reported in the *New York Times*, provoked the writer to retort, "It is unfortunate that science has not yet supported Mr. See's interpretation of Scripture by bringing to light the organic remains of the extinct babbling woman."[53]

See did not rest his case there. He claimed that the word *prophesy* in a passage in Acts that says, "Your sons and your daughters shall prophesy," means the same thing as to preach. Thus the passage commands women to preach. The *New York Times* writer challenged him to interpret another passage, "Your young men shall see visions and your old men shall dream dreams," by ordering the young men of his congregation to see visions and by providing comfortable pews and headrests for his old men.[54] See's final argument was that he regarded a pulpit as "no more sacred than a barrel on a sidewalk." To this, the *New York Times* author responded, "There is not a passage in the Old or New Testament which says that women may not enter ash-barrels."[55]

Craven replied to See at the next meeting of the presbytery six days later, speaking throughout the morning and again after lunch. He reinforced his belief that First Corinthians and Timothy meant that women should not preach and teach in the church and that this was the opinion of the Presbyterian Church. He discussed the 1874 General Assembly action when it "expressed no opinion" on the question of women speaking at weekly prayer meetings and insisted that since the Assembly had not considered the subject, the weight of the opinion was with the 1832 deliverance.[56]

The case continued a week later when See had an opportunity to make concluding remarks. On January 3, 1877, the presbytery sustained the charge, with the final count indicating divided opinion among the presbyters: 16 to sustain (11 ministers, 5 elders); 12 not to sustain (4 ministers, 8 elders); 1 to sustain in part (1 minister).[57] The elders' greater reluctance to convict See indicates that the church members were perhaps more ready for change than were the clergy and denomination.

The presbytery declined to condemn See as guilty of "conscious and willful disobedience of a divine ordinance" but rather stated:

We hold that the passages of Scripture referred to in the charge do prohibit the fulfilling by women of the offices of public preachers in the regular assemblies of the Church. And, while we admit that a different interpretation of them may be honestly held, we think that the action of Brother See in inviting women to preach in his pulpit at the regular public services on the Sabbath Day was irregular and unwise, and contrary to the views of the Scriptures and of Church order derived from them, as ordinarily held among us; and, as such conduct may open the way to disorder and mischief, we affectionately counsel and admonish Brother See to abstain from it in the future.[58]

Despite this initial statement, the presbytery included a commendation for women's participation in the church's life: "While maintaining this position, the Presbytery highly appreciates the services of women in all the departments of Christian evangelization and benevolence, and the large indebtedness of every good cause to their sympathy and co-operation."[59]

Although the subject of women's speaking and praying in the smaller social meetings of the church was not contained in the charge, the subject was prominent in the debate. Therefore, the decision noted, "With reference to it the Presbytery abides by the direction of the General Assembly of 1874"[60] that the whole subject should be committed to the discretion of the pastors and elders of the churches.

Neither Craven nor See agreed with the decision, each for different reasons. They both appealed to the Synod of New Jersey. The *New York Times* reported, "Mr. See objects to the decision because it went too far, and Dr. Craven because it did not go far enough."[61]

See's appeal was based on nine points, but primarily that a Presbyterian minister was not restrained by law from allowing a woman to publicly speak and teach at public worship. See did not feel his conduct was contrary to Scripture and thought the reasons given were inconsistent with the Presbytery's vote to sustain the charge. He objected to being condemned for honestly interpreting Holy Scripture according to his conscience and further stated that not permitting women to speak at regular public services while allowing them the floor at so-called social meetings had no scriptural authority. His other complaints were procedural.[62]

Craven's appeal, or complaint, was more complex and far lengthier. First, he pointed to the ambiguity of the use of the words "by women of the offices of public preachers" in the first paragraph of the decision. He said it may mean "the exercise of the functions of public speaking or teaching or *as licentiates or ordained ministers.*"[63] Lest this be misconstrued, Craven called for a correction. If the presbytery intended the latter, however, Craven sought to show that the question of ordaining or licensing women was not at issue, contemplated, or implied.[64]

Second, he complained about the presbytery's abiding by the 1874 General Assembly action to allow women to speak and pray in social prayer meetings. He challenged the Assembly's action being used because it was *obiter dictum* and therefore without judicial force. He further objected to the use of the opinion of the Assembly, as it "does not rise to the dignity of an opinion," and to the action taken without full discussion.[65] *The Presbyterian* commented, "Dr. Craven evidently wishes a clear, unequivocal judgment of an ecclesiastical court on the whole question, and not a deliverance against the preaching of women, with exceptions which may be considered as destroying the whole force of the deliverance."[66]

The Synod of New Jersey met on October 16, 1877, and arrived at a decision on See's appeal and Craven's complaint on October 19. Following basically the same proceedings as had the presbytery, the synod voted not to sustain the complaint of Craven nor the appeal of See, using the identical language of the presbytery. As did the presbytery, the synod put on record its appreciation for the services of women in other departments of Christian evangelization and benevolence.

See carried his appeal to the General Assembly of 1878, which found nothing in the proceedings of the Synod of New Jersey to warrant a reversal of the judgment and findings. Again a church body articulated its commendation of women's efforts and influence.[67]

The judgments in this case reflected the denomination's unwillingness to back away from its biblical interpretation. Nevertheless, the wording of the judgments and the relatively mild treatment of See indicated its equally strong unwillingness to take a binding stand that would obviously not hold up in practice. As a result, the door was still ajar, and the decisions rendered on the Craven–See case neither quieted the controversy nor stemmed the flow of publications on the subject, "Shall Women Speak?".

During the decade of the 1870s, however, two things had become evident. One, women were quantitatively and qualitatively important to the work of the church, as demonstrated by their contributions both financially and in service to the mission-oriented congregations. Two, the very fact that women were becoming more active meant that they inevitably would speak in church. Silence was no longer feasible given their leadership roles, and, although not many openly asked for the pulpit, the woman speaker, whether she preached, prayed, or lectured, broke the traditional barriers each time she appeared in front of congregations.

A woman arguing for females' being allowed to pray in public pointed out that the foreign women converted by the missionaries regularly prayed aloud. "The truth is that, with limitations which we Presbyterians are not likely to be allowed or to wish to overstep, women must have the blessed privilege of uniting their prayers for the objects near their hearts."[68]

7

SEEKING OFFICIAL RECOGNITION:
Widening Women's Sphere, 1880-1920

While theologians and church leaders discussed the unresolved issues of the Craven–See case and its implications for the future of
American Presbyterianism, women pursued activities that made them
increasingly visible in denominational life. In his recapitulation of important events at the 92nd General Assembly in 1880, the editor of *The
Presbyterian* enthusiastically affirmed the church's burgeoning women's
movement. " 'Place aux dames!' This was the constant cry in the General Assembly. 'Woman's Work,' and the grand success achieved there-
in was the theme of praise in many of the reports and speeches and the
tributes were hearty and generous."[1]

By the 1880s, most Presbyterian denominations had national women's
boards of home and foreign missions as well as auxiliary societies on the
synod and presbyterial level, with the Presbyterian Church in the U.S.
the notable exception. The growing network of Presbyterian Sabbath
schools was due in large measure to the cadre of female teachers and
superintendents whose volunteer services provided the basic religious
education for young persons in the United States. Despite sporadic
protests from sessions and presbyteries, women also mounted platform
and pulpit to speak on issues of temperance, Sabbath observance, and
some aspects of social reform.

Like other mainline Protestant denominations, the Presbyterian
church gradually accommodated to the changing role of women in
society and modified its practices in order to offer women more status in
church life. In 1891, the General Assembly acknowledged alterations in
attitudes in the denomination-at-large. Evident to a committee reporting
on deaconesses was that "a majority in the church are in favor of securing in some orderly way the services of godly women to assist in
religious work, and are desirous of clothing them with some measure of
authority."[2] Although the General Assembly envisaged neither ordination nor full equality for women, it recognized a need for adjustment in
the time-honored definition of "woman's sphere." To do so would

enable the church to utilize in its expanding program the energies and talents of the increasingly better educated and more sophisticated churchwomen.

Adaptation to social change was aided in the latter part of the nineteenth century by the introduction of a new biblical hermeneutic that gave intellectual respectability to a sociological and historical interpretation of the Bible. As a result, popular preachers such as Henry Ward Beecher, Lyman Abbott, and Washington Gladden could advocate a more liberal interpretation of Scripture than had been acceptable only a generation before. More important for women, the new approach to biblical texts gave proponents of sexual equality some ground on which to argue publicly against what most people believed to be the biblical definitions of women's proper place in secular and ecclesiastical life.[3]

George P. Hays applied this exegesis to the ecclesiastical status of women in a booklet published in 1889 entitled, *May Women Speak?* Hays, former president of Washington and Jefferson College, moderator of the General Assembly in 1884, and distinguished pastor and theologian, figured prominently in the theological controversies of the day over "higher criticism." In terms of the biblical references to females both in the Old and New Testaments, he concluded that a critical examination of relevant texts placed no restrictions on areas of service for women. "Surely the day has come," Hays said, "when the missionary spirit brought into the Church of God in the present century may have liberty to mould and use women as well as men in every form of work which shall tend to proclaim the Gospel."[4] Published under the auspices of the WCTU, Hays' book received wide circulation among churchwomen throughout the country. His ecclesiastical prominence also guaranteed the book a careful consideration among scholars who could not dismiss his views as either eccentric or superficial.[5]

Despite such indications of theological change during the last two decades of the nineteenth century, the inherent conservatism of the Presbyterian church caused social customs and traditions to be modified only slowly and not without tension and turmoil. Old attitudes and new convictions frequently clashed. Early in the 1880s, for example, Sophia B. Loring, a missionary from Syria, accepted an invitation to address the Synod of Geneva in New York. The elderly moderator, Henry A. Nelson, was horrified at the thought of ministers and elders sitting in a constituted church court and listening to a woman speak, citing Paul's injunction, "I will not suffer a woman to speak." Although he adjourned the meeting, most of the synod members remained in their seats to hear Loring's eloquent address on the importance of women's missionary work. When she concluded, the synod reconvened and continued its deliberations.[6]

Overtures from presbyteries to the General Assembly indicated two factors on the local level: that practices regarding the role of women in church life varied from church to church and that judicatories increasingly desired the Assembly to define more precisely denominational standards. In 1892, the Presbytery of Zanesville, Ohio, asked the Assembly if Paul's prohibitions of women's right to speak (I Cor. 14:33–37 and I Tim. 2:11—13) were still binding in Presbyterian churches and if the Assembly would give an authoritative definition of "public promiscuous assemblies."[7] Four years later, responding to a visitation of women temperance speakers in a number of Baltimore pulpits, the Presbytery of Baltimore referred a similar overture to the General Assembly. Noting that the presence of women in Presbyterian pulpits "had excited much unfavorable comment in our Presbyterian community," the presbytery asked the Assembly to "indicate clearly" what principles should dictate the practice of individual congregations.[8] In each instance, the General Assembly continued its practice of answering the overtures with some ambivalence. On the one hand, it referred petitioners to the deliverances of 1832 and 1872, which restricted the right of women to pray and speak in public, and on the other hand, it resisted attempts to introduce restrictive legislation by committing resolution of the problem "to the wise discretion of pastors and elders in each particular church."[9]

Such pronouncements at the General Assembly level did little to resolve the question of women's ecclesiastical status in the local churches. As one elder observed, "Some questions are settled by referring them to committees where they receive funeral rites, but not so with the Woman Question. It will not down!"[10] In response to the persistence of an interested female constituency, Presbyterian judicatories in the latter part of the nineteenth century cautiously granted women some role, recognition, and praise. Although reluctant to offer ordination as elders and ministers and access to decision-making bodies, by the 1880s a number of Reformed churches were considering opening the diaconate to women as a means to implement a limited status.[11]

Diaconal service by women had proof-text support in the New Testament (Romans 16:1), and its nurturing, service-oriented function seemed especially appropriate in the light of prevailing role models. The diaconate would provide women a measure of status but would withhold voice in church courts. In arguing for a female diaconate, one Presbyterian minister differentiated between two areas of ecclesiastical service, the presbyterial and the diaconal, and declared that "woman's work belongs in the Diaconal sphere." He further identified two methods of forming the diaconal ministry: ordination as female deacons on a par with men and election or appointment as deaconesses. A deaconess would not serve as an elected officer of any congregation but

would be prepared by prayer and special training for service in a benevolent or educational ministry. This might include work as pastors'
assistants, social workers, and practical nurses. Concentrated primarily
in large city parishes, the deaconess movement was the forerunner of
the modern director of Christian education.[12]

Impetus for the deaconess movement came from Theodore Fliedner,
pastor at Kaiserswerth, Germany, who founded an evangelical diaconate for women in 1936 to help alleviate suffering in the new industrial society of his day. Fliedner toured the United States and influenced
a number of American clergymen to institute similar charitable and
beneficent institutions. Methodists and Episcopalians were among the
first to establish deaconess orders in the United States, but by the end of
the century Lutheran and German Reformed churches were making
extensive use of deaconesses, and Congregationalists, Baptists, and
Presbyterians were considering similar programs.[13]

A number of prominent Presbyterian theologians including Archibald
A. Hodge, Charles A. Briggs, Alexander T. McGill, and Benjamin B.
Warfield approved the deaconess movement as a means of utilizing the
services of women in inner-city missions. When Hodge and Briggs began
publishing the *Presbyterian Review* in 1880, the first issue contained an
article by McGill proposing that deaconesses be organized into a series
of boards corresponding to presbyteries, synods, and the General
Assembly, all of which would be under the direct control and supervision of judicatories composed of ministers and elders.[14] Referring to
McGill's article, the editor of *The Presbyterian* predicted that the proposal
"was a foreshadowing of the elevation of women which may be at
hand." He concluded, "And if there is any place where pious and
zealous women should be honored, it is in the Church of God."[15]

Even before the General Assembly formally considered diaconal recognition for women, individual ministers and congregations were
making such appointments on an ad hoc basis. George P. Hays, pastor
of the Central Presbyterian Church in Denver, reported twenty-four
deaconesses at work in his congregation in 1884. In 1881, the Corinthian
Avenue Presbyterian Church in Philadelphia, influenced by a visit from
Fliedner's son, placed the care of its poor and sick in the hands of five
deaconesses, so designated by the session without ordination. In 1889,
the Third Presbyterian Church of Los Angeles empowered its board of
deacons to choose three women from the congregation to "cooperate
with them in their work" especially with responsibility for the poor and
needy in the neighborhood. Similar actions by Presbyterian sessions in
the latter part of the nineteenth century were not uncommon.[16]

After receiving a number of overtures requesting denominational
sanction of deaconesses, the General Assembly in 1889 appointed a
special committee led by B. B. Warfield to present recommendations the

following year. The committee thought that "the time was ripe for the reconstitution of the office of deaconess in the Church" but was reluctant to recommend legislation regarding structure and duties of the new order, assuming such details would evolve gradually after a period of experimentation. While acknowledging the usefulness of a sisterhood on the Kaiserswerth model, the committee suggested instead that the Presbyterian church have only congregational deaconesses supervised directly by local sessions. Although the committee cited biblical and historical precedent for deaconesses, it emphasized the practicality of providing women this ecclesiastical status: "The work is immense; it must be done; it is being done; and the only question is whether the Church will give its official recognition to the abundant labors already being performed voluntarily."[17]

With Warfield's endorsement, the Assembly sent down an overture in 1890 that recognized the apostolic origins of deaconesses and specified the "election" (not ordination) of deaconesses "in a manner similar to that appointed for deacons, and set apart by prayer." Strong opposition to acknowledging the biblical basis of deaconesses, however, brought the measure down to defeat.[18] A similar overture in 1892, which omitted the question of apostolic origin of deaconesses and provided for sessional appointment of "godly and competent women . . . for the care of the poor and sick, and especially of poor widows and orphans" was approved. Synods and presbyteries were urged to establish institutions and training schools "as opportunity offers" so that Presbyterian women could be adequately prepared for this diaconal service.[19]

Not until the first decade of the twentieth century did the Presbyterian church actually support its own training school for deaconesses. In 1903, the Presbyterian Training School opened its doors in Baltimore, offering a two-year course for women that stressed biblical studies, Presbyterian doctrine, practical Christian work, and a short course in nursing and care of the sick.[20] The Philadelphia School for Christian Workers, sponsored jointly by the Presbyterian Church in the U.S.A. and the Reformed Church in America, began its operations in 1908, the same year in which the Presbyterian College of Christian Education opened in Chicago. In addition to deaconesses, these schools trained women for careers as pastors' assistants, social workers, missionaries, church secretaries, and evangelists.[21] (See chapter 11.)

Although deaconesses served effectively, primarily as nurses and social workers, the movement never became a significant factor in Presbyterian life because of both theoretical and practical obstacles. The question of the apostolic origin of the office cost the movement considerable approval during its formative period and a prevailing anti-Catholicism added to the erosion of support. Many Presbyterian clergymen in general opposed a concept that set women apart by special garb and called for a highly disciplined life in a communal-type setting. As one writer expressed it, he feared that "the odor of a Catholic nunnery might surround an order of Protestant deaconesses."[22] Moreover, the deaconess movement did not have a strong appeal among middleclass Presbyterian women because of its minimal educational requirements and its close identification with the tedious work of nursing. With other options available for church service, such as teaching and missionary work, very few Presbyterian women were attracted to the calling as a deaconess.[23]

As the biblical argument against the ordination of women as deacons became less pronounced in the twentieth century, Presbyterian denominations modified their constitutions to provide for female deacons without a great deal of publicity. The UPNA church opened up the office to women in 1906, and the Cumberland Presbyterian Church followed suit in 1921.[24] The PCUSA ratified an overture from the Presbytery of Translyvania in 1922, granting women the privilege, but because framers of the overture had forgotten to remove masculine language from the ordination service in the *Form of Government* (ordinands were referred to as "brothers"), it was not until 1923 that the action, minus the incorrect language, officially became operative.[25]

Beyond the bounds of diaconal recognition, some of the smaller Presbyterian denominations sought to widen women's sphere by appointing them to serve as lay evangelists. The Cumberland Presbyterians had a number of female evangelists in the latter part of the nineteenth century, especially in rural areas where congregations were small, ministers few, and the home mission challenge demanding. Although the UPNA church stopped short of a formal provision in its *Book of Government*, it did not prohibit presbyteries from designating women as lay evangelists. One of the best known was Edith Livingston Peake, who began her labors in the early 1890s on the west coast where the UPNA had an active home mission program. A member of the First United Presbyterian Church of San Francisco, she was appointed as Presbyterian evangelist by the Presbytery of San Francisco on May 21, 1893. With her services much in demand, she traveled extensively on the Pacific coast and in 1898 came to the Pittsburgh area. One observer described her as an extraordinary woman. "As a public speaker and an able expounder of the doctrines of the gospel, she is much superior to the average evangelist, whether man or woman. . . . There are not very many men, even in the ministry, who hear her and cannot learn anything from her in regard to preaching the gospel, earnestly, tenderly, and fully."[26]

With such expanding incidences of women actively participating in American church life, it was only a matter of time until Presbyterian judicatories had to face the question: If a woman could be a deacon, deaconess, Sunday school teacher, missionary, and evangelist—all nineteenth-century innovations—why could she not fulfill other ecclesiastical functions? One disgruntled elder predicted the ultimate outcome of the expansion of "woman's sphere" taking place in the last decade of the nineteenth century: "The doors are to be flung wide open. Let no one be deceived in this matter. We are face to face with the woman's rights question in all its fullness. Unless we, as a denomination, are prepared to clothe women with *all* the functions of ministry, we must call a halt and face about at once."[27] This elder and other Presbyterian churchmen must have recognized that women were taking important roles in other denominations.

As early as the mid-nineteenth century, a few American denominations admitted women either as licentiates or as ministers. Most of these were Universalists, Unitarians, and Quakers, with a few women preachers among Baptists, Congregationalists, and Methodists. Nevertheless, even at the end of the nineteenth century, clergywomen were still few in number and considered by most church people to be an aberration or a novelty. The attitude of the average congregation was probably represented by the oft-quoted anecdote about the farmer who said of an exceptionally able young woman candidate, "I'd ruther have a man that wa'nt so good."[28]

Perhaps no Reformed denomination struggled more with the question of ordination and ecclesiastical parity between men and women than did the Cumberland Presbyterian Church. Its revivalistic and frontier origins and its willingness to exercise flexibility in ordination requirements made the denomination more receptive to exceptions. Moreover, as the fastest growing American Presbyterian church in the nineteenth century, the Cumberland church faced a shortage of ministers and evangelists, especially in rural areas where few congregations could sustain a full-time minister. Not surprisingly, women gradually began to fill some of these leadership positions.[29]

Efforts by Cumberland Presbyterian women to be accepted as ruling elders met with a mixture of ambivalence and resistance. In 1887, the Oregon Synod permitted women to attend its meetings as unofficial "advisors" with speaking privileges, which evoked a protest from some disapproving commissioners to the General Assembly. The Assembly adroitly avoided the major issue of women's rights, however, by ruling that the Cumberland Presbyterian *Book of Government* did not provide for the admission of lay members into a church court regardless of sex.[30] In 1892, by a narrow majority (105–90), the General Assembly adopted a minority report that the ordination of women to the eldership was not prohibited by church law and empowered lower judicatories to make decisions based on local attitudes and needs.[31] The following year, Pollie L. Clagett, ordained as an elder by the Nolin Presbytery in Kentucky, was seated as a commissioner to the 1893 General Assembly only after what an eyewitness described as "hours of quibbling, dodging, and fillibustering."[32] Attempts to secure a more definite ruling from the General Assembly were unsuccessful as several overtures endorsing the ordination of women as elders failed to secure approval from the presbyteries. In 1896, the General Assembly reversed its earlier ruling and declared the Synod of Indiana out of order in seating Mrs. S. K. Hart as a commissioner, but in 1897 the same body acknowledged as legal the Kansas Synod's seating of a woman as a ruling elder. Unable to develop a consistent policy, the Cumberland Presbyterian Church entered the twentieth century with the issue of women elders unresolved.[33]

Full ministerial status for women also captured the attention of Cumberland Presbyterians. The focal point in the debate was Louisa L. Woosley, a remarkably talented and self-disciplined woman who overcame educational deficiencies and personal hesitancy to become the first Presbyterian woman of record to be formally ordained by a presbytery. Petite, quiet-spoken, and dignified, yet capable of captivating audiences with her exposition of the gospel, Woosley took her defense of female ordination to the floor of the General Assembly. She aroused both ire and interest by publishing in 1891 a small book entitled, *Shall Women Preach? or The Question Answered.* Arguing primarily from biblical grounds, Woosley contended that the church would have to accept the pleas of women for ordination or run the risk of denying the Holy Spirit and contradicting its original mandate of freedom and equality in Christ. "A religion that does not give woman the liberty, privileges, and blessings, that it does a man," she contended, "will not stand the test; it falls far short of being the religion of the Bible."[34]

Shall Women Preach? was much more than an apology for female ordination. It contained an autobiographical account of Woosley's struggle for self-acceptance as one worthy of a ministerial call and of her rejection by friends, family, and church people who were not prepared to accept the validity of a women cleric. Told in the prevailing idiom of theological introspection, Woosley's personal odyssey dramatizes the ambivalences and convictions likely shared by many other churchwomen in the nineteenth century.

Louisa Layman Woosley's experience began in 1874 when as a young girl she was converted at a Baptist revival meeting in Grayson County, Kentucky. Her immediate impulse, she recalled, was to become a preacher even though she had never met any female ministers and knew that any effort to become a "lady preacher" would encounter opposition. Moreover, her youth and lack of formal education presented barriers to her hopes for ministerial status. Faced with these realities, Woosley tried to convince herself that it was not right for women to aspire to such a high and holy calling. In 1879, she married Curtis G.

Woosley, a Cumberland Presbyterian layman from Caneyville, Kentucky, secretly praying that he might become a minister and that her service to God could be as a minister's wife. Her hopes along these lines never materialized. The birth of two children and temporary health problems made her goal of ordination even more remote.[35]

Louisa Woosley, however, could not suppress her sense of an inner calling to the ministry. In the fall of 1882, she began to study the Bible in order to understand what the scriptures said about the role of women in the church. A year later, she had completed her self-directed studies, her convictions strengthened. "I was now convinced," she said, "of the fact that God, being no respecter of persons, had not overlooked the women, but that he had a great work for them to do. My impressions were felt more sensibly than ever before."[36] Again, however, Woosley deferred implementing her convictions because of the pressure of domestic responsibilities and because of a recurring lack of self-confidence. She told herself, "Now I am slow of speech, I am not educated, and the people will not hear me. And perhaps my husband will not be willing."[37]

In extreme personal anguish and unwilling to share her burdens with family and friends, Woosley suffered a physical and emotional collapse in the fall of 1885. For nearly six months, she was bedridden. Then, in a moment of crisis, she prayed that if God restored her health, she would make an irrevocable decision to preach the gospel. "Though unable to raise myself in bed, I laid myself, my husband and two dear children upon God's altar. . . . By faith I put my hand in His and He reached out to help me."[38]

Following this decision, Woosley's health improved and within several months she was back to a normal routine. Still telling no one of her determination to preach, she waited for an appropriate opportunity to make her decision public. The occasion came on the evening of January 1, 1887, in a small Cumberland Presbyterian church in Caneyville, Kentucky. When the minister failed to arrive for the service, the elders, as custom dictated, selected a layperson to lead the congregational worship. Possibly because of her reputation as a student of the Bible and as a woman of deep personal piety, the session requested Woosley to take charge. Initially hesitant, she finally gave an affirmative answer. "For the first time in my life," she recalled, "I went to the sacred desk and opened my mouth for God. Oh, that was a precious hour."[39]

Woosley's initial optimism faded when opposition to her precedent-breaking intentions surfaced. Former friends became distant and hostile. Even her father rejected her for a time because of what he thought were unscriptural and "unladylike" aspirations. Remaining adamant, however, Woosley requested permission and was accepted by

Nolin Presbytery of the Cumberland Presbyterian Church as a candidate for the ministry on November 5, 1887. The following year she received a license to preach "when and where she may choose, but not to involve the presbytery in a debt, but to appropriate all she may receive for her labors, to her own use and benefit."[40]

If presbytery statistics can be trusted, Louisa Woosley clearly was an energetic and productive evangelist. In 1888, she preached 267 sermons and received 306 professions of faith, 119 additions to the church, and $383.15 in contributions. The following year, she delivered 286 sermons, witnessed 453 professions of faith, added 168 members to the Cumberland Presbyterian Church, and amassed $421.25 in free-will offerings.[41] In November 1889, by action of Nolin Presbytery, Louisa Woosley became the first Presbyterian woman of record to be ordained to the full work of the gospel ministry. Her evangelistic career ended at her last revival meeting in 1937 at the age of seventy-five, but she continued writing sermons and "quoting scripture by the yard" until her death in 1952.[42]

Woosley's success did not prevent her ordination from precipitating among Cumberland Presbyterians a series of heated debates at the synod and the General Assembly, which displayed the same ambivalence as regarding women elders. In 1890, the Kentucky Synod ordered the Nolin Presbytery to remove Woosley's name from its roster of ministers but did not take action to rescind her ordination. The Nolin Presbytery, in direct defiance of the synodical directive, elected Woosley as an alternative delegate to the General Assembly. The Kentucky Synod responded by declaring her ordination invalid and again ordered the presbytery to strike her name from the roll.[43] The Nolin Presbytery refused to relinquish its right to be the final arbiter in determining ordination standards and challenged the Synod once again by electing Woosley as a commissioner to the General Assembly in 1894.[44]

As was expected, the General Assembly questioned Woosley's credentials as a commissioner. In the ensuing debate, which evoked all the traditional arguments on women ministers, pro and con, it became evident that commissioners were sharply divided over the validity of Woosley's credentials. More than the question of women ministers, they raised the sensitive issue of presbytery rights. The Cumberland denomination had been founded because of this principle, and many commissioners found themselves in the uncomfortable position of supporting female ordination in order to protect judicatory autonomy. By a surprisingly narrow margin of fifteen votes, however, the Assembly did endorse her as a lay evangelist and praised her "eminent usefulness and her womanly behavior, under the most trying circumstances."[45] Although there was some talk among commissioners to offer an amendment to the church's *Constitution* in order to eliminate sex discrimination in ordination standards, there was not enough interest to generate action. As one church reporter concluded, "There was a conviction that the Church is not yet ready to settle this question."[46]

As the nineteenth century ended, there was little doubt that Presbyterian judicatories were "not yet ready to settle" the issue of women's rights to ministerial ordination. After the tumultuous decade of the 1890s, which saw concerted efforts to secure political enfranchisement for women as well as equal opportunity in education and employment, the first decade of the twentieth century was relatively quiet. In particular, churchmen and women recoiled from the radicalism expressed so vividly in Elizabeth Cady Stanton's publication of the *Woman's Bible*, an attempt to reinterpret and retranslate the Bible so as to exclude all sexual discrimination. Coming as it did at a time when biblical authority was a burning issue, the *Woman's Bible* was an easy target for opponents of female ordination. No self-respecting, decent, Presbyterian churchman or woman, the argument went, would want to associate himself or herself with such crass antibiblicalism. The inspiration of the Bible itself was being called into question. Moreover, from a Presbyterian perspective, it was only the "deviant" denominations such as Unitarians, Universalists, or Quakers who openly espoused female ordination and even there clergywomen were numerically insignificant. The mainline groups either rejected ordination for women out of hand or displayed the same cautious, conservative attitudes common among Presbyterians.[47]

Even though the subject of female ordination failed to capture judicatorial attention in the opening decade of the twentieth century, a gradual change in public sentiment about the extent of "woman's sphere" emerged in the period prior to and following World War I. The Cumberland Presbyterian Church, which had narrowly voted down female ordination in the nineteenth century, was the first Presbyterian denomination to resolve the question in the twentieth century. Following the invalidation of Louisa Woosley's ordination in 1894, Cumberland presbyteries had continued to exercise their ordination prerogatives by accepting women as candidates and ordaining them to the ministry. In 1903, Walla Walla Presbytery accepted a woman as a probationer, but the stated clerk of the General Assembly ordered her name to be erased from the presbytery's list. Dallas–Bonham Presbytery received Bessie C. Morris from the Methodist Episcopal Church as an ordained minister in 1907, and in 1911 Leitchfield Presbytery, successor to Nolin Presbytery, added Louisa Woosley's name to its ministerial roster. Between 1916 and 1920, at least four other women were ordained as ministers despite rulings from the General Assembly questioning the validity of such ordinations.[48]

Almost annually the question of female ordination came before the

Cumberland Presbyterian General Assembly without any resolution. In 1920, the General Assembly attempted to resolve the "woman question" once and for all and appointed a committee to draft an amendment to the constitution.[49] After lively debate, the General Assembly in 1921 adopted a statement that effectively ended discriminatory rules regarding women's status. The word *man*, the Assembly ruled, is a generic term and as used in Scriptures and the *Constitution* has no reference to sex, "but should be construed to, and does, in fact, include the human being whether male or female."[50]

The PCUSA also devoted considerable attention to the subject in the first two decades of the twentieth century. A harbinger of future developments was the efforts of the Chemung Presbytery in central New York to permit women to occupy pulpits within its bounds. In 1912, the presbytery voted to take Rachel Gleason Brooks under its care as a "student of theology" and the following year by a vote of 11–10 agreed to take her under the care of the presbytery as a candidate for the ministry. No further mention of Brooks is made in the Chemung Presbytery minutes, but it is known that she later left the Presbyterian church to become an ordained Congregational minister.[51]

Five years later, the same judicatory licensed Lillian Herrick Chapman to preach within the bounds of the presbytery so that she could supply the pulpit of the North Presbyterian Church in Elmira, New York, while its pastor, Herbert Harris, was serving overseas as a chaplain in World War I. In licensing Chapman, the presbytery supported its action by noting that the new world being formed by World War I was already giving women equal standing with men in political suffrage and challenging the church to give women "at least a larger authority in Church work." It also argued that the church would lose its trained and qualified women unless time-honored customs and rules were revised or discarded.[52]

A lone dissenter, Robert C. Hallock, immediately questioned the presbytery's action. He filed a complaint with the Synod of New York, stating that licensing a woman was "irregular, unconstitutional, and unscriptural."[53] In 1919, the Synod of New York ruled that Chapman's licensing was irregular but did not deal with the other two substantive points of Hallock's protest. At the same meeting, synod commissioners voted down a proposed overture to the General Assembly requesting permission to license and ordain women, primarily because the Assembly had already received similar overtures from several other judicatories.[54]

Reflecting the spirit of the denomination's "New Era Movement," three presbyteries—Dallas, Columbia River, and Saginaw—sent overtures to the General Assembly in 1919 dealing with the status of women. Columbia River requested that women be eligible for ordination both as ministers and as elders, and the Presbytery of Saginaw asked for ordination of women only as ruling elders.[55] The Presbytery of Dallas requested a thorough investigation of the possibility of enlarged opportunities for women because of the imminent passage of the suffrage amendment and "in view of the fact that there seems to be a growing sentiment among the women of the Presbyterian Church, USA for more direct representation in the courts of the Church."[56]

As commissioners gathered in St. Louis in May 1919 for the 131st General Assembly, these overtures caused church papers to predict that the "woman question" would be a controversial issue. Rumors circulated that J. Frank Smith of Dallas, Texas, the retiring moderator, would publicly endorse his presbytery's overture and urge its immediate adoption. Smith had been quoted as saying that he favored the Dallas overture "because he could see what was coming and did not want to be run over."[57] While opponents rehearsed their traditional arguments, an editorial in the *Presbyterian Banner* warned that "leaders of the suffrage fight will fortify their demand with liberal quotations from the Bible."[58]

The three overtures were referred to the Standing Committee on Polity chaired by S. Hall Young, a former missionary associate of Sheldon Jackson in Alaska, who was sympathetic to the cause of women's rights. A majority in the committee (thirteen members) thought that inasmuch as only three presbyteries in the entire denomination had raised questions about women's ecclesiastical status, there was no imperative for "such radical action" and recommended "no action."[59] A minority report (seven members) presented by Chairman Young proposed the appointment of a committee consisting of three ministers, two elders, and two Presbyterian women to study women's positions in the church and to report to the next General Assembly.[60] In the brief and spirited debate that ensued, both sides were well represented. J. Frank Smith said, "If we fail to recognize the equality of man and woman before the cross, I fear we are standing in the way of the kingdom of God."[61] Alexander Mackie, a minister commissioner from Pennsylvania, sharply countered, "This Assembly has too many old ladies now without electing any more to membership."[62] Although he personally favored full equality for women, Young sensed that an effort to force the issue of ordination to a vote at the St. Louis Assembly would result in certain defeat. Young assured commissioners that the minority he represented was not advocating ordination of women "at this time" but was simply asking for a committee to investigate the question. "I don't propose to introduce any radical changes," he said, "but I have too much respect for the fairer sex not to take up this question in their favor."[63] With these assurances, the Assembly readily approved the minority report, and the moderator appointed Young to serve as chair man of the committee. The provision for two female members was removed, however, because of a standing Assembly rule that only ministers and elders could serve on Assembly committees.[64]

In preparation for its report to the General Assembly in 1920, Young's committee focused attention on three major areas: scriptural authority, practices of other leading Protestant denominations, and consensus of male and female leaders in the Presbyterian church. First, the committee consulted professors in various seminaries and concluded that "the Scriptures do not forbid either women elders or women preachers."[65] Second, it gathered evidence from other Reformed denominations that seemed to indicate support for women elders but was on the whole unfavorable for women ministers. Third, it compiled results from a representative sampling of approximately 140 Presbyterian leaders that revealed that 60 percent of the men favored ordaining women as elders or giving them some form of representation on church courts and that an even larger percentage of women supported the right of ordination to both eldership and ministry.[66]

In presenting his report to the 132nd General Assembly meeting in Philadelphia, Young informed commissioners that his committee "declined to express an opinion upon the merits of this important question" because "it was divided in sentiment, a majority having expressed themselves as conservative." Because the question of admitting women to the office of ruling elder seemed to have strong support from both male and female church leaders, however, he recommended that the stated clerk be directed to send down the following overture: "Shall the Constitution of the Presbyterian Church in the USA be so amended as to admit properly qualified and elected women to ordination as Ruling Elders, with all the rights and duties pertaining to this office?"[67]

In contrast to the sharp debate that marked the discussion in 1919, Hall's proposal hardly ruffled the calm of the Philadelphia commissioners. Even Hall himself was taken aback when interest in his motion was so languid that not a single commissioner cared to voice an opinion. By an overwhelming voice vote, the Assembly referred the overture to the presbyteries for their consideration. The editor of *The Continent* could suggest no explanation except to say that "General Assemblies differ."[68] A more likely answer, however, is that commissioners were in agreement that there was sufficient interest in ordaining women to the eldership and that individual presbyteries, the heart of the Presbyterian government, should be permitted to discuss the question and render a final decision.

The equanimity of the Assembly did not extend to the local judicatories, as church members publicly debated the propriety of women elders with considerable fervor. David S. Kennedy, editor of *The Presbyterian*, led the attack with a scathing critique of the notion of equality of function for men and women. In the rhetoric of the nineteenth century, he contended that the Bible had once and for all settled "God's exalted purpose and commission for women. . . . It is the mother's prerogative to arrange her home and her children about her table according to her own plan. It would be a violence for any other to alter her plans. Who are we that we should attempt to arrange God's house or to question his order?"[69] Other prominent Presbyterian clergymen such as Benjamin B. Warfield of Princeton Theological Seminary and Clarence E. Macartney, pastor of the Arch Street Presbyterian Church in Philadelphia, supported Kennedy's editorial stand and argued forcefully that passage of the overture would represent a defection from biblical standards and would create havoc in church courts.[70]

No men of similar ecclesiastical stature rose to defend the eldership overture in denominational newspapers. Young remained aloof from the controversy and officers of the women's Boards of Home and Foreign Missions maintained a public neutrality. In fact, the only major article written by a woman, Blanche Dickens-Lewis, Synodical President of Home Missions for Ohio, opposed the overture. "In the minds of many Presbyterian women," she said, "there is no desire to fill this sacred office, which we feel is still 'man's' special task and responsibility, in God's great program of the world's work."[71] Even the editors of the *Presbyterian Banner* who had supported ordination of women in principle argued that it was not "expedient" to do so at this time, because the denomination was too divided on the question.[72]

Despite this lack of public support, the overture was doing well based on early reports from the presbyteries. It might have secured the necessary majority had not some presbyteries refused to cast a vote. A sizable number of judicatories declined to respond because they thought that the question on the ordination of women was not an "overture" in the strict legal sense because it did not specify the chapter and section of the *Form of Government* to be amended.[73] In addition, the overture was further confused by a ruling from the Judicial Commission that permitted the original version to be amended to admit women also to the diaconate. The final wording, however, was ambiguous as it read "ruling elders *or* deacons" indicating a possibility of choosing one or the other.[74] Although reference to such technicalities may have been only a subterfuge, there can be no doubt that the careless wording of the ordination overture proved to be crucial in the final analysis. The results reported in 1921 showed that 139 presbyteries favored ordination, 125 opposed and 37 recorded no action. Because a majority of 152 presbyteries was needed to pass the overture, the "no action" votes caused the proposal to be defeated.[75]

In retrospect, efforts to widen women's sphere between 1880 and 1920 had met with limited success. Most Presbyterian churches provided a diaconal ministry for women, and their *de facto* if not *de jure* status as teachers and speakers was no longer seriously questioned as a matter of practice. Nevertheless, the crucial issue of ordination as elder and minister had not been resolved except in the small, continuing remnant of the Cumberland Presbyterian Church where necessity as much as principle may have been the dominant factor in opening the doors to women. Presbyterian women remained outside the ecclesiastical power structures so long as ordination, and, therefore, representation was withheld. Few denominational leaders at that time were likely to acknowledge that women's sphere was not a closed circle but had an infinite and indeterminable radius. Most seemed to be in agreement with the editor of *The Continent* who reported the negative vote on ordination with this comment: "The women can well be patient. There are other years coming, and they are in no hurry."[76]

8

CHALLENGING CHURCH POLICY:
Unrest in the Church, 1920-1930

While Presbyterian women waited with varying degrees of patience for church fathers to grant ecclesiastical equality, they continued their entry into the secular and religious workplace. Traditional delineations between a "man's job" and a "woman's calling" blurred in the 1920s with females engaging in tasks ranging from logging and dairy farming to banking and civil engineering. Also available to women were more opportunities for church vocations in missions, Christian education, and the administration of the women's boards. Especially in foreign missions, where women workers consistently outnumbered male missionaries, was the impact significant.[1] Such professional role changes led one Presbyterian editor to comment that old arguments prohibiting churchwomen from sharing certain privileges and responsibilities should be considered "childish." He further predicted that within a few years "women will be restored to our great councils and courts in proportion to their devotion and gifts."[2]

Denominational magazines repeatedly cited success stories, portraying various Presbyterian women as models for the rising generation of young churchwomen. Ella A. Boole, president of the national WCTU, made headlines by announcing her candidacy in the Republican primaries for United States Senator from the State of New York. Alice M. Robertson of Muskogee, Oklahoma, a former home missionary, in 1920 became the first Congresswoman to serve in the United States government. As assistant to the Director–General of Railroads, Frances H. Brady, a member of the Church of the Covenant in Washington, D.C., proved that a young woman could withstand the pressures of difficult decisions and long working hours. Like many women, Brady had entered government employment during the wartime labor shortage and had remained to work her way up to a position of considerable executive responsibility.[3] Other Presbyterian women were known to be active in a variety of secular political, social, and educational positions, and many in the mission fields who served as physicians, teachers, and evangelists received extensive publicity, especially in the religious press. Some of the executives who administered the women's boards for foreign and home missions were highly visible to church members, especially among the denominational and ecumenical leaders.[4]

Despite women's vocational advancement in church and society, however, Presbyterian women continued bereft of voice or vote except at the congregational level. Ordination as elders and ministers, which involved the right to election as commissioners to presbytery, synod, and the General Assembly, where denominational policy was forged, remained the prerogative of men. One nationally known Presbyterian woman told her friends, "The Presbyterian Church does little less than insult the intelligence of its womanhood. . . . In the Presbyterian Church, all that is expected of her is just to sit."[5] This was an unusual assertion, for Presbyterian women rarely voiced such criticism, or when they did it was private and off-the-record.

Rather than protest, younger women pursued careers outside the church. Older churchwomen continued to work in a volunteer capacity through their separate mission boards and local societies. As long as the boards existed, even those women unhappy with the lack of official status found themselves invested with some degree of power through the economic and program responsibilities of women's work. Consequently, Presbyterian women received a shattering blow in 1923 when a denominational reorganization resulted in the termination of the Woman's Board of Home Missions and the Woman's Board of Foreign Missions (see chapter 4). Apart from the disappointment in seeing their power base destroyed, the women bitterly resented the fact that they had been excluded from any vote in the entire reorganizational process. Both the decision and the method of arriving at it constituted a unilateral "take-over," as some women referred to it, and stirred advocates of sexual equality, both men and women, to marshal support for an amendment to the Presbyterian *Form of Government* that would end the anomaly of an organization where 60 percent of its members were denied official status.[6]

Initial efforts to secure equality proved ineffective largely because the denomination was engaged in a heated modernist–fundamentalist controversy. This controversy, which originated in the latter part of the nineteenth century, dramatically revived in the 1920s when Harry Emerson Fosdick became the regular "guest preacher" at the First Presbyterian Church of New York without transferring his membership from the Baptist to the Presbyterian ministry. The Fosdick case also evoked the famous Auburn Affirmation that condemned the denomination's biblical literalism and called for a broader interpretation of theological doctrine. The same modernist–fundamentalist struggle later centered on the Princeton Theological Seminary where J. Gresham Machen triggered a reorganization of the seminary and the formation of the Westminster Seminary and the Orthodox Presbyterian Church. These and other divisive issues caused the Moderator of the General Assembly, Charles R. Erdman, to propose a special commission to consider "the causes of unrest in the church" and to propose actions to resolve them.[7]

The Commission of Fifteen appointed by Erdman submitted its findings to the General Assembly in 1926. In an effort to promote the "peace, purity, unity, and the progress of the church," the commission identified a number of significant issues that the Presbyterian church would have to face in the immediate future. The last item in the long list of contributing factors was the status of women. "There are many women in the church who are not satisfied with present administrative conditions," the commission reported. "Some of them fear the loss of organization through which they have worked so long. Some regard as unjust the lack of representation of women in the church."[8] As a result, the General Assembly referred the subject of women to the General Council for study and recommendations.

In the spring of 1926, the General Council appointed Katharine Bennett and Margaret Hodge, ex officio members of the Council, to investigate the causes of unrest among Presbyterian women.[9] Neither of the two women wished to accept this appointment on such a controversial issue, even though their leadership in women's work qualified them for it. Nevertheless, during the next year they conducted careful research on the status of women, consulted churchwomen, and examined their own thoughts. They produced a carefully written study entitled *Causes of Unrest Among Women of the Church*, the first such critical analysis written by women rather than by clergymen.[10]

The report acknowledged that unrest among women did not constitute a comprehensive, organized, or articulate movement and candidly admitted that most churchwomen were either unaware or uninterested in issues of freedom and equality. The authors however, identified a group of women, "not large but intellectually keen," who seldom participated in church organizations because they were dissatisfied with restrictions imposed by the church. Even these women, influenced by inherited standards and traditions, reported Bennett and Hodge, preferred to accept the status accorded them rather than to criticize the church openly.[11]

Within the context of the history of women's work in the nineteenth and twentieth centuries, Bennett and Hodge posed a number of underlying causes of female unrest. Most prominent was dissatisfaction with the consolidation of the two Woman's Boards and their respective

Assembly Boards. Beyond this specific issue of reorganization, the report attributed much of the female unrest directly to reactionary and visionless male leadership. Citing one prominent churchman whose response to the burgeoning women's movement in the nineteenth century was, "Let it alone—all through history like movements have started. Do not oppose these women and it will die out," the report charged, "Popular male opinion with a few notable exceptions seems to have been equally divided between the above type and a benevolent paternalism which felt it to be a pleasant thing for the women to organize and raise funds but which utterly failed to recognize a new force that had been unleashed."[12]

Although Bennett and Hodge argued strongly for full equality of men and women, they noticeably downplayed any demand by women to occupy the pulpit. While recognizing sex-role stereotyping as inconsistent with the gospel, the authors acknowledged that few women "as yet" had any interest in preaching. What Presbyterian women wanted immediately was representation on local and denominational councils, even if without the formalities of ordination.[13]

In spite of this apparent ambivalence about ordination, Bennett and Hodge concluded with a forceful plea for recognition of full personhood for women:

Most [women] ask for no one thing, only, that artificial inhibitions that savor of another century having been removed, they may take their place wherever and however their abilities and need of the church may call. Woman asks to be considered in the light of her ability and not of her sex. She recognizes that being as one woman said, 'the first generation out of the kitchen,' she has much to learn, but she cannot be a 'new woman' in all phases of her life and willingly accept the position accorded to her in the church. Her mind rebels even if her heart keeps her tongue quiet.[14]

As chairman [sic] of the two-person committee, Bennett read the report on November 30, 1927, to the churchmen who composed the General Council. Even though the Council temporarily suspended the reading of her manuscript ("through the courtesy of Mrs. Bennett") in order that the Budget and Finance Committee could report, Bennett's thorough presentation stunned the Council whose minutes refer to it as a "thoughtful and disturbing paper."[15] Her oral presentation was even more colorful than the published version, which omitted a number of humorous illustrations. For example, Bennett told the Council the story of an old farmer who took his wife and drove into a nearby town. After hours of shopping and gossiping, he drove home, laden with packages. Placing them all on the kitchen table, he counted them out to his interested daughters—gingham for Mary's dress; muslin for Ellen's waists; and sugar, tea and flour for the pantry. Examining all his purchases, the farmer scratched his head and exclaimed, "I know that I had one more thing I just can't remember." After fruitless efforts to recollect, one of the girls hoping to quiet her father said, "Never mind, Pa, we'll ask Ma." Slapping his thigh, the old man said in disgust, "That's it, I forgot Ma!"[16]

Bennett's and Hodge's "thoughtful and disturbing paper" placed the General Council in an awkward position. On the one hand, having requested a comprehensive study (and apparently having received much more than it expected), the Council could not simply receive the report with "thanks to the ladies" and dispatch it into oblivion. Such a well-documented indictment of sexism in the Presbyterian Church coming from the pens of two respected "establishment" women demanded a response. On the other hand, for the General Council to accept the report (it contained no specific recommendations) and to prescribe remedial legislation to the General Assembly would require considerable prophetic courage. In a milieu of theological and cultural unrest, the Council questioned how well radical changes in ecclesiastical organization and government would set with an essentially conservative constituency already weary from a decade of controversy. Moving cautiously, it thus neither approved nor rejected the report. Instead, it referred it to a Committee of Four (Katharine Bennett, Margaret Hodge, Lewis S. Mudge, and Robert E. Speer) for study and recommendations.[17]

Despite individual differences in personality and background, each of the four committee members had mutual characteristics. Their theological position was conservative, evangelical, and ecumenical, representing both the breadth and the depth of historical Presbyterianism. They were all deeply committed to the institutional church and were willing to work through traditional denominational procedures. All avoided controversy, especially if it augured schism or dissension. Although Speer on occasion spoke out passionately about sexual equality, all four were extremely sensitive about being labeled "radical" or "liberal." Nevertheless, they were dedicated to sexual equality both as an empirical fact and as a biblical principle. Their ambivalence, a crucial factor in subsequent decisions, centered on the extent to which practical realities should be permitted to influence the actualization of principles.[18]

In answer to the question, "What action should the General Council take in regard to the unrest among Presbyterian women?" the Committee of Four recommended that a representative group of Presbyterian women be invited to attend a conference. The Council agreed and empowered the Committee to select fifteen women to meet with the General Council in November. This marked the first time in the history of the Presbyterian Church in the U.S.A. or of any other American

Reformed denomination that male and ordained church leaders met together with women specifically to discuss questions relating to sexual equality in the functioning of church government.[19]

The conference convened in Chicago on November 22, 1928, with fifteen members of the General Council present, among whom were Mudge, Speer, Hugh K. Walker, chairman of the Council, and Henry C. Swearingen, vice-chairman. Hodge attended as a corresponding member of the Council, but Bennett was absent because of her husband's illness. From all indications, the fifteen representative women covered a spectrum of attitudes. Among those present were Louise Blinn, generator of the Cincinnati petitions of 1924 and 1926; Emma Speer, a talented churchwoman who, despite being married to a church executive, left Presbyterian women's work because of its restrictions to serve in an interdenominational group; a number of younger women including Florence G. Tyler, a former student secretary of the two mission boards; and several presbyterial and synodical leaders who had been active in women's work for many years and were inclined to believe that the so-called "unrest" in the church was only in the minds of a few avant garde feminists.[20]

Opening remarks by Speer and Mudge briefed participants on events leading up to the conference and on the positions taken by other Reformed denominations regarding the status of women. Even though the ensuing discussion dealt with a variety of interrelated topics, comments by both men and women centered on the issue of sexual equality. Were men and women equal in the eyes of God and of church government or were they in some way divinely circumscribed in an inferior/superior relationship? Did Presbyterian Church government reflect the apostolic imperative that there was "neither male nor female" in Jesus Christ? Was it willing to accept some compromise dictated more by cultural considerations than by theological principles? The answer to the first question was a resounding Yes; to the second a reluctant No; and to the third an ambiguous no, but. . . .[21]

Because of the meeting's significance, Henry Barraclough, assistant stated clerk of the General Assembly, took detailed notes that were later mimeographed for limited distribution. A representative sampling of comments illustrates the scope and intensity of positions expressed and indicates that both women and men recognized the question of sexual equality to be preeminent:

I fancy if you took a vote from the women here on the matter of eldership and the ministry, that would occupy far less space in the thinking of women who are in the group here than the matter of representation and bearing our share in the courts of the church. . . . In our form of church government, in congregational matters, but beyond that, you see the whole field of representation is closed to the womanhood of the church. (Mrs. Dan E. Waid)

I have a fine intelligent girl in college, and she is going to have the finest education I can provide. I have served the Church for twenty years or more, but under the present conditions, I never would think of suggesting to her that she look to the Church for the outlet of her energy. (Mrs. Charles A. Blinn)

Are we not in the process of catching up with public opinion? Public opinion has gone so much faster than the legislation of the Church. We are not quite ready for changes in many parts of the Church. I wonder if there is as much opposition throughout the Church as some of the leaders think there is? (Mr. George Nicholson)

I do not believe we would find many men or women who would expositorily deny the equality of men and women as members of the Church. They feel they are equal, and if that is the case, it is for us to press the logical consequences of that principle. The position of the Church is illogical and indefensible. It is a very serious question as to how far and how fast we ought to go just now. (Reverend William R. Taylor)

Women have an inferiority complex, bred in the first place through their education. I doubt if any woman of my generation would feel free to express all her ideas before a company of men, because there was too much put into our education that implied inferiority. (Mrs. Robert E. Speer)

Frankly, coming into the Presbyterian Church from the Congregational Church I felt a difference. It was a difference in atmosphere. I felt there was a premium on dumbness. You weren't to have opinions on this or that—opinions were not asked for. I said, this is easy, because it is easy for me to be dumb. (Mrs. Frederick Paist)[22]

As the daylong conference drew to a close, Speer asked for specific recommendations for the General Council to consider at its spring meeting. Louise Blinn quickly proposed "that the right of the members of the Presbyterian Church to share and participate in defining its faith and determining its policy shall not be abridged because of sex."[23] Mudge advocated a change in the constitution to permit women to be ordained as ruling elders "as our line of least resistance and of most rapid progress."[24] Henry Swearingen summarized the position of several other General Council members when he acknowledged the theoretical aspects of sexual equality but felt that there were a number of unanswered practical questions in his mind. "I am going home tonight with my pencil in hand," he said, "And I am preparing to make a list of questions that I want to ask myself."[25] In lengthy summation, Speer described his perceptions of viewpoints as expressed at the conference and admitted the unlikelihood that anyone present could draft a single statement that would represent a consensus. He suggested that the Committee of Four be empowered to draft such a document on behalf of the group and present it to the General Council for action. His motion to that effect prevailed, and the conference was adjourned.[26]

Between January and March 1929, the Committee of Four circulated letters and held several meetings as they carefully worked out a recommendation for the General Council's spring meeting. Mudge maintained a consistent position throughout the proceedings. He favored proposing an overture to ordain women as ruling elders, leaving the question of ministerial ordination to a later date, because he was convinced that this was as far as the Presbyterian church was prepared to move. He preferred not to press for full ordination and lose everything. In a letter to Bennett, Mudge maintained that once ordination as elder was secured, it "would gradually introduce itself, in a perfectly natural way, a considerable number of women in our Presbyteries, Synods, and the General Assembly."[27]

Speer's avowed ardor for sexual equality was not highly visible in his first attempt as chairman to formulate a recommendation to the General Council. In a memorandum to Mudge, Hodge, and Bennett on January 11, 1929, Speer outlined a report consisting of five major sections. The first four were primarily informational, describing the background of the conference, previous efforts of the church to deal with the question of equality, and scriptural evidence supporting ordination of women as elders. Only in part five did Speer propose an overture to admit women to the eldership and suggest that the question of ordination as evangelists be submitted "whenever Presbyteries believe that it is desirable." He hesitantly concluded his memorandum: "Do you think that in the last section we would be going too far, or not far enough?"[28]

Hodge responded by raising serious questions about placing so much emphasis on ordination. She reiterated to Speer that the fundamental cause of unrest among the women "is not so much a desire to be admitted to the diaconate, the eldership, or even the ministry, as it is to have removed all discrimination against them as women." If the committee felt confident enough to recommend ordination, Hodge queried, why not go all the way and advocate the end of sexual discrimination? She reminded Speer, however, that most women at the Chicago conference were wary about pushing ordination because they did not want to risk another negative vote such as was taken in 1920. While Hodge retained her acceptance of the principle of equality, she qualified her approval with a suggestion that a postponement of the question for at least a year would provide time to prepare both men and women for this radical change in church policy.[29]

Bennett's reply followed the general lines suggested by Hodge but went further in defending the principle of sexual equality. Bennett noted that she and other leading Presbyterian women had not themselves raised the issue of ordination but had asked only for representation in decisions regarding women's work. Since the broader discussion was now before the church, however, she was not willing to support an overture limited only to ordination of women as ruling elder. "If it is right that women have equal place with men in the church, then it should be given to them; if it is not right, then let them not be given the eldership." She was convinced that the "fundamental rightness or wrongness of the matter must be faced, and action taken accordingly. Let the Church deny further 'rights,' or remove restrictions and inhibitions that are based on sex."[30]

Bennett's sharply worded letter left Mudge unmoved. In a letter to Speer, Mudge mentioned that he was "considerably impressed" with Bennett's arguments for sexual equality. Nevertheless, he insisted, "We must proceed, I still feel, with moderate speed lest we antagonize more people than we win."[31] Speer, on the other hand, was motivated to accommodate the views expressed by Hodge and Bennett. In a revised version of the committee report, Speer suggested three alternative proposals, putting on the General Council the responsibility to make a final decision: ordain women as ruling elders; ordain women as ruling elders and evangelists; or (the new feature), remove from the *Form of Government* all language that implied or acknowledged sexual inequality.[32]

The committee met on February 13, 1929, to discuss Speer's revised report. Mudge urged caution. He wanted to "test the mind of the church" on ordination as elders and licensure as evangelists (an intermediate step before ordination) before attempting to remove all sexual distinctions from the *Form of Government*.[33] Speer, Hodge, and Bennett felt that the time had come to take a stand on principle rather than expediency despite the problems it would raise. They wanted the General Council to overture the General Assembly to guarantee both men and women the right to serve the Presbyterian Church in any capacity without proscription because of gender. With some misgivings, Mudge agreed to support the majority opinion and approved the final draft to be presented to the General Council in March.[34]

Beyond its prefatory and explanatory sections, the final committee report contained two major recommendations that reflected specific points raised by Hodge and Bennett. In the first place, on Bennett's insistence, it incorporated questions raised by reorganization. Supported by a resolution from the Council of Woman's Committees of the Boards of Missions, the report recommended that the General Council call another conference of representative Presbyterian women to discuss the future of women's work in the light of revamped denominational structures.[35] The second recommendation related to the ecclesiastical status of women. The final version listed the same three alternatives as the second draft but added this significant sentence: *"Your committee is unanimously in favor of the principle of the third suggestion* [complete equality] *and if it meets with the approval of the Council, we would propose a recommendation by the Council to the Assembly of an overture to this effect;* or if the Council deems this unwise, then we would recommend an overture embodying the second proposal." Having taken its stand on principle, the Committee of Four left the final decision to the wisdom of the General Council.[36]

Speer read the report of the Committee of Four to the General Council that met in Philadelphia on March 6, 1929. With a forceful and at times dramatic defense of sexual equality, Speer stated the two basic questions that needed to be answered: "It is right? Is it expedient?" On both counts, he answered affirmatively. He concluded: "If it is right, I think we ought to go ahead with it and trust the Lord."[37] No direct account of the discussion following Speer's report is included in the minutes of the General Council, but the thrust was evident in correspondence and other sources. The members showed unanimity on principle but considerable difference of opinion on expediency. The minority, led by Mark A. Matthews, John Timothy Stone, and Joseph A. Vance, thought that the times were not propitious for presenting an overture on equality. They argued that consideration of the "woman question" would exacerbate the general unrest in the denomination and would have a disruptive effect on delicate union negotiations then going on with the Presbyterian Church in the U.S. The dissidents promised that they would support submission of appropriate overtures in 1930 but that they could not in good conscience vote favorably at this time.[38]

Nevertheless, when the discussion concluded, the General Council voted 13–6 to accept the third proposal: "removal from the *Form of Government* of any form of speech which is inconsistent with the recognition of the complete equality of men and women in the life and work of the Church." The stated clerk was directed to draw up "overtures" (note the shift from singular to plural) necessary to recommend this action to the General Assembly.[39] Bennett immediately telegraphed a friend to report the good news: "Recommendations of the committee asking that all disabilities be removed adopted and will be sent to the Assembly. Making history fast these days."[40]

The General Council specified overtures because of Mudge's caution on modifying the Presbyterian *Form of Government*. Aware that careless wording of previous overtures on women's status in the church had caused confusion and opposition, Mudge wanted to avoid imprecise language that might sidetrack commissioners from the main issue of sexual equality. He therefore proposed two separate and distinct overtures, one to modify the *Form of Government* and one to alter the *Constitution:* Overture A, "On Admission of Women to Full Ecclesiastical Standing," and Overture B, "On the Amendment of Constitutional Rule No. 1." The first overture specified word changes in two sections of the *Form of Government* (Chapters Three and Thirteen) so that the offices of minister, elder, and deacon could be filled by either sex, and that all references to the three offices should utilize both personal pronouns *he* and *she*. Presbyteries were instructed to approve or disapprove the over- ture as a whole by giving a single affirmative or negative answer. The second overture was designed to amend the *Constitution* so that local evangelists could be any communicant church member regardless of sex. Again, presbyteries were instructed to answer simply Yes or No.[41]

Denominational papers publicized the General Council's decision to petition the General Assembly for consideration of Overtures A and B. Predictably, *The Presbyterian*, a conservative Philadelphia periodical, responded negatively. Its editor, David S. Kennedy, accused Mudge of taking advantage of his position as stated clerk "to exercise undue influ- ence in the affairs of the church." He further lamented that the General Council could be supportive of "this ungodly and unscriptural plan and purpose" and prayed that God would give the Presbyterian Church a "full and prompt deliverance from this violence and sin."[42] The *Pres- byterian Banner*, a liberal publication in Pittsburgh edited by James H. Snowden, endorsed the Council's stand but predicted that there would be "reasons in plenty urged against it" and that the success of the movement for full equality was in doubt, given the mind of the Pres- byterian church at that time.[43]

Behind the scenes, influential Council members and other denomi- national leaders urged Speer and Mudge to modify the Committee's stand on sexual equality on the side of gradual change rather than on one decisive action. Speer was the first to feel the brunt of such pres- sure. A week after the March General Council meeting, Mark A. Matthews, pastor of the First Presbyterian Church, Seattle, Washington, spokesman for west coast fundamentalists, wrote Speer asserting, "In days gone by you spoke as a prophet; you have been speaking as an echo recently. What is the matter?" Matthews claimed that it would be a serious tactical error to send to presbyteries overtures on women's rights and that he personally would lead a movement on the General Assembly floor to postpone action unless Speer's committee would make such a recommendation at the May meeting of the General Council.[44] Speer refused to yield to Matthew's threat of organized opposition. Acknowledging that people of good will and honest con- science might differ on important issues, Speer contended that the basic question was "what is right in principle and the light of the teaching of the Scriptures? If this is clear must we not stand on it and act accord- ingly?" Speer acknowledged the possibility that the General Council could reconsider its action in May prior to the General Assembly, but personally he saw nothing to be gained by postponing action on a matter of principle.[45]

In his capacity as stated clerk, Mudge was an obvious target for those who opposed the ordination of women. He was extremely sensitive to criticism from denominational conservatives who quickly labeled as "modernists" those who differed with them on matters of biblical interpretation and ecclesiastical procedures. Still chafing over the bad press he had received in *The Presbyterian*, Mudge received a telegram from Mark Matthews demanding on behalf of Council dissidents that the stated clerk append a note in the General Assembly *Blue Book* that the action on woman's status in the church had not been unanimous and the names of the six churchmen who opposed it be listed. On this point, Mudge complied.[46]

The stated clerk also had to respond to an editorial in the *Christian Century* that correctly identified Mudge and Speer as supporting equality and naming Matthews, Stone, Vance, and others as Council members who had cast negative votes. On April 3, the same day on which he received Matthews' telegram, Mudge dictated a letter to the editor of the *Century* declining to write a brief article explaining Presbyterian plans to amend its *Form of Government* so that women could have full participatory rights. Mudge indicated that the General Council might be having some second thoughts about its March action. "My reason for this judgement," said Mudge, "is that our General Council may decide at its meeting in May just prior to the opening sessions of the General Assembly that we had better wait a year before advocating the submission to our Presbyteries of the necessary overtures."[47]

As pressure for reconsideration mounted, The Committee of Four met on April 16 in Philadelphia to decide on a unified course of action. They discussed Matthews' request for a delay of one year in presenting any overtures and decided to poll the other five dissidents—Swearingen, Stone, Shipp, Shattuck, and Vance—to ascertain their opinion. Of the five, only Stone took a hard line on postponement, with others professing to be willing to go along with any majority decision reached at the upcoming Council meeting. In a conciliatory letter to Matthews on April 17, Speer reaffirmed his committee's determination to move ahead with the overtures. At the same time, however, he promised that all four members would come to the May meeting of the General Council in St. Paul "eager only that we may all find together the right way and be able to determine the right time."[48]

Despite this display of solidarity, the Committee of Four had left the door open for last-minute modifications in the contested action taken at the March meeting of General Council. Unfortunately, there is no correspondence on the subject after Speer's April 17 letter to Matthews. The editor of *The Presbyterian* hinted that Matthews and his supporters were beginning to wear down the Council majority. The editor reported that he had been "officially" advised that the General Council would reconsider its recommendation to send down the overtures to the presbyteries. What action the Council would take was not yet clear but it appeared doubtful that it would hold fast to its original proposal.[49]

On the eve of the May 22 meeting of the General Council, the Committee of Four had one last opportunity to hear what Presbyterian women thought about the controversial equality overtures. At the Conference on Women's Status and Service in the Church that met in St. Paul on May 20–21, with Margaret Hodge presiding, the delegates considered two questions that had been submitted to them by the General Council: (1) Should the General Council take the overtures to the General Assembly or should it postpone action for one year? (2) Should the General Council seek full ecclesiastical status for women (as approved on March 6) or should it seek it by degrees—ruling elder now and minister and evangelist later?[50] Before making a decision, the delegates requested Mudge and Speer to make brief presentations. Both gave noncommittal addresses. Mudge summarized the position of women in other Protestant denominations, and Speer described the work of the Committee of Four and the arguments for and against the ordination of women. After the two men had left the room, the women discussed the questions at length before voting against postponement and affirming their support of equality now rather than by a gradual process.[51]

With this clear mandate from the women of the church, the Committee of Four went to the meeting of the General Council on May 22, 1929. Exactly how or when the following decision was made is unclear. Nevertheless, "At the request of the Special Committee" (Speer, Mudge, Bennett, and Hodge), the General Council amended the March 6 resolution to propose that *three* overtures (instead of two) be sent down to the presbyteries. Overture A specified ordination as ministers and elders; Overture B (the new overture) called for ordination as ruling elders only; and Overture C provided for licensure as evangelists.[52] As Mudge later explained, Overture B gave presbyteries "an opportunity to vote separately on every aspect of the question."[53]

This compromise, initiated by the Committee of Four, apparently quieted the Council minority who had been vigorously compaigning for postponement. A motion to defer action was defeated 19–2 with Matthews voting with the majority. Nevertheless, the decision to stand solely on the principle of equality had been undercut. The presbyteries could, if they chose, take only a half step without either rejecting or approving the fundamental issue of "neither male or female in Christ."[54]

When the 141st General Assembly convened May 26, 1929, the election of Cleland B. McAfee, professor of Systematic Theology at McCormick Seminary, a moderate who favored the expansion of women's ecclesiastical rights, seemed to be a hopeful sign for the women's overtures. The General Council selected the popular Speer to present Overtures A, B, and C to the General Assembly. By a large majority the commissioners voted to send the overtures down to the presbyteries, with the only opposition based on procedural objections. A few commissioners argued that the overtures should first have been referred to the Bills and Overtures Committee instead of coming directly out of the General Council's report, but Moderator McAfee, supported by Mudge, cited precedent for this procedure and overruled their objection.[55]

Although commissioners were aware of the amended overtures, the denomination-at-large was never fully advised of the significant change from two to three overtures. In fact, the report in the 1929 General Assembly *Minutes* is blatantly misleading. After citing "Minutes of the General Council" for March 6, which concluded with the words: "That the Stated Clerk be instructed to send to the Presbyteries for their action the following overtures," the overtures given are not the two from the March 6 meeting but the three from the May 22 meeting! This without one word of explanation. "Overtures" (two) by ecclesiastical legerdemain became "overtures" (three).[56] Even Bennett and Hodge acquiesced in this conspiracy of silence. In *An Open Letter to Presbyterian Women* encouraging support for Overtures A, B, and C, they described the process by which the Committee of Four arrived at its recommendations: "The above findings [committee report] were sent to the General Council and that body recommended to General Assembly the overtures which were noted in the early part of this letter."[57] Again, there was no mention that the "full equality" overtures had been amended at the May meeting of the General Council.

The "women's overtures" generated an unprecedented volume of articles and letters in Presbyterian journals and newspapers during the year between General Assemblies. The editor of the *Presbyterian Banner* had predicted that the discussion would "develop much heat and possibly little light," and his estimation was not far off the mark.[58] Opposition was led by Kennedy, editor of *The Presbyterian;* Matthews and Swearingen, of the General Council; Ethelbert D. Warfield; and Clarence Macartney, pastor of the Arch Street Presbyterian Church in Philadelphia and former moderator of the General Assembly (1924). These churchmen used traditional arguments, laying heavy emphasis on the authority of biblical texts, especially Pauline injunctions about women's submission to male authority, raising questions about the "natural order" of society, and enumerating practical problems that might arise if women were ordained.[59]

Proponents of Overtures A, B, and C worked hard to counteract their well-organized opposition, even though they had difficulty in finding respected Presbyterian leaders who were willing to write and speak for sexual equality. As stated clerk, Mudge decided to remain neutral, so he did not publicly support the overtures. Ignoring criticism from those who thought that as a Board secretary he, too, should observe an official silence, Speer on the other hand spoke and wrote on behalf of the overtures. He also privately encouraged colleagues to contribute favorable articles to the Presbyterian papers. Joining him were such notables as Cleland McAfee; Samuel Tyndale Wilson, president of Maryville College; and James H. Snowden, editor of the *Presbyterian Banner* and professor at Western Theological Seminary.[60]

Unlike the 1920 debate on ordination when Presbyterian women were virtually silent, they now took up pens to defend their goals. As acknowledged leaders, Katharine Bennett and Margaret Hodge wrote candidly about their convictions and asked presbyters to give careful consideration to the basic principles of human rights embodied in the overtures.[61] Other women acknowledged their support in articles and letters to denominational papers. In some presbyteries, women in numbers occupied the visitors galleries when commissioners voted on Overtures A, B, and C. At least one minister complained to Mudge that he had been forced to vote under the watchful eyes of a delegation of women who applauded and booed as a roll-call vote was taken.[62]

By early spring, an unofficial tally of presbytery votes indicated that Overture A (full equality) would not pass but that Overtures B and C still had a good chance of being approved. Speer conveyed this information to Matthews, commenting that the Seattle pastor would not have to hear "the sweet voice of any authorized woman ministers in the Presbyterian pulpit." Speer warned him, however, that he was "not absolutely safe yet against the presence of women elders in the Synod of Washington and the General Assembly."[63] Speer's predictions proved to be correct. The final tabulation showed that Overture A had been defeated 170 no, 108 yes, and 7 not voting. Overture B, granting women ordination as ruling elders, passed by a margin of 158 to 118, with 7 not voting. Although Overture C, licensing women as evangelists, received more affirmative votes (144) than negative votes (130), it did not have the minimum number of votes (147) required by the *Form of Government*.[64]

An analysis of the voting on Overture A shows that its strongest support came from presbyteries in western states, where women had received suffrage rights in the nineteenth century and where the influence of egalitarian frontier missions had prevailed. Utah, Wyoming, Colorado, Arizona, and New Mexico judicatories all voted three to one in favor of the overture for sexual equality. Even in Washington state where Matthews had considerable influence, five out of eleven presbyteries voted for Overture A. Midwestern states were almost three to one against full ordination, and in the east where traditional Presbyterian patterns and attitudes dominated, judicatories were overwhelmingly negative. New York state was an exception. With many small rural churches and a strong Congregational influence where it was not unusual to have ordained women ministers, the vote was almost even, with 15–14 in favor of Overture A.[65]

A number of factors contributed to the defeat of full equality for women at this time. Opponents were well organized, articulate, and eminently respectable. They utilized effectively the argument that biblical proof–texts were on their side and relied on centuries of ecclesiastical tradition to rebut divergent interpretations of relevant texts. Moreover, as Speer admitted privately, many Presbyterian women displayed little enthusiasm about ordination rights and consequently did little to support Overture A at the local level. The fact that the overtures originated with the General Council rather than from individual presbyteries apparently convinced some ministers and elders that a vote against the overtures was a vote against church bureaucracy. Finally, the dexterity with which some writers identified Overture A with all forms of radical political, social, and religious movements likely fostered its downfall. Neither reactionary nor radical, the middle-class constituency of the Presbyterian church could with good conscience defeat Overture A in the name of conservatism and with the same good conscience approve Overture B in the name of progressivism.[66]

According to one eyewitness, the results were accepted by the General Assembly in 1930 with only perfunctory interest. The vote to deny women the right to the pulpit "hardly occasioned a murmur, and the victory of the second part of the overture, which gives women the right of being elected as elders, was received with only feeble applause."[67] This tepid reception marked the end of any immediate movement to secure full ordination rights for women. The denomination had spoken through its judicatories, and there was little prospect that it would change its mind in the near future. The Committee of Four reported to the General Council that its work was completed and requested to be dismissed.[68] Mudge, who never had been wholehearted in his support of ministerial ordination for women, made no effort to introduce new overtures before his retirement in 1938. Speer, whose later years were marked by personal family tragedy and professional harrassment concerning his leadership of the Board of Foreign Missions, was absorbed in defending his position in the denomination. Bennett and Hodge devoted all their attention to preserving the integrity of women's organizations torn by the prolonged Syllabus Controversy of the early 1930s (see chapter 4). Another generation of church leaders would raise again the issue of Presbyterian women receiving full ordination in the denomination.

9

SECURING ORDINATION RIGHTS:
No Legal Barriers, 1930-1958

Efforts to secure full ordination rights for Presbyterian women during the 1920s were only one facet of the progressivism and moral idealism that had characterized American life since the early years of the twentieth century. By the mid-1920s, however, there was a mood of disenchantment among Americans. The Great War had not won a lasting peace, and there had been little idealism evident in postwar treaty negotiations. President Warren G. Harding's call for a return to "normalcy" led many to lay aside their crusades and retreat into inactivity. The institutional church reflected these general cultural trends. By 1925, the usual indexes of denominational strength—church attendance, Sunday school enrollment, and missionary giving had declined, and it continued to do so for nearly a decade. What historian Robert T. Handy has described as "The American Religious Depression" was well under way by the time the Presbyterian Church admitted women to the eldership in 1930. That achievement proved to be not the crest of the wave in the drive for equality but rather was hidden in the strong pull of a receding tide.[1]

Following the publicity given to the first five female commissioners to the General Assembly in 1931, the subject of the ordination of women disappeared almost immediately. Denominational papers carried no articles, editorials, or even letters from correspondents dealing with sexual equality. Having dismissed the Committee of Four, the General Council turned its attention to other problems facing the denomination, and its minutes have no references to eccelesiastical equality during the 1930s. Even the opponents of the ordination of women elders apparently accepted the status quo so long as no one attempted to reopen the question of male–female roles in church life. W. Courtland Robinson, a leader in the opposition to the ordination of women, summarized his position in 1931: "One may like it or not like it, think it good or not so good; it is written in the law of the church and the results will follow."[2] Beyond that comment, Robinson expressed no further interest.

Although Robinson and others had predicted that a majority of women would be commissioners to the General Assembly "not many years hence," admission to the eldership, in fact, did not bring a significant number of females into judicatories at any level. After the Wauwatosa Presbyterian Church of Milwaukee Presbytery elected Sarah L. Dickson as a ruling elder only two days following the approval of Overture B, the denomination as a whole seemed little inclined to press for much more than token representation of women at local and national levels. Initially, only "exceptional women," such as Dickson, who had been active professionally as deacons, deaconesses, religious educators, and missionaries or who were acknowledged leaders in women's missionary organizations and Sunday schools sought or were elected elders. Few churches applied the same high standards to prospective male elders as they did to women.[3]

Since congregations and judicatories did not identify elders as either male or female in the 1930s and 1940s, accurate statistics are not available for those years. A study conducted by the Federal Council of Churches in 1940, however, showed that only 6.6 percent of the Presbyterian churches that responded had women elders. Several presbyteries and at least one synod had no women elders at all within their bounds.[4] Fifteen years later, more reliable figures indicated that only 4.5 percent of the total eldership in the Presbyterian Church in the U.S.A. were female, representing about 3,000 out of a total of 65,744 elders.[5] As late as 1970, women comprised only 17.8 percent of the eldership, and a third of all the churches, about 2,900 congregations, had no women elders.[6]

To a certain extent, these figures reflected continued reluctance by Presbyterian men to work with women as equal partners. Although the Ruling Elders Association officially welcomed women into its ranks in 1932, noting that women were "sincere and enthusiastic missionary propagandists," the resolution endorsing women elders was the only one among others that did not pass unanimously.[7] The disregard of women's role, however, went beyond the question of eldership. One Presbyterian woman recounted that during the 1930s the report of the presbyterial society was never entered on the docket. The women's report was received by mail and put into the records without comment or acknowledgment. When the presbytery met in the hometown of the presbyterial president, she requested permission to make the report in person. Although the stated clerk assigned her a time on the docket, no request came for the report. As the morning session was about to close, the woman asked for the privilege of presenting her report to the "fathers and brethren," and received a courteous but extremely cool reception. "During the noon hour when the women served dinner," she noted, "we all became very popular."[8]

Nonetheless, male opposition or disinterest alone cannot account for the relatively small number of women elders. In most Presbyterian congregations, women outnumbered men three to one and, theoretically at least, could have selected a fair representation of women on local sessions. Their failure to do so is explained, in part, by the results of a questionnaire sent out to Presbyterian women leaders prior to World War II. While 65.1 percent of the respondents felt there should be at least a minority of women on church boards and sessions, 10 percent thought that their service should be restricted to certain boards, and another 8 percent wanted women on boards only if there was a shortage of men. Among these women, 16.8 percent believed that such official responsibilities as eldership and representation on official boards and committees should be left entirely to the men. These statistics reflected the opinions of active churchwomen who were in a position to exert influence over other women in the local congregations and presbyterials.[9]

Besides the women's obvious reluctance on the issue, the severe impact of the Depression precluded any reconsideration of the question of ministerial ordination. By 1933, there was widespread concern regarding the unemployment of Presbyterian clergymen. The Department of Vacancy and Supply of the Office of the General Assembly reported a great increase in the number of capable and highly desirable ministers out of work. The Depression had forced many congregations to share pastoral services, to discontinue the services of associate and assistant pastors, and to reduce the number of local, field, and headquarters representatives of the Boards. With presbyteries reporting 1,390 candidates for the ministry in 1931–32, the situation was not conducive to the General Assembly discussing opening the pulpit to women in an already overcrowded field.[10]

Despite the seeming impossibility of women having access to the ministry, a few Presbyterian women served as stated supplies, lay preachers, and evangelists in the 1930s. Judicatory record keeping makes it difficult to identify precisely how many women were so employed, but it is not likely that their number was great. Those who served usually were in small, rural churches that had a paucity of male leadership and a limited budget. Mary Jane Turner, a ruling elder in the Memorial Church of Gig Harbor in Olympia, Washington, served a congregation of forty-four communicants. In the 1930–31 fiscal year, the congregation reported a total budget of $834, which included $65 for benevolences.[11] Lena L. Jennings of Loudenville, Ohio, labored in two rural congregations, Perrysville and Clear Fork, as interim pulpit supply under the direction of the Presbytery of Wooster. When she retired in 1950, the presbytery bestowed upon her the honorary title of "minister emeritus" and provided her with a modest pension of $60 a month.[12]

Mrs. F. E. Smiley, whose husband was stated supply at the Aurora and Valverde churches in the Presbytery of Denver, frequently conducted morning worship at Valverde while her husband was at Aurora. Although she questioned the legality of such procedures, she was told that it was acceptable "on the authority of the bishop" (her husband). [13]

Some women who filled Presbyterian pulpits had been ordained by another Protestant denomination. Again, documentation of their presence is limited because of incomplete records. Louise Eby, ordained by the Congregational Church, served the Bethlehem Chapel of the First Presbyterian Church of New York City for a number of years. Her insightful article "Can Women Make Their Way Into the Ministry?" written in 1929 and overlooked by most modern scholars, described both the problems and possibilities of a nonsexist ministry in Protestant denominations. [14] Margaret Ruth Eddy served in a federated (Congregational/Presbyterian) congregation in Cincinnati, Ohio, and later with her husband, Norman Eddy, worked in the East Harlem Parish in New York City. [15] Hanna L. Almon, wife of a Presbyterian minister, was ordained in 1930 at the Kidder (Kansas City) Association of the Congregational Church. Various Presbyterian churches in Kansas and Missouri appointed her to fill vacant pulpits as a full-time pastor. In the early 1950s, she was listed as a stated supply at the Presbyterian Church in Hollister, Missouri. [16]

In one exceptional case, the Presbytery of Cedar Rapids, United Presbyterian Church of North America, ordained a woman to the ministry in 1943. Elizabeth Brinton Clarke made an urgent request for ordination because she was seeking an appointment in the Women's Auxiliary Army Corps as a chaplain. Clarke reportedly had the equivalent of a college education, had attended some pastoral theology classes at Pittsburgh-Xenia Seminary, and had completed correspondence courses with the Moody Bible Institute. In addition, she had served as a city missionary and pastor's assistant. Early in 1942, she became the stated supply at the Pratt Creek UP Church in Vinton, Iowa. The commission appointed by presbytery to study her request concluded that she had "a definite call of God to the ministry" and recommended that the presbytery proceed with her ordination. Because Clarke was not being installed as a pastor, the presbytery waived the usual congregational notice and ordained her to the gospel ministry. [17] This action was later overruled by the UPNA General Assembly in 1944.

Despite these rare situations, the General Assembly declined to raise the question of women's ordination betwen 1930 and 1945. During this time, women turned—indeed were actively guided—into the field of christian education as an alternative form of service not requiring ordination but meeting pressing needs in the denomination. (See chapter 11.) Relying on the traditional and still prevailing cultural standards, church leaders viewed women as particularly suited to work with children and young people because of their God-given nurturing attributes. William C. Covert, general secretary of the Board of Christian Education, expressed this oft-repeated theme in an article entitled, "Leadership—In the World of Christian Education—A Call To Women." Covert praised the increased number of women joining staffs of churches as directors of religious education and serving on presbytery education committees and challenged them to become leaders in the "great task of saving the youth of our nation."[18]

Even though the General Assembly ignored the question of ordination for women, it had not been forgotten by many Presbyterian women. According to Katherine McAfee Parker, some churchwomen repeatedly reminded denominational executives that they had never completed the action begun in 1930 with the ordination of women as elders. Parker admitted that women did not utilize confrontation tactics nor did they marshal any organized movement to remove prohibitions against their full participation in church life.[19] Nevertheless, through their national meetings Presbyterian women kept visible the subject of ordination. At Buck Hill Falls in 1938, Georgia Harkness, a Methodist minister and professor at Mount Holyoke College, addressed the group and referred to the church as "the last stronghold of male dominance."[20] They also heard one of their own members, Mrs. Charles Kirkland Roys of the Board of Christian Education, remind them that in no other area of activity were women so hesitant as they were in the field of religion: "Men have for so long a time assumed that in these matters they alone are the mouthpiece of God. And we have let them get away with that happy fiction. We have let them cherish the illusion that it is their divine right to mediate religion to us, the weaker sex (not too weak, let us add, to serve church dinners and to raise a tidy budget!)." Roys challenged the churchwomen present to "study, discuss, experiment. Work up public opinion. Arouse our own church."[21]

Again social upheaval intervened, with the onset of World War II diverting any organized movements to respond to Roys' call for action. While women secured the approval of the General Assembly for the creation of a national organization, The National Council of Presbyterian Women's Organizations (PWO) in 1943, they also devoted considerable energy to programs such as assisting the War Time Service Commission and caring for refugees and displaced persons (see chapter 5). Under the limited travel conditions imposed by fuel rationing, women could not meet as frequently and in such large numbers as they had during peacetime.

The wartime conditions, however, indirectly influenced the General Assembly to consider ways in which women might be more effectively utilized in ministerial roles. With many clergymen and seminary students in the armed forces as chaplains or in some related government service, a considerable number of small Presbyterian congregations needed leadership. In 1942, the Synod of New York reported "an urgent need for the services of consecrated and qualified laymen" to minister to vacant congregations and requested the General Assembly to give them some official status. The General Assembly deferred action and ultimately decided not to recommend such an overture to the presbyteries.[22] In 1945, however, the Synod of New York sent up another overture that requested modifying the *Form of Government* to enable presbyteries to grant local commissions for teaching and preaching "to properly qualified men and women who shall be known as Missioners." The overture made no provision for missioners to perform marriages, administer the sacraments, or moderate sessions. The missioners' sphere of authority was limited solely to "the authority to teach and preach." The General Assembly referred the overture to the General Council for study and directed it to make a report the following year.[23]

The General Council committee of Jesse Herrmann, Henry Sloane Coffin, and Helen Weber was instructed to consult synod executives and other field representatives from every geographical area of the denomination before making any recommendations. Most of these people sympathized with the need for status of worthy lay workers and praised the work being done by women in various missionary and educational capacities. Some expressed reservations, however, about having a different (and lower) set of standards for those performing ministerial duties.[24] Reacting to the response, the committee reported favorably on the overture, making only minor alterations in the original text, such as changing the title of "missioner" to "lay preacher." The General Assembly sent the overture down to the presbyteries in 1946 and it passed by a vote of 138–93.[25]

The same General Assembly also sent down an overture to grant women equal ordination rights with men. The overture, presented by the General Council, was the outcome of a controversy over whether an ordained Japanese woman could officiate at a communion service held during a PWO national meeting in May 1946. The PWO executive committee had invited Tamaki Uemura, an ordained minister of the Church of Christ of Japan and graduate of Wellesley College and the University of Edinburgh, to be the first Japanese civilian to visit the United States following World War II.The churchwomen intended that their invitation to Uemura and her acceptance provide a visible symbol of forgiveness and reconciliation between the two former enemies. Because PWO was not a church court, it had to request approval from the General Council to hold a communion service. The executive committee wished the retiring Moderator of the General Assembly, William Lampe, to preside, and specified to the General Council that the women also wanted Uemura to assist Lampe in the service.[26]

Even before the General Council meeting in March 1946, Lampe and Stated Clerk William B. Pugh informed the executive committee that they interpreted church law to mean that since women could not be ordained in the Presbyterian Church they could not administer the sacraments at a service under denominational sponsorship. Given such an interpretation, they could not condone Uemura's participating in the communion service.[27] Informed of this by PWO leaders, several members of the General Council came to the March meeting to challenge Lampe's and Pugh's interpretation of the *Form of Government.*[28]

A prolonged and at times acrimonious debate followed, with Pugh and Lampe on the defensive. At one point in the discussion, Pugh reportedly threw his rulebook across the room and stated that it might be hypocritical to exclude women, but in good conscience as stated clerk he had to enforce the rules as he understood them. One of the chief arguments was that one denomination should not judge the ordination standards of a sister church; if Uemura could administer communion in Japan, the Presbyterian Church had no right to question her authority to do so in the United States. Wilbur LaRoe, Jr., a lawyer and laymember on the Council, proposed a motion that appeased Pugh and at the same time enabled the women to invite Uemura. "We record it as the unofficial view of the General Council, that it would be a calamity in this day, if arrangements could not be made whereby our Japanese friend might participate in the communion service . . . and we express our unofficial view that a way should be found whereby it can be done."[29] Ironically, after this ecclesiastical maneuvering, Uemura was delayed in her travel and arrived the day after the communion had been celebrated.

With Pugh's concurrence and support, the General Council at its May meeting proposed an overture to the General Assembly that would grant ministerial ordination to women.[30] Lampe, in presenting the overture to the General Assembly, never referred to the Uemura incident, but unquestionably it was an important factor in his remarks. Lampe offered three reasons for approval of the overture: Women were rendering helpful service to the church, women could be ordained in other denominations, and women already had the right to be ordained as elders and deacons.[31] With Moderator Frederick W. Evans reminding commissioners to consider before they voted that a report of what happened might reach home and that they "might have to give a hard accounting to their wives," they voted overwhelmingly in favor of sending the overture down to the presbyteries.[32]

Unlike the public debate that characterized the "women's overtures" in 1929–30, Overture D ("the office of minister may be either men or women") generated little national debate. Although the executive committee of PWO sent a copy of the ordination overture to presbyterials "for their sympathetic interpretation throughout the year," churchwomen mounted no organized campaign to lobby for passage of the overture.[33] Denominational periodicals carried only a few articles on the subject. Methodist Georgia Harkness was the only female contributor to *The Presbyterian* who favored ordinaton.[34] The sole Presbyterian woman who expressed her views did so only after the issue had been decided. In an article entitled, "Why I Do Not Wish to be Ordained," Mae Ross Taylor, a staff member of the Fourth Presbyterian Church in Chicago, argued that "no lone woman could ever know and meet the needs of a community, could ever in the fullest sense of the word be a pastor."[35]

When the Committee on Bills and Overtures reported to the General Assembly in 1947, it announced that only one overture sent down in 1946 had not passed. That lone exception was Overture D, which received 100 yes, 128 no, and 8 no action votes.[36] Again, the negative votes were concentrated in the eastern section of the United States, with presbyteries in Pennsylvania and New Jersey almost solidly opposed to female ordination. One of the few public reactions to the vote came from a Presbyterian clergyman who had been asked by the *New York Times* to write an article on the pros and cons of women ministers. He concluded, "I feel that women get what they want, given time, and will get the privilege of the pulpit and the pastorate in the Presbyterian Church as they got the vote in the affairs of the nation. . . . Women may not win this year, but win they will, and God bless them. But also, God keep too many of them from taking up this new field all at once."[37]

The defeat of Overture D in 1947 did not usher in another long period of inactivity as had been true in 1930. Even though women did little to influence the passage of the overture, they had been alarmed by the Uemura incident to the inequities of denominational policies. In addition, social conditions in America and indeed throughout the world were quite different; during the war period, women had assumed leadership roles in both secular and ecclesiastical spheres. With the postwar population boom and the subsequent expansion of church plants and programs, the demand for trained workers increased dramatically, and there could be no question of women competing with men for limited positions.[38]

Reflecting these conditions, the newly organized World Council of Churches (WCC) at its initial assembly at Amsterdam in 1948 gave prominent consideration on its agenda to expanding the role of women, with delegates studying "The Life and Work of Women in the Church" as one of the featured "Concerns of the Churches." A provisional report called for the appointment of Kathleen Bliss of England to collect and organize information from various countries in order to develop a balanced interpretation of the current situation and to suggest possible future actions. W. A. Visser 'T Hooft, general secretary of the WCC, personally endorsed the study and suggested that a whole new era of church history might open up if Christians began to ask seriously "what the will of God is concerning the diversity of gifts of men and women and concerning the one spirit in which they are to serve together their common Lord."[39]

As part of the research for Bliss' study, the Presbyterian Church in the U.S.A. sent out approximately 1,500 questionnaires to women throughout the country. Evelyn Luchs, the Presbyterian survey coordinator, reported to the executive committee of the PWO in 1948 that the findings indicated fewer opportunities for women to utilize their abilities in church work than in most secular fields. Moreover, she pointed out that "American women find it strange that they have less opportunity to serve than in the same denominations abroad." Luchs also recounted a conversation with a group of Presbyterian women and Visser 'T Hooft in which the general secretary encouraged them to press their denomination to give women more participation in the total life of the church.[40]

On hearing Luch's comments, the PWO executive committee requested that she develop an educational plan for acquainting and arousing interest among Presbyterian women toward professional opportunities and services on official church boards. The committee also proposed that articles be written for *Outreach* and *Presbyterian Life* that would focus from time to time on World Council personalities, programs, and projects in order to stimulate interest and action by Presbyterian women. The executive committee compiled a cumulative list of women elders who might be qualified for positions of wider leadership on both denominational and interdenominational levels and who could communicate with women to support them in fulfilling the responsibilities of eldership.[41]

The publication of Kathleen Bliss' book, *The Service and Status of Women in the Church*, in 1952 evoked a wide-ranging, positive response in the United States. *The Christian Century* called for Protestant churches to implement ordination for women. It also produced a series of articles "intended to make better known to the American public women who are playing conspicuous parts in the church life of this country."[42] In the same year, the United Church Women initiated a study of the status of women in denominations associated with the National Council of Churches (NCC). Mossie Wyker, who was authorized to appoint a committee, asked the president of the NCC, Bishop Henry Knox Sherill, to select three male representatives so that the project would not appear to be a feminist uprising. The committee prepared a survey instrument and sent it to twenty denominations having women's organizations. Each denomination appointed a committee composed of both men and women to make a study of its own constituency. The results were collected and presented at the assembly of United Church Women in Atlantic City in 1953.[43]

The report contained revealing statistical information. According to the federal population census for 1950, there were 6,777 women ministers in the United States, or 4.1 percent of the total number. This marked an all-time high for women clergy and represented a doubling of the number reported in the federal census of 1940. A study of the data available in the 1951 *Yearbook of American Churches*, however, revealed only 2,897 pastors and 5,791 ordained or licensed women ministers. Of the pastors reported, only 608, or not quite one-tenth, were in churches affiliated with the National Council of Churches. Almost 60 percent of the total number of women ministers were in three denominations: The Church of God, The International Church of the Foursquare Gospel, and Christ Unity Science. More than one-tenth were in the Methodist church. Practically two-thirds (66.1 percent) of all *Protestant* women ministers were in four groups: The Church of God, the International Church of the Foursquare Gospel, the Methodist Church, and the Volunteers of America.[44] Clearly, women ministers were a negligible factor in most mainline Protestant churches.

According to reports from various denominations, nontheological factors continued to be used to justify not admitting women to the ministry. Although many of the arguments seemed trivial, they apparently were taken seriously: Women's voices carry less well and therefore are a handicap to a preacher; women have no wives, and churches like to have two leaders when they call one; churches dislike having a woman pastor, whom they hesitate to call out at night; women ministers drop their careers after marriage. One denominational committee candidly admitted: "It is a generally accepted fact that the woman parish minister has first to be twice as good as a man to overcome the resistance of many churches to the idea of a woman minister and secondly, that her acceptability to many churches is based solely on the fact that she can serve more cheaply than a man."[45]

The Presbyterian portion of the 1953 report indicated that women were increasingly predominant in denominational activities despite their exclusion from the ministry. Approximately 3,000 served as elders, and many functioned as Commissioned Church Workers, Christian educators, and lay preachers. Moreover, women elected by the General Assembly constituted one-third of the membership to the program and administrative boards of the church and were included on the General Council and on the Board of Pensions, although in a smaller ratio to the total membership of the latter groups. There were no policy-making boards on which women could not serve as regular members. Women also served as co-opted members of standing committees and subcommittees of synods and presbyteries, and women members of the various boards and staffs represented the denomination on the NCC Assembly and General Boards as well as on its divisions and departments.[46]

Regarding ministerial ordination, the Presbyterian committee stated that their denomination had not ordained women to the preaching ministry "largely because of its interpretation of the New Testament texts which have seemed to be against this service." It admitted, however, that "in the newer and less atomistic interpretation of the gospel," it appeared probable that there would be a reconsideration of this subject. Acknowledging that "there is no doctrine which prohibits the ordination of women as ministers," the committee nevertheless concluded that there "should not be an effort to force the issue of ordination," but "rather a calm re-thinking of the whole question by both men and women in the light of the desire for a truer interpretation of the Bible and for a fuller realization of the mission of the church in which all members must participate."[47]

Following the presentation of the complete report to the assembly of the UCW, Mary E. Lyman, professor at the Union Theological Seminary of New York, presented a paper on "Goals, and Some Steps to Take." Recommending that various committees be appointed to keep the NCC and participating denominations aware of the inequalities in their structures, Lyman concluded with a call for action. "With no chip on any shoulder, with no plea for rights, with no feminist crusade in our thought," she said, "we do pledge ourselves to be concerned and to arouse concern about this issue in the life of the American churches."[48] The ovation given Lyman's address indicated that the ecumenical churchwomen in attendance supported her position and themselves wished to achieve ecclesiastical parity in their respective denominations.

While ecumenical organizations discussed long-range strategy for elevating the ecclesiastical status of women, a member of the Third Presbyterian Church in Rochester, New York, supplied the spark that ignited a movement to modify the Presbyterian *Form of Government* so that women could be ordained to the ministry. Lilian Hurt Alexander, a ruling elder in Third Church, had been an unabashed "feminist" since her days as a college student at Vassar when she marched in suffragette parades. Although active in congregational life and a member of the PWO, Alexander was not aware of the WCC and NCC studies on the status of women. In fact, Alexander did not even know that the Presbyterian church officially barred women from the pulpit. She learned of this only when a friend described how her daughter had graduated from seminary but could not be accepted as a ministerial candidate simply because she was female. Aroused by what she considered as a blatant sexual discrimination, Alexander contacted colleagues on the session and her pastor to see what could be done to rectify the situation. Told that it would take a change in denominational government to end such an anomaly, Alexander drew up a petition and submitted it for sessional approval. In her petition she emphasized: "When a woman is led of God so to dedicate her life, it would be difficult to discover truly Christian grounds to deny her request."[49]

The Rochester session forwarded its action to the Presbytery of Rochester and that judicatory overtured the General Assembly on February 17, 1953, "to initiate such actions as may be necessary to permit the ordination of women to the Ministry of Jesus Christ." David W. Moody, pastor of the church, said that the session took the action because it "seemed the logical sequence of the constitutional provisions for ordaining women as Ruling Elders" and because, biblically speaking, "it emphasized the great teaching of Paul in Galatians 3:28 regarding the equality of men and women in the eyes of Christ."[50]

When the Rochester overture became known, it attracted considerable support from the church-at-large. Before the overture actually reached the floor of the General Assembly, sixty-five other presbyteries had formally endorsed it.[51] Nevertheless, some observers predicted a clash on the Assembly floor between "conservatives and liberals" when the overture came up for discussion. C. Ralston Smith, chairman of the Committee on Bills and Overtures, a noted denominational conservative, surprised many commissioners by stating that his committee had no objection to the overture and strongly endorsed it. Because the action necessitated a change in the *Constitution,* and because negotiations with the PCUS and UPNA denominations were in progress, however, Smith thought it best to wait for the outcome of those discussions. He therefore recommended "no action" but urged the Assembly to appoint a committee to conduct further study, a request that commissioners overwhelmingly approved.[52]

The moderator appointed a committee of eight ministers and elders, two of whom were women, with Stated Clerk Eugene Carson Blake serving as an advisor. The committee proceeded slowly and deliberately partly because of its desire to make a thorough theological and biblical study of women's role in church life and partly because it was aware of the possible impact of its report on the union negotiations. When the PCUS voted down a three-way reunion in 1954, however, the committee presented its findings to the General Assembly in 1955.[53] The committee decided unanimously that there were no biblical or theological barriers in the Reformed tradition to the ordination of women to the ministry. Moreover, it saw no significant policy considerations impeding ordination and acknowledged that there were no ministerial functions or responsibilities that women could not perform. On the practical side, the committee noted that the increasing diversification of ministry in the denomination would provide women ample opportunity for service as pastors, preachers, teachers, missionaries, directors of religious education, chaplains, social workers, and other related vocations. The ordination of women would also give women deserved status in the church and encourage others to undertake the work of the ministry. The committee concluded by recommending that the General Assembly approve the addition of a brief sentence to the end of the section of the *Form of Government* headed, "Of Bishops or Pastors, and Associate Pastors." The sentence would read: "Both men and women may be called to this office."[54]

Upon the endorsement of the recommendation, the Assembly sent down an overture calling for the revised standards. As on previous occasions, Presbyterians publicly debated the issue with old arguments, refurbished and modernized for contemporary audiences, indicating that the major contentions had not changed radically since Presbyterians began dealing with the "woman question" in the nineteenth century. Nevertheless, the language was much more restrained than it had been in earlier debates. *Presbyterian Life Magazine* featured a pro and con presentation in November 1955, in which John E. Burkhart, university pastor at the University of Southern California, took the affirmative, and John D. Craig, minister of the Central Presbyterian Church in Houston, Texas, defended the negative. Interestingly, both articles concluded with a reference to the impact of ordination of women on union efforts with other Presbyterian bodies, an indication that practical matters still carried considerable weight with the reading public.[55]

A new feature of the discussions in 1955 and 1956 was the formal participation of organized churchwomen. In 1929 and 1946, they had been conspicuous by their absence from the public forum, and women who contributed letters and articles did so as individuals rather than as representatives of women's organizations. This time, an aroused constituency of Presbyterian women openly supported the ordination overture and sought to win determinative votes in the judicatories. The executive committee of the PWO distributed a statement supporting the ordination overture and used it widely as a study paper at leadership training schools and presbyterial and synodical meetings. The statement expressed confidence that a sound theological base for ordination had been established and that the basic issue was not what men or women want but "what God wills for the life of the individual person. We believe that our Church is enriched as it receives the varied ministries of many kinds of persons, all working together for the glory of Jesus Christ and His kingdom."[56]

In addition to this formal statement, the PWO executive committee solicited a series of articles for *Outreach* supporting ordination, authored by respected churchwomen in the United States and overseas. The irenical tone of the articles and their appeal to traditional churchwomen removed some of the residual opposition to ordination still prevalent among some women in the denomination. Tokuko Inagaki described the successful implementation of female ordination in Japan, and Dorothy Foster, a black Presbyterian, explained how her experience as a national missionary supported the need for ordination. Helen Woolson, a member of the Assembly committee that proposed the overture, repeated the positive arguments set forth by the committee and noted that women could be doctors, lawyers, engineers, professors, architects, and even ball players and bus drivers. "If then," she concluded, "God calls a woman to preach the gospel and chooses to speak through her, dare man or the Church question His choice?"[57]

As the results of presbytery voting began to filter into the General Assembly offices, denominational leaders were already predicting that the overture on female ordination would pass easily. By March 1, 1956, the necessary majority had been secured, even though 102 presbyteries had not yet indicated their vote.[58] On the eve of its 250th anniversary, the Presbyterian Church in the U.S.A. had at last granted women full ecclesiastical parity with men. Inez Moser, former president of the PWO, interjected a note of caution into the victory celebrations. Moser warned Presbyterian women that this was not an occasion for self-congratulation. "It is a new responsibility," she said, "that is meaningful only through what we do with it, and it demands consecrated recruiting."[59]

Despite the overwhelming affirmation of female ordination by the 168th General Assembly, one obstacle continued the debate. When the PCUS rejected a three-way union with the PCUSA and UPNA in 1954, the latter two denominations immediately began negotiations to consummate a merger on their own. In 1956, the Commission on Inter-Church Relations presented to the Assembly a Plan of Union with the UPNA that, if approved, would go into effect in 1958. The smaller, conservative UPNA did not ordain women either as elders or ministers and had historically shown little enthusiasm toward changing its attitude on the subject.[60] One commissioner raised the question: "What if the United Presbyterians refuse to accept the ordination of women?" Ralph Waldo Lloyd, chairman of the Commission on Inter-Church Relations, replied, "We and they both know that this sets up a hazard to union, but our commission could not omit this provision in good faith to our church."[61]

During 1956 and 1957, Presbyterians hotly debated the question of ordination of women as a possible impediment to union with the larger denomination. The number of articles and letters published in *The United Presbyterian* and *The Christian Union Herald* indicated that they had serious reservations about the biblical authority for ordaining women and that there were many congregations unwilling to accept women on sessions or in the pulpit.[62] At Pittsburgh-Xenia Seminary, the denomination's only theological institution, the majority of students either opposed the ordination of women in principle or indicated that they personally did not choose to implement it when they became ordained ministers. Statements supporting women's ordination by respected denominational leaders like Theophilus M. Taylor and Samuel W. Shane, however, tended to calm some of the undecided. Private assurances from both PCUSA and UPNA executives that no congregation would be forced to accept women elders or ministers against their will helped secure passage of a union that otherwise seemed natural and desirable. Eventually the most prolonged debate centered on the name of the new denomination, which finally came to be known as The United Presbyterian Church in the United States of America (UPUSA).[63]

Although it is not possble to present precise numbers, a significant number of UPNA ministers and congregations entered the 1958 union convinced that the ordination of women was neither biblical nor expedient. Many former UPNA congregations continued to elect only men to the eldership and would not entertain calling a woman minister. One young Pittsburgh-Xenia graduate quickly learned that old traditions die slowly. In 1960, when he invited a woman missionary to occupy the pulpit during his absence, session members were apprehensive about a woman preaching on Sunday morning. They agreed to her appearance only when the bulletin specified that the missionary would give a "talk" and not a "sermon," and that an elder would preside and lead the worship service.[64]

As supporters of female ordination had predicted, granting women *de jure* equality did not result in a flood of women into seminaries or pulpits. Margaret Towner, a 1953 graduate of Union Seminary in New York, became the first PCUSA woman minister when she was ordained on October 24, 1956. Towner had taken the Bachelor of Divinity course in preparation for her work as a director of Christian education. By her own admission, Towner did not seek ordination to have a pulpit and did not think that many Presbyterian women would seek pulpits in the future. "Ordained women," she predicted, "may prove the solution to the smaller churches' problem. A woman minister could help with pastoral duties and guide the educational program, too."[65] Towner's sentiments were shared by the executive committee of PWO, which also acknowledged that "it is unlikely that many women would respond to the particular calling which demands ordination."[66]

The culturally ingrained reluctance of women to enter the ministry was reinforced by the attitude of male leaders in the Presbyterian hierarchy. Those men who voted for the ordination overture faced some inconsistencies in their understanding of ecclesiastical equality. On the one hand, they were intellectually committed to the principle of equality, which they saw emanating from basic theological convictions. Their sincerity in affirming that no one should be denied access to ordination on the basis of sex was beyond question. On the other hand, they assumed little or no responsibility for breaking down the *de facto* inequality that persisted in most aspects of church life. Executive positions continued to be held almost exclusively by men. Male commissioners dominated the proceedings of the General Assembly. Seminaries, for the most part, remained insensitive to problems encountered by female students studying for ordination in a predominately male faculty and student body.

These ambivalent attitudes are discernible in the experiences of Eugene Carson Blake, stated clerk of the General Assembly from 1952–66 and later general secretary of the World Council of Churches. Involved early in his career in the cause of minority rights and social justice, Blake did not hesitate to exert the considerable influence of his office to end formal sexual discrimination in the Presbyterian Church. As a special advisor, he participated actively in committee discussions preparatory to presenting an overture on the ordination of women in 1955. Through his participation in the National and World Council of Churches, Blake had become sensitized to the issues of sexual discrimination and to the enlightened position taken by many European churches where women already labored as equals with men. Because of his openness on this subject, Presbyterian churchwomen recognized him as an important ally and sought his advice and counsel at virtually every stage of their efforts to secure the ordination of women.[67]

While Blake was convinced that there were no valid theological reasons that women should not function as equals with men in church life, he carefully disassociated himself from any form of "feminism" and considered his task completed when the General Assembly approved the ordination overture. With legal barriers removed, Blake told churchwomen that he saw no need "to lift a hand beyond that."[68] He shared the commonly accepted view that only a few women would avail themselves of ordination and doubted if women in general could perform all the necessary functions of ministry as satisfactorily as men. Nevertheless, he affirmed that the few women who had such talents should not be prohibited from exercising their call in the Presbyterian church. Blake did concede, however, that women would not receive their full share of leadership "so long as society itself is masculinely dominated and so long as churches generally are represented at the top level by men." Like most churchmen of his time, Blake offered no strategy to alleviate this basic inequality except to affirm his conviction that when all legal impediments had been removed, "the churches and their councils will gradually make fuller use of women's leadership."[69]

In a "Letter to Miss Candidate" published in *Monday Morning Magazine*, in 1962, a biweekly publication for Presbyterian ministers, another church executive gave expression to his pervasive male ambivalence. Speaking approvingly of women's "great strides in gaining equality with men at the economic and vocational level," he warned that potential female ministerial candidates make a fatal mistake when they "try to live as equals with men in other spheres." With proper qualifications, he said, a woman can be a minister. "But as a woman, you will need to remember that such you must remain; you will need to maintain your femininity and learn to be a *woman* minister. You will never be able to do many of the things men ministers do. . . . And heaven help you if you expect groups of men, such as a ministerial society, to be able to treat you with equality. There are certain times and places when men simply do not want women along."[70]

In another article, ostensibly defending the proposition that women should become an integral part of the Presbyterian ministry and should have opportunity to develop as a leader, Arthur B. Cooper, a minister in Denver, Colorado, cited statistics in 1956 to demonstrate how many vacant churches existed in both urban and rural settings. To fill these vacancies, he saw the need for competent, younger women who would respond to the urgent call of "additional spiritual leaders adequately trained and consecrated." While emphatic that women should have equal training with men, Cooper described the ministerial opportunities available to women in terms reminiscent of nineteenth- and early twentieth-century role definitions. Women, he wrote, "can conduct junior congregations, relieve or supplement the pastor in calling, assist in the pulpit, take the sacraments to the sick and aged, perform certain types of personal work, counsel with young women on personal problems, even marry them, and lay away those of their sex."[71]

In the years following the approval of ordination for women, many Presbyterian churchwomen became increasingly aware that the struggle for genuine equality was only beginning. Encouraged by the growing impact of feminism on American life, a few voices asked the denomination to align its policies and procedures with its formal statement on sexual equality. Janet G. Harbison wrote a number of articles for *Presbyterian Life Magazine* in the 1950s and 1960s in which she incisively analyzed the prevailing patterns of discrimination based on sex and called for denominational leaders, both male and female, to respond with remedial actions.[72] Perhaps Mildred McAfee Horton most bluntly expressed the issues in an article entitled, "Second Class Citizens or Partners in Policy," published in 1958. "The crucial questions about the place of women in the church," argued Horton, "is whether or not the church will accept the pattern of the secular society (with which most women are fully content) or will take the lead within its own life demonstrating the truth of its age-old teaching that human personality is of ultimate worth, whether it be male or female."[73] This public challenge remained unanswered for another decade.

PART THREE

The Professional and Lay
Participation of Women

10

WOMEN IN MISSIONS:
Entering Church Professions

Nineteenth-century American women increasingly attempted to enter professions that might offer self-satisfaction, monetary reward, and upward mobility. Although limited by the societal view of women's participation in public life, their professional opportunities actually benefited from those aspects of "woman's sphere" that allowed women influence in the educational, moral, and religious interests of the family or extended family. Consequently, if women looked toward a career, they often found that education, reform, and missions provided some chance of a vocational entry.[1]

Just as the developing public education system in the country opened the teaching profession to women, so the expanding missionary enterprise led toward positions for females. Among Presbyterians, the interest in "woman's work for women and children" prompted leaders to sanction denominational careers in two areas: missions and education. Another possibility, that of ecclesiastical administration, grew from the volunteer leadership developed by the women themselves and from the bureaucratization of the various female boards for home and foreign missions. The denomination, reacting to the cultural and social changes in America and responding to the ramifications of the "social gospel," also looked approvingly on women's temperance activities, humanitarian projects, and other such reform-minded operations that offered many volunteer and some paid positions in the organizational, institutional, or speaking areas.[2]

Some writers have suggested that women's move into church professions might have paralleled men's retreat from those jobs.[3] This might be demonstrated in the Presbyterian experience, particularly in the area of foreign missions. At the same time, one must take into account the attitude of women, who eagerly sought the positions rather than just tolerated them; the feeling among these women that the positions were "within their sphere"; and the influence of the churchwide recruitment and training for female professionals coming from the missionary societies. Any explanation may reside in a practical fact: Women outnumbered men on church rolls and tended to invest considerable time and emotional energy in the denomination's needs, while men, ostensibly pulled away by the pursuit of their occupations, drifted farther and farther from American religious life.[4] Such a situation, coupled with a better educated womanhood oriented to vocation and a mission-minded church supporting and staffing an expanding program of evangelization, education, medical support, and social efforts, set up conditions for women's professionalism.

Influenced by the culturally induced insistence that women were by nature religiously inclined, females not surprisingly took the initiative in applying for careers in missions. A writer in the *American Missionary* who claimed that "woman has the instinct for religion" saw this "spiritual faculty" as having found its natural outlet in missionary work.[5] More important, however, was a "call" that could come to male and female alike, although how the female responded was determined by church policy.[6] Both men and women were assumed to have been motivated toward missionary work by claims on them from God. Arthur Judson Brown, distinguished historian of Presbyterian foreign missions, saw three primary motives that led missionaries "from the associations and opportunities of home and country": the soul's experience in Christ, the world's evident need of Christ, and the command of Christ. Brown acknowledged, however, a secondary list of motives based on humanitarian, commercial, and practical ideas, especially among second-generation missionaries. "The idea of saving men for the present world appeals more strongly than the idea of saving them for the next world, and missionary sermons and addresses give large emphasis to these motives."[7]

In the case of women, the promotional facilities of the women's mission societies greatly reinforced females' "instinct" and "call." While Brown could report, "The boards do not send the pale enthusiast or the romantic young lady to the foreign field, but the sturdy, practical, energetic man of affairs, the woman of poise and sense and character," the women saw to it that the female candidates fulfilled the description.[8] Once the woman's boards began recruiting and screening, financially supporting, and helping train women for mission work, the church offered a substantial number of positions to women, often describing opportunities in pragmatic terms—the need for trained females to minister to native women and children abroad and to exceptional populations at home.[9]

Aside from the mission societies, the group vital in paving the way for women's professionalism in missions were the wives of missionaries, the first sizable group of women serving. Taking on responsibilities for the education and training of native women and children and opening their homes so that their methods of house management, interpersonal relationships, child rearing, and spiritual exercises might serve as a model, the wives functioned as co-professionals with the men. Toward the end of the century, a missionary acknowledged this, writing, "It is the missionary's wife, who, by years of endurance and acquired experience in the foreign field, has made it possible in these later years—the years of the woman's missionary societies—for unmarried ladies to go abroad and live and work among the people of eastern lands."[10] The same could be attributed to the wives of home missionaries, who participated in the building and acculturation of western America and who helped introduce educational and medical services among the non-English speaking populations.[11]

In general, missionaries were encouraged to marry. Rufus Anderson, head of the American Board of Commissioners for Foreign Missions (ABCFM), wrote Elisha P. Swift, secretary of the young Presbyterian Western Foreign Mission Society, the forerunner of the Board of Foreign Missions (BFM), in 1832 that the ABCFM considered missionaries "more useful for being married," but left it to the men to decide. If the man was to be married, the group required testimonials of the suitableness of the female "before the Committee receive her, by a formal act, as an assistant missionary."[12] Experience convinced many missionaries of the wives' usefulness. R. M. Mateer, Presbyterian missionary in China, for one told an assembly, "It is unfair, inexcusable, and unwise; irrational from every standpoint, to undertake to establish a station without women." Arguing against a suggestion that men should go out alone, at least for the first few years, Mateer said of the wives, "Let them have an equal chance with the men."[13] The "first white women over the Rockies," immortalized in Clifford Drury's multi-volume treatment, and the many teachers to the Indians and home mission wives chronicled in church literature demonstrated the usefulness and hardiness of women on the American frontier.[14]

The Roll of Presbyterian Foreign Missions (the work including at the time the American Indians) listed missionary wives as early as 1833.[15] The Roll of Missionaries compiled by Florence Pinder for Brown's *One Hundred Years* demonstrates the large numbers who served in each station, along with their maiden names and dates of service. Letters and memoirs confirm that some wives had gone out prior to 1833, either with the ABCFM or independently, particularly as a result of the revivals of the 1820s.[16]

As early as 1839, a traveler abroad commended the missionary wife's adaptability. Noting the effect of uprooting herself from her family and friends into an alien culture and environment, the traveler was impressed wiith the change from a "tender and helpless girl" into the "staff and support of the man."[17] After some two decades, the Presbyterian BFM considered the wife first as an assistant, later as an associate missionary,[18] and articles describing her "qualifications" began to appear. Qualifications usually emphasized piety, using the word to connote Christian belief and faith, love, and steadfast endurance in the midst of testing, humility and meekness, and self-examination. One wife added energy and perseverance, a good mind, the ability to labor with one's hands, and resourcefulness in managing home and children.[19] Unquestionably the wives needed all these attributes, along with good health, stamina, a fair education, "all tempered with and regulated by the blessed commodity—common sense."[20] Reports show that the women not only managed their homes and families and served as their own children's teachers but also instructed and counseled native women and established schools for children, taught English, read and interpreted the Bible to groups of women and young people, translated the Scriptures, opened their houses to visitors, accompanied their husbands on evangelistic tours, and handled much of the correspondence and writing tasks.[21]

Many husbands sought to publicize their wives' value to the mission. A home missionary extolled the work of missionary wives in general, but particularly praised his own spouse. In one year, he reported, she had made 700 formal calls independent of incidental visits, taught in the Sabbath school, participated in female prayer meetings, social committees, and sewing circles, and managed household duties and the care of their two children. "In a word," he wrote, "if you want *efficient missionaries*, be sure that they are *married*, and carry with them to the field the tact, energy, and devotion of a good wife."[22] Another man did not think his wife was an "extraordinary exception" because "a good wife is one of the Lord's compensations to most missionaries." He felt it only fair to record, however, that she had a large class of young girls, was his aid and counselor during revivals, led the singing at prayer meetings, assisted in parish work, besides doing all her own housework and most of her sewing.[23]

The wives' outside activities were expected to be secondary to the home, in which resided woman's responsibility.[24] Home, however, in the mission environment was not only a refuge for the missionary but also an "object-lesson" to those to whom the missionaries ministered.[25] Consequently, even the duties of house management and childrearing related to the wives' position of assistant missionary. This principle of presiding over an instructive and exemplary home, along with the quantity and nature of the work among women and children, influenced a change in the traditional view of the wife's sole duties as related to the husband and children.[26] Brown, defending the missionaries' hiring of servants, asked, "Would it be common sense to send an educated Christian woman as a foreign missionary, and then force her to spend her time in cooking meals and washing dishes?"[27] A missionary in Asia said, "I demand that the missionaries keep servants. They are paid to give their time to missionary work, and, especially in the case of a wife and mother, I claim she has no right to do housework, sewing, etc. and give only her leisure from such things to that service for which she has a regular salary."[28] R. M. Mateer said at a missionary conference, "The Church in this country [China] expects and practically demands that a missionary's wife should be something more than a mere wife, occupied with the care of him and his family, and doing no missionary work. Our American women are first and always missionaries; and their work and their influence are not one whit behind that of the men."[29]

Letters indicated the wives' enthusiasm toward ministering to the women and children around them. Some even paid their own expenses to travel out from the station to begin day schools, Sabbath schools, and prayer-meeting groups.[30] Commented one reporter, "The wives of missionaries are usually among the most useful laborers."[31] Random samples indicate the varied professional "spheres" of the nineteenth-century foreign missionary's wife: In four years, one wife learned a new language, opened a school, made visits, had two children of her own, adopted a native child, held classes in areas reached only by horseback. Another had a "husband, a house, a garden, a herd of goats, five children to care for and teach" as well as responsibility for writing reports and entertaining the native women who constantly visited.[32] Letters and articles told of meticulously scheduled days, and the women's magazines reported on the wives' entry into zenana, purdah, palace, and hovel to teach and preach.[33] R. Pierce Beaver, in his description of women entering the mission field, saw American wives as "personalities in their own right . . . known and celebrated."[34]

Wives of home missionaries had much less status than their sisters abroad, for the Board of Home Missions (BHM) gave them no "assistant" title. Noting the arduous conditions of life on the frontier, the Board reported to the General Assembly in 1877 that since it was not customary to commission the wives, they had no statistics on deaths among them, "yet it is believed that there is no higher rate of mortality among ministers' wives in any other part of the world than among our Home Missionaries." Although the report emphasized their usefulness, it did not request status or benefits for them but rather asked the women of the church to send contributions to the general budget of the BHM.[35] Why the status of these wives' differed from that of the foreign workers perhaps can be attributed to the general view that mission work in America was primarily to establish churches—an ordained minister's responsibility—and the wife was seen to have little or no impact on the development of such work. When the BHM supplemented its church-development emphasis with educational and medical assistance to exceptional populations in the Southwest and the West and with work among freedmen, mountain whites, immigrants, and other groups, it increased the status and role of women workers.[36]

Although the BHM moved too slowly for some, at the end of the century one woman wrote, "Our women who are called to be missionaries are now free to follow their calling within the United States without being limited to missions schools. Hallelujah!" This woman had applied to the BHM in 1892 but was refused because she wanted to pursue evangelistic work. She "was happily accepted by the Foreign Board." In the foreign field, she noted, "such restrictions could not live—have never prevailed; why should they here? Why in one building in New York should one Presbyterian Board of Missions be fifty years ahead of another?" Various other women who had been rejected by the Home Board either changed to another denomination or joined nondenominational missions, but this particular individual reapplied, writing "for the last time, in mere decency, almost without a hope, to the Home Board, before throwing in my lot with some other Church." This time she was accepted as a Bible reader among the southern mountain whites.[37] With the organization in 1878 of the Women's Executive Committee (WEC), later the Woman's Board of Home Missions, its officers kept close touch with all the women workers, including the missionary wives. Besides maintaining financial support, they undertook the training and oversight of the mission teachers, seeing to it that they and the medical workers had adequate provisions and facilities. Eventually this Board also gave attention to work among immigrants, freedmen, mountain people, and other groups.

The great surge of unmarried females to the mission field coincided with the development of women's missionary organizations in the 1870s, although the BFM had solicited "unmarried female teachers" as early as 1840.[38] Only when the women's groups began to provide financial assistance, however, were large numbers motivated to apply. Beginning with Sarah Doremus' nondenominational Women's Union Missionary Society in 1861, and continuing with the development of the seven regional women's boards and the WEC of the Presbyterian Church in the U.S.A., the Women's General Missionary Society (WGMS) of the United Presbyterian Church in North America, and the women's groups of the Cumberland Presbyterian Church, those Presbyterian women desiring to serve at home or abroad sought appointment through these groups. A pamphlet containing "Rules and Recommendations for Foreign Missionaries" of the UPNA, issued in 1861, extended an invitation to women: "Similar qualifications [for males], so far as applicable, are called for in the case of all females, who go out to the missionary work."[39] By 1889, the WGMS underwrote all medical work in the foreign fields, support for two-thirds of the un-married women on all fields, and an extensive building program over-seas.[40] The manual of the Board of Foreign Missions (PCUSA) specified that single women, including physicians, should make application through women's groups. The same manual directed that "so far as is consistent with their strength and household duties," wives of mis-sionaries "will learn the language and take part in missionary work."[41]

The sheer numbers of single women missionaries abroad in the 1870s was staggering. D. L. Leonard, associate editor of the *Missionary Review of the World*, claimed that in the 1870s, ordained missionaries numbered slightly more than 4,300, while unmarried women accounted for more than 3,400 workers.[42] By 1877, the BFM reported fifty more women than men in the foreign field, fulfilling roles in evangelism, education, and medicine.[43] In 1880, Calvin Mateer of the China mission observed that the work "seems to be going into the hands of the ladies not only at home but also on the foreign field."[44] Arthur Judson Brown, who served as secretary of the Foreign Board for thirty-four years, stated that "a majority of the foreign missionaries of the Church are women. Wives, and single women evangelists, teachers, physicians and nurses have for many years formed approximately two-thirds of the total missionary force."[45] In the face of the possibility of a feminine takeover, the BFM in 1879 called for more men to balance the work, giving credit to the women for applying, but adding, "so far as the laborers and missions are concerned it is not wise to permit the disproportion between the numbers of the two classes to increase."[46]

As opportunities presented themselves, though, women responded readily. Some felt they had a compelling "call." Others not so confident of a call still had a sense of vocation and of wanting to do something meaningful.[47] Some pragmatically wanted a change in their life-style, while others wanted a chance for more power and authority in their work. The Civil War experiences had proven to women that they had hardy constitutions and could perform well in arduous and remote areas. Quite a few were swayed by the promotional literature supplied by the women's organizations; others were influenced by their parents, by returning missionary speakers, or by friends already serving.[48] Undoubtedly a few of the women wanted a chance to "preach," even without ordination and felt they could speak freely in the mission en-vironment. In the case of women physicians, many went out of a sense of duty and call; others went for professional satisfaction; and some saw it as a chance to practice their profession without sexual discrimination.[49]

Historian Barbara Welter has raised an interesting possibility that mission careers might have saved some from facing up to the questions raised by the American women's movement.[50] Certainly, Presbyterian spokesmen regularly denounced the women's rights participants, and many Presbyterian women themselves seemed reluctant to voice support of the movement. In fact, a few, even though active in non-traditional roles, spoke against expanded rights of women.[51] One long-time Presbyterian missionary wife, giving counsel to new missionaries in 1905, apologized for having written her essay too exclusively for women, "a natural consequence, perhaps, of my old-fashioned notions of the impropriety of a woman's presuming to attempt to teach men!",[52] even though her own adjective, old-fashioned, indicated alternative opinions already existing. Whether the women were escaping a stand on rights or not, their increasing participation in missions and in the Sunday-school movement influenced the church to reflect on issues relating to women in a way it had never before done. In 1896, the PCUSA Assembly issued an unprecedented statement: "In view of the fact that nearly one thousand women are employed as missionaries by the Boards of our Church, over sixty thousand are teaching in our Sunday-schools, and a very great number are teaching in colleges and schools in all parts of the world, it is evident that the teaching of these teachers is a matter of very great interest to the Church." Therefore, the Assembly commended "the cause of higher education for women to the generous consideration of the whole Church."[53]

The professional woman missionary of the nineteenth century, despite her growing status, understood her role to be limited to work among women and children. Recruitment appealed to her in terms of sharing the freedom offered by Christianity with her sisters in need. "Our work is woman's work for women; not high to low, not rich to poor; but wife to wife, sister to sister. The City of God has gates on all sides, for all nations."[54] To this purpose, the missionaries committed themselves, agreeing to do the work no man could—entering the isolated woman's areas to preach and supply medical care to women and to teach the girls. In those places where women were less confined, the women missionaries held their evangelistic gatherings in a convenient spot, and if men chose to listen to the sermons or sit in on the class sessions, evidence indicates that they were not turned away. In fact, one of the principles undergirding the work with women was that "if wives and mothers would be won, . . . their men might well follow them to Christianity."[55]

The manual in 1889 stated that "women of the mission who are actively engaged in mission work . . . are entitled to vote on what is known as Woman's Work." In a second version, the manual gave all missionaries, including women in full-time mission work, the right to vote in the local mission council, apparently on all subjects. In 1920, however, at a post-war conference of the Assembly's Board, it appeared that the vote depended on the rules of the individual mission station. The consensus of the conference was that all missionaries should have the right to vote, and Arthur Brown, as he had stated ten years earlier, reiterated his position that "the proper course is to eliminate the sex line altogether." The BFM manual subsequently was amended to eliminate all distinction between men and women with regard to the transaction of the general business of the missions. In the UPNA, single women did not become regular members of the mission until 1927; wives were designated associate members.[56]

As women entered the mission ranks, they encountered various practical problems: of acceptance, housing, marital restrictions, and salaries. That openings for women were available did not allay reservations about their appointment on the part of the Board members, some missionaries and wives, and church members in general.[57] To lessen problems, the Boards exercised care in the selection of appointees. As one woman cautioned, "try and be careful to send *experienced* women, and if they are not very *handsome*, don't let it trouble you, it will be all the better, especially if they are earnest devoted Christians, who have known something about the work at home, and are self-reliant and judicious."[58]

Although some criticism concerned women's suitability for professional service, other criticism focused on practical matters. For instance, living accommodations for single women presented problems immediately upon their entry into the profession and proved to be a continuing dilemma for decades. Rufus Anderson, as early as 1836, felt that sending out unmarried females would "imply the existence of families where these could find a home." He recognized the difficulty of the congeniality of such an arrangement but could see no alternative. By 1860, Anderson acknowledged that securing appropriate housing had limited women to a large extent to serving in female boarding schools.[59] In 1866, a Presbyterian observer wrote, "It is not an easy matter to provide a suitable home for an unmarried lady at most stations. There are hardly ever any families with whom she could board except those of missionaries." Listing overcrowding, uncongeniality, differing habits, the writer noted that such situations presented sensitive issues.[60] A decade later, a medical missionary from Japan recommended that single women be sent out in twos and threes and that they should "live together in a comfortable home of their own, and in a building suited to their work," alluding to a continuing question on this issue.[61]

The Board, when possible, tried to send more than one to a field, but this led to complaints from the women about "unnatural, uncongenial 'marriages' " as one missionary called them. Writing with some emotion, the woman charged that "none of the married people sense it unless the wife has been a single missionary who has had to live and work with another single woman or more than one of a very different temperament. . . . For many, living alone is incomparably easier."[62] Another wrote of "a terrible experience" during her first ten years out, "where four of us, earnest, conscientious Christian women nearly died trying to live with one another, a thing that was impossible from the very nature of the case for we were not congenial either by birth, training or temperament." This experienced missionary suggested an apartment as suitable housing. "I find the ones who ridicule the idea of small apartments for women workers are married men who do not know what they are laughing at or the women who dominate a place and have never suffered the torture which they inflict on others."[63]

This woman and others pointed out the importance of relationships in a mission environment that was often isolated, lonely, and arduous. Uncooperativeness assumed huge proportions when a small group was thrown together, and the woman's boards took early note of this. A handwritten document for the candidates and appointees under the care of the women's societies addressed some "minor points" that the women should consider. Women missionaries would do well to be "very careful of insisting on views of their own which are opposed to those of the mission as a whole or of the older and wiser members thereof." While the mutual relations of missionaries should not differ from other Christian workers, the "necessarily close association together and isolation from those around them, the often debilitating and nerve-trying climate—the different habits of thought—and work brought thither by those who now join hand in hand to build up the Lord's Kingdom in any enemy's country—the absence of the helpful sympathy and varied social intercourse of a Christian land—all these things surrounding and pressing on the soul and spirit of missionaries, render the need more imperative for mutual confidence and fervent charity, while yet making it more difficult always to secure the presence of these desirable companions."[64]

The manual recommended that the missionary not confine herself to her own work but try to see needs of the entire mission. A narrow view "will almost certainly lead to undue magnifying of what is but a part of a whole, to jealous dissatisfaction with the estimate put by others on their work and to a onesided, partial, distorted judgement in financial and other questions arising with regard to it." Especially did the manual recognize that "woman's work for woman" was new and untested, and that problems would have to be solved gradually.[65]

Although the church expected missionaries to serve for life except in special cases,[66] they could not prevent single women from getting married. Both the Woman's Board and the BFM discouraged early marriage by rules of service—the women because they wanted the appointee to repay their expenses of outfitting her and underwriting her travel by at least three years of service. In 1894, the BFM manual was amended to require that "*single women* will not *marry* within the circle of our own missions in less than three years from date of arrival, or outside . . . in less than five years. Single women medical missionaries . . . not within our missions or outside in less than five years."[67] Prior to that, between 1832 and 1891, some forty-seven marriages of 372 appointed single women were noted in the Roll of Missionaries.[68] A "List of Resignations 1834–1899," showed that 143 women wed out of the mission during that period.[69] The women frequently married single missionaries, widowed workers, or persons in another denomination's mission. One listing recorded in the roll indicates a woman worker married a native. Marriages continued to concern the Boards in the 1900s, with Margaret Hodge writing in 1922 about "a few marriage casualties apparently aided and abetted by the missionaries" in Japan. When one young woman on the field asked Hodge if the rules and time limit against marrying meant anything, she answered that they did "but that my observation leads me to believe that the masculine part of Executive Council is more lenient than the feminine!"[70]

Salaries paid by the BFM were broken down into one sum for married missionaries, another sum for single men, and a lower amount for unmarried women. Brown explained the disparity in 1907, "Single men usually receive a little more than single women, not because they are considered as worth more, but because it costs them more to live, as they more often require separate establishments, while single women can usually live with some family or in a school."[71] Not until 1922 did the Board vote to raise salaries of all single women to the level of the single men, approximately 60 per cent of a married man's salary.

Questions occasionally arose about the single salary given to the married couple. In 1894, *Woman's Work for Woman* discussed the missionary wife's compensation, a subject "which we had thought long ago settled and laid away among relics of the past." The response detailed the history of women's support for missionary wives: the situation of the wives' "doing quite as much active work among the women where their lot was cast as any of the single women sent out"; the women's boards wanting to aid these wives; the BFM suggesting that the women be responsible for the difference of salary given to a married missionary over that of one unmarried. "The wife herself would not receive money, any more than does the wife of a pastor or teacher in America, but the husband receives from the Board a larger salary because of his having a helpmeet in his life and work."[72] In 1903, the same publication again addressed "the same old bogey about the missionary wife's salary," adding other justifications for the manner of remuneration: that the salary would be the same whether the women's boards aided or not; that her supplement was credited to her name on the women's books not because the income was divided but in recognition that she also was "sent" out by the Church; that the women raised the funds to assist the Board and to put themselves alongside their sisters; and finally that only a living salary was furnished missionaries anyway.[73] In 1885, the PCUSA Assembly extended benefits from the Board of Ministerial Relief to missionary women "upon the same conditions as ministers."[74]

Of special importance to the professionalization of American women in general, and to church women in particular, was the active recruitment and financial support of female physicians for work in missions. Sarah J. Hale, editor of *Godey's Lady's Book*, raised the need for women doctors in missions in the early 1850s.[75] She founded a Ladies' Medical Missionary Society in Philadelphia in 1851 to recruit and assist women to study medicine and then go to the foreign field. The first woman physician, a Methodist, went to India in 1869; the first PCUSA medical woman went to Korea in 1886; and the UPNA sent its first to India in the same year. By 1893, reports presented at the Woman's Congress of Missions showed that PCUSA women's societies supported twenty-one physicians, more than any single society in the world. In all, seventy women doctors, serving some 5,000 to 25,000 patients in each locale, were in foreign work at that time.[76] By 1936, the medical staff totals also included missionary nurses and national physicians, assistants, and nurses.[77]

Medical missionaries, male and female, were expected to have general knowledge of medicine and surgery, to operate dispensaries for the poor, to make house calls, to work in the hospital, to engage in medical itineration, and to teach medicine to native students.[78] Although this entailed a grueling schedule, it gave women a chance to practice medicine in a more diverse manner than if they had remained in the United States. Underlying these medical expectations placed on the doctors was that they would also be "evangelists." "Many patients come one or two hundred miles, sometimes more, and in addition to the treatment they usually hear the doctrine, and if any interest is shown they receive tracts. In this manner the Word is carried to distant place," wrote one reporter.[79] Pierce Beaver found that the writings and speeches of the women medical missionaries "make it clear that they considered themselves evangelists."[80]

The nineteenth-century missionary woman—evangelist, teacher, physician—tried to convert and build character in the women and children of the station through example, education, translation of Scripture into the native language, medical care, and visiting. Her primary goal was to "feed the Word" to the women and encourage them to spread it to their husbands, children, and friends."[81] In the mission schools and hospitals, the women taught not only reading, writing, and medicine but also Christian dogma. With the political, economic, and educational changes of the twentieth century in the countries in which

Presbyterian missionaries resided, with the increase of international communication and travel, with the growth of nationalism, and with the effect of wars, the missionaries faced changing conditions. A Board of Missionary Preparation, reporting on the preparation of missionaries appointed to the educational service in 1920 and speaking mainly to women since they predominated in that area, called for more training, more physical preparation, and higher adaptability. Una M. Saunders, listing special types of work for unmarried women, emphasized the need for specialized professional leadership abilities. "Where men missionaries are called off to some other field, this may mean that women missionaries are left to cope with some important phase of church organization, or, again, to cooperate with men in larger spheres of service heretofore." Saunders also called for social workers able to found settlements and neighborhood houses in industrial centers. Lastly, she listed the need for women prepared to deal with the "woman's movement." Admitting that in some places "missionaries are still living with their people the life of the primitive centuries," she pointed to other missionaries who "are almost breathlessly following the work of the women leaders who agitate for laws enforcing the same rights that women in the most advanced lands have but newly received." Saunders attributed the opportunities given women missionary doctors and educators to the woman's movement of the West and suggested that "new opportunities accorded women in some Christian lands of sharing in administrative work and of lifting their citizenship onto a higher plane may form a special preparation in the purpose of God, for their leading some of the thoughtful eastern women to His service."[82]

Two years later, the candidate secretary of the Woman's Board of Foreign Missions printed a series of brochures on the requirements for the general, educational, and medical missionary that blended nineteenth-century language and twentieth-century demands. "The Woman Missionary" called for "the counterpart of the ordained man, by whatever name she is called, evangelistic, or general, missionary." Described as the one "who goes among the women in their homes . . . to hold Bible classes or instruct the Bible women that they may teach after she had moved on to the next town,"[83] the woman missionary's basic role seemed not to have changed. Added requirements, however, implemented the needs as expressed by the Board of Missionary Preparation report. Necessary training included a college or equivalent degree and a course in a missionary training school; the study of the history of missions; knowledge of the history and religious beliefs of the people with whom she would work; a course in sociology in relation to modern missionary problems and practical experience in philanthropic work; a facility in language; a thorough preparation for Bible teaching, including practical knowledge; and systematic Bible study.[84]

Although Presbyterians tentatively had projected readjustments, they faced in the 1930s a reexamination of both mission concepts and personnel in the foreign fields. Of special impact was one report, *Rethinking Missions: A Laymen's Inquiry After One Hundred Years*, giving results of a fact-finding and appraisal commission that criticized past efforts and recommended changes in all areas. Although the report claimed national attention and widespread media coverage, the PCUSA General Assemblies of 1932, 1933, and 1934 rejected its criticisms.[85] Robert E. Speer published a rebuttal, missionaries almost universally disapproved, and Brown could ultimately write, "In the Presbyterian Church, the Report is dead."[86] Nevertheless, *Re-thinking Missions* had been widely circulated, discussed, studied, and quoted, and its conclusions were supported by many individual Presbyterians.

One of the most controversial comments dealt with mission personnel. Although having met many missionaries of power, saintliness, and devotion, the inquiry members reported, "The greater number seem to us of limited outlook and capacity." The report especially criticized the efficiency and adequacy of missionaries in the areas of teaching and medicine and in interpreting Christianity to the Orient. This they traced to deficiencies of leadership, professional biases, or incidents of inept organizational machinery.[87] In its study of women's interests and activities, the report pointed to teachers with little specialized training in religious education, "interpreted only through conventional media of Bible teaching and formal religious services, bearing little relationship to the students' environment, and showing little awareness of the correlation of Christian teaching with major social problems and with the development of a fuller life."[88]

The report recommended a reorganization of the missionary enterprise to bring women's work into a closer relationship with the general program. The report also called for the missionary women to reorient their point of view to take into account the changing status of women and to adjust their service and technique accordingly.[89] Speer called the chapter on "Women's Interests and Activities" the most satisfactory part, although not without qualification. Primarily he was pleased with its general attitude of appreciation of the influence of women's work. To its critics, Speer wrote, "Missionary women know well the weaknesses and inadequacies of their work, but we dare to say, with care and deliberation, that it is the best work being done in the world today."[90]

Women in home mission work also faced changes, especially after 1890 when attention was directed to urban areas. A diversified approach to church development included work with foreign-speaking populations in metropolitan locations, social services, church–labor relations, and suburban growth. These areas demanded professionals distinct from the Sunday school, itinerating, or single medical missionaries. Although the social-service projects opened positions for some women, the church development tasks called for ordained ministers for the "settled pastorate," and at that point the Assembly subsidized pastors rather than sent missionaries.[91] Until women gained ordination rights, their roles in national missions resided in social work and religious education.

Of great influence on the role of women professionals both in this country and in others was the implementation of equality for women in the Presbyterian Church that began in 1958 and reached a milestone in 1967, when the 179th Assembly affirmed that "the freeing of women to be equal and responsible partners in the mission of the Church is necessary for the health and soundness of the Church's body and the vigor of its witness and proclamation in the world."[92]

As noted in Part One, the administrative details of supplying and supporting women missionaries had fallen to the women's boards as soon as they were established in the 1870s. For some decades, the leaders of these groups were unsalaried volunteers, although serving on a continuing basis. These early officers demonstrated knowledge of office management, fund raising, promotion and public relation methods, vocational training, and political influence.[93] As they implemented the work, new positions occurred that necessitated paid, full-time office staff. Into such positions came educated women who would assume the authority held by the male Board leaders. These women officials became national figures, respected and consulted by Presbyterians from all levels of the denomination. Although some men found it hard to accept women executives and even to listen to them make reports on the floor of the Assembly or other judicatories, most accepted and admired their abilities. Some, such as Robert E. Speer, changed their former opinions on the role of women and openly called for equal status.[94] After the dissolution of the women's boards, women stepped into various professional positions in the new structure with few questions raised.

It is not within the scope of this study to discuss the ramifications of the woman missionary's influence on the theology and doctrine of Presbyterian missions. The preponderance of women—single and married—even though coming from a culture that disenfranchised, subordinated, and for half the nineteenth century undereducated females, obviously gave a distinctive character to the theology, philosophy, and administration of Protestant mission efforts. This subject seems to be worthy of further study. Our interest here has been to study the opportunities that missions offered in professionalizing women.

11

WOMEN IN EDUCATION AND MINISTRY:
Opposition and Opportunities

Presbyterian women in the nineteenth century found their presence in the field of religious education welcomed. Clergy horrified at the prospect of having a woman in the pulpit supported a woman as a Sunday school teacher because in that position she was fulfilling an acceptable role as a spiritual nurturer of children. Only a handful of men recognized the implications of women Sunday-school personnel. One warned, "These women will be in the pulpit next," while another mused about the ambiguity involved in deciding "where the 'lecturing' ends . . . and the sermon begins."[1] Such observations proved prophetic, for the future would demonstrate a progressive movement from women as Sunday-school teachers to deaconesses, directors of Christian education, commissioned church workers, and finally ordained ministers.

The incorporation of women into the network of Sunday schools that developed within evangelical Protestantism in the 1800s was facilitated by the revivalistic milieu and by subsequent revisions of dominant Calvinistic theology. The revivals of the eighteenth and nineteenth centuries had focused attention on a theological link between conversion and emotion. Since women were traditionally considered to be more emotional than men, they were deemed more able to relate readily to the experiences of children and adolescents. Moreover, a shift in the theology of conversion from that of viewing children as sinners who could be redeemed only by sudden repentance to that of describing children as wax-like creatures "pliable . . . tender, and capable of impressions" gave rise to the idea that Sunday schools could consciously mold the lives of children in a positive fashion and counteract negative influences.[2] In particular, theologians like Nathaniel Taylor and Charles Finney influenced Protestant thinking to consider children morally neutral until an age when they could make decisions for themselves. Women, by nature and God's plan, seemed to be one group who could put these theological principles into action.[3]

The career of Joanna Graham Bethune, sometimes called the "mother of Sabbath Schools in America," typified the role that Presbyterian women played in the development of that institution. Visiting Scotland in 1801, she observed some Sunday schools in operation and became convinced of their evangelistic potential. On her return to New York, Bethune tried to interest local ministers and congregations in setting up their own Sunday schools. When she received no response, her husband reportedly said, "My dear wife, there is no use in waiting for the men; do you gather a few ladies of different denominations, and begin the work yourselves."[4] Under Bethune's leadership, the Female Union Society for the Promotion of Sabbath Schools was established in 1816. From its modest beginnings, the organization eventually promoted an enrollment of 8,000 pupils. As administrator, Bethune supervised the entire operation and coordinated the work of a large staff. Although the society eventually became an auxiliary of a larger organization led by men, Bethune remained active in religious and secular education, especially in the area of infant schools for children left unattended by working parents.[5]

The significance of women's involvement in Presbyterian Sunday schools lies not with identifiable leaders but with those whose contribution to the history of religious education is recognized by nothing more than a mention in a congregational history or a name in an old Sunday-school register. Yet in most Presbyterian churches in the United States, women provided most of the leadership except for the position of superintendent usually reserved for a man. By the end of the nineteenth century, there existed more than 8,000 Presbyterian Sabbath schools with nearly 1,000,000 pupils enrolled. Adding missionary schools and independent programs, the number would be considerably higher.[6] When the Board of Publication and Sabbath-School Work was organized in 1887, its initial report stated that "the Sabbath-School is the best known agency for reaching millions upon millions of children who have no religious training from parents or any others, and saving them from godless lives with all their disastrous consequences."[7]

Especially in rural areas did Presbyterian women play pivotal roles in creating and sustaining Sunday schools. With a paucity of ordained ministers and elders in small, struggling congregations, only the imaginative contributions of women kept many institutions alive. Under such conditions, theoretical considerations about the status of women in the church did not loom large in religious education. One small congregation in Temple, Oklahoma, for example, had only one male member in addition to an itinerant missionary who visited the church several times a month. Even though there were not enough men to constitute a session, the work of the congregation continued through a "council" of women and a lone elder who kept the church in good repair and who

maintained a Sunday school twice the size of the usual church attendance. The women even assisted with the communion service, though
they lacked ordination. According to the writer who described the
Temple church, the women were married and mothers, "well educated,
refined and devout Christians. They are not only leaders in the church
but leaders in the social, civic, fraternal and business enterprises of the
town."[8]

Despite their popularity, lay-oriented Sunday schools were not without their detractors. By the end of the nineteenth century, professional
educators were criticizing Sunday-school pedagogy for its inadequate
standards, curriculum, and staff. Outmoded Sunday schools, critics
argued, should be replaced with week-day religious education through
released time in public schools and by vacation church schools, where
children could be exposed to religion in an academically respectable
context. Utilization of the term "church school" for Sunday or Sabbath
school by the major Protestant denominations in the early part of the
twentieth century reflected changing attitudes regarding Christian
education. To facilitate this reform, William Rainey Harper, president of
the University of Chicago, established the Religious Education Association in 1903, which rapidly made an impact on denominational boards
of education. In 1922, the International Council of Religious Education
organized to encourage curriculum reform and teaching training programs as a means of upgrading religious education programs.[9]

These changes influenced the appearance of a new type of educator in
the Presbyterian Church in the U.S.A., one not formally ordained but
who by special training in religious education was more qualified than
the traditional lay Sunday-school teacher. By the 1920s, the Board of
Christian Education reported an expansion in the areas of weekday
religious education and released-time activity. Between 1921 and 1925,
for example, the number of Presbyterian churches having such programs grew from fifteen to more than 500. The church also began
appointing field representatives for religious education at presbytery
and synod levels, a number of whom were women.[10] With heavy
demands for such qualified educators, especially from large city
churches, the denomination responded by opening schools designed to
prepare lay workers for a variety of parish tasks. The Presbyterian Training School in Baltimore (1903), the Philadelphia School for Christian
Workers (1907), and the Presbyterian College of Christian Education in
Chicago (1908) were the three major training centers in the early part of
the twentieth century. Although the schools were open to both sexes,
residence facilities were provided only for women, and the student body
was predominantly female.[11]

The evolution of the Philadelphia School for Christian Workers
mirrored the changing trends in lay service as it gradually altered its

original program to meet the needs of a modern generation. Founded as a response to the deaconess movement of the nineteenth century, the Philadelphia school offered courses for deaconesses and directors of religious education (three years), pastors' assistants (two years), and church secretaries (one year). Most of the early graduates either became deaconesses or entered some form of home or foreign missionary service. By the 1920s, however, a discernible interest in religious education among its student body prompted the school to offer a four-year course leading to the degree of Bachelor of Religious Education (B.R.E). In 1931, the B.R.E. became the sole degree offered. At the same time, the school changed its name to the Tennent College of Christian Education. By the time Tennent College closed in the 1940s it had produced more than 300 graduates, most of whom were active in the field of Christian education.[12]

With the increased demand for Christian educators, the General Assemblies in the 1920s encouraged the development of graduate schools for lay workers in order to upgrade their skills and to present a more professional image to the denomination-at-large. In 1921, Auburn Seminary opened a program for men and women that required a baccalaureate degree for entrance and offered a two-year course in Bible, church history, and doctrine along with field-work experience. During its years of operation (1921–39), the School of Religious Education at Auburn had a student body composed largely of women. A similar course was inaugurated at the Presbyterian Training School in Baltimore in 1922. Later, other Presbyterian seminaries provided opportunities for women to study religious education even though denied entrance into the Bachelor of Divinity curriculum. By the 1940s, three Presbyterian seminaries—McCormick, Princeton, and San Anselmo— had become coeducational to the extent that they accepted women in the Christian education program.[13]

The growing popularity of Christian education had some negative aspects for women. Those who attended religious education training schools found upon graduation low-paying positions serving under clergymen who considered their education inferior compared with a traditional seminary course. Lay leaders in Sunday schools often viewed suspiciously the new breed of female professional religious educator whom they saw as meddling with the curriculum and implying that long-standing teaching methods did not attain acceptable educational standards. With no status in presbyteries, male and female educators lacked a power base from which to operate and often found themselves overruled by both ministers and lay leaders who made unilateral decisions affecting the direction of local church schools. By the same token, they personally had no support system or recourse if their theological or

educational views were challenged and thus felt isolated and unpro-
tected.[14] When such problems came to the attention of the denomination, the General Assembly in conjunction with reorganization in 1923
appointed a special committee to study religious education offerings in
seminaries and to make recommendations about the future course of
such training. One section of the report focused on women and their
potential contributions. Noting that the church had not successfully
attracted many women into professional religious education, the committee appealed to "the heroic spirit in our young women" to make
professional preparation for educational services. The committee noted
that one of the principal obstacles in the way of securing qualified
college women for service in the church was the failure "to establish and
define a professional status for women with heroic appeal to service and
sacrifice with adequate tests for appointment, reasonable compensation,
and appropriate title." The committee suggested consideration of such
status as a way of "creating a professional consciousness such as exists
among teachers, trained nurses, or certified public accountants."[15]

The General Council recommended an overture to the General Assembly that provided for a licensed director of religious education under
the jurisdiction of a particular presbytery. Each applicant for this
position would be required to have a college education and a three-year
seminary course with a specialization in religious education, or a major
in religious education in college and two-years' teaching experience in a
public school. The validity of the license would not extend beyond the
initiating presbytery and had to be renewed annually. Despite the support of the General Council and the Board of Christian Education, the
overture did not receive a majority vote in the presbyteries. Presbyters
attributed defeat of that overture and a subsequent one on licensing
evangelists to a historical reluctance within the denomination to accept
any standards lower than a full seminary course at an approved theological institution.[16]

Efforts to provide a formal status for religious educators did not cease
with the defeat of the 1929 overture. Among others, Robert L. Sawyier,
president of the Presbyterian College of Christian Education in Chicago,
urged the Board of Christian Education to recommend a form of lay
commissioning that had already been accepted by individual presbyteries on an ad hoc basis.[17] In 1937, the Presbytery of Chicago, in whose
bounds the Presbyterian College of Christian Education was located,
overtured the General Assembly "to prepare standards for the
admission of such lay workers to a classification to be known as
'Commissioned Lay Workers.'"[18] The following year, the General
Assembly approved the position of Commissioned Church Worker
(CCW), which set the following basic standards for religious educators

in the Presbyterian Church: Membership in the PCUSA; a high school diploma plus four years of study in approved schools (two years of which were to be in religious training schools); a personal appearance before the presbytery; and an annual examination while under the care of the presbytery. The names of all CCWs were to be reported by presbytery clerks and listed in the General Assembly *Minutes*.[19]

Even the framers of the CCW overture admitted after a time that its results were unsatisfactory for the recipients or the denomination as a whole, primarily because the designation conveyed status without corresponding power. CCWs had no official standing in the presbytery and without ordination could not participate in committee work even when qualified to do so. Moreover, because qualifications were so vague as to leave considerable room for individual interpretation, presbyteries varied greatly in establishing procedures to receive and dismiss CCWs. Many CCWs reported that they had never been formally installed or recognized by presbyteries and that they were in the final analysis "at the mercy of the whim of a pastor or the changing attitudes of a session or a committee."[20]

A typical complaint lodged with Stated Clerk Pugh involved the case of Alla Belle Cropp, a CCW in the 1940s. Cropp had been commissioned by the Presbytery of Helena in 1941 as a Director of Christian Education and had resigned in February 1943 to seek employment in California. In June 1943, she accepted a position as housemother in a Chinese girls' home that operated under the auspices of the Board of National Missions. In the meantime, the Presbytery of Helena discontinued her CCW status at its spring meeting because she was no longer laboring within the bounds of that judicatory. As a result, Cropp had to reapply for status as CCW, undergo a long examination process by the California presbytery, and be recommissioned. All this took several years of embarrassment and frustrating correspondence and caused Cropp to wonder aloud if the whole process of commissioning was worth the meager benefits obtained.[21]

Despite the inherent problems in the commissioning process, the number of CCWs grew rapidly in the 1940s and 1950s as Christian education became an integral part of the denominational program. Approval of the new Faith and Life Curriculum in 1948 accelerated the demand for professional educators, and women especially, having few other outlets in the denomination, responded. In 1946, there were ninety-nine CCWs listed, only ten of whom were men.[22] About the same time, a survey of church vocation candidates in colleges and Westminster Foundations indicated that 253 women were considering positions in the field of Christian education.[23] By 1956, there were 237 registered CCWs, and of that number only sixteen were men.[24] Since many presbyteries failed to list CCWs in their annual report, the number of women so employed may actually have been considerably higher.

As early as 1942, the General Assembly requested the Board of Christian Education to restudy the status of CCWs and to make recommendations to correct the inadequacies of the 1938 overture. After several years of study, prolonged because of wartime conditions, the Board proposed changes that were approved by the General Assembly in 1949. The Board recommended raising the standard of commissioning to two years of specialized training in an accredited seminary or a master's degree or its equivalent and requiring the presbytery to examine and approve the terms of call to a local church and to preside over his or her installation. These alterations in procedures provided CCWs with some measure of job security and heightened their formal status in the eyes of judicatories.[25]

Resolution of another aspect of the CCW status came when the General Assembly approved a distinction between church educators who held graduate degrees and those with only undergraduate training. An overture to the General Assembly in 1958 proposed the creation of the position of Certified Church Educator for men or women who had a bachelor's degree from an accredited Presbyterian college having an approved program of preparation for service in Christian education. This certificate could be renewed on a yearly basis, provided the individual continued advanced studies toward a full commissioning as a CCW. The General Assembly approved this overture in 1960 and added the office of Certified Church Educator to the *Form of Government*.[26]

Interest in improving the status of CCWs diminished rapidly following the decision to admit women to full ministerial ordination in 1956 and the decline of the Christian education movement in the 1960s and 1970s. An overture presented to the General Assembly in 1963 that would have permitted CCWs to vote in presbytery received a no-action response from the Special Committee on the Nature of the Ministry.[27] Subsequently the number of CCWs dwindled, and by 1974 there were only 114 women and twenty men listed in that capacity.[28] Finally, in 1976 the Vocation Agency proposed an overture to dispense with the office of CCW. No new candidates were to be accepted after 1976, and those commissioned before July 1, 1976, could either retain their commission or qualify for ordination before June 1, 1981. Presbyteries were permitted to accept "experience, continuing education, and self-study" in place of the formal educational requirements for ordination. After June 1, 1981, however, all candidates for ordination were expected to proceed under the specified requirements of the *Form of Government*.[29]

In her analysis of the decline of the female Christian educator in the Presbyterian church, Elizabeth Verdesi collected data from a representative group of congregations for the period 1950–72. Selecting churches known to have traditionally employed staff persons for Christian education, Verdesi concluded that the professionally trained female CCW had become caught in a "double squeeze" between ordained men and nonprofessionally trained women. Due in part to a decrease in denominational membership, generally unsettled economic conditions, and high inflation rates that meant smaller church budgets, women were being replaced by ordained men who could perform other pastoral functions as well as Christian education or by nonprofessional women who were willing to work part time or at greatly reduced salaries.[30]

Questionnaires sent to CCWs in 1972 requesting information about their experience with commissioning revealed considerable ambiguity and frustration. The major recurring complaint concerned lack of official standing in the presbytery. One woman wrote: "I think the inability to vote in presbytery rankles me most. An ordained session member can vote at presbytery with no theological training, but I am not allowed to. And they call women illogical."[31] Another common theme was salary discrimination. When the question of a raise was introduced at a session meeting, one CCW reported, "There was always an embarrassed laugh. . . but no move to face reality and tackle the problem. . . . Not only the fact of being a woman, but that of being unmarried and having no children contributed to the absolute refusal of pastors or congregations to look at poverty wages."[32]

The internal inconsistencies and shortcomings of the CCW status notwithstanding, professionally trained Presbyterian women utilized this opportunity to make some significant contributions to the field of Christian education. Women served the Board of Christian Education in leadership roles as editors and program secretaries as well as on university campuses and in local congregations. Their influence in Christian education departments of Presbyterian seminaries made an impact on predominantly male students who were introduced to Christian education for the first time as a respectable and potentially powerful means of evangelism and spiritual enrichment. With the era of the specialist in Christian education past, the rhetorical question posed by Elizabeth Verdesi points up the contributions so many made: "Where today are the Margaret Hummels, the Dorothy Fritzes, the Julia Tottans, and others like Jean MacDougal, Miriam Jones, Myrl Jean Hughes, Jean Stewart, and Neva Palmeter?"[33]

The first woman to be ordained in the PCUSA, Margaret E. Towner, typified both the background and vocational interest of the majority of Presbyterian women who entered the ministry in the 1950s and 1960s. Towner, ordained by Syracuse–Cayuga Presbytery, New York, in 1956, left a career as a medical photographer at the Mayo Clinic to take education courses at Syracuse University prior to becoming director of Christian education at the East Genesee Presbyterian Church in New York. Towner then took a three-year Bachelor of Divinity course at

Union Seminary in New York because she felt that it was the only way that she would receive adequate training as a Christian educator. By her own admission, however, Towner considered herself to be a poor preacher and did not seek ordination in order to have a pulpit. She also did not think that many other Presbyterian women would seek pulpits in the future. "Ordained women," she predicted, "may prove the solution to the smaller churches' problem. A woman minister could help with pastoral duties and guide the education program, too."[34] Although Towner later changed her views and became an advocate of sole pastoral ministries for women, she acknowledged in a 1978 interview, "At that time, I guess, I didn't know better and that statement has come back to haunt me."[35]

Another of the first women ministers in the PCUSA, Wilmena Rowland, began her ordained career as an associate pastor but discovered rather quickly that there were more opportunities for a woman to serve as a church administrator in the field of Christian education than there were in the pastorate. After serving briefly as an associate pastor (1957–60), Rowland became director of educational loans and scholarships for the Board of Christian Education of the PCUSA. Although ordination was in a sense optional for much of her professional career, Rowland had no doubt that the status of ecclesiastical recognition added much to the effectiveness of her ministry: "It is difficult to explain why," she said. "Perhaps it is because parishioners are more likely to turn and respond to an ordained person who is visibly performing all the functions of the traditional ministry." Moreover, ordination opened up vocational possibilities that otherwise would have been closed. The job description for the director of educational loans and scholarships, for example, called for an ordained person; thus Rowland would not have been eligible to serve in that capacity had she been unordained.[36]

A few women broke the traditional Christian education pattern and sought calls as pastors. One of the first to receive such a call, Priscilla Chaplin, did so only after having been rejected by several congregations on the grounds that they did not want a woman minister. As pastor of a small rural congregation in upper New York state, Chaplin overcame some initial opposition and stereotyping to initiate a number of successful programs. As Chaplin described her work in 1958, she was optimistic about her future as a minister even though she admitted that the rarity of women ministers sometimes caused her problems. "Some people seem to think I'm a cross between a public monument and a three-headed freak," she told a reporter for *Presbyteran Life* magazine. "My congregation, however, has accepted me as a person, and no problems have risen because I am a woman."[37]

Not all Presbyterian women in the vanguard of the ordination movement were so positive in recounting their seminary experience and subsequent efforts to receive a ministerial call. In a survey conducted three years after the PCUSA approved ordination of women, a number of clergywomen listed "feelings of inadequacy and inferiority" and "suspicions that I could serve as well without ordination" as obstacles they faced. Other problems listed were discouragement by friends and professors who were convinced that churches were not ready for women ministers, theological questions regarding Paul's comments about the role of women in the church, and the lack of vocational opportunities for women ministers. Of the sixteen women interviewed in the survey, only four reported that they had met no significant obstacles either before or after ordination.[38]

Despite the enabling legislation of 1956, few women chose at that time to enter seminary and pursue a career as a pastor in a Presbyterian church. Women ministers were considered by most churchpeople to be an oddity or an aberration or at best a very special calling for an unusual and highly qualified woman who just did not fit into the ordinary ecclesiastical patterns. With the rise of feminism in the 1960s and its subsequent impact on religious institutions in the 1970s (see chapter 14), the status of ministry for Presbyterian women captured the attention of the denomination in unprecedented fashion. Largely through the efforts of the Task Force on Women and its successor COWAC, the UPCUSA sought to bring women into the mainstream of denominational life by concerted efforts in the area of equal employment opportunities and programs designed to encourage women to consider the possibilities of serving the church as ordained ministers.

Because of recruitment, feminism, and a conducive atmosphere, the 1970s saw a rapid growth in the number of women attending seminary and serving as ordained clergywomen. On January 1, 1970, there were seventy-six ordained women ministers who represented one-half of one percent of the total clergy in the denomination. Most of these women were associate or assistant pastors or were serving churches with less than 200 members.[39] By 1978, there were 315 ordained clergywomen, 18 percent of whom were in full pastorates and 41 percent of whom were serving in other than pastoral categories.[40] By 1981, the number of ordained women had almost doubled, and women represented about 40 percent of full-time seminary students.[41]

With few exceptions, the women who occupied Presbyterian pulpits in the years immediately following the decision to end sexual discrimination in ordination standards were single. Increasing numbers of married women seeking ministerial placement set up situations in which the women had to deal not only with the usual male/female stereotyping but also with societal expectations about their roles as wife and mother. The case of Anne Montgomery (a pseudonym), which formed the basis of a research report done by the Hartford Seminary Foundation in 1975, illustrated the problems encountered by a married woman seeking a ministerial appointment in the United Presbyterian Church in the U.S.A. A wife, mother, and school teacher, Montgomery decided in the mid-1960s to enter seminary and eventually accept a call to a pastoral ministry. Although she was not active in the feminist movement, Montgomery agreed with her feminist friends that ordination would give her ministry authority and validity in the eyes of the church.[42]

Montgomery graduated from seminary in June, 1969 and spent the next year and a half looking for a church position. Even though she stated on her dossier that she would consider part-time employment, no offers were received. Finally, with the help of a local pastor, she secured a half-time position as an assistant minister in a suburban Presbyterian church of approximately 600 members. This appointment came only after she had firmly resisted offers to be a director of Christian education. Even so, many members of the session and the congregation informally expected her to "do" Christian education rather than to function as a preaching and pastoral minister. While Anne Montgomery received the minimum salary for a half-time assistant, she initially did not receive all of the usual fringe benefits. During the first year, for example, she got no housing allowance because she was living in a home already provided by her husband's salary.[43]

Montgomery found the work at Calvary Presbyterian Church both stimulating and frustrating. As might be expected, she received an ambivalent response both in the congregation and in her family. Although her husband tried to be supportive, he found tensions created by a two-career family to be threatening. The couple required counseling to keep their marriage together. At church and in the presbytery, Anne stood out as the lone woman minister and was subject to the extremes of adulation and rejection. Her work as chairperson of the presbytery's Task Force on Women branded her as a "radical" in many male eyes and added greatly to her pressure and work load. "I was feeling so drained and alienated," she said, "I thought I'd better take care of myself. I had had it. I did not want to spend my energy running around, finding those little cracks where there would be a place for women. I wasn't sure there was a place for women."[44]

By the fall of 1973, Montgomery had decided that she needed a full-time position primarily to shore up a limited family budget. She initiated again the process of looking for a pastorate. Always hopeful, yet tempered by the realism of past experience, Montgomery prepared herself for another long and difficult process. Regarding her chances to find another pastorate, a colleague of Montgomery concluded somewhat uncertainly: "This presbytery is receptive enough that there should be churches that would also be receptive. Maybe there isn't and maybe there is. I would hope there is."[45]

The dramatic influx of women into seminaries in the 1970s also fostered the emergence of a new phenomenon in denominational history—clergy couples. By 1978, there were some 750 clergy couples nationwide serving thirteen Protestant denominations. Within the UPUSA, there were sixty couples on the field and more in seminary who would be graduating within the next two years.[46] Although many see the potential advantages of such a shared ministry serving as a model for the church to express the mutuality of Christian marriage and the collegiality of ministry, those attempting such a ministry have discovered that their path is often filled with bureaucratic and personal frustrations. Employment is complicated by the need to locate in the same geographical area. Tension frequently arises as the two try to combine the marital and the professional relationship. Stress occurs in the management of family life, particularly when there are children involved and when there are career decisions such as when and where to move. The lingering image of the woman as a "helpmeet" to the man who, in the eyes of the congregation, is the "real minister" with the woman as simply a well-trained minister's wife affects the professionalism of the spouses. As one couple expressed it, "The woman is open to the double jeopardy of pastor's wife and of traditional clergy-images. . . . Her work could be seen as a mere extension of her husband's work, while she runs the danger of being identified with male authority roles."[47]

As the 1980s began, the relation of clergywomen to the UPUSA appeared clouded. Opposition to women serving in ministerial capacities continued to surface. According to a survey conducted by the *Presbyterian Panel,* church members and officers expressed a strong preference for male pastors, especially in dispensing sacraments, in preaching, and in administrative activities. In only one pastoral activity—teaching small children—did an appreciable segment in the church believe women to be more effective than men.[48] Moreover, such opinions about women clergy were not confined to Presbyterian males. A number of sources indicate that women in local congregations often were the most vocal opponents of women ministers. As one report concluded, "This is not to say men leaders are really more open, but since women are outspoken in their resistance, the men can keep silent."[49]

Another factor influencing the placement of ordained women has been an overcrowded job market, especially in the mainline Protestant denominations. The rapid increase in seminary enrollment of women has not been matched by a corresponding growth in the denomination-at-large. In fact, the surge of women into the ministerial field has developed at a time of decreasing membership and reduced budgets. A study completed in 1977 entitled "The Clergy Job Market: Oversupply and/or Opportunity" indicated that 86 percent of women students anticipated ordination and approximately half of that number planned to become pastors; nevertheless, declining birth rates, a slowdown in new church development, and increasing longevity of clergy limit positions for seminary graduates as well as chances for advancement for those in pastoral and administrative positions. Based on trend data and reports from denominational agencies, the UPUSA, PCUS, Episcopal Church, and United Church of Christ have the most serious oversupply problem.[50]

Attitudes toward the ordination of women as ministers and as elders have been adversely affected in recent years by the denomination-wide controversy over the implementation of Overture L approved by the General Assembly in 1979. (See chapter 14.) In requiring a fair representation of women on sessions, the Overture provoked debate on the issue of congregational freedom of choice. With the specter of denominational schism over the issue of the status of women in the church, even some advocates of sexual equality have questioned whether the church has moved too far in the direction of using quota systems and of coercing local churches to accept ordained women against their collective wills.[51]

Another unresolved issue relates to the use of the Bible in determining denominational policies and practices regarding the status of women in the church. In their recent study on the ordination of women and on the function of the Bible, Mary Faith Carson and James H. Price have pointed out that the UPUSA church has never developed a clearly articulated hermeneutic to guide churches in their efforts to determine precisely what part or parts of Scripture are authoritative. The gradual acceptance of women's participation in the life of the church, culminating in official actions in the 1950s and 1960s, was based on an interpretation of biblical passages that in a previous period were used to oppose ordination. Despite sanction by the denomination, the leadership and some of the general membership of the church still tend to disagree on whether Scripture gives absolute directions regarding women's ordination. Although many cling to the conviction that I Corinthians 14:34 and I Timothy 2:11-12 prohibit women from serving either as ruling elders or ministers, Carson and Price conclude that there was "never a compellingly felt need to address their understanding of Scripture in the official discussions of the issues."[52]

Despite these factors, evidence indicates that actions taken in the 1970s to institute sexual equality will be maintained and expanded. Through the General Assembly and its agencies, the UPUSA church has attempted to work closely wth judicatories on the recruitment and employment of women ministers. In 1976, the Vocation Agency appointed a Task Force on Strategies for the Employment of Clergy-women, which completed its extensive research and study the following year. The Task Force recommended a Major Mission Fund five-year $500,000 Women in Ministry program to facilitate the placement of clergywomen and to develop a churchwide acceptance and support of their ministry. The Vocation Agency gave the program top priority, and the Major Mission funding began in 1977. An associate for Women in Ministry was employed in 1977 for a five-year assignment to work with the coordinator of employment opportunities in implementing the Women in Ministry program.[53]

Individual presbyteries have initiated action to make women as practicing ministers more visible. The Department of Ministerial Relations of the Presbytery of Seattle employed one woman seminarian to preach in churches throughout the presbytery in order to acquaint churches with women ministers and to provide women an opportunity to develop and enhance their own skills. The Presbytery of Albany provided funds to enable interested churches within presbytery bounds to hear women preach and to interview female or minority candidates. The Presbytery of San Gabriel called a Woman-Minister-At-Large as a member of the presbytery staff to serve three-fourths time as an interim pastor and one-fourth time as an executive associate.[54]

In discussing the future of clergywomen, one can only project a few observations. Denominational policies likely will be influenced by general cultural trends as they have been in the past. If a favorable, open climate regarding the status of women in society continues to develop, women ministers should be increasingly well received within the denomination. A reversal of such trends, however, would undoubtedly have an impact. In any event, acceptance will not come easily so long as deeply rooted cultural and theological preferences regarding the role of women in the church persist. In 1981, for example, while the number of ordained women had increased to 621 out of a total of 14,502 clergy, the ratio of women in the total actually decreased from 28 to 25 percent.[55] A recent Vocation Agency report noted that progress was made in placing women in church positions, but after citing several examples of improvement, the report concluded, "We still have a long way to go."[56]

12

MINISTERS' WIVES:
Untitled Professionals

When a nineteenth-century male defined the cultural and social limits of the sexes as "Let man then, exercise power; woman exert influence," he provided an accurate description of the relationship of women to the church in the 1800s.[1] Especially did such a definition reflect a role model for the minister's wife—that of a woman in the background but with some responsibility for her husband's vocation.[2]

"Influence" constituted a crucial element in all descriptions of the nineteenth-century minister's wife. Commentators advised against assertiveness on the part of the wife, reinforcing the subordinate and submissive role of women, but expecting her to have some culture and education. She was to use meek, affectionate insinuation; gently criticize her husband's preaching if need be; provide a softening influence on him and the parishioners; exude piety and selflessness.[3]

At the same time, common expectations among church members that the wives be part of a "team" ministry, sharing in the day-to-day activities of the parish, characterized the women as "professionals" and implied more than just influence. By not recognizing the wives as having professional status, however, the church withheld any power from them other than that wielded through the intangible "influence."[4] They received no salary, although by the end of the nineteenth century one boldly suggested in print that the church consider a stipend for the wives' services: "No church has a right to demand her [minister's wife] toil unless the finance committee has added somewhat to the stipend on her behalf." She recognized this to be a futile request, even though husbands and wives in other professions such as teaching each received salaries. "The most daring of deacons would scarcely suggest such an innovation; but if her work be worthy, why should not a trifle be added to his [minister's] income? It would make all the difference in the world to many a minister's helpmeet."[5]

Neither lack of status nor of salary inhibited the church activities of many of the wives, and their assumption of a quasi-ministerial role formed a permanent pattern. This came about for several reasons: Many felt they had a "call" similar to that of their husbands; some desired a career themselves but were thwarted by church restrictions and essentially worked through their husband's position; some liked the status but desired no professional responsibility; most seemed to feel that conditions in the denomination in the 1800s demanded that they function as "assistant ministers." In the parish ministry of the nineteenth century, the rise of denominationalism and the move to attract members as well as to nurture those already on the rolls introduced a more clearly defined people-and-program pastorate. The minister spent many hours in pastoral visiting, counseling, teaching, administering, soliciting donations, and attending to the various activities of the parish. To fulfill commitments required assistance, and his wife was the person to whom he often turned.

One facet of the wife's role surfaced because of the numbers of active women in American Protestantism in the 1800s. The wife became the one important in relating to members of her own sex. In one book on pastoral theology, for example, James M. Hoppin, professor at Yale University, declared, "There is a department in the Church in which the ministry of woman is indispensable, and that is, in religious counsel to those of her own sex."[6] More popular articles and books pointed out that she should not only be available to counsel the women parishioners but also to act as a buffer between them and her husband.

The wife's foremost duty, though, was as helpmeet to her husband. An early article in a Presbyterian church journal dwelled specifically on this responsibility to be supportive. John H. Rice, professor at Union Theological Seminary, Richmond, wrote a letter to his daughter in 1828, which was later published.[7] Rice expressed hope that his daughter, who had recently married a Presbyterian clergyman in Virgina, be "very *happy* and very *useful*." To do so, he advised her to cultivate a cheerful spirit in order to counteract the minister's wearying life of a student that might lead to despondency. He suggested also that she develop an "affectionate, conciliating, winning temper and manner" to provide a softening influence on her husband's temper.

Counter to the prevalent expectations, Rice discouraged her active participation in the congregation, although other sources indicated the impracticality of such a suggestion. "Many ministers' wives destroy their influence entirely by seeming to think that they have also a sort of official character, which gives them authority to dictate, prescribe, recommend, or oppose measures to be adopted in the congregation." Instead, the woman should use meek, gentle, and affectionate insinuation. Never should she demand too much of her husband's personal attention. She ought rather to allow him to study in peace. Rice insisted that this would be to her advantage, because "she is, in a certain sense, identified with her husband," and he emphasized that the respect and attention received would be based on how the congregation viewed her husband. Finally, Rice instructed her to be alert to correct mannerisms, improprieties, tediousness in her husband's preaching, teaching, and praying. "I have often heard it asked of a preacher's wife, 'Why doesn't she tell her husband about his long prayers?' and the remark has been made many a time—'That woman can't be much, or her husband would not have such rough and uncouth manners.' "

Rice's counsel of meek insinuation rather than active participation extolled influence and was supported by at least one Presbyterian clergyman's wife, who described what her role as helpmeet should be: "To keep the minister's heart unclouded from his own labors, to feel that she can occasionally give him a point for a sermon or a story to fit a text, to pray fervently for him and with him when things are difficult, to share his joy when souls are coming to the Father, these things ought to make any manse mother blessed among women, and to be a home-maker of this sort is vocation enough in life."[8]

In addition to such responsibilities for their husbands' welfare, however, ministers' wives of the nineteenth century had specific demands made on their time. In an early series of letters addressed to the wife of a clergyman in the 1830s, the writer warned that if the minister's wife does too much in the church she will be accused of neglecting her family, but if not enough, then she will be accused of want of interest.[9] A decade later, an article in The Presbyterian suggested a similar sentiment in a tongue-in-cheek manner. The minister's wife should be "always at home and always abroad, always serving God and always serving tables." Furthermore, when the church is about to call a pastor, the author wrote, a special committee should visit the wife and ascertain whether she is able and willing to perform the labor of five ordinary women without "any compensation except the crumbs which fall from her master's table."[10]

The types of demands on the wives depended on the size and location of the church. The needs of large urban Presbyterian churches were different from those of small and isolated frontier or rural churches. The Presbyterian Banner in 1879 reported that the urban churches by then did not seem to expect as much of a pastor's wife as formerly, although some "old fashioned" country churches expected a combination saint and angel to do a bit of everything, from visiting to singing to leading women's groups.[11] A daughter reminiscing about her mother, a nineteenth-century minister's wife in Ohio, could not remember a time "when there were not guests in the home. . . . Always the home was full to overflowing." Although the wife had seven children and suffered from malaria, she conserved what strength she had for "the outside demands which were constantly being made upon her."[12]

Notwithstanding the size, income, and sophistication of the membership of a church, all organized Presbyterian congregations seemed to want the lives of the ministers' families to conform to certain standards. Just prior to the turn of the century, a writer in *The United Presbyterian*, in suggesting the General Assembly might give a deliverance upon the subject of the relation of the minister's spouse to congregations, expected that it would declare that she did not sustain official relation to the congregation different from that of elders' wives, or of any other woman in good standing of the church. Yet, he argued, "we all know that the people usually expect service from her of a character and an amount not required of others." His view of her position confirmed that of other reports: assistant and counsel to the pastor, teacher in Sabbath school; member and/or leader of the women's prayer meeting, missionary society, and song service; pastoral caller, and hostess. [13]

Presbyterian church members undoubtedly hoped for the spouse to take a leadership role in the social life of the church. One minister's wife noted that the nineteenth-century church was so dominated by women that a church's kitchen and parlor were as important as the "audience room" and that most parishioners' social lives centered around the church. [14] A fictional clergyman's wife in *The Shady Side*, a novel based on actual events in the 1830s in a New England Congregational parish, felt that the people looked upon her as a "sort of public functionary." One of her church members wished her to "get up some parties, or sewing circles, or something else; it's so horribly dull here. We only want a person to take the lead, to have something going on here as well as in other places." [15]

Furthermore, the women expected her to be able to lead them in spiritual exercises. The young woman caused a furor when she refused to pray aloud at a female prayer meeting and sewing society, which prompted her father to explain to her that it was a service "which, in these days, is expected of a minister's wife." [16] Much of the literature of the women's organizations of the nineteenth century indicates that the pastor's wife was the spiritual leader as well as the convener of the local groups. Often she opened the meetings with prayer and devotions if her husband was not in attendance, and sometimes she read aloud from inspirational books while others sewed. [17]

Reports from the wives' journals and diaries confirmed that they taught in Sunday school, raised money, visited parishioners, organized women's groups, ran the manse economically, cared for the church's facilities, collected and supervised benevolences, and entertained guests regularly. Particularly obligatory were pastoral calls and social visits. The wife, "many a time, when she is weak and wearied, when the weather is disagreeable, and when the claims of home duties are pressing, must go forth—sometimes merely for a friendly call . . . to visit the sick, or to comfort the sorrowing, or to aid the needy, or to speak a word in season to one that is weary."[18] One observer noted that the life of a pastor's wife "is passed in the midst of mingled gladness and sorrow. While somebody is always rejoicing, somebody, too, is always sick or dying, or else weeping."[19]

Preparing the dead for burial, nursing the ill, aiding in births was not uncommon. One woman in 1865 noted in her diary that she "rubbed up Communion Service" the day before the sacrament was served.[20] Another indicated that she always made sure that the baptismal font was filled before a baptism.[21] The wives engaged in solicitation of funds for building and furnishing the church, which the wife of a midwestern Presbyterian minister, described in her diary as "begging."

Carried Miss Copeland [school mistress] to school and rode along to Mrs. Johnson's. She had just heard of the death of her brother. I took her out with me to beg money for carpets again. Called at Mrs. Randall's–Brownson's–Robinson's–McFadden's–Mittlers and Hanes. got 13.50. Called at Joel Scovell's on my return. snowed quite fast. [22]

"Good workers" were called for in a letter in *The Presbyterian* from a member of a church in a "mountainous State." In seeking a minister, the church members "would also be glad if the wife of our minister took an active part in church work, Sunday-school and Young People's meetings, for we are very scare [sic] of good workers." *The Presbyterian* suggested that young preachers take note of the requirements and "as to those venturesome young women who have their eyes upon a manse let them likewise read and reflect."[23] Such a busy life did not scare many women off apparently. The rather significant mortality rate among ministers' wives, especially the wives of home missions pastors, left widowers with large families, but there were "plenty of girls ready to slip into her slippers as soon as may be after her funeral."[24]

In addition to church duties, sometimes the pastor's wife might be called on to teach in the local school, particularly in small communities, simply because she was the candidate whom they considered fit for the task.[25] In fact, in some cases, a congregation filling a vacant pulpit would seek not only a minister but one with a wife who could teach. An advertisement in 1848 for a Cumberland Presbyterian pastor in Alabama used a headline: "A Preacher and a Teacher Wanted." The advertisement stated that a "married man, whose lady could take charge of a female school, would be prefered [sic]."[26] One such Presbyterian came to Illinois in 1832 with her minister husband and "commenced a school, being earnestly solicited to do so, as good teachers were so difficult to obtain." She taught school for about fifteen years, which supplied her with pocket money and helped support the family.[27]

Although the pulpit committees and officers took careful consideration of what the wives could or should do, it is not clear how much the church members demanded of the women and how much the women demanded of themselves; whether the church always pressed them to assume leadership or whether they worked for their own self-esteem. Some articles spoke of the women as "self-denying," and working for the sake of the Gospel. One observer, speaking in sentimental terms of the ministers' wives as "a class whose achievements had been seldom celebrated or sung," described them as "patient, zealous, benevolent; the angels of the bedside of suffering; the unfaltering helpmeets of the preachers of the world."[28] Some diaries and journals gave the impression that the women pushed themselves unmercifully to educate, nurse, comfort, and please parishioners with about as much zeal as they gave to their families. The same sources also indicated that the wives were sensitive to public opinion and made some choices accordingly.

The congregations expected much the same of their ministers. That similar attributes and activities were expected of the wife indicated that church members recognized her identity to be a reflection of that of her husband. "She is in many instances as conspicuously before the public as the man himself. If her husband be in charge of a church she is called to account for any error he may commit as surely as if she had made it herself."[29] Although some denied such an identification, one Presbyterian observer wrote, "Whether she desire it or not, the pastor's wife is first lady in the congregation, just as the President's wife is first lady in the land, and she cannot slip away from the loving watchfulness."[30]

Written materials indicated that the ministers themselves recognized and appreciated their wives' efforts. One Presbyterian minister, in describing his wife, wrote that "Not only did the heart of her husband safely trust in her but the entire congregation reverenced and respected her as their friend and counselor. In sickness and trouble, they always expected to see her and receive her sympathies and counsel. And often to the neglect of her own personal affairs did she engage in these missions of comfort and sympathy."[31]

On the twenty-fifth anniversary of Theodore Cuyler's ministry at Lafayette Avenue Presbyterian Church, Brooklyn, he said of his wife, "If you have any tribute of thanks for any good which I have done you, do not offer it to me; go carry it down to yonder home, of which she has been the light and the joy, and *lay it at her unselfish feet*." He reported that for the only time in his career he heard a murmur of applause run through the congregation.[32]

Bolstered by approval, many ministers' wives took on their roles serenely and comfortably, confident of their personal call and anxious to be a credit to their husbands. George Prentiss wrote of Elizabeth Prentiss, "What a helpmeet she was to her husband and with what zeal and delight she fulfilled her office, especially that of a daughter of consolation among his people."[33] Some few nineteenth-century wives had professional interests outside the church. One Presbyterian, Margaret

Junkin Preston, combined literary interests with parish duties. One year, 1877, she wrote forty-six book notices, 360 letters, corrected proof of one of her volumes, wrote articles, and composed nineteen new poems. From her letters, one finds in the same year she began a Woman's Foreign Missionary Association, dug a garden, put up thirty pounds of sweet pickles, tended a lawn, and pursued many other such activities.[34] Others performed publicly but within the confines of local churches or in judicatorial or evangelistic activities. One, Sarah Foster Hanna, by invitation in 1875 was the first woman ever to address the General Assembly of the United Presbyterian Church of North America when she presented a memorial seeking to constitute the General Missionary Society.[35] The "Thank Offering" for missions of the United Presbyterian Church originated with Eliza Clokey, married to a Presbyterian minister in Ohio.[36] Others were instrumental in professionalizing the women's boards for missions. The biographies of nineteenth-century women in Frances Willard's and Mary Livermore's *Notable American Women* indicate a sizable group of temperance leaders who were minister's wives.

A candid and lengthy essay in *Atlantic Monthly* sought to repudiate the popular nineteenth-century opinions about the abused pastor's wife. An anonymous minister's wife wrote, "I have been for some years in search of the abused clergyman's wife, in both city and country parishes. I have come to the conclusion that she is a myth." In the writer's opinion, she herself was neither an unsalaried assistant, a victim to female prayer meetings and Dorcas Societies, nor the mistress of a house open to all. "So far as my observation goes, the church makes no demand upon the minister's wife; what she does, or refrains from doing, is at her own volition. I have no sympathy with those women who say, 'The church engaged my husband, not me.' The clergyman's wife has the same interest in the church that every loyal member feels, plus the interest that every loyal wife has in her husband's life work."[37]

Despite her protestations, the description of her life indicated that she was indeed a teamworker and co-worker. She claimed that she shared responsibility for the movement and efficiency of the entire organization, including keeping up on theological literature, criticizing her husband's sermons, suggesting ideas. She kept track of the sick, the disheartened, the malcontent. She felt that the wife should suggest calls to be made, although she did not accompany her husband, observing that "our people always preferred to talk with the minister." She did call alone, believing that "the minister's wife has personal interest in all the members of the congregation, adapting herself to their various needs, and helping each to the best."[38]

These comments sound as though this woman were indeed "just the one to marry a minister" if the stereotypical role were desired. What then were her confessions? First, she confessed that she wanted neither

her son to be a minister nor her daughter to marry one. This was based on the frustrations and expectations on the minister, and thus on his wife and family. She blamed "ecclesiastical machinery," the pressure to attract money and members (particularly males), and the emphasis on philosophical thought. Furthermore, she was concerned with the insecurity of position, a constant cause of anxiety. She criticized the method of calling a pastor, with both minister and wife on display, and the criteria on which the selections were made. Relevant also was the economic strain, resulting from extremely low salaries.[39]

By 1900, *The Presbyterian* reported "spirited and even spunky" defenses against the demands without remuneration made on ministers' wives. One writer suggested that wives' positions involved obligation, even if they had no call nor salary, and that the churches "are right in expecting a great deal from the wife of the minister aside from her home duties." He cited support from "the best minister's wife I know," who indeed defined the role in terms of "a holy calling." Nevertheless, she too admitted that wives were liable to be imposed upon and to have too much expected of them.[40]

In the waning years of the nineteenth century and the early decades of the twentieth, women in America experienced enormous changes in educational, professional, and volunteer opportunities. Presbyterian women's lay leadership, particularly with the advent of the Commissioned Church Worker and the deaconess, assumed prominence in the church.[41] That wives of ministers, as a rule educated and sensitive to community currents, reacted to these factors is evident through subtle changes in materials relating to their roles. As the new century wore on, wives more boldly declaimed their dissatisfaction with the position of "assistant pastor" without status. Editorial comments responding to their complaints showed some sympathy but little capitulation on the basic ideals of the role of the minister's wife.

Apart from the discussion of what their roles should be, the activities of the women continued along the line of those developed in the nineteenth century. Even a woman preacher and feminist of the early twentieth century included in her book this story: "A successful woman preacher was once asked 'What special obstacle have you met as a woman in the ministry?' "Not one, she answered, 'except the lack of a minister's wife.' "[42] More typical was an article that began: "We may say as often as we please, and the minister may as confidently assert it in his turn, that the congregation has no claim upon the minister's wife. She is helpmeet to her husband, not a servant to the church. She receives no salary, and nobody has a right to call upon her for service not exacted from nor expected of any other woman who belongs to the particular church in which her husband officiates."[43] As a matter of fact, though, the article reiterated her special position, where people "look to her for certain phases of example and certain acts of leadership."[44]

The social, cultural, and political changes of the early decades of the twentieth century influenced the behavior of most American women, including the minister's wife. Observers realized that she was no longer "the meek, unintelligently submissive person who took that part in the novels of yesterday."[45] Despite all sorts of alterations in opportunities and life-styles, however, the parameters of the changes still were bordered by home and family. As a result, the ministers' wives argued not for freedom to move outside the parish but rather freedom to be a private person within it. The wives seemed to crave individualism, not equality or status. Such a sweeping generalization, however, included all types of women from varied backgrounds: Some wanted positions of leadership and liked to have people around them; others wanted to be spectators and preferred privacy; some gloried in being on a pedestal; others saw attention as a fishbowl; some defined church activities as opportunities; others called them tasks; some participated in the women's missionary endeavors that were becoming increasingly professional in their orientation; others shrank from public speaking or teaching.[46]

In a positive way, the twentieth-century pastor's wife could be "her husband's comrade, companion, counselor and chum in all his work, excluded from none of its perplexities, baffled by none of its technicalities, a side-line spectator of neither its successes nor its defeats."[47] Because the work of the minister in the early century often radiated from his home, one analyst suggested that it was to his benefit that he was not compelled to a daily "day-long divorce from his household."[48] Furthermore, since women, despite being engaged in business and industry, "continue to be much more interested in the sentiments of life and its human relations than in its commercial processes and industrial activities," the pastor's occupation of dealing with people in stress and difficulty, is "in full range of a good wife's natural and unforced interest."[49]

Such a personal situation, however, had to conform to the goals of the church. In a period when the church was encouraging lay leadership, the minister did not want to discourage congregational participation. One Presbyterian minister alluded to times when some ministers' wives might find it hard not to step in and take over, but contended that "it is not always best." Arguing that the "great revolution" in society had affected the relationship of the sexes, he pointed out, "Women have learned that they can do things efficiently and they want the scope and space to toss their ball. The wife of the minister must abdicate these places of parish influence when others are ready to occupy them."[50]

At the same time that such ideas seemed to downgrade the position of the wife as a "professional" church worker, a somewhat contradictory concept of the role of "minister's wife" as a career as well as a call emerged around the 1930s. A specific treatment of this topic appeared in a two-part article by Eloise H. Davison, who reported meetings between 1930 and 1940 with groups of ministers' wives "just starting off on their careers." Some were looking forward to opportunities of service, some were dreading the prospect, some were openly rebellious. Davison felt that "almost the only solution which has as yet been suggested for the present unsatisfactory status of the minister's wife is the personal one of finding the perfect wife who shall be all things to all in the congregation but not too much of anything to anybody." Feeling that the church had forced the minister's wife into a cubbyhole of outworn traditions, Davison felt it to be "unethical in expecting all sacrifices from her for the sake of the church and in refusing her any recognition as a spiritual leader or as a consecrated follower of Christ." Further charging the church with being conservative in witnessing women's position change in the financial, social, political, business, and professional world, but maintaining an outworn social order for the ministers' wives, she wrote, "If the men who steer the affairs of the church feel that the wives of ministers are unable to rise to the heights of their husbands in consecration and the service of Christ, and should therefore be given neither recognition nor responsibility, then they would be far wiser to free the minister and the church of this burden and insist on the celibacy of the clergy."[51]

Recognition and responsibility, at least on an official level, was not to come. In the mid-twentieth century, the whole question of the status of women was prominent.[52] Amid all the discussions of ordination, equal opportunities, unrest in the church, the status of women, however, no specific mention was made of ministers' wives. Nevertheless, along with other American Presbyterian churchwomen, the ministers' wives took part in the struggle for equal representation in the church. They, like others, faced the day-to-day inequities, as well as shared the rewards.

Influenced by the Depression, by World War II, and then by the returning veterans, women lost footing in professions, gained it during wartime, and then lost it once more in a competitive postwar job market. A resurgence of extolling the motherhood, family, housework, helpmate sphere in the 1950s emphasized subordination—a subordination with slightly different connotations than those of the nineteenth century but with essentially the same message: Live for and through the husband. Just as the advice to the minister's wife in the early part of the century was to restrict leadership activities in the church for the sake of developing lay leadership, so it became now that she should restrict herself for the sake of providing a calm, loving oasis in the home for the minister. Important to her identity as a career–wife was house and family care, although expectations of service to the church were never completely obscured.

A postwar conference of ministers' wives at San Francisco Theological

Seminary, San Anselmo, California, concluded that "a foremost qualification of a minister's wife is that she preside over a well-ordered
attractive home. Furthermore, she should be a woman who takes the
time, forethought, and care, necessary to insure good health for her
husband, her children, and herself. Again, she should be a woman
taking a share of responsibility in parish work, according as her strength
allows." Nowhere in the report's recommendations was there a hint of a
request for status, salary, or position. On the contrary, the thrust of the
article was one of reticence, care for husband, care for family and self-
effacement.[53]

The idea of the "specialness" of the minister's wife and of her identification through her husband was reinforced in the organizations for
wives of Presbyterian seminarians in the 1950s. Not all seminary wives
attended, but those who did participate in the groups, known by a
number of names such as Parsonettes, Divinity Dames, Seminaryannes,
Pastor Pushers, heard it emphasized that being a pastor's wife was a
"profession," that the woman must be a "living example," but that she
should not try to run the church.[54] The programs in these groups ranged
from offering special courses on Bible and theology, Old and New Testaments, church history, missions, Christian education, and public
speaking to having programs on "etiquette for the minister's wife,"
"organizing a youth choir," "rearing children in a parsonage," and "the
way of women in the church." One wives' club was interested in the
differences between a "regular housewife" and a "minister's mate."[55]

The late 1950s marked a decision that seemed to demand crucial alterations in the image of "ministers' wives." In 1956, the United Presbyterian Church in the U.S.A. granted women the right to be ordained as
ministers; thus a new designation, minister's spouse, came into being.
This change had no ascertainable influence on the literature concerning
the role of the spouse, however, and advertisements and articles still
centered around wives, not husbands. In fact, some pioneering studies
pertaining to the role of the wives appeared afterwards.

In 1958, influenced by the increased attention by the social sciences to
role theory and analysis and observing the public's interest in the roles
of wives of business and professional men, psychologist William
Douglas, an ordained Presbyterian minister, directed a major research
study on minister's wives. His evolving project attempted "to learn
more concerning the varying psychosocial situations of the many different kinds of women married to many different kinds of minister–
husbands, in varying geographical regions, religious traditions, and
church-community settings." This statement represented Douglas' increasing realization of the "irreducible individuality of people and
relationships" and the impossibility of discussing the so-called role of
the minister's wife in general terms. Thus, the study, dealing within the

individual differences, explored how the various ministers' wives perceived their own involvements in their husbands' vocation and their
satisfactions and frustrations in these involvements. Using interviews
and questionnaires, the researchers studied ministers' wives from
thirty-seven Protestant religious groups. Both the United Presbyterian
Church, U.S.A. and the Presbyterian Church, U.S. had response rates of
more than 90 percent, which would indicate high applicability of the
findings to the study of Presbyterian ministers' wives.

Douglas examined the written literature of the 1800s and 1900s and
found some similarities between the nineteenth-century role expectations and those of the twentieth. He also found differences—a lessening of the wives' diffuse responsibilities in churches and communities; a
decline in social status and leadership; a breakdown in the "mother"
image to the parish.

Similarities reinforced common stereotypes. The contemporary portrait demanded that she should be a good wife, a good hostess and a
dedicated Christian. She should accept his career, because, by marrying
him, she has chosen her way of life. She should actively encourage,
praise, comfort, and constructively criticize him. She should feel a call,
set an example, and serve the church. The women's response to the
"most important suggestion you would give to a young minister's wife"
was close between "Your first responsibility is to be a good wife and
mother" (33 percent total respondents, 36 percent subgroup including
Presbyterians) and "Face problems with your husband, or be your own
best self—don't worry about expectations of others, have a genuine
interest in people, become emotionally mature with sense of humor" (27
percent total; 24 percent subgroup).

Pointing out that the literature by and large had failed to deal with the
individual nature of each woman-husband situation, Douglas saw some
improvement in publications but admitted that a negative cultural image
persisted. Therefore, he suggested, "even though the *external* premise of
the cultural role model may have lessened, the *internal* pressure and
resulting guilt from nonconformity to the self-accepted ideal remain
great. In fact, potential conflict and frustration may be greater for ministers' wives today than in earlier periods, since expectations are less
consistent and more in flux, often deriving from earlier historical and
cultural epochs and therefore quite unrelated to present realities." Furthermore, a shift of the meaning of the ministry for many away from a
"set-apart calling toward a profession-among-other-professions" affects
the self-understanding and expectations of ministers' wives.

With this underpinning, Douglas pursued his study fully aware of
each woman's personal set of variables, and those of her husband,
denomination, church, community, and geographical location, but with
a corresponding understanding of the influence of the stereotypical role

model of a unique position. His important findings require careful study. A brief summary of the interests of his respondents pertaining to the question of the "professionalism" of the minister's wife indicated that 20.6 percent were very involved as a *teamworker* (11 percent subgroup including Presbyterians); 63.9 percent were very involved (69 percent subgroup) but in a *background supportive way*; and 15.1 percent (19 percent subgroup) were *"no more involved* than if he were in another profession."

In terms of general trends in the motivation and meaning of the minister's wife, Douglas again stressed each respondent's uniqueness. Some patterns reoccurred, however, including that the women found their major fulfillment in the home and that church activities provided them genuine satisfaction. The wife generally felt positively about herself but often wished "that she would increase in the sense of adequacy and security." Social and personal isolation concerned her, but she generally did not regard the church as a rival for her husband's affection. Although age brings some lessening of frustrations, problems continue, but "she admits that what more than compensates for these frustrations and limitations is believing in the importance of what her husband is doing, and being able, unlike most wives, to have a meaningful part in it."[56]

This formidable body of material stressed individuality against prevailing stereotypes. Yet nothing in it contradicted descriptions from the popular press: "I consider my role as a minister's wife as a supportive role"; "The minister's wife is not truly either laity or clergy, but partakes somewhat of each, so serves as a bridge of understanding between the two"; "To be a minister's wife does imply a certain unique status which cannot be evaded"; "She should be accepted as an individual without the artificial packaging into a standard container marked 'minister's wife' "; "[the role should be as a] person, a wife and mother, a Christian"; "We can conclude that it is reasonable to expect the preacher's wife, along with the rest of us church members, to live as a Christian in every area of life."[57]

Especially among those wives who still fulfilled the "team worker" role, however, arose the old complaint in the popular church press, never fully put to rest, of the lack of status for wives and the disregard by the church of their "professional" role. An article in *Concern* in 1963 accused pastoral committees of still behaving in a manner "much the same as that of fifty years ago. . . . What they seemed to expect is a perfect team, man and wife. They take financial responsibility for only the man, but require what amounts to full time service from the wife, also."[58] During the sixties and seventies, however, the political and social thrust of feminism changed both the church's stance toward women and the way women viewed themselves. Whether the wives agreed or disagreed with the aims of women's liberation, they inevitably were affected by the ramifications of the movement.

On the denominational level, the influence of the intensive series of pronouncements by the UPUSA General Assembly dealing with equality for women both in the church and in society had its effect on raising the question of the role of the ministers' wives. In 1974, the report of the Assembly Committee on Women in Church and Society dealt with the minister's spouse. "Recognizing that the Protestant ministry is a profession which offers the spouse of the minister a unique opportunity to be involved in the organization to which the minister is called; Further recognizing that the spouse is a separate individual with distinct talents and personhood that have often been restricted by congregational customs," the committee called for endorsement of a "Bill of Rights for Ministers' Spouses." This included four rights: to seek employment of his or her choice; to choose freely church membership or nonmembership; to serve the mission of the church as a member, without special obligations or privileges; to be considered, as a member of a congregation, for election to the session and other boards and committees. The 186th General Assembly approved this statement.[59]

A testing of attitudes occurred when the Research Division of the Support Agency, UPUSA, conducted a three-phase study on the minister's spouse in 1977: an exploratory study with selected spouses; a mail survey of samples of UP members, elders, and church professionals; a mail survey of a sample of approximately 600 pastors' wives. The survey of the ministers, national staff, Christian educators, nonparish clergy, and retired ministers and missionaries produced interesting results. At many points, their disagreements over certain descriptions of the role made obvious the changes in the expectations on the women. For example, the retired Presbyterians stood alone as a group in *disagreeing* that the pastor's spouse should have an equal right as a member of a congregation to be considered for election to the session and other boards and committees; a majority of this same group *agreed* that the pastor's spouse should be deeply involved in the life of the congregation.[60]

Such a study, although not conclusive, surely indicated that even the discussion of the role of the minister's wife was changing, not only among women themselves but also among church leaders. Old images had not completely disappeared, for although a majority of the respondents agreed that "the pastor's spouse has a right to serve the mission of the church as a member without special obligations or privileges," they equally agreed on a nineteenth-century axiom that "the pastor's spouse should always be publicly supportive of his/her spouse's ministry." Most members, elders, and pastors felt that a pastor's spouse is treated differently than other lay persons "some of the time," while all other groups seemed to feel that this was the case "most of the time."[61]

When offered a choice of statements regarding what the respondents considered their congregations' expectations of the role of the pastor's spouse, most chose the statement "the pastor's spouse should attend worship services regularly and take part in church activities to a certain extent, being careful not to discourage the leadership capacities of other lay persons." The statement least often chosen was "the role of the pastor's spouse has nothing to do with the pastor's ministry or my congregation's acceptance of the pastor. It makes absolutely no difference what participation the pastor's spouse has in the congregation."[62]

A third phase of the research involved sending a questionnaire to the some 600 ministers' wives.[63] This provided an interesting comparison of the way the previous respondents viewed the wives' roles and how the women saw themselves. Although a majority of members and pastors agreed that pastors' wives are treated differently than other lay persons in the church, the wives felt such less frequently. Most of the women agreed only that "the pastor's spouse is expected to attend worship services more regularly than other lay persons" and is "expected to be more informed about the lives of members of the congregation (illness, death, etc.) than other lay persons."

On the question of a spouse's holding elective offices in the church, members, pastors, and wives agreed that the spouse should have an equal right to be considered for election to leadership roles. Nevertheless, 21 percent of the wives said their church forbade or discouraged the pastor's spouse from holding the office of ruling elder; 14 percent said this was true of the position of deacon; 17 percent regarding the position of trustee; and 7 percent regarding other elected positions in the church.

The pastor's wives were more satisfied with their relationships with their congregations and with their spouses than with their own self-development and fulfillment of personal goals. In other areas, they indicated the difficulty in defining a role other than on an individual basis, the need for independent sources of support in times of personal and spiritual need; the impact of the pastorate on clergy marriage and family life and personal concerns of clergy spouses and families; and those factors which, in their eyes, would improve the lives of clergy families. Of special significance was the secondary finding that there were substantial differences of opinion and perspective among ministers' wives in different age cohorts. The report concluded: "These data seem to indicate that there is a new generation of pastors' wives entering parish life. . . . Considerable changes have already taken place in the status and roles of pastors' wives in recent years. The fact that about one half of the women in this study are employed outside the home cannot help but effect changes in their roles in the parish."[64]

The study discovered five areas in which the spouses felt changes could be introduced that would improve the lot of clergy families in general. These changes included higher salaries, income adequate to purchase a home, improved public understanding of the ministry, counseling for men and women who are or will become clergy spouses, and opportunities for continuing education for pastors and their spouses. A follow-up study to ascertain the importance attached to these areas a year later showed a clear consensus that the salary question and programs for ministers and spouses to deal with problems inherent in pastors' marriages continued to be of primary importance.[65]

This study and its results, although enlightening, reinforced a view of a relationship that rarely, if ever, showed a theological incompatibility, or even compatibility, between two spouses. The articles in the nineteenth- and twentieth-century popular journals dwelled on practical aspects of the lives of the ministers' wives, and most writers, men and women, seemed to take for granted that the wife believed as her husband did. Restrictions on women speaking in church and the slowness of the denominations to award ordination rights gave little opportunity for women to proclaim their theological beliefs.[66]

The lack of discussion of the wives' theological views coincides with the observation that the literature on ministers' wives in general has reflected the stereotype of the relation and has taken minimal account of the individuality of each wife. The nineteenth-century model—to be good wives and mothers, to be indefatigable church workers, to behave appropriately and piously, to be ever supportive of their husbands' concerns—eventually collided with another image, based on changing cultural expectations, evolving definitions of women's place in political, economic, and social life, and, ultimately, on the necessity for a new identification once women could be ordained as ministers.

Now, the "untitled, unsalaried co-pastor" may or may not be nearing extinction, depending on the location of the church and the personality of the spouse. Variables such as inflation, the divorce rate, the professionalism of women, influence the role inordinately. Future discussions inevitably will deal with questions of cultural norms and economic realities as well as with how the male spouse fits into the traditional discussions of the role of the "minister's wife."

PART FOUR

A Parallel History
and Modern Developments

13

THE EVOLVING ROLE OF THE SOUTHERN PRESBYTERIAN WOMAN:
Blessed Inconsistencies

Before the turn of the century, nearly every mainstream American denomination had some type of organized woman's work for missions. One exception was the Presbyterian Church in the U.S. (PCUS). Although the women of the South had participated in societies since the early 1800s and continued to do so after the denomination came into existence in 1861, they formed organizations only on the local level because of the prevailing attitude toward women's role.[1]

The southern women knew that their northern Presbyterian sisters were successfully building strong centralized boards, but their leadership did not develop concurrently. When it emerged, organizers envisaged a different concept, choosing an auxiliary union with no budgetary self-determination. Such a pattern undoubtedly stemmed from the denomination's consistently outspoken opposition to any role for women other than a subordinate and silent one, particularly condemning women as "preachers" but also objecting to any notion of a combined group of women autonomously developing programmatically. This position remained firmly articulated far longer than in the other Presbyterian denominations although a pioneer woman leader noted "blessed inconsistencies" because many churchmen actually were helping the women to organize.

Southern leaders early in the denomination's history expressed concern that women might demand a right to speak or preach to mixed audiences within the church. Deeming the few incidents noted as a northern intrusion, the editor of the *Texas Presbyterian* in 1879 warned that unless southerners were on guard, "the evil will, by degrees, steal in upon us."[2] James Woodrow, professor at Columbia Theological Seminary, lamented the increasing "perversion of women's influence" by the appearance in the South of "male women, female lecturers, public speakers and preachers, and all 'woman's rights' advocates" who, he insisted, were "the abomination of our people."[3]

Robert L. Dabney, professor at Union Theological Seminary and Austin Presbyterian Theological Seminary, who more than any other person shaped the theological perspectives of the PCUS in the nineteenth century, led in denying women's right to preach and to teach. Writing in the *Southern Presbyterian Review* in 1879, Dabney castigated southern ministers for yielding to public opinion and granting women a wider sphere of involvement in church life. He contended that public preaching by women was "a frontal attack on God's truth and divine kingdom and should be vigorously opposed with all the force that the church could muster."[4] Dabney later asserted that the women's movement was "part and parcel of French Jacobinism, that travesty of true republicanism, which caused the reign of terror in France, and which disorganizes every society which it invades."[5]

The subject moved from the periodicals into the church courts. In 1879, the Synod of North Carolina resolved that "public preaching by women, being opposed to the Word of God, is therefore opposed to the welfare of His people, and all our members are instructed to give it no countenance."[6] During the same year, the Synod of Texas requested the General Assembly to promulgate an unambiguous ruling on the practice of women preachers. The PCUS General Assembly in 1880 responded by stating that "the introduction of women into our pulpits for the purpose of publicly expounding God's Word is an irregularity not to be tolerated." Furthermore, the Assembly concluded, "It is the settled doctrine of our Church that women are excluded from licensure and ordination by the plain teaching of Scriptures, and therefore cannot be admitted to our pulpits as authorized preachers of the Word."[7]

Although the PCUS had spoken definitively, opposing the ordination of women, its position on the wider issue of women speaking in "mixed assemblies" was far from settled. In 1887, William Adams, pastor of the prestigious First Presbyterian Church of Augusta, Georgia, invited Mary T. Lathrop of the WCTU to address his congregation on a Sunday evening. The Presbytery of Augusta subsequently noted its disapproval of the incident but did not initiate any judicial process against Adams or the session.[8] In 1891, largely through the personal initiative of Samuel F. Tenney, the Presbytery of Eastern Texas again raised the question of women's right to speak at church meetings where men were present.[9] Almost unanimously the Assembly voted to deny the women the right to speak, lead in prayer, or participate in public discussions in mixed assemblies. The Assembly softened its prohibition, however, by affirming the propriety of women holding meetings among themselves "for mutual edification and comfort by pious conversation and prayer."[10]

The solidarity of southern Presbyterian men in their stand against the "woman's movement" as evidenced in the General Assembly's resolution appeared to be unshakable. Only two commissioners dared to cast dissenting votes, and neither one cared to have his name recorded for posterity. Nevertheless, there were indications that a few progressive clergymen might welcome women to address mixed congregations under certain circumstances. One contributor to the *Presbyterian Quarterly* identified "a small portion of our ministry" as "somewhat infected with error" by declaring themselves in favor of "a revolutional revision of the church's historic interpretation of Scripture concerning women's part in the public exercise of worship."[11] Another writer deplored the example of his brother clergymen, "very few in number," who had been permitting women to speak at prayer meetings, missionary gatherings, and young people's societies where members of both sexes were present.[12]

Reflecting a nationwide interest in the "woman question" in the 1890s, the PCUS General Assembly once more dealt publicly with the morality and propriety of female speakers. An overture from the West Lexington Presbytery in 1897, "shall our pulpits be occupied by women to lecture or make addresses to mixed audiences of men and women?" reportedly "engulfed the Assembly in much disputation." Alexander Pitzer of Washington, D.C., led a small minority of commissioners who opposed ordination of women but defended their right to speak publicly. Citing Gal. 3:28 ("neither male nor female") as biblical authority, Pitzer reminded commissioners that women were already doing an excellent job teaching in Sunday schools and participating in various interdenominational organizations. Spokesman for the opposition R. K. Smoot based his arguments on the "thus saith the Lord" nature of Scripture and the "God-ordained relations of the sexes." To loud applause, Smoot challenged proponents of women preachers to put a finger on one biblical injunction requiring it. "The advocates of women's preaching are always attempting to show the Bible does not forbid it," contended Smoot, "striking, however, a blow at inspiration as they do."[13] The Assembly overwhelmingly endorsed Smoot's exegesis. Referring to "clear deliverances of former Assemblies" and using the traditional language, the General Assembly of 1897 concluded: "To teach and exhort, or lead in prayer in public and promiscuous assemblies, is clearly forbidden to women in the Holy Oracles."[14]

Of special impact on the cause of women organizing was a report adopted by the Synod of Virginia in 1899. Discussing "the rights and duties of woman in the church of God and in the home," the synod considered the scriptural teaching on woman's role in the church. The report reiterated the common restrictions: she should not hold office or bear rule, and she should not preach, exhort, or lead in prayer at a public assembly. It allowed her to teach in her home and in the Sunday school, sing in the church, and form aid and missionary societies under the control of the session. The synod, however, found it "questionable, to say the least, whether under the polity of the Presbyterian Church, founded as it is professed to be, upon the word of God, union societies, presbyterial, synodical, or mixed denominational are legitimate."[15]

The PCUS gave little evidence in the opening decades of the twentieth century that it intended to consider the possibility of sexual equality within the church. In two lengthy articles written just at the turn of the century, P. D. Stephenson summarized recent developments in the "Woman Movement" and described in vivid terms its deleterious effect on church and society, especially in the Christian home. Nevertheless, Stephenson took obvious pride in three encouraging demographic facts. First, the South was still essentially agrarian and, therefore, tended to resist innovations such as "Womanism." Second, the South, as a rule, still had old-fashioned ideas and customs concerning "the home." And third, the South as a section stoutly maintained her old-fashion faith in and reverence for the Bible as God's Word. These three qualities, he concluded, "ought to enable her to resist the tide that's on her, flood tide though it be; or, if it passes over her, remain unscathed, unharmed, unshaken and unchanged, lifting her head high above the muddy and receding waves."[16]

Outwardly the PCUS fulfilled Stephenson's expectations in the first decade of the twentieth century. The ministers did not publicly advocate female ordination rights, and the women maintained low profiles. R. A. Lapsley, a prominent Christian educator, spoke for a majority of his colleagues when he said, "Logically, there is no safe spot on which to rest the sole of your foot between the old-time view of the woman question and all abominations of womanism."[17] When some commissioners raised a question about the practice of women speaking in public at the General Assembly in 1910, they received the abrupt response that "there has been no change in the settled policy of our denomination."[18]

Behind these affirmations of adherence to sectionalism, tradition, and Scripture, some changes in southern church life were quietly taking place. The entrance of women into the business and professional world and the growing visibility of the suffrage movement did not leave the church unaffected. Southern churchwomen, like their northern counterparts, assumed leadership roles as Sunday school teachers, missionaries, and temperance reformers. Referring to this period, Lila Ripley Barnwell recalled how her mother served as Sunday school superintendent of a small country church where she led in prayer, taught a class, played the organ, raised the hymns, "and did with earnest effort everything that would keep the church and Sunday school alive." The rhetorical question with which Barnwell concluded her reminiscences indicated that both practice and principle among southern Presbyterian women were changing: "Can anyone think that she was wrong?"[19]

A few prominent southern Presbyterian clergymen such as J. R. Howerton, Egbert W. Smith, and A. J. McKelway dared to go against public sentiment by permitting women to speak in their congregations even though only a handful of colleagues were willing to defend their action. Howerton permitted Mrs. Howard Taylor to give a talk on missions to a mixed audience in 1902. Moreover, he defended his action by saying that he would do it again under similar circumstances. Noting that his mind had changed since he wrote an article in 1893 opposing the right of women to speak in public, Howerton argued that neither Paul nor the Holy Spirit intended apparent restrictions on women's participation in church life to be universally and eternally binding.[20] Howerton's rejection of the biblical literalism that had characterized so much of the theological argumentation about women in the nineteenth century suggested that the PCUS was not impervious to theological innovation; nevertheless, in 1910, the General Assembly declared no change in its policy on women speaking before mixed assemblies.[21] Six years later, however, the conservative editor of the *Presbyterian Standard* admitted, "One is impressed with the fact that there is a spirit of rebellion against what some term 'the hidebound conservatism' of the past; and therefore, when an opportunity offers, the temptation will be too great to resist."[22]

Because of these changing conditions, the General Assembly in 1915 appointed an ad interim committee of five men to make a careful study of scriptural teaching on women's position in the Church and to report to the next General Assembly.[23] When the committee reported in 1916, however, it was unable to offer a unanimous statement. Instead, the committee of five presented four different reports, each of which indicated a preference for granting women wider participation in the life of the church short of ordination.[24] After lengthy and colorful debate between self-identified "conservative" and "progressive" spokesmen, the Assembly discarded all four reports and adopted (by a vote of 132–80) a substitute resolution that reaffirmed actions taken by the General Assembly in prohibiting women to "publicly expound God's Word" from the pulpit or to be ordained or licensed.[25] Significantly, however, the resolution omitted any reference to women's right to speak in promiscuous assemblies. It simply recommended that "other services of women be left to the discretion of the sessions and the enlightened consciences of our Christian women themselves."[26]

Even such a moderate response to the widening sphere of Presbyterian churchwomen generated a sharp conservative countermovement. Led by the retiring moderator, McF. Alexander, sixty-one commissioners immediately protested the Assembly's action on the grounds that it reversed the position of the PCUS on the subject without scriptural warrant, but the Assembly answered in terms of the position being influenced by practice. "The Scriptures may have their authority discredited not merely by a violation of their precepts, but also by any attempt on the part of ecclesiastical courts to bind the consciences of God's people on matters of doubtful interpretation."[27]

The *Presbyterian Advance,* reporting the incident, did not see the action of the General Assembly "drastic enough to call forth a protest" but admitted, "Everyone who knows anything of the spirit and genius of the church would know that this Assembly would be against women entering the ministry, and it is doubtful if there is a woman in the church who ever had any such thought." That they should be able to speak and pray in public worship indicated to the writer considerable progress.[28]

Southern Presbyterians entered the 1920s still unsettled over issues raised and left unresolved. Only the question of female ordination seemed to be settled with some certainty. A PCUS clergyman, Walter L. Lingle, emphasized this unanimity in his analysis of the denomination. "Our church could probably unite unanimously on the idea that we will have no women preachers or elders. When we go beyond that into details," Lingle admitted, "we at once strike a great diversity of opinions."[29] Certainly the actions taken by the 1916 General Assembly supported Lingle's analysis in which that Assembly left all areas of service by women excluding ordination up to women's judgments and the discretion of the local sessions.

Although this compromise measure by no means settled the perennial "woman question," it did mark a decisive turning point for the PCUS. Symbolic of the new spirit in ecclesiastical circles was the appearance of Hallie P. Winsborough, president of the Women's Auxiliary, before the 1920 General Assembly to address commissioners on the developments in women's work. While other Presbyterian denominations had allowed women to speak before church judicatories earlier in the century, Winsborough was the first female to address southern Presbyterians.[30] General Assembly commissioners voted to hear her again in 1923. Only one dissenting vote came from a minister who reminded his colleagues that they had forgotten St. Paul's instructions about women's place in the church. At this same Assembly, a proposal to add three women to each of the executive committees passed by a vote of 139–50, thus giving women a voice in matters affecting church policy. Petitions from one synod and five presbyteries in the following year to rescind the action were rejected decisively.[31]

Despite such innovations, events at the 1925 General Assembly demonstrated that conservatives who objected to women's participation still had a strong following among ministers and elders. An overture from the Presbytery of Concord opened the question of Winsborough's right personally to give a report to the Assembly. After considerable debate, the Assembly voted to reaffirm previous deliverances (especially in 1880 and 1891) forbidding women to speak or pray in church meetings and omitted or ignored the more liberal position taken in 1916.[32] The only exception the General Assembly allowed was in the case of the Women's Auxiliary and similar associations. Their reports could be submitted provided a female did not make a speech in conjunction with them. Furthermore, the Assembly recommended that a commissioner, who, of course, would be male, should read the report.[33]

The regressive stance of the 1925 General Assembly evoked vehement protests from southern Presbyterians both male and female. The debate that ensued filled pages of denominational papers. R. E. McGill, editor of the *Presbyterian Survey*, expressed his displeasure with the action of the Lexington Assembly and reported that there were "feelings of amazement and indignation throughout the women's organizations of our Assembly."[34] Lila Barnwell defended the right of women to speak and teach and noted that St. Paul's words about women keeping silent in church had been ignored for years "for wise and sufficient reasons." She queried whether women should be condemned by men for teaching, praying, and evangelizing. "If men should do so," she concluded, "I am sure that God will not."[35]

As the time for the 1926 General Assembly drew near, self-styled "conservatives" and "progressives" attempted to explain their respective positions. Typical articulation of the conservative position came from Judge F. B. Hutton of Abingdon, Virginia, who felt that Presbyterian women had no right to complain about the Assembly's ruling. "She joined our church freely, without any compulsion in any form or from any source . . . and has no right to be amazed or indignant when the actions of Church courts are in accord with the Constitution of our Church."[36] E. S. Campbell, a progressive, responded to Hutton by arguing that women had equality in government, education, and every other sphere of life except in the church. "To say that the Bible prohibits them from any public function in the church is placing the same narrow literalism upon Scriptural interpretation which was used in years gone by to prove that the earth was flat or that slavery was right."[37]

Both conservatives and progressives expected the 1926 General Assembly in Pensacola, Florida, to be a testing ground for denominational attitudes regarding women. Strangely enough, no presbytery had sent up an overture concerning women, which meant that the issue would have to be raised from the Assembly floor. Based on the previous year's ruling, H. H. Sweets rose to read the report of the Women's Auxiliary in lieu of Winsborough. At this point, Alfred D. Mason, a ruling elder, called for a point of order. "I would be most uncomfortable in facing my wife and daughter," he said, "if I return home and do not hear Mrs. Winsborough read her own report."[38] Mason entered a motion to hear Winsborough, which passed by a vote of 163–51. A group of commissioners immediately challenged the action, arguing that the moderator, J. W. Skinner, had allowed no opportunity for discussion. This precipitated a series of objections, motions, countermotions, and points of order. One eyewitness described the moderator's attempts "to agree with everybody, no matter how different he might be from everybody else." The arguments continued for about thirty minutes, until someone made a motion to adjourn. This motion quickly prevailed.[39]

After the recess, which lasted overnight, a measure of dignity was restored to the proceedings. No information is available on the behind-the-scenes events; however, at the request of Winsborough, Sweets read the Women's Auxiliary report. The Assembly then spoke to the issue by reaffirming by a large majority the 1916 deliverance that left women's activities, other than preaching, up to the discretion of church sessions. It also approved a new resolution that specifically permitted the superintendent of the Women's Auxiliary to read her own report at the General Assembly, thus negating the 1925 decision. The Assembly's only caveat was the notation that "she has a natural right to read her report to the Assembly; but this privilege does not carry any implication of membership in the Assembly or of any participation in its discussions."[40]

After this, the question of women speaking in religious assemblies would no longer be a major issue in the PCUS. Although for a number of years a few commissioners silently left the Assembly hall when the women's report was given, their departure was not considered controversial. This minimal acquiescence to women's role in the church did not affect the denomination's stand that women had no biblical right to be ordained as ministers, elders, or deacons, an issue with which the denomination would not deal for another quarter century.

In 1955, two overtures to the General Assembly indicated that the ambivalence evident in the 1920s still lingered in church courts. The Presbytery of Suwannee requested the General Assembly to make a definitive, unambiguous ruling on the question of women speaking in church courts even though that body had spoken numerous times to that specific issue.[41] The Presbytery of Granville, on a more positive note, overtured the Assembly to amend the *Book of Church Order* to make women eligible for the offices of ruling elder and deacon "on a permissive basis." The Assembly referred the overtures to an ad interim committee of five (four men and one woman) to do a "thorough Biblical study of both issues involved" and to make a report to the Assembly in 1956.[42]

The committee's final report indicated that theological currents in the PCUS were gradually pulling the denomination in the direction of a broader and more ecumenical interpretation of Scripture. Citing traditional Pauline texts historically invoked by church fathers to restrict women's sphere, the report admitted that taken literally and as a setting for "a rule that is permanent and without exception," the church had no choice but to deny ordination rights to women. To be completely consistent, it continued, the church should deny women the right to speak and to vote in congregational meetings. Rejecting this legalistic and static interpretation of Scripture that had dominated the denomination since its inception in the nineteenth century, however, the committee report pressed for a dynamic and inclusive understanding of the Bible that permitted more latitude for the ongoing illumination of the Holy Spirit. "From our study of the Bible," committee members said, "we are led to believe that the Holy Spirit will progressively lead God's people into a new understanding of the practice of the will of God."[43] The report concluded that biblical teaching did not forbid women to speak in church courts and that the request to ordain women as elders and deacons should be sent down to presbyteries for acceptance or rejection. After more than two hours of heated debate, the Assembly approved the report by a slim majority of 234–226.[44]

Throughout the year, as presbyteries voted on the overture, denominational papers kept readers informed about the highly emotional and controversial aspects of local debates. Much of the opposition to the ordination of women was of a "non-theological" nature, but the same Pauline texts (1 Cor. 14 and 1 Tim. 2) kept reappearing as non-refutable arguments. As was true in earlier discussions, southern Presbyterian women remained aloof from the conflict. At least they made no attempt to express their opinions publicly either as individuals or as members of women's associations. The final vote of the presbyteries showed that ministers and elders were not yet prepared to follow the directions suggested by its newly expressed theology. By a vote of 44 to 39, the overture was defeated.[45]

Rejection of the ordination overture in 1957 proved to be the final victory for opponents of women's participatory rights in the PCUS. The tide of opinion among leaders, reflected in the new theological stance of the 1956 report on biblical issues, was changing in favor of equality for women. During the next five years, even though the denomination officially showed little interest in the subject,[46] at least two of the moderators of the PCUS General Assembly publicly advocated the ordination of women during their travels throughout the denomination. Moreover, a few women began to make themselves heard primarily through the Board of Women's Work which endorsed the right of women to full ordination. In 1962, the General Assembly appointed a judicial commission to suggest changes in the Book of Church Order that would allow ordination to women at all levels—deacon, elder, and minister. Despite the substantive nature of this action, little discussion occurred within the churches. Moderator Edward D. Grant in 1963 was astonished at both the lack of comment and "the completeness of the silence of our Church women."[47] A final battle by dissidents on the floor of the 1964 General Assembly proved insufficient to stop ratification of the overture. By a vote of 240–145 commissioners acknowledged the right of women to be ordained in the Presbyterian Church in the U.S.[48]

Rachel Henderlite, a Ph.D. from Yale University who at the time was director of curriculum development for the Covenant Life Curriculum, was the first woman ordained in the PCUS. An author, scholar, and committed Presbyterian, Henderlite was ordained by the Presbytery of Hanover, Virginia, on May 12, 1965. She recalled having very little opposition, even though she received a few letters objecting. For the most part, "people were most cordial."[49]

Two women were elected commissioners to the 1965 General Assembly. According to an article in the May 1980 issue of *Presbyterian Survey*, six commissioners served in 1967, and in 1968 Henderlite became the first clergywoman to be a commissioner. In 1982, eighty-three out of 388 commissioners were women, with five of the thirteen Standing Committees chaired by women.[50]

In 1978, laywoman Sara Bernice Moseley served as the first woman moderator of the General Assembly. In 1981, Dorothy Barnard was elected to that position. Other women have served in positions of leadership on committees. Even so, a few female commissioners are said to have felt shy, uncertain, or intimidated. Nevertheless, one woman pointed out, "The church has come too far on the road of tapping the skills and resources of women to turn back now."[51]

The prescriptive role of the late nineteenth and early twentieth century suited a substantial number of southern Presbyterian churchwomen who believed they should not step out of their sphere and assume any but the most modest roles in the church's outreach. Although many women throughout the country shared this feeling, the southerners seemed to hold to it more conscientiously. One woman, writing to defend the idea of conferences of women for "mutual elevation in spirituality, stimulation and education," warned, "If there is anything which we women of the Southern Presbyterian Church need to hold fast, it is the Bible-womanliness that makes us willing and glad to work for the Master with all our souls—but within our God-given sphere, that is, in our Missionary Societies, Home and Foreign, helping the men by prayer, and by cheerful, dignified submission to the powers that be, which are ordained by God. . . . Above everything let us stay within that sphere, so beautiful—so full of possibilities, where God has placed us: and Aunt Remy [the columnist's pen name] believes that she voices a large number of the women of the Southern Presbyterian Church in writing thus."[52]

As in the northern church, however, a sizable number of more progressive female communicants and many of the traditional women as well were fervently interested in missions. The denomination's need to finance a significant program of foreign work as well as to restore war-damaged churches and rebuild their resources, extend the denomination farther west, and provide religious instruction to the blacks created an atmosphere in which those responsible for administering the denominational work sought help from all quarters.[53] This led the secretaries of the denomination's program areas for Sustentation, for Foreign Missions, and for Education and Publication to suggest that the women might more effectively support missions if they formed local missionary associations to raise funds and promote enterprises authorized by the proper ecclesiastical bodies.[54] Because of appeals to women and young people, in 1875 the Assembly reported that the gifts of the Sabbath schools and the women's missionary associations during 1874 had amounted to one-third of the entire sum contributed by the church to the cause of foreign missions.[55] In 1878, the Assembly recommended that all congregations form missionary societies.[56] This source continued to increase revenues, although never so much as in other denominations, where women's work was organized on a national or regional level.

Sensing that more could be accomplished, Jennie Hanna of Kansas City, Missouri, in 1884 proposed in articles in church newspapers that the southern Presbyterian women form educational, inspirational, and advisory presbyterial unions in which to share ideas on enlarging the work and promoting greater efficiency among the scattered groups. Mrs. Josiah Sibley of Augusta, Georgia, agreed with Hanna's views, and, although hundreds of miles apart, these two women sought to reach women in some 2,000 churches of the denomination in an attempt to form presbyterial organizations.

When the plan became widely known, even though it had the approval of M. H. Houston, secretary of the Board of Foreign Missions, it was denounced by ministers as "unscriptural, un-Presbyterian, unwomanly."[57] This surprised the women, who had assumed that a plan that would tap the "unused ability latent among our women, of consecrated service and money, withheld from a cause so sorely needing them" would be welcomed. Instead, it was met by a "storm of criticism, misconception and indignation."[58] Hanna later wrote that she would not have begun such an endeavor with hopes of success had she "known the Southern Church as I do now." Of Kentucky, Virginia, and Huguenot ancestry, she admitted, "I *thought* I was conservative and a loyal Presbyterian, but I found I did not know the alphabet of conservatism!" Her appeal to the women at large, published in the Louisville *Christian Observer* in 1888, seemed to Hanna moderate and temperate, but a reply from T. D. Witherspoon indicated, as she told it, that he could see "the cloven hoof of woman's suffrage under our petticoats."[59]

Although the adverse reaction was more prominent, the women received considerable support from men and women throughout the denomination. Hallie Winsborough, another pioneer in attempting to create a unified woman's work, noted the "blessed inconsistencies" of this period. "At the time General Assembly was limiting woman's activities officially and the different Presbyteries were forbidding the organization of Presbyterial Unions . . . there were throughout the Church a number of able, broad-minded, devoted Christian men who were helping the women to establish their organizations and guiding them into successful work."[60] Because of such unauthorized assistance, in 1888 two presbyterial organizations, one in East Hanover, Virginia, and one in Wilmington, North Carolina, promptly formed for foreign missions.[61] Within a decade, there were presbyterial unions in half of the synods, and by 1910 seventy-eight out of eighty-four presbyteries were organized.[62]

The women took another step in 1901, when synodical unions formed in Texas and Virginia. By 1911, however, when the Jubilee celebrating fifty years of organized women's work for missions called attention to the fact that "the Southern Presbyterian Church was the only evangelical denomination in this whole country which had no central organization of its women, no comprehensive records, no accurate reports of their splendid work," only five synods had formed.[63] Again one woman sensed the significance of the situation and personally attempted to correct it. Winsborough at her home in Kansas City wrote a document, "Some Reasons Why a Woman Secretary is Needed," and sent it to Mrs. D. A. McMillan, president of the Missouri Synodical. McMillan immediately circulated it to other synodical presidents, who approved its ideas. McMillan, Winsborough, and Hanna assisted by three ministers, W. R. Dobyns, Henry H. Sweets, and A. L. Phillips, turned the statement into an overture to the General Assembly, which was unanimously adopted by the synod of Missouri.[64]

The overture pointed out that women constituted three-fifths of the members of the church, raised a large proportion of mission money, promoted and planned mission education, and exerted great influence on the young as mothers and teachers. It charged that while the affairs of the church were being conducted along modern lines, "the work of the women had been allowed to drag, greatly hampered by inefficient organization, or none at all." To remedy the situation, the overture called for the appointment of a female General Secretary of Woman's Work to coordinate work, stimulate interest, disseminate information, increase gifts, organize local societies, presbyterial and synodical unions, and keep records and statistics of all women's work. The overture left it to the General Assembly to direct under what supervision the secretary should work.[65]

Because of earlier experiences, the women prepared themselves to argue their case. Winsborough very well understood what she called the "characteristic position" of the Presbyterian Church in the U.S. regarding women. The ministers and elders would vote against any infringement of the old order and then assume that the women would observe the rulings with great care. Winsborough agreed that "although the women may not agree with the wisdom of the deliverance, so long as Assembly has spoken, they will obey it even though they never have a chance to officially help change it."[66] In something of a break from the past, the leaders decided on this occasion to speak publicly for their case, even if they would be unable to vote for it.

Promoting the overture received substantial assistance from the Systematic Beneficence Committee, then the steering committee of the church. Chairman R. O. Flinn invited synodical presidents, representatives of women of various synods, and promoters of the overture to meet at the same time the committee was holding its pre-Assembly sessions. He further invited the women to present the overture to the committee for approval. Approximately twenty women accepted, probably the first church-wide meeting of southern Presbyterian women ever held.[67] Winsborough told of the inexperience and timidity of the women as they appeared before the male committee members; nevertheless, they persuaded the group to approve the plan unanimously.

Besides gaining an important ally in the committee, this gathering gave the women a chance to coordinate plans. Winsborough's account indicates that the women used astute political judgment in mounting their campaign despite their insecurity: "We were blazing new trails, seeking a plan of organization for woman's work adapted to our Church and unlike that formulated by any sister denomination."[68]

As predicted, the overture unleashed a torrent of discussion in pulpits, meetings, and church papers, with not only men but many women publicly opposing the idea. Several presbyteries and at least one synod expressed official disapproval. A local women's group—the Missionary Society of the Waynesboro, Virginia, Church—published a resolution claiming that "it is our belief that the great majority of women of the Southern Presbyterian Church are opposed to the appointment of said secretary."[69]

Those charged with promoting the overture countered with non-argumentative but informative replies. Probably their two most effective pre-Assembly tactics were the publication of a number of supporting statements from prominent ministers over each's signature and the dissemination of a leaflet called "The Nots."[70] Seeing misunderstanding as the primary problem, the women supplemented the overture's statement of what they *did* want with a statement of what they did *not* want: "We are NOT asking for more authority. We are NOT asking the handling of funds. We are NOT asking the creation of any new agency. We ARE asking more efficiency through better organization and closer union of our forces."[71] At the Assembly meeting itself, the opponents placed a church paper containing a strong denouncement of the overture in every commissioners' place; the women placed a copy of the overture with no comment.[72]

Winsborough attended the 1912 General Assembly in Bristol as the official woman representative to answer any inquiries from the committee. Perhaps the first time a woman ever appeared before an Assembly committee of that denomination, Winsborough recalled her apprehension. To her imagination, "every commissioner met was the author of one of the letters opposing the 'woman bishop' and the 'limited pope' in the Church papers."[73] She nevertheless appeared before the committee to which the overture was sent, although she could not understand "how it could be proper for a woman to address a *committee of men* of the General Assembly when, according to the Church law, no woman could address a group of women if even one man were present."[74] She left the "ecclesiastical propriety" question to the chairman, however, and answered the committee's questions. The committee recommended the appointment of the Secretary to the Assembly. When the time for the vote came on May 20, 1912, Winsborough, sitting near the front, expected speeches for and against. She was astonished that no discussion whatsoever ensued and that when the vote was taken there was no audible dissenting voice. As the moderator called out "Carried," she turned to a male supporter and asked "Is that all?" He replied, "That's all. You have your Secretary."[75]

The Assembly directed the four executive committees of the denomination to select a woman superintendent who should "give her whole time to the work of organizing our women into synodical and Presbyterial Unions, and local Societies under control of Synods, Presbyteries, and Sessions, respectively."[76] In addition, she would coordinate the groups already existing and stimulate interest by disseminating information. The supervisory committee met with the presidents of the six organized synodicals and representatives of the unorganized synods at Montreat in August, 1912. Winsborough was nominated as superintendent. She described herself as "a woman of no previous business experience, unknown to the great body of women in the Church, a woman laden with family cares and a member of the most remote church in our Assembly." This humble woman would serve from 1912–27 as superintendent; from 1927–29 as secretary of woman's work; from

1929–40 as secretary emerita and would greatly influence the character of women's work in the southern Church.

At Montreat, the synodical presidents organized into the Woman's Council, an advisory group. The representatives designated the new organization "The Woman's Auxiliary of the Presbyterian Church, U.S.," as Winsborough explained, "that its very name might express its desired place in the Church activities."[77] Differing from other denominational women's groups, its slogan was "All the women of the Church working for, praying for and giving to all the Causes of the Church," delineating the three distinctive features: *all* women communicants were automatically members, *all* causes were supported, *all* functions were auxiliary.[78] Winsborough received the title of superintendent rather than secretary to placate critics "who felt that the title 'Secretary' should not dignify one of the weaker sex."[79] Just as did the women organizing in New York in 1870, this group realized that they would begin with no money, no office equipment, no literature, no experience, and in the face of considerable opposition that was "bitter, unfair, and, hardest of all, conscientious."[80] Nevertheless, they left Montreat with a carefully thought out plan to set into motion.

As Winsborough was boarding the departing train, a young minister ran up to her companion, a leading Presbyterian U.S. pastor, and asked of him, "Dr. ——, which woman is the ecclesiastical suffragette? I want to see her." With everyone embarrassed, the minister replied that he did not know but introduced Winsborough to the questioner. With such attitudes awaiting, Winsborough returned to Kansas City to set up an upstairs room in her own home as her office.[81]

The southern Presbyterian women avidly preserved and collected their materials and first appointed a General Historian of Woman's Work in 1929. Much of this material is readily available, and several excellent historical publications have been prepared.[82] Consequently, the details of organizational changes, projects, study emphases, ecumenical endeavors, emerging national groups, and other outreach activities will not be repeated here. A chart from Janie McGaughey's book published in 1961 succinctly shows the highlights up to the years when feminism began to make a noticable impact on the church's life. A special issue of *Concern* magazine in 1977 by text and photographs brings the story up to that year, and an article in the *Presbyterian Survey* in 1980 relates the women's growing influence on the General Assembly.[83]

In 1978, a publication entitled *Reflection*, published by the Synod of the Virginias, summarized the various women's organizations for PCUS women: the Committee on Church-employed women, support; the Committee on Women's Concerns, advocacy; Church Women United, ecumenical; Office of Professional Development, support; Women's Advisory Council, link to the Committee on Women's Concern; Women

Janie McGaughey. *On the Crest of the Present* (Atlanta, 1961):200.

CHART—LANDMARKS IN HISTORY OF ORGANIZED WOMEN'S WORK

	FOUNDATION	PREPARATION		REALIZATION	EXPANSION		PROGRESSION		FRUITION
	Prior to 1884	1884	1912	1912	1929	1956	1956	1959	1959—
Organizations	In local churches: Female Societies (Bible, Tract, Missionary) Ladies' Aid and Missionary Societies	Beginning of Presbyterial Unions and Synodical Unions		1912. Assembly-wide: "The Woman's Auxiliary" Synodical, Presbyterial, Local Feb. 1912—1st Church-wide meeting May 1912—Assembly organization approved by General Assembly Aug. 1912—Woman's Auxiliary organized (Montreat)	1948 "Women of the Church"				
Assembly-wide Organization Leaders				Mrs. W. C. Winshorough 1912-1927 "Superintendent" 1927-1929 Secretary of Woman's Work	Janie W. McGaughey 1929-1950 Secretary of Woman's Work 1950-1956 Executive Secretary Board of Women's Work		Mrs. L. M. McCutchen 1956-1959 Executive Secretary Board of Women's Work		Evelyn L. Green 1960— Executive Secretary Board of Women's Work
Office Headquarters Place Name				1912—Kansas City, Mo. 1914—Atlanta, Ga. 1918—St. Louis, Mo. Office of Woman's Auxiliary 1928 Office of Department of Woman's Work	1931—Atlanta, Ga. 1931 Office of Committee on Woman's Work 1949 Office of Board of Woman's Work 1950 Office of Board of Women's Work		1954 Presbyterian Center		

Assembly-wide Administration	1912-1927 Supervisory Committee (Four Executive Secretaries of the Four Executive Committees) 1927 Sub-Committee on Woman's Work Committee on Assembly's Work 5 members	1931 Committee on Woman's Work 1934 6 members (women) 1934 8 members (women) 1945 10 members (women) 1950 Board of Women's Work, 14 women, 4 men
Assembly-wide Advisory Agency	1912-1914—Woman's Council 1914-1949—Woman's Advisory Committee	1950 Women's Advisory Council
Assembly-wide Church Organization Affecting Women's Work		1935—Beginning of Joint Committee on Adult Work 1950—Inter-Board Adult Council 1950—Executive Committees became Boards—World Missions, Church Extension, Christian Education, Annuities and Relief. General Council established. (Cause Secretaries became Chairmen of Committees corresponding to Assembly Agencies.)
	Basic principles of organized women's work have not changed—Program, Organization and Nomenclature changed in accordance with changes in Assembly organization and adapted to meet needs of women.	

NOTE: Names by which organizations and leaders were called during years indicated are used in this history in record of the respective period.

Sn: Taken from *On the Crest of the Present*, Janie McGaughey, Board of Women's Work, Presbyterian Church in the United States, Atlanta, 1961, p. 200. Used with permission, Office of Women, Mission Board, PCUS.

of the Church, network of women's groups in the local church; Presbytery task forces, advocacy.[84] According to a chart in *Matrix*, a connectional newsletter for Presbyterian Church, U.S. women, in September 1982, the four women's groups currently are Women of the Church Committee, Committee for Racial Ethnic Women, Committee on Church Employed Women, Committee on Women's Concerns.

The style of operation between the women of the southern and northern churches has differed primarily in organizational philosophy: auxiliary versus autonomous. Many leaders in the UPUSA women's work feel that their century-long experience indicates that an organization functions more efficiently and powerfully when it is not responsible to any judicatory but reports directly to the General Assembly.

As noted in this chapter, the shorter southern experience of women's organizations has evolved out of a more recent history of official rulings of the denomination limiting the role of women in the administration and leadership of the church. With the women's loyal adherence to the tenets of the church, they felt constrained by such policies to behave with all propriety and caution. During the early meetings of presbyterial unions, the presiding officers consciously avoided speaking in the presence of any man, even if he were there as speaker or representative of the denominational committees. The result was that men often conducted the meetings, and "No stranger would ever guess they were attending a woman's meeting."[85] Stories abound of husbands sitting in the rain or in the cold waiting to escort their wives home from the meetings. They often wanted to come inside, but the women stubbornly refused to break the rules of order.[86] The superintendent never addressed the General Assembly, even to read her report, until fifteen years after her appointment, even though she spoke in front of other denominations.

The northern women, on the other hand, by 1912 had not received voting privileges but already enjoyed substantial status and power through their Boards. When union talks between the two denominations occurred in 1913, according to Winsborough, the PCUSA women recognized the differences in style and influence. Consequently, a representative of one of the Woman's Boards of the PCUSA telegraphed her denomination's moderator at the General Assembly being held in Atlanta to oppose the union discussions because of the auxiliary type of organization the women of the southern church had adopted.[87]

Although seventy years have passed, the issue remains. During a period of new union negotiations, the same types of concerns are being expressed: auxiliary or autonomous, inclusive or programmatic, persuasive compliance or mandated equality.[88] At the 193rd General Assembly in 1981, women leaders openly discussed the commonality of the two approaches to organization and the implications of merging two heritages, two histories.[89]

14

THE CONTEMPORARY SCENE:
A Time for Equality

From its formation in 1958, the United Presbyterian Church in the U.S.A. (UPUSA) dealt with successive waves of crucial social issues. The integration episode at Central High School in Little Rock, Arkansas, that year ushered in a decade of demonstrations and riots. Blacks, Hispanics, Native Americans, and other ethnic groups refused to accept traditional establishment palliatives to their demand for equality. Concurrently the church, struggling with the ethical and theological ramifications of a widening conflict in Vietnam, like the country as a whole, had ambivalent responses to the demands of patriotism and the rights of individual conscience. The specter of human suffering and deprivation both at home and abroad triggered a comprehensive crusade against poverty, which had a significant impact on national and ecclesiastical budgets.

During the 1960s the denomination approved the *Confession of 1967* and adopted a new *Book of Confessions* amid acrimonious theological debate and denominational dissension. A proposal by Stated Clerk Eugene Carson Blake to unite major Protestant denominations resulted in the formation of the Consultation on Church Union (COCU) and increased interest in the ecumenical movement in the United States. Aside from these ecclesiastical issues, Presbyterians also contemplated the creation of regional synods and projected a major restructuring of its boards and agencies, the first such effort since 1923.[1]

Despite the prominence of the women's liberation movement in the early part of this same decade, the governing bodies of the church did not address the new feminism nor study the continuing dissatisfaction of churchwomen with their status in the denomination. The denomination had yet to grasp the significance of what one woman called the central issue: Although the church could remove restrictions and promote reform, "only education and consciousness-raising can bring about the changed attitudes necessary for full equality of both sexes in actual practice."[2].

In the 1960s, a small group of women professionals in the denominational offices of the Witherspoon Building in Philadelphia became increasingly unhappy with the lagging implementation of official policies of equality. According to one of the participants, Wilmina Rowland, a group caucused to develop a strategy with which to confront the church with issues important to women. They enlisted the assistance of Stated Clerk Blake, who suggested that they work through the Office of Church and Society. Consequently their concerns, referred to the Counseling Committee on Church and Society, resulted in a proposal to the General Assembly in 1967 for a "Study of Women in the Church and Society," which was authorized without a dissenting murmur.[3]

The Office of Church and Society anticipated that the projected study would be "a radical break in what has been termed a sub-Christian view of the relationship of men and women in the modern world."[4] When the committee completed its work two years later and presented its findings to the 181st General Assembly, it marked the beginning of a new era for male–female relationships in the church. From that date forward, the issues, concerns, and needs of women have had an unprecedented prominence in General Assembly deliverances and in denominational practices.

The report of the Special Committee on the Status of Women in Society and in the Church in 1969 candidly described the extent of sexual discrimination in ecclesiastical thought and practice and attempted to understand male–female relationships in wide sociological and theological perspectives. Although committee members could not reach any "theological consensus," they provided basic data for future study and pointed out crucial issues to which the denomination would have to respond.[5]

Central in the report was the thesis that "what happens in the Church to and through its ordained women, clergy and lay, to its commissioned women and elected church officers reflects in powerful symbolism the prevailing attitudes in the church as a whole toward its women in relation to its men."[6] Women constituted 57.4 percent of all members of the UPUSA church in 1967, but the report showed that their numerical dominance stood in sharp contrast to the proportion of women in church offices.[7]

	Male	Female	Female (percentage of total)
Ministers (ordained)	12,865	67	0.518
Elders (ordained)	76,695	14,268	15.7
Deacons (ordained)	37,733	25,999	40.8
Trustees	45,586	6,491	12.4

In discussing theological and biblical interpretations of the role of women, the report dismissed most of the traditional interpretations of biblical passages in which women are mentioned that reflected social attitudes of a specific period and not the "unchanging, revealed word of God." The committee saw the message of the Old Testament as representing the mutual relatedness of man and woman rather than the subservience of female to male. Furthermore, it subjected the Pauline passages, especially 1 Tim. 2:9-15 and 1 Cor. 14:14-25, to rigorous textual criticism and it questioned their validity as representing early Christian perspectives on sexual equality.[8]

Under the heading "Gender in the Church," the report dealt with several theological and sociological approaches to the problem of sexual discrimination. Describing the present situation as "critical, infectious, explosive," the committee warned that the church must take a lead in social change or become merely "a quaint club or historical artifact in a class with Virginia's Williamsburg."[9] In the concluding two sections, the report listed statistical implications for ecclesiology and theology and for the church's mission to the world. It also challenged Presbyterian women "to make your voice heard, not as second-class men but fully human women."[10]

The committee offered two specific recommendations, which the 181st Assembly approved. First, that UPW and the Office of Church and Society create a Task Force on Women to carry out a three-year study of the role and status of women in society. Second, that the Council on Theological Education be requested to produce a study that would include a biblical interpretation of the nature and role of women and male–female relationships, theological anthropology, and ethical issues of justice between men and women in contemporary American life.[11]

At this same Assembly, a Presbyterian woman spoke out on the Assembly floor as an aggrieved member of the "great minority." Diane Tennis, a minister from Rochester, New York, rose to protest against the use of the form of address: "Fathers and Brethren," comparing this ritual usage to the analogous unthinking use of the term *boy* in addressing a black man. Tennis also offered a substitute motion for the recommendation that the Council on Theological Education undertake a theological study of women's role in the church and in contemporary American life. She proposed a conference of women meeting by themselves and under the informal auspices of Church and Society. "My recommendation is essentially that the church permit women to be together without an agenda, without male interference, and without the traditional label of United Presbyterian Women's sponsorship." Although her motion failed, Tennis gained attention when she concluded, "I am sick of being told I am so smart I qualify as a man. . . . If you have millions for Blacks, as you should, give us a couple of bucks to conduct the conference."[12]

The actions of this Assembly ushered in what can be termed another "woman's decade." Primarily through the Task Force on Women and its successor, the Council on Women and the Church (COWAC) and UPW, women's concerns maintained a prominent place in the church's agenda. Presbyterian women gained unprecedented visibility as leaders in denominational activities. Between 1970 and 1980, the UPUSA church approved the creation of new women's support groups, initiated a series of overtures designed to guarantee women equal opportunity of service in church life, sponsored workshops and study sessions for intensive examination of problems facing women in the 1970s, wrestled with the issue of sexist language in theology and liturgy, took stands on controversial issues such as ERA and abortion, and opened up executive positions and committee assignments previously dominated by males.

A series of "firsts" for UPUSA women occurred in the 1970s. The first Standing Committee on Women chaired by ruling elder Ethel Lambert presented its recommendations to the General Assembly in 1970. The following year, Jane Cox, a middler at Pittsburgh Theological Seminary, became the first female page, a task previously assigned only to male seminarians. In 1973, Barbara Prasse and Alice Truman were the first women to be appointed to the Permanent Judicial Commission, and Helen E. Irvine, manager of the personnel office of the church's Vocation Agency, was selected as the first woman vice-moderator of the General Assembly by Clinton Marsh. In 1974, Katie Cannon became the first black Presbyterian woman to be ordained to the ministry, and in the same year Rachel Henderlite, an ordained PCUS minister, was the first woman invited to preach at the Sunday evening ecumenical service, which marked the opening of the annual meeting.[13]

For most Presbyterian women, however, the most significant "first" was the election of Lois H. Stair, a ruling elder from Waukesha, Wisconsin, as Moderator of the General Assembly in 1971. Her skill and poise and her ability to articulate the concerns of women during her moderatorial year did much to increase denominational acceptance of women. As the first elected head of the General Assembly Mission Council (GAMC), in 1973, Stair assumed leadership responsibility and established a role model for other women to follow. Noting that women were among her sharpest critics ("Don't you know what Paul said about women? A woman shouldn't speak in the church."), Stair described how her own attitudes about being a woman had changed in recent years. Once taking it as a compliment when someone said, "You think like a man," and finding her ego fortified when she was the only woman serving on a committee, she later believed she "should think and speak out as a woman." On one occasion, Stair as the sole woman on a national committee was asked to take the minutes and to get the coffee. She informed her colleagues that they already had a secretary and that she was present to discuss her ideas, not to serve refreshments. Stair recalled that she "could feel the shock waves going through the committee, but afterwards she had no trouble making her views known."[14]

A second woman moderator, Thelma C. D. Adair, was elected by the 188th General Assembly in 1976. A ruling elder from the Presbytery of New York, Adair served as professor of education at Queens College, University of the City of New York, and for several years as coordinator of educational systems for the Board of National Missions. She was also the first woman president of Black Presbyterians United, an affiliation of black Presbyterian men and women of the UPUSA church that sought to be a channel for making black concerns known to the church. Adair's active moderatorial year personalized to the denomination the problems of discrimination faced by women in ethnic minority groups. Her charismatic presence and effective speaking ability gave heightened visibility to the forgotten "third-world woman." "To me," said Adair, "the term Third World includes people of color around the world, those untold millions striving for justice and liberation, economic and social security."[15]

Complementing the contributions of individuals such as Stair and Adair in introducing women into the mainstream of church life was the Task Force on Women created by the General Assembly in 1969. By encouraging the formation of local task forces and identifying issues of concern to Presbyterian women, the Task Force provided a major advocacy voice for Presbyterian women. When the three-year mandate of the Task Force on Women ended in 1972, the General Assembly approved an Interim Task Force on Women for the period between the 184th General Assembly (1972) and the time that the new national structure would take effect sometime in 1973. At the same time, the General Assembly also instructed the Program Agency to establish a Consulting Committee on Women for a three-year period subject to renewal. The new committee was to advise and provide resources for judicatory task forces and through research and study support existing programs and initiate action on untouched issues such as minority women, male liberation, liberation of older women, and others as they might arise.[16]

Despite the approval of the Interim Task Force, tension among Presbyterian women pervaded the period during which the denominational reorganization was being put in final form. Some still remembered or knew of the 1923 reorganization with its sudden demise of the women's missionary boards and were concerned that gains of the early 1970s might be erased in the reorganization reshuffling. Others feared that the Committee of Eleven, chaired by Sherman W. Skinner, would not accept the concept of a woman's advocacy group apart from the traditional

UPW. In 1972, the Task Force on Women reported in its newsletter that restructuring was continuing without any definite assurance that women would be represented fairly. According to Virginia Mills, decisions were being made with few or no women participating.[17] In a subsequent newsletter, Mills reiterated her uncertainty about any successor to the Task Force on Women in the new structure and called for women to express their concerns to the Committee of Eleven and to lobby at the General Assembly for their cause. Mills warned that without national connections for women, "women could again become invisible through most of the church."[18]

Their efforts proved successful when the Committee of Eleven recommended the inclusion of a Council on Women and the Church (COWAC) under the aegis of the Program Agency to the General Assembly of 1973. Lois Montgomery was appointed coordinator of the Women's Program, which provided support, resources, and services for UPW, COWAC, and other women's concerns. COWAC's stated purpose became "to serve as the focal point to the identification of issues in churchwide policy relating to the status of women and their position within the church and in society."[19] In its role as advocate, COWAC monitored the General Assembly agencies to determine their compliance with policies of equal representation and employment of women, sponsored regional workshops, and provided resources for women's regional task forces. It initiated and approved funds on behalf of the General Assembly for experimental and emergency programs related to the status of women such as seminars for wives of clergy, for single parents, and for programs aimed at the prevention of sexual violence.[20]

In response to the large numbers in which women began entering theological institutions, COWAC gave high priority to improving the conditions of female seminary students. The Task Force had asked the 183rd General Assembly (1971) to direct the Council on Theological Education to request that all UPUSA seminaries institute a program to recruit women students, to establish priorities in faculty hiring of women, and to provide greater assistance to women students in field work, interim-year opportunities, post-graduate placement, and continuing education programs. Seminaries also were requested to evaluate and correct patterns of discrimination felt by many female students and to revise their publications to reflect more accurately the contemporary roles of women.[21] In 1974, COWAC began official on-site visits to the seminaries to assess the status of these efforts and to offer assistance in endeavors to improve attitudes toward women and opportunities for women. COWAC has continued to communicate with UPUSA Presbyterian women enrolled in non-Presbyterian seminaries and has encouraged meetings such as the National Training Conference held in Dallas in 1978, where seminarians and seminary administrators could share information and begin to form a support network.[22]

COWAC also encouraged the UPUSA church to take stands on a number of controversial social issues facing women in general. On its recommendation, the General Assembly affirmed its support of the Equal Rights Amendment (ERA) initially in 1971 and subsequently in 1974, 1975, 1976, 1978, and 1979. In 1977, the GAMC adopted a policy of holding meetings only in states where the ERA had been ratified.[23] Regarding abortion, the General Assembly in 1970 adopted a policy that the abortion of a pregnancy is a matter of "the careful ethical decision of the patient, her physician, and her pastor or other counselor, and therefore should not be restricted by law."[24] The following year, the Assembly added to its previous action that while abortion was "not regarded as an ordinary or usual means of birth control," it did recommend the establishment of medically sound, easily available, and low cost abortion services.[25] COWAC also spoke out against rape and other forms of sexual violence and called for recognition of children's rights in contemporary society.[26]

Other more specialized women's advocacy groups emerged in the 1970s and were endorsed and supported by COWAC and UPW. Church Employed Women (CEW) consisting of women clergy and Christian educators, first met as a Professional Women's Caucus at the 1971 General Assembly. The following General Assembly recognized CEW as an official organization whose goal was "the realization of an inclusive church which is a good steward of all its resources."[27] By 1973, CEW had a membership of approximately 350 women who worked as seminarians, pastors, Christian educators, church secretaries, judicatory and agency personnel, and overseas workers. CEW sponsored the first Church Employed Women's National Training Conference in 1974 and developed other workshops to provide support and skills training for secretaries, church educators, and clergy.[28]

The Third World Women's Coordinating Committee (TWWCC) was formed in 1972 to represent the concerns of the four racial caucuses of the UPUSA church: The Asian Presbyterian Council, Black Presbyterians United, La Raza Presbyterian Caucus, and the Native American Consulting Committee. TWWCC attempted to help women of racial and ethnic minorities enter more fully into the life of their church and their own societies. Recognizing the interrelatedness of racism and sexism, TWWCC in consultation with COWAC developed leadership training programs that reflected the cultural, racial, and social diversity of third world women.[29]

In 1974, TWWCC submitted a proposal to the Vocation Agency that the two groups work together on a project called "Minority Women's Study." Approval was given by the Vocation Agency and as a result the Minority Women Executive Group was created. The group embarked on a serious campaign to design models and programs of professional development geared toward enabling ethnic and minority women to assume leadership roles in the church. Since 1974, the Minority Women Executive Group has conducted numerous workshops covering a wide range of concerns and interests. As a result, minority women have been placed in a variety of leadership positions within the church, such as the Program Agency's professional recruitment office, personnel services, minority placement, benefits administrations and supporting services, and administration in the offices of the stated clerk and the general director of the Program Agency.[30]

With the advent of women's advocacy groups and the growing movement of women into denominational leadership, members of UPW found themselves in the midst of an identity crisis comparable to the one that churchwomen faced in the 1920s. UPW continued to be recognized as the quasi-official voice of Presbyterian women in the denomination-at-large, and, through its second-mile giving, it contributed upwards of $5,000,000 annually to the benevolence budget. Yet its status seemed jeopardized by younger women who moved more toward involvement in current social issues and who employed the methods of the women's liberation movement to denominational structures. The constituency of UPW primarily remained traditional, mainline, white, middle-class and middle-aged. Some of the women were unsure how to relate to the new feminism and were uncomfortable with the tactics of confrontation. Although Presbyterian women historically had been involved in social issues such as American Indian rights, the fight against polygamy, temperance, and other concerns, they found the radical style of questioning of the status quo to be threatening and potentially divisive.[31]

In March 1963, the National Executive Committee of UPW met with the presidents of thirty-three synodical societies to make preparations for the 1964 national meeting, which would in turn inaugurate the third triennium of UPW. The participants decided that there was a need for a serious study of the entire program of UPW in order to make it flexible and responsive to rapid changes in contemporary society. A study committee appointed in 1964 made its final report at the national meeting in 1967. UPW approved a new program structure focusing on four major areas of concern for understanding and action: technology, social revolution, the generation gap, and peace with justice. The program was given the acronym DARE (Discover the needs, Ask for resources, Respond in Action, Endure the difficulties). The new program encouraged women to become involved in service-oriented projects such as tutoring and preschool programs, services to the elderly and physically handicapped, adult literacy, and job-skill training programs. Support for the change in priorities was not unanimous, but the 1967 meeting marked the beginning of UPW's struggle to maintain its continuity with the past while at the same time coming to terms with contemporary issues.[32]

New editorial policies for *Concern* magazine reflected the determination of UPW leadership to project its new goals to its constituency and to the entire denomination. Under editor Sarah Cunningham, *Concern* became more than an informational and inspirational organ for Presbyterian women. It provided material for serious study and interpretation that attempted to be a "challenging mind-stretcher." One entire issue, for example, was devoted to "Women's Liberation in a Biblical Perspective," and beginning in 1971 *Concern* reported on the implications of actions taken at the General Assembly for women of the church. The innovations offended some churchwomen, who canceled their subscriptions and complained bitterly about the "secularization" of their magazine. By the early 1970s, however, the trend reversed and Presbyterian women seemed more willing to be outspoken on issues of equality and participation.[33]

Of specific concern to members of UPW was the creation of COWAC in 1973. No longer could UPW develop its programs without consulting other independent associations of women. Some women who feared that COWAC would usurp the prominence of UPW opposed the formation of COWAC as a potentially schismatic organization. Others, sympathetic with the goals of advocacy groups, were confused about how to relate both to UPW and to other organizations. The situation was analogous to mother-daughter relationships where the parent sympathized with the child's goals but could not identify with her methods of attaining them, and the daughter, recognizing her roots in the maternal tradition, nevertheless saw the parent as a well-meaning pietist who had not yet come to grips with the realities of a new age.[34]

In the 1970s, UPW consciously attempted to close what some perceived as the ideological gap between itself and the Task Force on Women and its successor, COWAC. At the 1970 General Assembly, Lois Boesch, UPW president, departed from her prepared text to support the movement for sexual equality. Boesch expressed her regret that among the 825 commissioners were just ninety-two women—a decrease of about twenty from the previous year. She also reminded commissioners that UPW was "one of the very few groups that bring a gift of five million dollars to the church instead of asking for five million," a remark that elicited an enthusiastic response from the Assembly. There was only polite applause, however, when she said: "There is a strong feeling developing that women should have a larger part in determining how these funds are used, and that they be included in decision-making processes across-the-board. This feeling is not confined to the young women's liberation groups or UPW—it is present in all women."[35]

During the triennium 1973–76 UPW moved intentionally into the mainstream of the political process of the UPUSA church, especially at the General Assembly level. Beginning in 1974, the UPW report was directed through working Assembly committees rather than through the Committee on Minutes and Reports. This new procedure meant that issues raised in the UPW report had to be dealt with at the Assembly rather than being received, applauded, and dismissed.[36] As a result, UPW has been able to take the initiative on a number of denominational involvements in social issues. In 1975, UPW recommended that the 187th General Assembly identify Global Hunger as its major mission priority and challenged the church to enter into "a united, substained effort in working toward the eradication of global hunger."[37] UPW also advocated in 1979 that the denomination boycott Nestle products because the company by its advertising and promotion in third world countries was encouraging the widespread use of infant formula products, a practice that discouraged breast feeding and was detrimental to the health and nutrition of children.[38]

UPW also provided financial support for a variety of projects that encouraged the participation of women in church life and helped to cope with specific societal problems and inequalities. The UPW Thank Offering to the Board of Christian Education for 1971–74 underwrote the project Women In Leadership (WIL), which was initiated to enable women to move to a new level of self-awareness as they developed personal capacities for leadership. WIL gave seed-money grants to forty-two local projects ranging in amounts from $500 to $4,000 in such areas as health, employment, aging, criminal justice, legal rights, and women in seminaries. In Montana, an ecumenical task force sought ways to bridge cultural differences between Native Americans and other local residents; in Philadelphia, a coalition of older adults and younger people shared common concerns for human liberation and social change; in Portland, women assisted Chinese newcomers through language instruction.[39]

Through its Opportunity Giving Fund, UPW also sponsored a variety of programs that assisted women throughout the world to become more independent and aware of alternatives to traditional sexual stereotyping. The fund supported such programs as a YWCA Battered Women Shelter in Cincinnati, Ohio, a Rape Crisis Center in Knoxville, Tennessee, a mobile counseling program in Seoul, Korea, a Children's Center in Lexington, Mississippi, and a Career Development Center for Women in Youngstown, Ohio. UPW also encouraged research and writing of women's history by subsidizing the publication of several projects, among which was a comprehensive history of mission work by the Woman's Board of Home Missions in the nineteenth century in New Mexico and southern Colorado. In 1980, UPW reported to the General Assembly that it had given $411,250 to similar projects and expressed its resolve to continue such support during the next decade.[40]

Along with the creation of women's advocacy groups and changes in the structures of UPW, the 1970s were also characterized by supportive legislation at the General Assembly level to ensure the full participation of Presbyterian women in all aspects of church life. In 1970, the General Assembly added "The Equality of Women" to its "Seven More Urgent Concerns" and in 1975 included in its Four Directions for Mission "Justice for Women and for Racial and Ethnic Minorities."[41] These general concerns were implemented in the passage of some seventeen overtures between 1970 and 1979, which amended the *Form of Government* to guard against women being the subjects of discrimination in the election to church offices and employment as ministers, executives, and staff workers. Overture D in 1971, for example, specified that in the election of elders and deacons, there should be a "fair representation of both male and female constituency of the congregation" and that all offices should be open to people "regardless of race, ethnic origin, sex, or marital status."[42]

Throughout the decade the General Assembly took strong stands to uphold its policy of full ordination rights for women when that policy was questioned in appeals to the Permanent Judicial Commission. One highly publicized case involved Walter Wynn Kenyon, a candidate for the ministry who sought ordination by the Presbytery of Pittsburgh even though he expressed his belief that the church was wrong in ordaining women according to his understanding of the Scriptures. Kenyon cited 1 Cor. 14 and 1 Tim. 2 as support for his position. He did, however, affirm his willingness to serve with women who were ordained, and he promised not to prevent the ordination of women, provided another minister conducted the service. Pittsburgh Presbytery voted in February 1974 to ordain Kenyon by the narrow margin of 147–133. Presbyter Jack M. Maxwell filed a complaint against the action, which was later sustained by the Permanent Judicial Commissions of the Synod of the Trinity and of the General Assembly. In reporting its final decision, the Permanent Judicial Commission of the General Assembly concluded: "It is the responsibility of our Church to deny ordination to one who has refused to ordain women." Stated Clerk William P. Thompson subsequently clarified the denomination's position in a written opinion that all ministers may be questioned about their adherence to the church's policy on the ordination of women when they accept a call to a different congregation.[43]

Resolution of the Kenyon case prompted efforts by several judicatories to modify ordination vows so that candidates who had reservations about the biblical bases of female ordination could be admitted into the UPUSA ministry. Overtures from Pittsburgh and Seattle Presbyteries, for example, proposed changing the fifth vow from "Do you *endorse* our church's government?" to "Do you *submit* to our church's government?" Advocates of the revised wording argued that it would help make the church more inclusive and would protect individual freedom of conscience. Opponents contended that such changes would undercut the church's long-standing commitment to the ordination of women. After debating for more than an hour, commissioners to the 189th General Assembly in 1977 overwhelmingly defeated the proposed changes, which leading churchwomen insisted would abridge women's rights and turn the clock of the church back in the area of human rights.[44]

Perhaps the most controversial action taken by the General Assembly to ensure equality for women was the approval of Overture L in 1979. Initiated by the Presbytery of Denver, the overture proposed amending the *Form of Government* to specify that "every congregation shall elect men and women from among its active members" to the office of deacon and ruling elder. This new wording was much more explicit and binding than previous language, which had required only that congregations should have a "fair representation" of men and women in church offices. On the floor of the General Assembly in 1978, the overture generated heated debate. The first vote to send it down to the presbyteries ended in a 267–267 tie and was passed on a second vote by a slim majority of 277–271. The final vote of the individual presbyteries reported in 1979 (79 yes, 70 no) reflected a sharp division in the denomination.[45]

Although eight presbyteries suggested amendments to the overture that they said "seriously jeopardizes" church unity and "destroys the principle of free election," the General Assembly resisted efforts to modify or to rescind Overture L in 1980 and 1981. It did, however, recommend an addition to the *Constitution* that would give nonconforming congregations an opportunity to apply for a waiver of the requirement, provided that the presbytery was satisfied that a genuine effort was being made to move toward compliance. A three-fourths vote of the presbytery was required to approve an exemption, and it could be granted for not more than three years at a time subject to revocation at any time by a majority vote.[46] The General Assembly also suggested that presbyteries should implement Overture L "by the exercise of pastoral patience and education rather than by the immediate exercise of church discipline."[47]

The passage of Overture L angered some clergy and lay people who maintained that mandatory ordination of women was unbiblical and unenforceable. They utilized Overture L as a rallying point for Presbyterians who had been unhappy with denominational social policies and property rulings since the mid-1960s. In October 1979, more than 300 ministers and lay people met at the nationally known Tenth Presbyterian Church in Philadelphia to form "Concerned United Presbyterians." Disturbed by what they identified as "liberal trends in the denomination," they threatened to withdraw "as a last resort" if no provision were made for those UPUSA congregations that would not ordain women as a matter of conscience. Even before the denomination had time to respond, however, some congregations had already departed. *The Presbyterian Layman* reported that between September 1979 and April 1980, eight churches with combined memberships of some 8,100 communicants had severed their connections with the denomination.[48]

While legislative pronouncements regarding ordination and equal employment frequently captured the headlines during the 1970s, the General Assembly also worked along other lines to make the denomination aware of the deep roots of sexism. With a great deal of the initiative coming from COWAC, various General Assemblies worked on the problem of removing sexist language which had permeated so much of the church's theological vocabulary. In 1971, the General Assembly ruled that "so-called generic usage of masculine nouns, pronouns, and adjectives is no longer acceptable in church documents" and recommended that revisions be made in the next three years. Judicatories were requested to replace the phrase, "Fathers and Brethren," with one more in keeping with their actual membership, and the General Assembly manual was amended to substitute "ecumenical delegates" for the traditional "fraternal delegates."[49] Church educators conducted studies of Christian education materials so that curricula and related publication would be "free of a double standard of morality which oppresses and stereotypes both men and women."[50] An effort to revise the new *Worshipbook*, which had been produced jointly with the PCUS and the Cumberland Presbyterian Church in 1970 failed in 1974 when the General Assembly rejected a proposal to make some 250 changes in the liturgical section at an estimated cost of $110,000.[51]

In 1973, the 185th General Assembly instructed the Advisory Council on Discipleship and Worship in consultation with COWAC to begin a two-year study on the biblical and theological interpretations of God that are not limited by masculine and exclusivistic language. The Assembly received and adopted the paper, "Language About God— Opening the Door," as a resource document in 1975. The study warned against limited interpretations of God, especially those utilizing language "built on a dualism of male and female which implies that the male is inherently superior." It also challenged the church to assume leadership in revising its language about God and to "avoid an idolatry of the masculine." The same General Assembly also commissioned another three-year study of the cultural and theological implication and impact of changing language about God for the total life of the church. The provocative study entitled "The Power of Language Among the People of God" was received and recommended by the 191st General

Assembly in 1979 for use as a resource document in congregations throughout the denomination.[52]

The church also encouraged and supported scholarly inquiry into issues relating to the role of women in denominational life. In 1975, Westminster Press published a revised version of Elizabeth Verdesi's thesis done at Columbia University and Union Theological Seminary under the title, *In But Still Out*. Verdesi's work traced the unfulfilled efforts of Presbyterian women to gain equality in church life in the first half of the twentieth century. The book was widely used in women's groups as a background to understanding contemporary issues facing churchwomen. The *Journal of Presbyterian History* devoted an entire issue to Presbyterian women in 1977, and under the editorship of James H. Smylie has frequently featured articles dealing with various aspects of women's history. Papers read at a symposium sponsored by the Council of Theological Seminaries and COWAC were published in *Theology Today* (January 1978). They dealt with such topics as "Women Clergy and the Cultural Order," "Women's Liberation: The Cultural Context," and "On the Way to Wholeness." Publications by theologian Letty M. Russell—herself a Presbyterian—including *Human Liberation in a Feminist Perspective* (1974) and *The Liberating Word: A Guide to a Non-Sexist Interpretation of the Bible* (1976) were some of the best-known theological studies produced by a new generation of Presbyterian women scholars.

Despite the signs that the General Assembly was committed to implementing a policy of sexual equality, wholehearted acquiescence by local church leaders, male and female, was not forthcoming. A questionnaire survey of attitudes toward sexism developed by COWAC and administered through the *Presbyterian Panel* in 1975 revealed that while approximately one third of the laity and more than one half of the pastors held somewhat positive feelings toward the women's movement, not many were willing to support actively the cause of women in American society. Large majorities of members, elders, and pastors endorsed the ordination of women as clergy, but approximately 10 percent of each group was negative, and a larger percentage (25, 14, 8 respectively) was neutral. "Fair representation" of women in church life received a strong endorsement, but only one third of the pastors and elders and 27 percent of the members defined "fair" to mean proportional representation. In terms of biblical principles, only a few of the respondents grounded sexism in scriptural passages or buttressed it with a specific theology. It appeared that sexist attitudes among Presbyterians persisted in spite of theological and biblical understandings held as normative by the church-at-large.[53]

According to reports from the GAMC's Equal Employment Opportunity Committee, males continued to dominate leadership positions despite the fact that women represented nearly 60 percent of the denomination's membership. Based on data from the period 1973–77, EEO reported that in the early part of the period there had been some significant gains in the hiring of minorities and women, but that trend had been reversed. Moreover, the concentration of minorities and women in the lower salary ranges remained fairly constant, with little movement "up the ladder" to top-paying positions.[54] In 1979, records indicated that only 12.8 percent of the administrators at synods and presbyteries were women, while 40.1 percent were administrators in General Assembly agencies.[55]

Optimism about the denomination's acceptance of clergywomen was at best guarded. Although the Vocation Agency had given top priority to the employment of clergywomen in the 1970s and statistics indicated that more women were going to seminary and receiving ordination, figures for the period 1971–78 showed that there were only 141 women pastors, or less than 2 percent of the pastors and associate pastors in the denomination.[56] In 1981, while the number of ordained women had increased to 621 out of a total of 14,502 clergy, the ratio of women in the total actually decreased from 28 to 25 percent. As the Vocation Agency spokespeople admitted, "We still have a long way to go."[57]

One of the most articulate and incisive Presbyterian observers in the 1970s, Janet Harbison Penfield, summed up her observations about the decade in an article for the *Christian Century* entitled, "What's a Nice Woman Like You Doing in a Male-Dominated Church Like This?" Although appreciative of strides made in the drive for racial and sexual equality in mainline Protestantism, Penfield saw more frustration than fulfillment in the efforts of women to become equal partners with men in serving Christ through the church. She cited "horrendous tales of difficulties encountered by women who are ordained to professional ministries but can't find any jobs," and repeated instances of "tokenism, insensitive males, and lack of women in positions of top leadership." Penfield also noted that female theologians had made few inroads in altering male-oriented views about women's place in the church and that no first-rate woman thinker or writer had offered "a defense of the church-as-it-is, or, on the other hand, a model of the church as it ought to be." Expressing her own personal frustration with the pace of change, Penfield concluded, "All we women seem to do is to pick away at the edges, congratulating ourselves each time a heretofore male post is held for the first time by a woman."[58]

Historians today are too close to the decade's events to draw firm conclusions. Movements and trends have a way of altering course without warning. Who, for example, would have thought that the feminism of the 1920s would have been followed by the disinterest of the 1930s? Nevertheless, a prediction made by Patricia Doyle in her address to the General Assembly in 1970 is a fitting conclusion to a study of this nature. "The equality of women," she said, "is related to every other search for freedom. It will be the single most difficult item to achieve on the agenda of the church and the world. As such, it will need years of strong effort on the part of the Church."[59]

NOTES

Unless otherwise indicated, the location of all primary sources, such as correspondence, memoranda, reports, journals, memoirs, unpublished materials, etc., is in the Presbyterian Historical Society archives, Philadelphia, Pennsylvania. Such materials that are in Record Groups are cited by RG with category, box, and folder designations. When General Assembly *Minutes* are cited, the entry refers to *GAM* with the denominational identity in parenthetics, the year, and the page number, e.g., *GAM*(USA) 1893: 114. All citations identified as interviews represent an "Oral History" interview on cassette tape. The tapes are catalogued and stored at the Presbyterian Historical Society. Other abbreviations and shortened references are noted throughout; however, for the convenience of the reader, the following is a list of the most common abbreviations used:

CHA   *The Church at Home and Abroad*
CP   Cumberland Presbyterian Church
GAM   *General Assembly Minutes*
HFR   *Home and Foreign Record*
HMM   *Home Mission Monthly*
MF   Microfilm
OMF   *Our Mission Field*
PCUS   Presbyterian Church in the United States
PCUSA   Presbyterian Church in the United States of America
PHS   Presbyterian Historical Society
PMR   *Presbyterian Monthly Record*
PPM   *Presbyterian Pioneer Missions*
PW   *Pioneer Women of the Presbyterian Church, United States*
RG   Record Group
RMP   *Rocky Mountain Presbyterian*
SJ   Sheldon Jackson (Collection, Correspondence, Scrapbook)
UPNA   United Presbyterian Church in North America
UPUSA   United Presbyterian Church in the United States of America
UPW   United Presbyterian Women
W&M   *Women and Missions*
WWW   *Woman's Work for Woman*
YY   *Yesteryears*

Chapter 1: Pious Females

1. General Assembly *Minutes* 1789–1820, 1817:26. Hereafter cited as *GAM*.
2. That many who joined organizations believed the millennium was nigh was evident in the annual reports of the American Board of Commissioners for Foreign Mission begun in 1810: "It is not only practical for multitudes to unite in the great purpose of evangelizing the world; but such a union is absolutely necessary, in order to bring about this event in the shortest time. All the power and influence of the whole Christian world must be put in requisition, during the course of those beneficent labors which will precede the millennium." *First Ten*

Annual Reports of the American Board of Commissioners for Foreign Missions (Boston, 1834), as quoted in H. Shelton Smith, Robert T. Handy, Lefferts A. Loetscher, *American Christianity: An Historical Interpretation with Representative Documents 1607–1820* (New York, 1960), pp. 549–50.

3. Certainly the purpose of one of the earliest British societies influenced later American societies in determining their goals. The "end proposed" was the propagation of the Christian faith and the salvation of souls. The aim, however, was further extended: "And the Serious Reader must be much affected with the Endeavors of the Society, towards planting Religion and Virtue, *and the Due Ordering* the Life and Manner of numerous People." David Humphreys, *An Historical Account of the Incorporated Society for the Propagation of the Gospels in Foreign Parts Containing their Foundation, Proceedings, and the Success of Their Missionaries in the British Colonies to the Year 1728* (London, 1730), p. iv.

4. Some of the most helpful literature includes Clifford S. Griffin, "Religious Benevolence as Social Control, 1815-1860," *Mississippi Valley Historical Review* 44 (December 1957): 423–44; Lois W. Banner, "Religious Benevolence as Social Control: A Critique of an Interpretation," *The Journal of American History* 60 (June 1973): 23-41; John L. Thomas, "Romantic Reform in America, 1815-1865," *American Quarterly* 17 (Winter 1965): 656-81; Elwyn A. Smith, "The Forming of a Modern American Denomination," *Church History* 31 (March 1962): 74-99; Keith Melder, "Ladies Bountiful: Organized Women's Benevolence in Early 19th-Century America," *New York History* 48 (July 1967): 231-54; Anne Firor Scott, "What, Then, is the American: This New Woman?" *Journal of American History* 65 (December 1978): 679-703; and many others.

5. Margaret Fuller, *Woman in the Nineteenth Century* (New York, 1855; Norton Library edition, 1971), p. 35.

6. *Woman in Missions: Papers and Addresses presented at the Woman's Congress of Missions, October 2-4, 1893, in the Hall of Columbus, Chicago*, comp. Rev. E. M. Wherry, D. D. (New York, 1893): 90.

7. Mary Stone to Mrs. M. Ward, 20 August 1806. (Located in Presbyterian Historical Society archives; hereafter cited as PHS.) Ward obviously supported female groups, for she organized and became the first president of the Rochester Female Charitable Society (Mabel Ward Waters to Katharine Bennett, 6 June 1942, PHS).

8. "Female Missionary Societies," *The Presbyterian*, 23 July 1842:118.

9. Claude Welch, *Protestant Thought in the Nineteenth Century*, vol. 1, 1799-1870 (New Haven and London, 1972), p. 129. The revivalistic spirit was conducive to women's participation in worship, and the earlier "Great Awakening" had stirred some women to form "praying groups" during the eighteenth century. Mary Sumner Benson, *Woman in Eighteenth-Century America: A Study of Opinion and Social Usage* (New York, 1935; reissued Port Washington, 1966), p. 259, and Dorothy Bass Fraser, "Woman with Past: A New Look," *Theological Education* 8 (Summer 1972):215. Mary P. Ryan has demonstrated links between revivals and women's organizations in the Utica (New York) First Presbyterian Church between 1814 and 1838 in her article, "A Women's Awakening: Evangelical Religion and the Families of Utica, New York, 1800-1840," *American Quarterly* (Winter 1978):617-23.

10. Ashbel Green, *A Historical Sketch, or A Compendious View of Domestic and*

Foreign Missions in the Presbyterian Church of the U.S.A. (Philadelphia, 1838), p. 31.

11. *Woman's Work for Woman*, May 1883:169. Hereafter cited as *WWW*.

12. *GAM 1789-1820*, 1816:298.

13. Joanna Graham Bethune, *The Power of Faith, Exemplified in the Life and Writings of the Late Mrs. Isabella Graham* (New York/Boston, 1843), p. 250.

14. Matthew La Rue Perrine, *Women Have a Work to Do in the House of God. A Discourse Delivered at the First Annual Meeting of the Female Missionary Society for the Poor of the City of New York and Its Vicinity*, 12 May 1817.

15. Mary Stone to Mrs. Ward, 20 August 1806, PHS. See also Florence Hayes, *Daughters of Dorcas: The Story of the Work of Women for Home Missions since 1802* (New York, 1952), pp. 8, 10; R. Pierce Beaver, *All Loves Excelling: American Protestant Women in World Mission* (Grand Rapids, 1968), p. 23.

16. Bethune, *Power of Faith*, 233.

17. Walter Harris, *Discourse Delivered to the Members of the Female Cent Society in Bedford, New Hampshire, July 18, 1814* (Concord, 1814), pp. 14-15. Also referred to in Beaver, *All Loves Excelling*, 13. The first male benevolent and missionary organizations were centered in New England, particularly in Boston, and an early women's missions group, the Boston Female Society for Missionary Purposes, composed of Baptist and Congregational women, also was formed in Boston on October 9, 1800. In this history of women's organizations, Beaver observed that the "Bostonian example was powerful in the land, and the women of Boston knew it. The example they set would be followed by others" (Beaver, 19). Indeed it was, including by Presbyterian women. See "The Articles of the Boston Female Society, for promoting the Diffusion of Christian Knowledge" in *New York Missionary Magazine* II (1801):379-81 for more information on this early organization.

18. Elizabeth Verdesi, *In But Still Out* (Philadelphia, 1973 and 1976), p. 38.

19. Beaver, *All Loves Excelling*, 16. See, for instance, the constitution of the Boston Female Society, *New York Missionary Magazine* 2 (1801): 379–85.

20. Hayes, *Dorcas*, 9.

21. *GAM 1789-1820*, 1817:15.

22. Winthrop Hudson, *Religion in America*, 2nd. ed. (New York, 1973), p. 151.

23. Hayes, *Dorcas*, 146.

24. Mrs. Charles F. Cole, *History of Woman's Work in East Hanover Presbytery* (Richmond, 1938), p. 61.

25. Hayes, *Dorcas*, 144.

26. Bethune, *Power of Faith*, 144.

27. Perrine, *Women Have a Work to Do*, 25.

28. *GAM*, 1824:130.

29. "Answer to a Letter from the Secretary of a Female Cent Society,"*Panoplist and Missionary Magazine* 12 (1816):256-60.

30. Arthur Judson Brown, *One Hundred Years: A History of the Foreign Missionary Work of the Presbyterian Church in the U.S.A.* (New York, 1936), p. 114; also *Woman in Missions*, 85.

31. Hayes, *Dorcas*, 154.

32. Ibid., 24 (italics mine). This same story is recounted in the histories of other denominations' women's work.

33. Ibid., 147; Cole, *East Hanover*, 54.

34. J. H. Agnew, *Harper's New Monthly Magazine*, October 1851:657.

35. *Thirteenth Annual Report of the Free Home for Destitute Young Girls* (New York, 1880).

36. *GAM* 1815:600.

37. *The Homiletic Review* 12 (July 1886):76.

38. Hudson, *Religion in America*, 142. Whitney Cross, *The Burned Over District: The Social and Intellectual History of Enthusiastic Religion in Western New York, 1800-1850* (New York, 1965), p. 152. Admittedly this society was far more organizationally sophisticated than other groups. It not only employed missionaries but also established branch societies. The society disbanded in 1827, absorbed by the male Western Domestic Missionary Society. See Page Putnam Miller, "The Evolving Role of Women in the Presbyterian Church in the Early Nineteenth Century" (Ph.D. dissertation, University of Maryland, 1979), pp. 175-81, for an extensive description of this group. See also Ryan, "A Women's Awakening."

39. Harris, *Discourse*, 15.

40. Hayes, *Dorcas*, 143; Mrs. F. S. Bennett, comp. *How It Grew: The Story of Woman's Organization in the Presbyterian Church in the United States of America.* Narrative and Drama presented at Quadrennial Meeting, Atlantic City, New Jersey, May 15, 1942, p. 14. An interesting sketch of the Religious Female Cent Society of Bridge Hampton Presbyterian Church (1815) indicates how significant was the sacrifice of even 1 cent a week "in days when farmers' crops went in exchange for the commodities of life" and little real money was handled. Pamphlet, PHS.

41. Hayes, *Dorcas*, 151.

42. Cole, *East Hanover*, 50-51.

43. Mrs. Mary Feeney, "The Female Heathen School Society," *Women and Missions* 17 (January 1941):329. The parent group, the Female Heathen School Society, began in 1817.

44. Mary L. Hall, "Historic Sketch of Spencer Presbyterian Church, Spencer, New York," *Journal of the Presbyterian Historical Society* 9 (September 1918):315-16.

45. "Female Missionary Societies," 118.

46. *Woman in Missions*, 93.

47. Even though the Assembly had established a Standing Committee on Missions in 1802 and later a Board of Missions in 1816, these groups had no salaried staff and relied on volunteers. Home and foreign mission work mostly followed the European pattern, which was to use independent boards especially formed for missions, such as the American Home Missionary Society and the American Board of Commissioners for Foreign Missions, comprised of representatives of various denominations. A "Plan of Union" with the Congregational Church designated geographical areas for which the Presbyterians and the Congregationalists each had specific mission responsibility. After the Old School–New School split, the New School branch of the Presbyterian Church continued for a time to support the Plan of Union, although it established its own Home Mission agency in 1861. The Old School branch immediately established the Presbyterian Board of Foreign Missions and the former Board of Missions continued for home mission work. It later was renamed Board of Domestic Missions. During this split, the Old School took a strong "denominational" line and began to solicit support for Presbyterian mission work. One account of the Old School–

New School split is in William O. Brackett, Jr., "The Rise and Development of the New School in the Presbyterian Church in the U.S.A. to the Reunion of 1869," 2 parts, *Journal of the Presbyterian Historical Society* 13 (3 & 4) (September 1929, December 1929):117-40; 145-74.

48. Brown, *One Hundred Years*, 118. "Until 1831, Presbyterian concern for world missions had found expression through interdenominational societies, especially the American Board of Commissioners for Foreign Missions. The stiffening denominationalism of the 1830s led the Synod of Pittsburgh to expand its Western Missionary Society—so as to include its foreign work. In holding that missionary effort is not a voluntary matter but is obligatory on all church members, the synod was far in advance of the Church. In 1838, the WFMS became the Assembly's Board of Foreign Missions." *The Presbyterian Enterprise: Sources of American Presbyterian History*, ed. Maurice W. Armstrong, Lefferts A. Loetscher, Charles A. Anderson (Philadelphia, 1956), p. 149. See "Constitution of the Female Missionary Society of the First Presbyterian Church, Cincinnati" for one example of a woman's group organized as an auxiliary to the Western Society, RG 31-1-1.

49. Board of Missions' *Annual Report*, 1834, pp. 39-40.

50. E. P. Rogers, *The Obligations and Duties of the Female Sex to Christianity* (Augusta, 1849), p. 5.

51. Ibid., 7.

52. J.F. Stearns, *Female Influence and the True Christian Mode of Its Exercise*, (Newburyport, Ma., 1837), p. 23.

53. Hayes, *Dorcas*, 35. During these same times, the judicatories were setting up bureaucratic procedures for administering church extension and foreign missions. The administrative decisions, of course, were entirely in the hands of men.

54. Hayes, *Dorcas*, 28.

55. Numerous examples are in letters, diaries, and books in the archives of the PIIS. Some responses were printed in women's mission magazines.

56. Lois W. Banner, *Elizabeth Cady Stanton, A Radical for Woman's Rights* (Boston, Toronto, 1980), p. 15. See also p. 158.

57. Eleanor H. Porter, *Pollyanna* (New York, 1913), p. 126.

58. "Confessions of a Minister's Wife," *The Atlantic Monthly* 87 (1901):211-12.

59. Scott, *This New Woman*, 679.

60. Rev. F. F. Ellinwood, D.D., "Early Years in Our Woman's Foreign Missionary Societies," *WWW* 20 (February 1905):47.

61. *The Presbyterian*, 10 January 1863:2.

62. Thomas Murphy, *Pastoral Theology: The Pastor in the Various Duties of His Office* (Philadelphia, 1877):290-97, esp. 293.

63. Annie C. F. Cunningham, "Woman's Work in the American Church," *The Catholic Presbyterian* 9 (January-June 1883):362.

64. See chapters 2, 7, and the preface.

Chapter 2: Church Woman's Decade

1. M. Katharine Bennett, "How It Grew," 29 and Bennett, "The Past a Promise for the Future," *Home Mission Monthly* 38 (March 1924):106. Hereafter cited as *HMM*.

2. "Christian Women in America," *WWW* 1 (April 1871-January 1872):25.

3. Mrs. Annie Wittenmyer, "Plea for Christian Woman's Work," *Rocky Mountain Presbyterian* (November 1876). Sheldon Jackson Collection, PHS; hereafter cited as SJ.

4. *HMM* 1 (November 1886-November 1887):17.

5. "Report of Foreign Secretary," Sixth Annual Report, Woman's Presbyterian Board of Missions of the Southwest (1883), p. 9. Microfilm 3; hereafter cited as MF with number of reel (PHS).

6. Mrs. M. H. Faris, "Women's Work," *Presbyterian Banner*, 4 December 1878:2.

7. Mrs. F. S. Scovel, "Woman's Executive Committee of Home Missions; History of Its Organization," paper read at Annual Meeting, 23 May 1879. Clipping, Sheldon Jackson Scrapbook, "Woman's Home Missions, 1875-1884," Volume 62:135; hereafter cited as Scrapbook 62.

8. The preceding listing was compiled from various sources: Hayes, *Dorcas*; *Woman in Missions*; Bennett, "How It Grew"; Brown, *One Hundred Years*, 113-57; Scrapbook 62. See also "A Historical Sketch of the Board of Home Missions of the Presbyterian Church in the United States of America, 1802-1888," pamphlet (ca. 1889):17-23.

9. First Annual Report, Ladies' Board, January 1872, MF 2, reel 1, "Annual Reports, 1871-1923."

10. Minutes, Ladies' Board of New York, MF 1, reel 1, "Minutes, 1876-1914."

11. *GAM* 1874:80. All *GAM* in this chapter are from the USA church unless otherwise noted.

12. Scrapbook 62:135. Scovel, "Woman's Executive Committee."

13. *GAM* 1875:489.

14. Ibid. See also "A Historical Sketch of the Board of Home Missions," 17.

15. *GAM* 1875:489. See also "Women's Work in the Synods and Presbyteries," Scrapbook 62. This anonymous clipping lists organizations in the Synods of Erie, Albany, Wisconsin, Pittsburgh, and Harrisburg. Several presbyteries were also listed.

16. *GAM* 1876:31.

17. *GAM* 1877:512.

18. Cornelia W. Martin to Sheldon Jackson, 26 June 1875. SJ Correspondence.

19. Hayes, *Dorcas*: 64-65.

20. *First Report, New Mexico, Arizona and Colorado Missionary Association* (New York, 1869):1.

21. Clifford Merrill Drury, *Presbyterian Panorama* (Philadelphia, 1972), p. 191. The General Assembly transferred to the Home Board all responsibility for work among Indians in the English language in 1884.

22. "One Decade," *HMM* 3 (January 1889):52.

23. Robert Laird Stewart, *Sheldon Jackson* (New York, 1908):277.

24. Alvin Keith Bailey, "The Strategy of Sheldon Jackson in Opening the West for National Missions 1860-1880" (Ph.D. dissertation, Yale University, 1948), 381.

25. "Woman's Work for Missions," *RMP* (November 1872). SJ.

26. Bailey, "Sheldon Jackson," 386.

27. Julia M. Graham to Sheldon Jackson, 5 January 1874. SJ Correspondence.

28. Bailey, "Sheldon Jackson," 386.

29. Sheldon Jackson to Mrs. Haines, 4 July 1878, RG 51-1-2. Undeniably he was far more enthusiastic for national missions.

30. Stewart, *Sheldon Jackson*, 257-60.

31. Ibid., 273. See also Emily J. Paxton to Sheldon Jackson, 21 November 1905, RG 51-1. The women undoubtedly had been influenced in part by a strongly worded circular sent by Frank F. Ellinwood, secretary of the Foreign Board, to Woman's Foreign Mission Societies in January 1878. Distributed among churches in Pennsylvania and New Jersey, where Jackson had been advertised to address a series of meetings, Ellinwood said, among many other things, "I shall assume, what you and all our intelligent ladies know, viz: that the *chief* aim of this movement is to make a break in woman's work for [heathen] women." Circular sent 1 January 1878, in *Presbyterian Pioneer Missions*, 229: hereafter cited as *PPM. SJ*.

32. Melissa P. Dodge to Mrs. W. N. Paxton, 15 May 1878. SJ Correspondence.

33. Mrs. Arch McCoure to Sheldon Jackson, 9 May 1878. SJ Correspondence.

34. Scrapbook 62:116-17. Written in 1876.

35. Julia B. Kendall to Sheldon Jackson, 16 May 1878. SJ Correspondence.

36. *Presbyterian Monthly Record* 25 (November 1874):326.

37. Scrapbook 62:1.

38. H. Kendall to Sheldon Jackson, 30 August 1875. In *PPM*:697-98.

39. *GAM* 1877:513.

40. Ibid.

41. Ibid.

42. *GAM* 1875:489.

43. *GAM* 1877:512.

44. Scrapbook 62:108.

45. *WWW* 8 (January 1878):9.

46. Ibid., 9-14.

47. Sheldon Jackson to Mrs. F. E. H. Haines, 4 July 1878, RG 51-1-2.

48. SJ Correspondence, MSS VIII, May 1878:60-69. At this Assembly, commissioners approved a statement that "it is suicidal to foster the idea that there is any radical distinction between the two great departments of mission work" and recommended that pastors present to the women the principles and the history of women's groups and secure "harmony of method." *GAM* 1878:110.

49. RG 51-1-2. Also in Scrapbook 62. A letter to Jackson from Emily Paxton in RG 51-1, written in 1905, attempted to reconstruct the events. A private group met the night before to plan the conference, draw up the constitution, and select the officers to be nominated. This group included Dr. and Mrs. Kendall, Myra Scovel, Mrs. William Thaw, Mrs. Oscar E. Boyd, Paxton, and Jackson.

50. *PPM*: 75-76. F. E. H. Haines to Sheldon Jackson, 27 June 1878, RG 51-1-2.

51. Jackson to Haines, 4 July 1878.

52. Scovel, "History":137.

53. Ibid.

54. Ibid.

55. Ibid.

56. Julia McNair Wright to Sheldon Jackson, 1 August 1878. *PPM*:82-83.

57. Scovel, "History":138.

58. Ibid.

59. Hayes, *Dorcas*: 79-81.

60. "One Decade," 53. Minutes, Monthly Meeting, Ladies' Board, 16 December 1879, MF 1, reel 1.

61. *GAM* 1879:593.

62. SJ Correspondence, May 1878.

63. Ninth Annual Meeting Report, Ladies' Board, MF 1, reel 1.

64. Rev. Robert W. Patterson, D.D., "Woman's Work for Woman," *The Interior*, 25 November 1880; "Woman's Work for Woman," by H. Kendall, D.D., 22-24, and R. W. Patterson, "Woman's Work for Woman Once More," 54-56 (both clippings in SJ Scrapbook, 24-25).

65. "Woman's Work for Woman," SJ Scrapbook, 56-57.

66. The following summaries are taken from an examination of reports of the woman's boards, on microfilm (PHS): the reading of *Our Mission Field* and *Woman's Work for Woman*, and some helpful books, including, among others, Brown's *One Hundred Years*, pp. 113-57, and Hayes, *Dorcas*, 53-58. Also helpful were two unpublished manuscripts on the history of women's mission work: one by Mrs. Hareen, written in 1944 and one by Mary W. (Mrs. Halsey L.) Wood, n.d. Periodical articles useful were Mrs. William E. Waters, "Fifty Years of Women's Work for Missions," *The Continent*, 13 May 1920:649-50, 659, and "History of the Ladies' Board of Home and Foreign Missions," *Our Mission Field* (July 1879):61-64.

67. First Annual Report, MF 2, reel 1, Annual Reports 1871-1923.

68. Hareen, 8.

69. Brown, *One Hundred Years*, 122.

70. Ibid., 123.

71. Ibid., 122. Quoted from Mrs. W. C. Perkins, "The Story of Twenty-five Years."

72. Ibid., 124-25.

73. Ibid., 129.

74. Ibid., 130. See also Mrs. J. W. Allen, "Historical Sketch of the Woman's Presbyterian Board of Missions of the Southwest, 1877-1892," p. 1. Quoting J. J. Marks in an article in the *St. Louis Evangelist*. This historical sketch gives a good summary of this particular Board's work, RG 81-40-17.

75. The information on the UPNA women's association is from Wallace Newlin Jamison, *The United Presbyterian Story* (Pittsburgh, 1958), pp. 163-74; Evlyn Fulton, "A Brief History of the WGNS of the UPCNA," *Concern* (February 1977):10; a paper read by Mrs. B. T. Leitch at the Allegheny Presbyterial Association and published in *The Women's Missionary Magazine* 3 (August 1889):142-47; and Annie R. Herron, "Foreign Missions and the Women's General Missionary Society," *Foreign Missionary Jubilee Convention of the United Presbyterian Church of North America*, Pittsburgh, December 6-8, 1904, pp. 232-35, 237.

76. Leitch, 143.

77. Ibid.

78. Ibid., 144.

79. Ibid.

80. The following is from Ben M. Barrus, Milton L. Baughn, and Thomas H. Campbell, *A People Called Cumberland Presbyterians: A History of the Cumberland Church* (Memphis, 1972), pp. 173-75.

81. Cumberland *GAM* 1881:52-53.

Chapter 3: Woman's Boards

1. M. Katharine Bennett, "The Past a Promise for the Future," 106-7.

2. The materials in this section are drawn chiefly from primary sources in the Records Groups 51 and 105, PHS, and from reading through issues of the *Home Mission Monthly (HMM), Our Mission Field (OMF)*, and *Woman's Work for Woman (WWW)*. Specific references will be cited as needed. The women conscientiously kept records and preserved written materials. Various "histories" were written or typed, some with neither date nor author listed. Katharine Bennett (the most reliable observer since her leadership carried her through the WEC, the Woman's Board, and the reorganization) wrote several such histories. Her "A Fiftieth Anniversary" (1920) was particularly helpful; hereafter cited as "A Fiftieth Anniversary."

3. Bennett, "How It Grew," 35. These charges continued until the dissolution of the Woman's Board in 1923, with overtures, letters, and articles suggesting that the women were not only setting up an independent agency but also diverting their gifts from the regular budget of the church. See, for example, an overture to General Assembly, PCUSA, from the Presbytery of Madison (Wisconsin), April 16, 1912, RG 105-9-32; letter from Cora Lee (Mrs. Bion B.) Williams, president, Woman's Missionary Society of Redstone Presbytery of the Synod of Pennsylvania, to Mrs. F. S. Bennett, 30 March 1920, RG 105-9-32.

4. The "Appreciation" is in RG 105-6. "Where Does the Fault Lie?" *WWW* 13 (December 1883):425-26. George E. Hunt, a presbyter of Madison Presbytery, wrote George F. McAfee, 26 April 1912, complaining of "recent tactics in this neck o'the woods." He admitted that he did not think the Woman's Board was to blame. "Fancy it is a local movement." He cited instances of loss of revenue and accused the women of "unfortunate discrimination against the 'Men's Boards.' " He claimed to have tried to reason with some of the women, but they thought it was the policy of headquarters; besides, they were sure "that the men should take care of their own affairs, leaving the women to do the same." The official statements of the Woman's Board did not support the ideas of these women about how the women at headquarters felt.

5. Rev. F. F. Ellinwood, D.D., "Address Delivered at the General Meeting of Woman's Missionary Boards, at Cincinnati, May, 1885," *WWW* 1 (January 1885):5-8.

6. Manuscript. A typed history of the Presbyterian Women's Foreign Missionary societies by Mrs. Hareen, 1944. See also, a similar typed history by Mary F. Wood (Mrs. Halsey L.), the second general secretary of the Central Committee (n.p., n.d.), RG 81-50-17. See also Hayes, *Dorcas*, and Brown, *One Hundred Years*.

7. Mrs. A. E. Arnold, "The Power of Woman," *HMM* 4 (April 1890):131. (Italics hers). Full records of the WEC are located in the PHS archives.

8. Elizabeth Osborn Thompson, *Woman's Board of Home Missions: A Short History* (New York, n.d. [ca. 1922]), pp. 5-6. Hereafter cited as *A Short History*.

9. *A Short History*, p. 25. There was some confusion on the exact date James took over as president. Mabel M. Sheibley, secretary for education and publicity of the Board of National Missions, after some research thought the date should be 1886. Mabel M. Sheibley to Mrs. F. S. Bennett, 28 December 1943 and 14 January 1944, RG 101-18-11.

10. Hayes, *Dorcas*, 108. Issues of the *HMM* have copious information on this subject.

11. Hayes, *Dorcas*, 107-9. The political behavior of the officers of the WEC is an area that should be explored. Besides their stand on Mormonism, the women petitioned the President to appoint honest men to Indian affairs, to supply food to starving Indians, to apportion money for a reservoir to supply Pima Indians with water for irrigation. Although most evidence shows the churchwomen to be keeping to their "sphere" in the church courts, these incidents demonstrate a profound political energy despite disenfranchisement in government and church.

12. Emeline G. Pierson to Mrs. T. C. Hamlin, 10 April 1900, RG 51-4-17.

13. Mary E. James to Sheldon Jackson, 11 December (no year listed), RG 51-1-2. The office of Superintendent of Schools began in 1893. The work had become so demanding that a person was needed to devote full-time to the school work, visit the fields, and preach. This person related both to the BHM and the WEC, but the WEC paid his salary. Superintendents were Rev. George F. McAfee, 1883-1905; Rev. Robert M. Craig, 1905-1908; Dr. David R. Boyd, 1908-1912; Marshall C. Allaben, 1912-1920; Edna R. Voss, 1920-1923. *A Short History*, 26. "A Fiftieth Anniversary," 18-19.

14. The first officers were Mrs. Ashbel Green, president; Myra (Mrs. S.F.) Scovel and Mrs. J. B. Dunn, vice-presidents; F. E. H. (Mrs. Richard) Haines and Mrs. A. R. Walsh, corresponding secretaries; Mrs. J. D. Bedle, recording secretary; Mrs. O. E. Boyd, treasurer. Julia (Mrs. J. L.) Graham was nominated for vice-president but declined after consultation with the Ladies' Board because of her position on that Board.

15. *GAM* 1890:43.

16. See chapter 1.

17. F. E. Haines to Mrs. C. L. Garleck, Youngstown, Ohio, 19 February 1881, RG 105-2-7.

18. F. E. Haines to Mrs. Rebecca Hyatt, Cambridge, Ohio, 25 February 1881, RG 105-2-7.

19. Hayes, *Dorcas*, 95.

20. Ibid., 102.

21. *HMM* 1 (18 January 1887):52-53; 58.

22. The Ladies' Board transferred its home work to the Synodical Committee of New York on April 18, 1883. (Ladies' Board, Annual Report, 1883).

23. "Report of the Woman's Executive Committee of Home Missions, March 31st 1883 To the Board of Home Missions of the Presbyterian Church in the United States of America." Handwritten report, RG 105-1-9.

24. "Report of the Freedmen Department of the Woman's Executive Committee of Home Missions, Mrs. C. E. Coulter, Cor. Sec'y, Pittsburgh, Pa., March 31, 1885," RG 51-1-7.

25. "How to Organize a Home Missionary Society," n.d. Filed in 1881 folder, RG 105-2-7.

26. "How to Hold a Home Missionary Meeting," n.d. Filed in 1881 folder, RG 105-2-7.

27. "To Members of Synod Com[tees] of Home-Missions," n.d., RG 105-2-5.

28. The magazine had only two editors in its history: Mrs. D. E. Finks (1886-

1911) was succeeded by her daughter, Theodora Finks. Issues are available at PHS and on microfilm. Biographies of these two women are in RG 101-18-11.

29. *HMM* 1 (February 1887):89-90.

30. Ibid., 1 (December 1887):18.

31. Mrs. S. H. McMullin to her Sisters in Ohio, 15 November 1882.

32. *HMM* 1 (May 1887):158.

33. Ibid. (June 1887):181.

34. Ibid.

35. Ibid. (July 1887):192.

36. Ibid. 192-97.

37. *HMM* 2 (December 1887).

38. "Diagram of the Plan of Work of the Woman's Executive Committee," *HMM* 2 (February 1888):88-89.

39. "Copy of the Paper read by Mrs. Wm. M. Ferry of Park City, Utah before the Presbyterian Teachers Convention, assembled at Monti, Utah Aug 26th 1887." Handwritten, RG 51-1-5.

40. Ibid., 9.

41. "To Our Missionary Teachers." Typescript, n.d., RG 51-1-5.

42. Handwritten. Signed by S. B. Brownell, rec. sec., 12 December 1889, RG 51-1-7.

43. Ibid.

44. Typescript of Report presented to the BHM, 24 December 1889 and referred to Woman's Executive Committee. Attested by O. E. Boyd, Rec. Sec., RG 51-1-24.

45. Typescript of Rules adopted by Board of Home Missions, 25 February 1890. Attested by O. E. Boyd, Rec. Sec., RG 51-1-25.

46. *GAM* 1890:43.

47. The missionary box program was dropped in 1912. It formed a large part of women's activities in the nineteenth century, but as the church began to pay better salaries and as mail-order houses opened, the need for such diminished. *A Short History*, 6.

48. *GAM* 1892:82.

49. Typescript. "Young People's." RG 105-10-6. The secretaries for Young People's Work were E. M. Wishard (1893-1896), M. Katharine Jones (later Katharine Bennett) (1896-1898), and M. Josephine Petrie (1898-1920).

50. Ibid. and *A Short History*, 6-7.

51. "Young People's."

52. Ibid.

53. Typescript. "The Woman's Board of Home Missions and Work Among Immigrants" by M. Katharine Bennett. Dated by hand in upper right corner of first page, 1914, RG 105-9-32.

54. *GAM* 1895:45.

55. Quoted in "Work Among Immigrants," 3-4.

56. Ibid., 4.

57. Typescript, "Policy Concerning Work Among Foreign Speaking People. Adopted March 9, 1920," RG 105-9-32.

58. *GAM* 1898:234. Although funds seemed uppermost in the reports, spiritual exercises were not neglected.

59. Ibid.

60. *GAM* 1899:220.

61. "Report of Standing Committee on Home Missions," *GAM* 1902:60.

62. *GAM* 1903:73.

63. "Report of Standing Committee on Home Missions," *GAM* 1908:329.

64. Verdesi, *In But Still Out*, 65.

65. *GAM* 1910:363-64.

66. Ibid.

67. "Standing Rules of the Woman's Board of Home Missions of the PCUSA. Adopted June Nineteen Hundred and Ten." Pamphlet, RG 105-1-2.

68. The following is put together from various documents of the period, but particularly from Katharine Bennett's "Detailed Statement Made to the Woman's Board of Home Missions, March 2, 1915, Regarding the Incorporation of Said Board." Typescript. Also very useful was a report by letter of the first committee set up to study the issue, submitted by Mrs. S. P. Harbison, Mrs. S. B. Brownell, and Mrs. M. V. Richards on May 6, 1911. Materials on incorporation are in RG 105-6-7 through 14.

69. "Detailed Statement," 2.

70. Letter from the Committee to "Madame President & Sisters," 16 May 1911, RG 105-6-7.

71. J. E. MacCloskey, Jr. to Mrs. S. P. Harbison, 17 February 1911, RG 105-6-7.

72. John E. Parsons to Dr. Charles L. Thompson, 9 May 1911, RG 105-6-7.

73. Mrs. D. E. Waid to Committee on Incorporation, 20 July 1911, RG 105-6-7.

74. Ibid.

75. Emma Jo (Mrs. S. P.) Harbison to Mrs. D. E. Waid, 2 August 1911, RG 105-6-7.

76. Agnes M. Mitchell to Mrs. D. E. Waid, 5 September 1911, RG 105-6-7.

77. Eva (Mrs. D. E.) Waid, to Miss [Julia] Fraser, 6 February 1912, RG 105-6-7.

78. Charles L. Thompson to Mrs. D. E. Waid, 16 October 1911. The plan called for a membership on the Board of twenty men and ten women, RG 105-6-7.

79. M. Katharine Bennett, "Relation of the Woman's Board of Home Missions to the Board of Home Missions." Dated by hand: Received Feb. 14, 1912, RG 105-6-8.

80. Ibid., 3.

81. Typescript, "Statement Made by Mrs. F. S. Bennett, President in re Incorporation of the Woman's Board of Home Missions," 2 June 1914, RG 105-6-9. An excerpt from a letter to Mrs. M. W. Wood, secretary for Specific Work of the Board, from Marian Hall Blackburn of the Albany Presbyterial Society, 28 September 1912, indicates that their organization had been involved in a drawn-out court case apparently over a challenged legacy. This woman wanted their presbyterial to incorporate so that they might receive and be credited with legacies with no fear of litigation; surely, the national Board had even more reason to need to do so.

82. "Memorandum of Mrs. Bennett's Statement to the Woman's Board, 2 March 1915. Regarding the Incorporation of the Woman's Board," Typescript, RG 105-6-10.

83. Ibid., 1.

84. Letter attesting this, with extract from the Minutes included, from John Dixon, Clerk of the Board, to Edith Grier Long of the Woman's Board, dated September 18, 1914, RG 105-6-9.

85. Edith Grier Long to Mrs. F. S. Bennett, 25 September 1914, RG 105-6-9.

86. Ibid., 2.

87. "Detailed Statement," 2.

88. A. W. Halsey to the Executive Council, New York, 30 August 1915, RG 81-40-19.

89. Verdesi, *In But Still Out*, 70.

90. This phrase occurs occasionally in the minutes and reports of the women's Boards. None of the official documents include arguments for or against various issues but only allude to the attitudes of the women. Most of the reports and minutes deal with the specifics of mission work and occasionally with a restatement of women's responsibilities such as in the Sixth Annual Report of the Woman's Board of Foreign Missions of the Southwest, 1883, MF 3, "Annual Reports 1883-1905."

91. A full report of this committee's charge and report is in the "Thirteenth Annual Report of the Ladies' Board of Missions," 1883, MF 2, reel 1, Woman's Board of Foreign Missions, Annual Reports, 1871-1923. Hereafter cited as "Annual Reports, WBFM," with year and microfilm reference.

92. *OMF* (February 1883):288. Other Boards gave up home mission projects by the end of the century.

93. In 1908, this group, the Woman's Presbyterian Foreign Missionary Society of Northern New York, voted to unite with the New York Board.

94. Report of Saratoga Conference, May 23, 1884, MF 1, reel 1, Records and Minutes, Woman's Board of Foreign Missions, 1876-1914. Hereafter cited as "Records and Minutes," with year and microfilm reference. The Central Committee also published *Children's Work for Children*, which later merged with the children's publication of the Woman's Home Board and became *Over Sea and Land*.

95. Mabel M. Roys, "Happy Birthday to You!" *W&M* (May 1945):36.

96. Ibid., 36 and Mrs. Hareen, History, 23.

97. "Jubilee Address by Mrs. Henry N. Beers," Annual Reports, 1895, MF 2, reel 1.

98. Annual Reports, 1887, MF 2, reel 1.

99. "Jubilee Address," 1895, MF 2, reel 1.

100. Annual Reports, 1909, 1921. MF 2, reel 1.

101. Annual Reports, 1909, MF 2, reel 2.

102. Roys, "Happy Birthday," 36.

103. Advertisement, *New Era*, 1920.

104. Margaret E. Hodge to Dr. White [Rev. Stanley White], 10 November 1919, RG 81-40-19. The letter reporting the recommendation of the Board of the Northwest to Robert E. Speer, Secretary of the BFM, was from Alice Wood Coy, 25 March 1919, RG 81-40-19. Speer had to convince at least one woman that the idea had not come from the male Board. Speer to Miss A. M. Davison, 15 April 1919, RG 81-40-19. The details of the negotiations, planning sessions, and consultations are in RG 81-40-19 and contain the minutiae of consolidation and restructuring.

105. Annual Reports, 1921, MF 2, reel 2.

106. Annual Reports, 1922, MF 2, reel 2.

Chapter 4: Reorganization Controversies

1. *Forty-Third Annual Report of the Woman's Home Board*, 1922, pp. 6-7; *Eighty-fifth Annual Report of the Board of Foreign Missions*, 1922, pp. 18-19; and Bennett, Katharine, and Hodge, Margaret, *Causes of Unrest Among Women of the Church* (Philadelphia, 1927), p. 19.

2. "General Council Minutes," 15 May 1934, pp. 28-42.

3. *Causes of Unrest*, p. 18.

4. Ellen Louderbaugh to Robert E. Speer, 31 March 1931.

5. Katharine Bennett, "Why These Overtures?" *The Presbyterian Magazine*, December 1929:624.

6. Esther B. Strong, "That 'Younger Generation' of College Women," *Women and Missions*, September 1937:195-96. Hereafter cited as *W&M*.

7. Interview, Katherine McAfee Parker to Barbara Roche, 1973, #5, pp. 26-28.

8. "The Woman's Society of the First Presbyterian Church of Berkeley, California," Program Booklet for 1927-28. This is typical of many other similar booklets in the PHS archives.

9. "Conference of Fifteen," pp. 15-16.

10. In 1933, five synods (Kentucky, Oklahoma, West Virginia, Texas, and Tennessee) sent formal protests to the Board of National Missions and the General Council about budgetary procedures within their bounds. They claimed that the women's budgets were having an adverse effect on general benevolence giving. See also "General Council Minutes," 22 May 1934, pp. 28-42.

11. *GAM(USA)* 1923, I:58-188. See also Clifford M. Drury, *Presbyterian Panorama*, pp. 225-32.

12. John Timothy Stone to Cleland B. McAfee, 2 April 1931. According to an editorial in the *Illinois Presbyterian News-letter*, March 1931:5, the Stone Committee wanted the presbyterial and synodical groups to be purely "educational and inspirational" and to make the financial aspects part of the unified budget. "But the prejudice of fixed groups seemed too strong, and a compromise was made."

13. *GAM(USA)* 1923, I:111.

14. Ibid., 126.

15. The General Assembly later provided for three women to serve on the General Council with full voting rights. *GAM(USA)* 1932, I: 213. Women on the Board of Foreign Missions were unhappy that their Woman's Committee was made a subcommittee of the Home Base Committee rather than having independent status as was the case in National Missions. Margaret Hodge complained that the chairman of the Home Base Committee never attended their meetings and only perfunctorily reviewed their minutes. The Woman's Committee could not make any policy decisions without Home Base approval. Margaret Hodge to Cleland B. McAfee, 15 August 1934.

16. *The Presbyterian Banner*, 8 June 1922:8.

17. Margaret Hodge, "Votes for Women," *Women's Work for Missions*, January 1923:89-90.

18. These and similar letters are found in PHS archives, Record Group 121-7.

19. See Stone Committee correspondence in PHS archives, Record Group 81,

especially boxes 7 and 8. Much of the correspondence focused on protecting the home mission work.

20. *GAM(USA)* 1923, I:131. The motion to have women represented on the Board of Christian Education came from the assembly floor and was made by Joseph W. Cochran, who had previously served as corresponding secretary of the Board of Education. See *GAM(USA)* 1922, I:145.

21. Ellen Louderbaugh to Robert E. Speer, 31 March 1931.

22. Ella Rogers to Lucy Dawson, 23 February 1926.

23. Margaret Hodge to Robert E. Speer, 23 January 1929.

24. "Comments Received during the Syllabus Controversy," 1931, p. 6, RG 81-41-19. These comments were printed without any title and represented a cross-section of women and men responding to the issue of including Christian education in the women's budget. Hereafter cited as "Comments."

25. *Causes of Unrest*, pp. 13-14.

26. *Second Annual Report of the Board of Christian Education*, 1925, p. 8, and Josephine Petrie to Katharine Bennett, 6 June 1923.

27. *First Annual Report of the Board of Christian Education*, 1924, p. 7.

28. *The Continent*, 10 December 1925:2. In *The Presbyterian Advance*, 20 December 1928, back cover, the advertisement concluded: "The Board of Christian Education depends entirely on receipts through the church budgets. It has no auxiliary organization of women."

29. Katharine Bennett to Margaret Hodge, 28 February 1925.

30. Katharine Bennett to Lucy Dawson, 24 February 1925.

31. The Cincinnati *Enquirer*, 6 December 1924:2; *The Continent*, 31 January 1924:158.

32. A copy of this petition is in RG 81-41. Blinn sent up another petition in 1926. See *GAM(USA)* 1926, I:33. A copy of this petition is in PHS archives, RG 125-6.

33. *GAM(USA)* 1924, I:29.

34. Clarence Macartney to Louise Blinn, 29 July 1924. See also "General Council Minutes," 25 June 1924:10.

35. Katharine Bennett and Margaret Hodge to Synodical and Presbyterial Presidents, 5 April 1924.

36. Gertrude Schultz to Lucy Dawson, 15 April 1926.

37. "Minutes of the Woman's Conference April 29-May 2, 1925," pp. 14-19.

38. "Discussion of the Woman's Conference of the Boards of Missions of a Woman's Organization, April 30-May 1, 1925," pp. 14, 15, and 49, RG 81-41-15.

39. Ibid., 25.

40. Ibid., 45.

41. William C. Covert to Katharine Bennett, 7 October 1925.

42. Cited in "General Council Minutes," 25 May 1932, pp. 42-43.

43. "Comments," p. 14.

44. *Causes of Unrest*, p. 22.

45. "General Council Minutes," 22 February 1928, p. 2.

46. "Conference of Fifteen," pp. 31-42. "My own opinion in the matter has been very clear from the beginning, and I have thought that the women's societies should be left to themselves to do what they think best." Robert E. Speer to Emma De Forest, 16 March 1931.

47. Margaret Hodge to Robert E. Speer, 6 February 1929, and "General Council Minutes," 6 March 1929, p. 4.

48. *Findings of the Conference on Women's Status and Service in the Church* (Philadelphia, 1929), pp. 3-4.

49. *The Presbyterian,* 17 October 1929:13. See also "General Council Minutes," 5 March 1930, pp. 57-59.

50. Gertrude Schultz to Robert E. Speer, 15 May 1931.

51. "Comments," pp. 5-6.

52. "General Council Minutes," 20 November 1929, p. 5.

53. Cleland B. McAfee to Organized Churchwomen, March, 1930. A similar letter was sent out by Lewis S. Mudge on March 18, 1931.

54. Helen Meister to Lewis S. Mudge, 24 January 1931.

55. Gertrude Schultz to Robert E. Speer, 15 May 1931.

56. *Eleventh Annual Report of the Board of Christian Education,* 1934, p. 45.

57. Cleland B. McAfee to Hiram Foulkes, 21 January 1931; Hiram Foulkes to Cleland B. McAfee, 28 January 1931; Cleland B. McAfee to Lewis S. Mudge, 30 January and 5 February 1931.

58. Hiram Foulkes to Ann Elizabeth Taylor, 3 October 1930, and to Lewis S. Mudge, 28 October 1930.

59. Cleland B. McAfee to Lewis S. Mudge, 30 January 1931, and Lewis S. Mudge to Cleland B. McAfee, 4 February 1931.

60. Members of Seattle Presbyterial published an open letter in *The Presbyterian,* 4 June 1931:27. Others sent letters to the General Council and the Committee on Financial Cooperation. Mudge informed Bennett and Hodge through Foulkes that they should take "prompt, firm, and definite steps to bring to an end at once such communications." Lewis S. Mudge to Hiram Foulkes, 30 January 1931.

61. Anonymous to William C. Covert, 12 February 1931.

62. "Report of the Syllabus Correspondence," *W&M,* May 1932:68. See also James E. Clarke, "Women's Relation to the Boards," *The Presbyterian Advance,* 14 April 1932:16.

63. According to Gertrude Schultz, many societies refused to vote, believing that their silence was the best form of protest against procedures followed by General Council. Gertrude Schultz to Robert E. Speer, 15 May 1931.

64. "General Council Minutes," 27 May 1931:38. Mudge said: "There may have been a day when National Missions, Foreign Missions, and Christian education could be thought of as in quite distinct categories. Certainly, if ever this was possible, it is no longer so." Lewis S. Mudge to Robert E. Speer, 15 May 1931.

65. "The Pittsburgh Biennial Meeting," *W&M,* July 1931:124-25.

66. "Notes on a meeting supporting vote on Syllabus," 23 May 1931:2-7.

67. "General Council Minutes," 25 May 1932:46, and "Report of Findings Committee, Third Biennial Meeting of Woman's Missionary Societies, May 22 to 27, 1931," p. 2, RG 81-42-30.

68. "General Council Minutes," 18 November 1931, p. 22.

69. "General Council Minutes," 2 March 1932, pp. 35-47.

70. Katharine Bennett, "On-going Processes," *W&M,* March 1938:416.

71. Margaret Hodge to Lewis S. Mudge, 22 October 1934, and Lewis S. Mudge

to Hiram Foulkes, 4 October 1930. Mudge considered asking General Assembly to take direct action to include Christian education but finally rejected that alternative, fearing that such a step would only exacerbate unrest among women. In his letter to Foulkes, Mudge predicted that women had only one choice for the future: "co-operation or competition."

72. "General Council Minutes," 22 May 1934, p. 2. These actions were supported by Lucia P. Towne, editor of W&M in the 1930s. She frequently featured articles on social issues such as world peace, industrial relations, alcohol and drug abuse, and race relations. Lists of study books always included titles other than the usual missionary publications.

Chapter 5: National Organization

1. For a background of these movements, see Katharine Bennett et al., The Emergence of Interdenominational Organizations Among Protestant Church Women (New York, 1944); Margaret Hummel and Mildred Roe, The Amazing Heritage (Philadelphia, 1970); Margaret Shannon, Just Because (Corte Madera, California, 1977).

2. Report of the Fourteenth Council of the World Alliance, 1933, pp. 188-92.

3. Marcel Pradervand, A Century of Service (Grand Rapids, 1975), pp. 45, 91-95, 123-24.

4. Margaret Hodge to Cleland B. McAfee, 26 March 1935, and Katharine Bennett to Robert E. Speer, 24 March 1938.

5. Louise Blinn to Katharine Bennett and Margaret Hodge, 9 March 1935. Original of the petition is in RG 81-40-17.

6. Margaret Hodge to Cleland B. McAfee and Robert E. Speer, 12 March 1935.

7. Mrs. Samuel D. Wingate to Margaret Hodge, 9 April 1935. Mrs. Wingate was a member of Matthews' congregation.

8. Robert E. Speer to Margaret Hodge, 16 November 1937.

9. W&M, July 1935:114-15.

10. Ibid., July 1938:113-15 and February 1939:390.

11. "Minutes of the First Meeting of the National Council of Women's Organizations of the Presbyterian Church, U.S.A.," 23 September 1942, p. 2.

12. W&M, September 1943:148.

13. Elizabeth Engler to Mary Amelia Steer, 11 November 1940.

14. W&M, October 1943:182; January 1947:3; and GAM(USA) 1956, I:551.

15. William B. Pugh to Katharine Strock, 24 March 1942.

16. Interview, Katherine McAfee Parker to Barbara Roche, 1973, #5, pp. 17-18, and Concern Magazine, February 1977:11.

17. Katharine Strock to William B. Pugh, 24 March 1942.

18. "General Council Minutes," 2 March 1943, p. 11.

19. "General Council Minutes," 26 May 1943:17-18.

20. W&M, July-August 1943:116.

21. GAM(USA) 1943, I:278-79.

22. W&M, March 1943:378-79.

23. Hummel and Roe, The Amazing Heritage, 80-84.

24. Katharine Bennett to Gertrude Berbey, 6 December 1943.

25. *GAM*(USA) 1945, I:122-23.

26. *The Christian Century*, 11 June 1947:735-36.

27. *GAM*(USA) 1954, I:91.

28. Ibid., 90-91.

29. *W&M*, July 1942:117.

30. *GAM*(USA) 1955, I:75-76.

31. Inez Moser, "Our High Calling," *W&M*, July-August 1943:109.

32. *GAM*(USA) 1954, I:94 and 1955:45.

33. *W&M*, 1 August 1931:190.

34. Marian Clements to William B. Pugh, 30 December 1949. Correspondence between Oxnam and Ocean Grove officials is in RG 122-3-6, PHS.

35. UPW reports in the 1950s give details of the various leadership opportunities for women. In 1953, for example, more than 1,500 women attended leadership schools sponsored by the three national boards. *GAM*(USA) 1953, I:92-93.

36. *GAM*(USA) 1949, I:46.

37. *GAM*(UPUSA) 1959, I:128. The blending of the two denominations seems to have been worked out with a minimum of friction. Some of the UPNA congregations were reluctant to give up their missionary society emphasis but apparently there were no significant defections or controversies over this issue.

38. *GAM*(UPUSA) 1958, I:262.

Chapter 6: Questioning Women's Role

1. John Calvin, *Commentaries on the First Book of Moses Called Genesis*, vol. 1 (Grand Rapids, 1948), pp. 129-30 and *The First Epistle of Paul the Apostle to the Corinthians* (Grand Rapids, 1960), p. 233. See also Georgia Harkness, *John Calvin: The Man and His Ethics* (New York, 1958), pp. 154-56 and T. H. L. Parker, *John Calvin: A Biography* (Philadelphia, 1975), pp. 101-3.

2. Albert Barnes, *Notes Explanatory and Practical on the Epistles of Paul to the Corinthians* (London, 1837), p. 189.

3. *The Presbyterian*, 2 March 1872:2. Signed H.J.V.

4. *Case of the Rev. E. R. Craven Against The Rev. I. M. See, in the Presbytery of Newark and The Synod of New Jersey*. General Assembly Study Document, p. 13. Hereafter cited as *Case*.

5. J. F. Stearns, *Female Influence, and the True Christian Mode of Its Exercise* (Newburyport, Mass., 1837), p. 20.

6. "The Woman Question," *The Presbyterian*, 21 April 1877:1. Charles G. Finney's revival in Utica, New York, occurred in 1826, but its relation to this incident is not determined.

7. Charles C. Cole, Jr., "The New Lebanon Convention," *New York History* 31 (1950):385-97 and Page Putnam Miller, "The Evolving Role of Women in the Presbyterian Church in the Early Nineteenth Century" (Ph.D. dissertation, University of Maryland, 1979), pp. 76-80.

8. James M. Moorhead, "Social Reform and the Divided Conscience of Antebellum Protestantism," *Church History*, 48 (December 1979):423.

9. *GAM* 1832:378. See the report of the Assembly meeting in two issues of the *Presbyterian* (18 June 1832 and 20 June 1832) and "Pastoral Letter," *GAM* 1832. In

1831, the General Synod of the Dutch Reformed Church issued a deliverance against the introduction of women as leaders in public assemblies of the Church. In a Pastoral Letter, ordered to be read in every pulpit of the church in America, a sentence read, "We witness with pain, in some parts of the Christian Church, the introduction of females to lead the devotions of a *promiscuous* assembly, a practice which we believe to be not only contrary to the word of God, but ruinous to the benign and permanent influence of pious females in the Church of Christ." *The Presbyterian,* 16 November 1872. Eleven years later, the Ohio Synod of the Reformed Church formally disapproved of women praying aloud in promiscuous assemblies or prayer meetings. "Woman Preaching Viewed in the Light of God's Work and Church History," *Reformed Quarterly Review* 29 (January 1882):124.

10. "Minutes of Presbytery of North River," 19 April 1836 and 20 September 1836.

11. *The Presbyterian Magazine* 1 (1851):181-82.

12. Ibid. 2 (1852):303.

13. Ronald W. Hogeland, "Charles Hodge, The Association of Gentlemen and Ornamental Womanhood: A Study of Male Conventional Wisdom 1825-1855," *Journal of Presbyterian History* 53 (Fall 1975):239-55.

14. This admonition fit with the domestic character of "woman's sphere." Orators and writers usually defined women's roles in terms of the married or to-be-married. The eventual broadening of woman's sphere to include the freedom of education and associations presumed that these activities were linked to improving the woman's function as a wife and mother to a large extent.

15. Charles Grandison Finney, *Revivals of Religion,* 2d ed. rev. and ed. William Henry Harding (London, 1913), p. 291.

16. Keith Melder, "Ladies Bountiful: Organized Women's Benevolence in Early 19th-Century America," *New York History* 48 (July 1967):247.

17. Elizabeth Cady Stanton, Susan B. Anthony, Matilda Joslyn Gage, eds., *History of Woman Suffrage,* vol. 1, 1848-1861 (New York, 1969, facsimile; originally published New York, 1881), p. 67.

18. Ibid., 72.

19. From typed pages entitled "From Old Letters and Journals," at Presbyterian Historical Society.

20. "Feminine Oratory," *The Presbyterian* (6 January 1872):8. In 1876, the *Congregationalist* reported the reaction of "one refined and cultivated woman" to a female temperance speaker's behavior in insisting on addressing the General Association. Her opinion: "disgusting!" "The Woman Question," *The Presbyterian,* 24 June 1876:14. In response to a Presbyterian minister's support of women speaking, Augusta Moore admitted that she had both wanted to speak and had spoken but had gone back to Scripture and become concerned that God forbids it. *Congregational Quarterly,* 16 April 1874:279. She was responding to an article by a Presbyterian minister who had tried to get a Presbyterian journal to publish his article but had it refused by all.

21. "Woman's Rights," *The Presbyterian,* 10 February 1849:22.

22. Catherine H. Birney, *Sarah and Angelina Grimke: A Biography* (Boston, 1885):188.

23. William Henry Black, "The Cumberland Presbyterian Church: Its Origins,

Distinctive Features, and the Grounds for Preserving its Denominational Integrity," *Journal of Presbyterian History* 1 (December 1901):193, 200.

24. J. B. Logan, *History of the Cumberland Church in Illinois, Containing Sketches of the First Ministers, Churches, Presbyteries and Synods; also a History of Missions, Publication and Education* (Alton, Illinois, 1878), pp. 136-37, as quoted in Barrus *et al., A People Called Cumberland Presbyterians*, p. 174.

25. *The Presbyterian*, 10 January 1863:2.

26. S. G. Bulfinch, "Priscilla's Preaching," *Monthly Religious Magazine*, 40 (July 1868):18.

27. For a report on nineteenth-century women in the ministry, see Phebe A. Hanaford, "Women Preachers," in *Daughters of America, or Women of the Century* (Augusta, Maine, 1882), pp. 415-76. Occasional articles in *The Presbyterian* reported by name several women preachers in the 1870s from other denominations.

28. "A Woman in the Pulpit," *Harper's Weekly*, 2 March 1872:1.

29. Ibid.

30. Ibid.

31. Ibid.

32. "Encouragement to Christian Women," *The Presbyterian*, 2 March 1872:1.

33. "Protest Against Women in the Pulpit," *The Presbyterian*, 4 May 1872:1.

34. "The Rights of Women in the Church," *The Presbyterian*, 20 June 1874:8.

35. *The Presbyterian*, 6 July 1872:4.

36. "Minutes of the Presbytery of Brooklyn," 12 January 1874 and 26 January 1874. The "Minutes" did not name Smiley, but the Presbyterian *Occident* did, according to an article entitled "Miss Smiley" in the *Herald and Presbyter*, 4 March 1874:4. A "shoulder church" of Lafayette Church, Memorial Church, was also involved in this situation.

37. *Herald and Presbyter*, 4 March 1874:4.

38. Ibid.

39. "Semper Femina Est," *The Presbyterian*, 18 April 1874:4.

40. "Shall Women Pray?," *The Presbyterian*, 20 June 1874:2.

41. Ibid.

42. *The Presbyterian*, 13 June 1874:9.

43. Ibid.

44. "The Woman Question," *The Presbyterian*, 1 August 1874:9.

45. *The Presbyterian*, 27 October 1877:10.

46. Mrs. S. M. Henderson, *Methods and Motives for Enlarged Activity* (Pittsburgh, 1876):4-5.

47. See Lois A. Boyd, "Shall Women Speak?" Confrontation in the Church 1876," *Journal of Presbyterian History* 56 (Winter 1978):281-94 for a full account of this trial.

48. The specifics of the Craven-See case used throughout this portion of the chapter are from the "Minutes of the Presbytery of Newark" for the period of the proceedings, and from the General Assembly Study Document entitled *The Case of the Rev. E. R. Craven against the Rev. I. M. See, in the Presbytery of Newark and the Synod of New Jersey* (see note 4).

49. "Newark Presbytery and Rev. I. M. See," *The Interior*, January 1877:1.

50. Case, 10.

51. *New York Times*, 23 December 1876:4; reprinted in *The Presbyterian*, 6 January 1877:5, and *History of Woman Suffrage*, 780-81. Neither the proceedings nor the presbytery minutes reported on the addresses or discussion; therefore, the newspaper accounts and the women's account must be relied upon.

52. *History of Woman Suffrage*,780-81.

53. *New York Times*, 26 December 1876:4.

54. Ibid.

55. Ibid.

56. Ibid., 28 December 1876, 5.

57. Case, 13.

58. Case, 1.

59. Ibid.

60. Ibid.

61. *New York Times*, 10 February 1877:8.

62. Case, 2.

63. Case, 3.

64. Ibid.

65. Case, 4.

66. *The Presbyterian*, 24 February 1877:1.

67. GAM(USA) 1878:102-3.

68. "Women's Prayer," *WWW* 13 (January 1883):91-92.

Chapter 7: Seeking Official Recognition

1. *The Presbyterian*, 5 June 1880:3.

2. GAM(USA) 1891:139.

3. Lefferts A. Loetscher, *The Broadening Church* (Philadelphia, 1954), pp. 18-39 and Winthrop Hudson, *Religion in America*, 3d ed. (New York, 1981), pp. 267-81.

4. George P. Hays, *May Women Speak?* (Chicago, 1889), p. 85. In the same year, Frances E. Willard wrote *Woman in the Pulpit* (Chicago, 1889) in which she defended the right of women to ordination.

5. Samuel M. Smith reviewed Hays's book in *The Presbyterian Quarterly* IV (1890):152-54. Although Smith disagreed with Hays, he acknowledged that Hays's "distinguished name" would "doubtless secure a wider reading than would otherwise be accorded to the pamphlet."

6. *The Presbyterian*, 15 July 1920:10.

7. "Minutes of the Presbytery of Zanesville" (USA), 14 September 1892.

8. "Minutes of the Presbytery of Baltimore" (USA), 22 April 1896.

9. GAM(USA) 1893:114 and 1896:148. Newspaper accounts of the General Assembly discussions indicate that there was no prolonged discussion over the overtures relating to women. Extensive coverage, however, was given to the Briggs and McGiffert trials and issues relating to biblical criticism. See *The Presbyterian*, 5 July 1893:1.

10. The St. Louis *Observer*, 1 June 1893:9.

11. In the 1870s, for example, the UPNA church debated the propriety of establishing the office of deaconess or female deacon. Although they concluded that there was no scriptural justification for the ordination of women to the office

of deacon, United Presbyterians approved the recognition of "pious women" as "assistants of the Deacon" without ordination provided that they not form "sisterhoods living apart from ordinary society after the manner of certain Popish devotees, or even of some associations found in certain denominations of the Protestant Church." *GAM*(UPNA) 1878:567-68.

12. *The Christian Observer*, 24 May 1916. This was a frequent theme in the latter part of the nineteenth century. For the distinction between deacons (female) and deaconesses, see *The Presbyterian Advance*, 8 June 1920:17.

13. Hudson, *Religion in America*, 297. For an analysis of the deaconess movement in the Methodist Church, see Rosemary Skinner Keller, "The Deaconess Movement: Liberating or Constricting? A Case Study of the Chicago Training School" (Paper presented at the Missouri Valley History Conference, Omaha, Nebraska, March 11, 1978).

14. Alexander T. McGill, "Deaconesses," *The Presbyterian Review* I (1880):268-90. See also Benjamin B. Warfield, "The Deaconess as Part of the Church," *Presbyterian Deaconess Quarterly* I (June 1905):1-3.

15. *The Presbyterian*, 5 June 1880:3.

16. Benjamin B. Warfield, "Presbyterian Deaconesses," *The Presbyterian Review* 10 (1889):287-88.

17. *GAM*(USA) 1890:118-21.

18. *GAM*(USA) 1892:169-70.

19. Ibid., 170. See also *The Presbyterian Journal*, 16 April 1891:242-43 and Joseph F. Jennison, "Deaconesses in the Primitive and Later Church" (Baltimore, 1891), pp. 16-17.

20. *Catalog of the Presbyterian Training School 1912-1913*, pp. 3-5.

21. *Tennent College Bulletin*, 1936, p. 9. See also Elizabeth Verdesi, *In But Still Out*, pp. 117-19.

22. John Richelsen, "Protestant Deaconesses," *The Presbyterian Journal*, 11 April 1889:3.

23. For a modern analysis, see Virginia Lieson Brereton and Christa Ressmeyer Klein, "American Women in Ministry: A History of Protestant Beginning Points," in *Women in American Religion*, Janet Wilson James, ed. (Philadelphia, 1980), pp. 178-80.

24. *GAM*(UPNA) 1906:595 and *GAM*(CP) 1921:200.

25. *GAM*(USA) 1922, I:197-98 and 1923, I:52. The General Assembly amended the *Form of Government* in 1915 to permit the election of women as deaconesses "in a manner similar to that appointed for deacons" with the stipulation that they be under the supervision of local sessions in all aspects of their work" (1915:202).

26. *The United Presbyterian*, 5 April 1894:215 and 10 February 1898:4. Another UPNA woman, Winifred Wirts Dague, was licensed as an evangelist in 1919 by the Presbytery of Cleveland. Her request for ordination in 1920 was denied by the General Assembly. Nevertheless, Dague continued to serve a congregation in Ohio and conducted numerous revivalistic meetings. *The United Presbyterian Magazine*, 26 February 1925:11.

27. The St. Louis *Observer*, 1 June 1893:9.

28. See Willard, *Woman in the Pulpit*, 47.

29. For an excellent survey of the Cumberland Church, see Barrus, *A People Called Cumberland Presbyterians.*
30. *GAM*(CP) 1887:20.
31. Barrus, *Cumberland Presbyterians*, 279-80.
32. The St. Louis *Observer*, 1 June 1893:9.
33. Barrus, *Cumberland Presbyterians*, 279-80.
34. Louisa M. Woosley, *Shall Women Preach? or, The Question Answered* (Caneyville, Kentucky, 1891), p. 95.
35. Ibid., 190.
36. Ibid., 191.
37. Ibid., 194.
38. Ibid., 194-95.
39. Ibid., 195.
40. "Minutes of Nolin Presbytery" (CP), 5 November 1887 and 4 November 1888.
41. Ibid., 4 November 1887 and 7 November 1888.
42. There is a lacuna in the Nolin Presbytery Minutes for 1889. The precise date of Woosley's ordination is not recorded. From her own testimony, however, it was in November 1889. The latter information about Woosley is based on letters from people who knew Woosley personally. See Evelyn B. Crick to Joseph Snider, 11 September 1975 and Robert E. Campbell to Joseph Snider, 21 November 1975.
43. Barrus, *Cumberland Presbyterians*, 280.
44. "Minutes of Nolin Presbytery" (CP), 24 November 1893.
45. *GAM*(CP) 1894:7-9, 22-29. The Assembly rejected another appeal from Nolin Presbytery in 1895, pp. 34-37.
46. The St. Louis *Observer*, 7 June 1894:9.
47. For a good background of this decade, see Aileen Kraditor, *The Ideas of the Woman Suffrage Movement 1890-1920* (New York, 1971), esp. pp. 64-81.
48. Barrus, *Cumberland Presbyterians*, pp. 429-30. For an interesting account of the ordination of another Presbyterian woman, see Sidney Slaton, *Mama Was a Preacher: The Life and Work of the Reverend Mrs. Ada Slaton Bonds* (Memphis, 1971).
49. *GAM*(CP) 1920:114-15.
50. *GAM*(CP) 1921:33 and 200.
51. "Minutes of the Presbytery of Chemung" (USA), 15-16 May 1912. See also the discussion of this in Verdesi, *In But Still Out*, 91-93.
52. "Minutes of the Presbytery of Chemung," 24 September 1918:78-79.
53. "Minutes of the Presbytery of Chemung," 22 April 1919:87.
54. "Minutes of the Synod of New York," 22 October 1919:29-32.
55. *GAM*(USA) 1919, I:267.
56. "Minutes of the Presbytery of Dallas" (USA), 12 April 1919.
57. *The Continent*, 29 May 1919:688.
58. *The Presbyterian Banner*, 15 May 1919:3.
59. *The Presbyterian Advance*, 29 May 1919 and *The Continent*, 29 May 1919:688.
60. *GAM*(USA) 1919, I:267-68.
61. *The Presbyterian Advance*, 29 May 1919:17.
62. The Philadelphia *Public Ledger*, 24 May 1919:9.

63. Ibid., 9 and *The Continent*, 11 September 1919:1091.

64. *The Presbyterian Advance*, 29 May 1919:17. A substitute motion offered by U. S. Bartz proposing that presbyteries be overtured to see if they wished to have women ordained as ministers and elders was overwhelmingly defeated. *The Continent*, 29 May 1919:688.

65. *GAM(USA)* 1920, I: 126.

66. Ibid., 126-28.

67. Ibid., 131.

68. *The Continent*, 3 June 1920:798.

69. *The Presbyterian*, 20 May 1920:2. Although the *Presbyterian* published articles both pro and con, its editorial commitment clearly was in opposition to the ordination of women. See also 23 September 1920:3-6 and 17 February 1921:6.

70. Benjamin B. Warfield, "Paul on Women Speaking in Church," *The Presbyterian*, 20 May 1920:8-9 and Clarence E. Macartney, "Shall We Ordain Women as Elders and Deacons?" *The Presbyterian*, 13 January 1921:8-9 and 31. Other major articles opposing the ordination of women were: George P. Doneho, "Feminism in the Church," *The Presbyterian*, 20 January 1921:10 and 26; Richard Montgomery, "The Overture on Women and Deaconesses," *The Presbyterian*, 3 February 1921:9; Euclid Philips, "Woman's Place in the Church," *The Presbyterian*, 16 September 1920:10. In defense of female ordination, the major articles were William H. Bates, "Paul (and Others) on Women Speaking in the Church," *The Presbyterian*, 15 July 1920:9-10; F. L. Hitchcock, "The Eldership and Women," *The Presbyterian*, 3 February 1921:10-11; A. Mackenzie Lamb, "The Ecclesiastical Rank of Women," *The Presbyterian*, 9 September 1920:8-9; and J. Wallace MacGowan, "God's Word about Women Speaking in Church," *The Presbyterian*, 15 July 1920:11 and 26. We have examined other Presbyterian periodicals during 1919-1921 (*The Continent*, *The Presbyterian Advance*, and the *Presbyterian Banner*) and have found only a few other editorial comments and letters to the editor bearing on the ordination of women. The issue was not debated as fully as it was later in 1929. In our examination of the periodicals, we could find no articles by S. Hall Young except one reply to a letter to the editor in the *Continent*, and no articles by women church leaders such as Katharine Bennett and Margaret Hodge, presidents of the Women's Board of Home and Foreign Missions. One pro-letter to the editor appeared in the *Continent*, 4 September 1919:1060. It was written by Julia D. Brainard of Payette, Idaho.

71. Mrs. Blanche Bickens-Lewis, "The Ordination of Women," *The Presbyterian*, 7 October 1920:10. In relevant issues of *Home Mission Monthly*, we found only one reference to the status of women in the church. In a brief paragraph, the action of the 1920 General Assembly was described without comment (July 1920:207). Again, without comment, it reported the defeat of the overture (July 1921:200).

72. *The Presbyterian Banner*, 28 October 1920:7.

73. *The Presbyterian Advance*, 7 April 1921:4. Pittsburgh Presbytery, one of the largest in the denomination, refused to approve the overture because it was not in proper form. *The Presbyterian Banner*, 23 December 1920:6. Grand Rapids Presbytery refused to take action for a similar reason. *The Continent*, 30 September 1920:1210.

74. *The Presbyterian Advance,* 8 June 1920:17; *The Presbyterian,* 3 February 1921:9.

75. *GAM(USA)* 1921, I: 20 and 44.

76. *The Continent,* 28 April 1921:476.

Chapter 8: Challenging Church Policy

1. *Eighty-seventh Annual Report of the Board of Foreign Missions,* 1924:380-98.

2. *The Presbyterian Banner,* 6 February 1919:7.

3. *The Presbyterian Advance,* 9 October 1919:7; *The Presbyterian Banner,* 10 February 1921:18; and *The Presbyterian,* 10 April 1919:17.

4. Lull Martin, "Milady's Occupations," *The Presbyterian Advance,* 9 October 1919:7. Many news items and articles in church papers featured the rising prominence of women in professional business worlds.

5. Bennett and Hodge, *Causes of Unrest,* 18-19.

6. Ibid., 4-5.

7. *GAM(USA)* 1925, I: 88. For a background of this period, see Loetscher, *The Broadening Church,* pp. 90-155.

8. *GAM(USA)* 1926, I: 70.

9. "General Council Minutes," 31 May 1926, p. 11.

10. Katharine Bennett, "Those Restless Women," *The Presbyterian Banner,* 18 April 1929:13.

11. Bennett and Hodge, *Causes of Unrest,* 4-10.

12. Ibid., 9-10.

13. Ibid., 25ff.

14. Ibid., 27.

15. "General Council Minutes," 30 November 1927, p. 26. See also, *GAM(USA)* 1929, I: 186.

16. Bennett and Hodge, "Unrest in the Church" (manuscript), p. 4. The original manuscript is in Record Group #105.

17. "General Council Minutes," 30 November 1927, p. 26.

18. These generalizations are based on an analysis of the correspondence of Speer, Mudge, Bennett, and Hodge in the PHS archives.

19. "General Council Minutes," 22 February 1920, p. 2.

20. A summary of the conference and list of participants can be found in *The Presbyterian Advance,* 8 December 1929:24-25.

21. "Conference of the General Council With Fifteen Representative Women, November 22, 1928," Record Group #105, p. 2. Hereafter cited as "Conference of Fifteen."

22. "Conference of Fifteen," in order of quotation: 10, 11, 13, 12, 9.

23. Ibid., 29.

24. Ibid., 29-30.

25. Ibid., 30.

26. Ibid., 31-34.

27. Lewis S. Mudge to Katharine Bennett, 6 January 1928.

28. Robert E. Speer to Mudge, Bennett, and Hodge, 11 January 1929.

29. Margaret Hodge to Robert E. Speer, 28 January 1929.

30. Katharine Bennett to Robert E. Speer, 5 February 1929. Earlier Bennett had proposed the creation of a third class of representation in addition to ministers and elders "so that women might through gradual training come to participate more largely in the affairs of the denomination." Katharine Bennett to Lewis S. Mudge, 7 February 1928. Mudge was opposed to the idea and argued that it would ultimately work against full equality for women.

31. Lewis S. Mudge to Robert E. Speer, 9 February 1929.

32. Robert E. Speer to Lewis S. Mudge, Katharine Bennett, and Margaret Hodge, 7 February 1929.

33. Lewis S. Mudge to Robert E. Speer, 9 February 1929.

34. There is no verbatim account of this particular meeting in Philadelphia. Our reconstruction of the discussion is based on subsequent letters exchanged among the participants where references to these decisions were made.

35. "General Council Minutes," 6 March 1929, p. 6.

36. Ibid., 7.

37. Margaret Hodge, "Causes of Unrest Among the Women of the Church, Steps Leading To, and the Action by General Council, March 6, 1929," Typescript, n.d. (appears to have been written in April or May, 1929). Hodge attended the meeting of the General Council when the report was given.

38. Mark Matthews to Robert E. Speer, 12 March 1929.

39. "General Council Minutes," 6 March 1929, p. 4.

40. Katharine Bennett to Ann Elizabeth Taylor, 7 March 1929.

41. Lewis S. Mudge to Robert E. Speer, 26 March 1929. The original overtures here cited can be found in *Reports Relating to the Status of Women in the Church for the Information of the Delegates to the Conference of Women, St. Paul, Minnesota, May, 1929* (Philadelphia, 1929), pp. 14-16.

42. *The Presbyterian*, 28 March 1929:5.

43. *The Presbyterian Banner*, 14 March 1929:8.

44. Mark A. Matthews to Robert E. Speer, 12 March 1929.

45. Robert E. Speer to Mark A. Matthews, 25 March 1929.

46. Lewis S. Mudge to Mark A. Matthews, 4 April 1929.

47. Lewis S. Mudge to Paul Hutchinson, 3 April 1929. The editorial appeared in *The Christian Century*, 21 March 1929:379-80.

48. Robert E. Speer to Mark A. Matthews, 17 April 1929.

49. *The Presbyterian*, 2 May 1929:5.

50. *Findings of the Conference on Women's Status and Service in the Church* (Philadelphia, 1929), pp. 3-4.

51. Ibid., p. 4. For a background of this conference, see Katharine Bennett, *Status of Women in the Presbyterian Church in the USA with Reference to Other Denominations* (Philadelphia, 1929), pp. 1-21.

52. "General Council Minutes," 22 May 1929, p. 6.

53. Lewis S. Mudge to William L. Darby, 3 June 1929.

54. "General Council Minutes," 22 May 1929, p. 6.

55. *The Presbyterian Advance*, 10 May 1929:28.

56. *GAM(USA)* 1929, I: 189.

57. Katharine Bennett and Margaret Hodge, "An Open Letter To Presbyterian Women," *W&M*, September 1929:232.

58. *The Presbyterian Banner*, 30 May 1929:10.

59. Representative articles are: Mark A. Matthews, "Why Women in the Pulpit?" *The Presbyterian*, 16 January 1930:7-9; Clarence Macartney, "Shall We Ordain Women as Ministers and Elders?" *The Presbyterian*, 7 November 1929:6-9; and W. Courtland Robinson, "The Unwisdom of Ordaining Women," *The Presbyterian Advance*, 30 January 1930:7.

60. Robert E. Speer, "The Place of Women in the Church," *The Presbyterian Banner*, 18 April 1929:12; Samuel Tyndale Wilson, "Give the Women Full Opportunity," *The Presbyterian Advance*, 30 January 1930:10-11; and Cleland B. McAfee, "Women and Official Church Life," *The Presbyterian Banner*, 16 January 1930:13 and 32.

61. M. Katharine Bennett, "Why These Overtures?" *The Presbyterian Magazine*, December 1929:624; Ella A. Boole, "May Women Speak?" *The Presbyterian*, 17 October 1929:8-9; Margaret E. Hodge, "Woman's Service in the Church," *The Presbyterian Banner*, 25 April 1929:11-12; and Mary Herron Wallace, "A Woman's Reaction: A Woman Speaks Her Mind," *The Presbyterian Banner*, 20 March 1930:11-12.

62. Claude T. Reno to Lewis S. Mudge, 29 November 1930.

63. Robert E. Speer to Mark A. Matthews, 12 May 1930.

64. *GAM(USA)* 1930, I: 48-54.

65. Ibid.

66. Robert E. Speer to Katharine Bennett, 8 May 1929.

67. *W&M*, July 1930:123.

68. "General Council Minutes," 5 March 1930, p. 21.

Chapter 9: Securing Ordination Rights

1. Hudson, *Religion in America*, 3d ed., pp. 357-58, and Robert T. Handy, "The American Religious Depression, 1925-35," *Church History*, 29 (1960):2-16.

2. *The Presbyterian*, 4 June 1931:5.

3. *The Presbyterian Banner*, 12 June 1930:10, and *The Presbyterian Magazine*, July 1930:409. See also Frederick W. Loetscher's optimistic comments about the future of women elders in *The Presbyterian*, 12 February 1931:12.

4. Information Service, "Women's Status in Protestant Churches," *Federal Council of Churches Bulletin*, 16 November 1940:8.

5. "Statement Regarding the Position of Women in the Presbyterian Church," Typescript, 1953:1-2.

6. *Presbyterian Life Magazine*, 15 November 1970:5. Hereafter cited as *Presbyterian Life*. The Cumberland Presbyterian Church reported in 1977 that there were only 429 women elders and that only six women had been elected commissioners to the General Assembly that year. *GAM(CP)* 1978:81.

7. *The Presbyterian*, 2 June 1932:31.

8. Information Service, "Woman's Status in Protestant Churches," *Federal Council of Churches Bulletin*, 16 November 1940:4-5.

9. Ibid., 8. Another Presbyterian report indicated that only 5 percent of the Presbyterian trustees in the country were women. A Presbyterian woman described how a woman who had been elected to the board of trustees resigned because she thought it was "a man's job." Ibid., 12.

10. *Ninth Annual Report of the Board of Christian Education*, 1933, pp. 19-20.

11. *The Presbyterian Banner,* 8 October 1931:31.

12. *The Presbyterian Advance,* 13 March 1930:18, and "Minutes of Presbytery of Wooster," 26 September 1932. See also Lois A. Boyd and R. Douglas Bracken-ridge, "Lena Jennings and Her Unordained Ministry," *A.D. Magazine,* July-August, 1980:15. Hereafter cited as *A.D.*

13. *The Continent,* 3 July 1919:829.

14. The *New York Times,* 19 May 1929:26. See also Louise S. Eby, "Can Women Make Their Way Into The Ministry?" *Christian Education* (June 1929):534-38.

15. *Presbyterian Life,* 7 July 1951:22.

16. Ibid., 1 September 1951:3.

17. "Minutes of Cedar Rapids Presbytery of the United Presbyterian Church of North America," 2 and 4 July 1943, and *GAM*(UPNA) 1944:43.

18. *The Presbyterian,* 13 June 1929:9.

19. Interview, Katherine McAfee Parker to Barbara Roche, 1973, #5, p. 50.

20. *Report of the National Meeting of the Women's Missionary Organizations Buck Hill Falls, Pennsylvania, May 18-25, 1938* (New York, 1938), pp. 100-108.

21. *The Biennial Book: Addresses and Recommendations Made in Asheville, North Carolina, 1935* (New York, 1935), pp. 168-73.

22. *GAM*(USA) 1945, I: 40-41.

23. Ibid., 172.

24. "Report of the Committee on Communication 27 to the General Council," Typescript, 1-3. See also *GAM*(USA) 1946, I: 255-60.

25. *GAM*(USA) 1947, I: 124.

26. Interview, Margaret Shannon Meyers to R. Douglas Brackenridge and Lois A. Boyd, 18 June 1981. Shannon succeeded Gertrude Schultz as Secretary for Women's Work for the Board of Foreign Missions in 1939 and served in that capacity until 1959 when she became Associate General Secretary of the Commission on Ecumenical Relations.

27. PWO Executive Committee Memorandum, Typescript, 10 May 1946 in RG 81. Reference is made in this memo to a note of Lampe's dated 25 January 1946 in which he informed them that he could not invite Uemura to participate.

28. Interview, Margaret Shannon Meyers to R. Douglas Brackenridge and Lois A. Boyd, 18 June 1981.

29. "General Council Minutes," 13 March 1946, pp. 2-3. The editor of *The Presbyterian Tribune* reported some of the details of the General Council meeting (May 1946:6-7), which evoked a response from the General Council. See *The Presbyterian Tribune,* July 1946:3, and November 1946:4.

30. "General Council Minutes," 21 May 1946, p. 6.

31. *GAM*(USA) 1946, I: 187.

32. *The Presbyterian Guardian,* 10 July 1946:204.

33. "Minutes of the Executive Committee of PWO," July 16-19, 1946, p. 15.

34. Georgia Harkness, "Shall Women Be Ordained?" *The Presbyterian,* 15 March 1947:6-7.

35. Mae Ross Taylor, "Why I do Not Wish To Be Ordained," *The Presbyterian,* 5-12 July 1947:8.

36. *GAM*(USA) 1947, I: 129.

37. Lyman Richard Hartley, "Women as Ministers: The Pros and Cons," *New York Times*, 13 April 1947.

38. Interview, Margaret Shannon Meyers to Lois A. Boyd and R. D. Brackenridge, 18 June 1981.

39. Kathleen Bliss, *The Service and Status of Women in the Church* (London, 1952), p. 10. See also Visser 'T Hooft, ed., *The First Assembly of the World Council of Churches*, vol. #5 in the series, *Man's Disorder and God's Design* (New York, 1949), pp. 146-52.

40. "Minutes of the Executive Committee of PWO," 22 May 1947, pp. 28-30.

41. Ibid., 30. See also Inez M. Cavert, *Women In American Church Life* (New York, 1948).

42. *The Christian Century* 69 (May 1956):606-07.

43. Mossie A. Wyker, "Church Women in the Scheme of Things," *Outreach*, February 1954:35.

44. *Information Service*, National Council of Churches, 6 March 1954:1.

45. Mildred McAfee Horton, "Summary of Reports From Denomination Representatives on the Status of Women," Typescript, n.d., pp. 5-6.

46. "Statement Regarding the Position of Women in the Presbyterian Church, U.S.A.," Typescript, n.d., pp. 1-2.

47. Ibid., 3-5.

48. Wyker, "Church Women in the Scheme of Things," 36.

49. Interview, Lilian Hurt Alexander to R. Douglas Brackenridge, 17 June 1981, and "Minutes of the Session of Third Presbyterian Church, Rochester, New York, 13 January 1953.

50. *GAM(USA)* 1953, I: 23-24.

51. *Presbyterian Life*, 16 May 1953:6.

52. Ibid., 27 June 1953:12.

53. *GAM(USA)* 1954, I: 111.

54. *GAM(USA)* 1955, I: 95-98. For a more detailed analysis of the committee's biblical perspectives, see Mary Faith Carson and James H. Price, "The Ordination of Women and the Function of the Bible," *Journal of Presbyterian History* 59 (Summer 1981):249-52.

55. *Presbyterian Life*, 26 November 1955:19-21 and 35-38. For other comments, see 7 January 1956:3-5 and 38, and 4 February 1956:3.

56. "Minutes of the Executive Committee of PWO," 31 May 1955, pp. 11-12. The statement was subsequently published in *Monday Morning Magazine*, August 1955:18-19, and *Presbyterian Life*, 23 July 1955:16-17.

57. Tokuko Inagaki, "On the Ordination of Women in Japan," *Outreach*, February 1956:39-40; Dorothy Foster, "Some Reflections on Ordination for Women," *Outreach*, April 1955:115-16; and Helen C. Woolson, "Shall Women Be Ordained?," *Outreach*, August-September 1955:199-200.

58. *Presbyterian Life*, 17 March 1956:16.

59. Ibid., 9 June 1956:29-30.

60. The UPNA Church approved the ordination of women as deacons in 1906 but rejected a memorial from Cleveland Presbytery in 1920 requesting that women be ordained as ministers and elders. *GAM(UPNA)* 1920:40. The subject did not come up again until 1944 when the Assembly overruled the action of

Cedar Rapids Presbytery in ordaining Elizabeth Brinton Clarke. See *GAM* (UPNA) 1944:43.

61. *Presbyterian Life*, 23 June 1956:9. See also W. W. Mckenney, "Why Rush Union With the U.P. Church?" *Presbyterian Life*, 27 October 1956:26-27.

62. See, for example, Clifford Smith, "Questions Concerning Church Union," *The United Presbyterian*, 4 June 1956:9-10, and Gordon H. Clark, "Does the Bible Forbid the Ordination of Women?," *The United Presbyterian*, 30 December 1956:9-10.

63. Theophilus M. Taylor, "Women and the Christian Ministry," *The United Presbyterian*, 14 October 1956:5-6, and A. H. Baldinger, "Church Union Now," *The United Presbyterian*, 11 September 1956:6 and 21.

64. Personal experience of R. Douglas Brackenridge, pastor, Cross Roads United Presbyterian Church, Washington, Pennsylvania, 1957-60.

65. *Presbyterian Life*, 27 October 1956:18.

66. *Monday Morning Magazine*, August 1955:19.

67. R. Douglas Brackenridge, *Eugene Carson Blake: Prophet with Portfolio* (New York, 1978), pp. 56-76.

68. Eugene Carson Blake to Mossie A. Wyker, 9 March and 16 June 1961.

69. Eugene Carson Blake to Margaret Shannon, n.d. See also Eugene Carson Blake, "The Scripture and the Ministry, Sermon at the Ordination of Miss Wilmina Rowland, November 24, 1957," Typescript, and Interview, Eugene Carson Blake to R. Douglas Brackenridge and Lois A. Boyd, 28 February 1977.

70. *Monday Morning Magazine*, 21 May 1962:7-8.

71. Ibid., 24 September 1956:3-5.

72. Janet G. Harbison, "We The Females," *Presbyterian Life*, 15 June 1958:10-13 and 41-42.

73. Mildred McAfee Horton, "Second Class Citizens or Partners in Policy?," *Presbyterian Life*, 15 June 1958:26-27 and 42.

Chapter 10: Women in Missions

1. Among the most helpful secondary sources for this chapter were R. Pierce Beaver, *All Loves Excelling: American Protestant Women in World Mission* (Grand Rapids, 1968); two books by Arthur Judson Brown, *One Hundred Years: A History of the Foreign Missionary Work of the Presbyterian Church in the U.S.A., With Some Account of Countries, Peoples and the Problems of Modern Missions* (New York, London & Edinburgh, 1936) and *The Foreign Missionary: An Incarnation of the World Movement* (New York, Chicago, Toronto, London & Edinburgh, 1907); Barbara Welter, "She Hath Done What She Could: Protestant Women's Missionary Careers in Nineteenth-Century America," *American Quarterly* 30 (Winter 1978):624-38, reprinted in *Women in American Religion*, ed. Janet Wilson James (Philadelphia, 1980):111-26; "The United Presbyterian Church in Mission: An Historical Overview," *Journal of Presbyterian History* 57 (Fall 1979). Andrew T. Roy compiled "Overseas Mission Policies—an Historical Overview" (186-228), and Everett L. and Margaret T. Perry compiled "New Church Development Policies—an Historical Overview" (229-71). Hereafter cited as "The United Presbyterian Church in Mission."

2. It was in the Hillsboro (Ohio) Presbyterian Church where women met to plan and pray before they ventured on their first procession to the barrooms. The Woman's Christian Temperance Union historian, Helen Tyler, attributed the crusade in part to women's consciousness of their potentialities in peacetime social reforms because of their wartime humanitarian services. Furthermore, she identified the "opening wedges for women in business and the professions" as factors in giving them self-assurance and money of their own for philanthropic purposes. *The WCTU Story: 1874-1949* (Evanston, Ill., 1949):12-17. Various Presbyterian periodicals wrote approvingly of Presbyterian women's activities. One particularly interesting example is entitled "The Arrest of the Women," *Herald and Presbyter* (3 June 1874):4, and describes the arrest of a number of women demonstrating on the street outside a saloon in Cincinnati, including the wife of the minister of the largest Presbyterian Church in town. The writer commended them as a class "who do not make the Church a mere convenience for getting safely to heaven . . . but deem it a duty and a privilege to do what they can for the good of humanity while passing through the world, and they look upon the Church as chiefly designed to fit them for life's work." The crossover between reform and church women's groups has not adequately been addressed, however. Evidence indicates that in mid-century Presbyterian women did much work in autonomous, nonaligned groups. When the denominational women's boards became so large and powerful a part of the church's outreach, many Presbyterians seemed to put most of their time in these activities.

3. Welter, "She Hath Done What She Could," 624.

4. See chapters 1 and 6.

5. Quoted in *HMM* 1 (April 1887):124.

6. One particularly interesting firsthand account of a vow to honor a "call" is described in Marjorie Barnhart's *Prisoners of Hope: A Search for Mission 1815-1822* (Philadelphia, 1980):1. Betsy Beach, later Mrs. Elisha Swift, promised the Lord on January 1, 1815, that she would never "shrink from any known duty" if he would restore health to her parent and grant the family comfortable circumstances. Two years later, she found herself drawn by the young people going out through the ABCFM and "felt strongly urged" to give herself up to the work. After a proposal of marriage, she wrote in diary, "I find it requires a far greater degree of grace to consecrate myself now to the Lord for his service in heathen lands when the opportunity is given than . . . when I had no prospect of the offer." (15) Luckily her leaning toward missionary work was supported by her fiance's commitment to missions.

7. Brown, *The Foreign Missionary*, 13-28, esp. 13-17, 25. Practically speaking, developments in screening, selecting, and preparing candidates, the broadening of work from purely evangelical to educational, medical, and industrial assistance, and the emerging self-interests of the countries themselves led to such a change in missionary motive.

8. Ibid., 67 and Brown, *One Hundred Years,* 67.

9. See chapters 1, 2, and 3.

10. George F. Herrick, *Missionary Herald,* as quoted in *The Church at Home and Abroad* 5 (March 1889):296. A particularly useful document is *The Missionary Wife:*

Her Preparation, Place and Program by Mrs. Charles Kirkland Roys, prepared under the auspices of the Committee of Missionary Preparation, 1923. Roys was a missionary of the BFM in Shantung, China, from 1904-1920. She then assumed an administrative position with the Board.

11. See chapters 2 and 3.

12. R. Anderson to Rev. E. P. Swift, 31 August 1832, RG 31-1-1. The ABCFM was criticized by some for their sending wives; for instance, in 1839 an article in a New York newspaper did not think women should go to Siam. A correspondent writing in *The Presbyterian*, 16 November 1839, strongly supported their going and suggested the critic saw the wife only in terms of comfort to the missionary when indeed she should also be nurturer and teacher of "heathen children." The correspondent, whose initials were S. C., argued for woman's being allowed to labor "for the extension of that system which has done so much for her."

13. Rev. R. M. Mateer in *Ecumenical Missionary Conference*, 2 vols. (New York, 1900), I: 315-16.

14. *First White Women Over the Rockies: Diaries, Letters, and Biographical Sketches of the Six Women of the Oregon Mission Who Made the Overland Journey in 1836 and 1838*. Intro. and ed. Clifford Merrill Drury, 3 vols. (Glendale, 1963).

15. "Roll of Missionaries, 1832-1891," Presbyterian Church in the U.S.A. Handwritten ledger, PHS.

16. One example is Laura Fish Judd. A Finney convert in the Utica Revival of 1826, she married Gerritt Judd, also a convert. She and her husband, a missionary doctor, served in the Sandwich Islands. One of her letters to Lydia Finney is reproduced in "Awakening the Silent Majority: The Changing Role of Women in My Church, Past, Present, Future," a study guide by Mary O'Hara, Auburn Studies in Education, 1975, pp. 25-27. Also see Laura Fish Judd, *Her Life . . . from 1828 to 1861* (1880, reprinted 1928).

17. "The Missionary's Wife," *The Presbyterian*, 23 February 1839:4.

18. "The United Presbyterian Church in Mission," 193, 200.

19. "Qualifications for the Wife of a Missionary," by the wife of a missionary, *Home and Foreign Record* 7 (October 1856):302-5. Hereafter cited as *HFR*.

20. *Church at Home and Abroad* 20 (November 1896):385; Ibid. (July 1896):69. Hereafter cited as *CHA*.

21. See, e.g., *HFR* 5 (September 1854), 281; (October 1854), 312; 10 (October 1859), 307-11; 23 (May 1872), 142-43; 24 (January 1873), 2-3; 27 (July 1876), 197. See also "Awakening the Silent Majority," 25-27.

22. "The Missionary's Wife," *HFR* 24 (May 1873):141-42.

23. *HFR* 27 (July 1876):197.

24. Edward A. Lawrence, *Modern Missions in the East: Their Methods, Successes, and Limitations* (New York, 1895):196-98, 210-13; Mrs. James S. Dennis, "Our Foreign Missionary Women," *CHA* 24 (May 1897):352. II.R. Potter (Mrs. J. L.), "Home Life of Missionary Wives," *WWW* 15 (July 1900):187-88; Mary Schauffler Platt, *The Home with the Open Door: An Agency in Missionary Service* (New York, 1920), p. 5; and many other references in the mission literature.

25. Helen S. C. Nevius (Mrs.), "The Home Life of Missionaries," in *Counsel to New Missionaries: From Older Missionaries of the Presbyterian Church* (New York, 1905), 76.

26. Florence E. Smith, *The Missionary and Work for Women* (New York, n.d.),

5-6. A statement exemplifying the change, "woman's sphere in this world is in the home" to "The *centre* of woman's sphere is in the home," grew out of the experiences of the missionary wives. *CHA* 8 (June 1890), 487.

27. Brown, *The Foreign Missionary*, 127.

28. Quoted in ibid., 127.

29. *Ecumenical Missionary Conference*, I: 315.

30. *Presbyterian Monthly Record* 31 (February 1880):49. Hereafter cited as *PMR*.

31. Ibid., 31.

32. "Sphere of the Missionary Wife," *WWW* 13 (June 1898):148-51. Pearl Buck recalled that her Presbyterian missionary father was often traveling, but her mother would not leave the children, "and when she had to go we went with her. This meant, too, that many visitors came to see her." Pearl S. Buck, *My Several Worlds* (New York, 1954; Pocketbook edition, 1956), p. 28.

33. "Are a Man and his Wife One?" *WWW* 9 (March 1894):59.

34. Beaver, *All Loves Excelling*, 55. Such fame extended to America through the publicity and promotion methods of the women's missionary societies and because the wives took a part in writing and speaking when on furlough.

35. *GAM* 1877:5-10. Appeals of financial support from the home missionary wives were plaintive and numerous, and those very appeals were used in attempting to get women interested in establishing a national women's organization solely devoted to aiding home mission work. See, e.g., "Inside View: A Missionary's Wife Speaks for Many Others—Self Denials," *HFR* 18 (June 1867):121-23; *PMR* 22 (May 1871):132-33. See also *HFR* 24 (January 1873):2-3.

36. After 1890, the emphasis in urban missions altered the "frontier missionary" role. Although ordained men played a much more important part in the work, women were needed also for service as social workers, teachers, nurses, Bible readers, and translators. "The United Presbyterian Church in Mission," 266-67.

37. "A New Departure in Home Missions," *Occident* (17 August 1898):13. Signed B. A. R. S.

38. "The United Presbyterian Church in Mission," 193. Applications were to be in writing, although "For a *female* this information may be given through a *third person.*"

39. *Rules and Recommendations for Foreign Missionaries and Candidates of The United Presbyterian Church* (Philadelphia, 1861):10.

40. *The Women's Missionary Magazine of the United Presbyterian Church* 3 (August 1889):144. Elizabeth McConnell, retired missionary to India, remembers that as late as her appointment in the 1930s, she received a letter from Mrs. H. C. Campbell, head of the UP Women's Board, saying that McConnell would be the last single woman she was sending out until the Men's Board sent out some men. Whether this was said in jest or not, it reflected the continuing trend of more women than men joining the mission professions. Interview, Elizabeth McConnell to Lois Boyd and R. Douglas Brackenridge, 4 March 1977.

41. Extract from "Manual" of the Board of Foreign Missions of the Presbyterian Church for Use of Missionary Candidates. Printed sheet, n.d.

42. D. L. Leonard, *Missionary Annals of the Nineteenth Century* (Cleveland and New York, 1899), p. 180. Mr. Leonard gave no reference to the source of his figures.

43. *The Presbyterian,* 27 October 1877:10.

44. As quoted in Irwin T. Hyatt, Jr., *Our Ordered Lives Confess: Three Nineteenth-Century American Missionaries in East Shantung* (Cambridge, Mass., & London, 1976). Thirty years later, in Mateer's province in China, there were seventy-nine Presbyterian and Southern Baptist women missionaries as compared to forty-six males.

45. Brown, *One Hundred Years,* 114. A list of "New Missionaries sent out to Foreign Field" from 1837-1942, broken down by "Men" and "Women," totaled 2,653 women, 1,779 men. RG 81-5-1.

46. *PMR* 30 (January 1879):18.

47. One particularly interesting account was in a taped oral history interview with a modern missionary, Lynda Carver, to Lois Boyd, Philadelphia, 4 March 1977. She said, "I had a good job. I had a car and was living at home and had friends and so on, but it just seemed there was something—I don't know whether I was searching for something or just what, but I just wasn't particularly satisfied with my life." Mission work had never entered her thinking nor had she had any contact with mission people until she met a female missionary from China who was visiting her church. With the assistance of this missionary, Carver received an appointment as principal of a girls' school in Baghdad and left the States in 1946.

48. Pearl Buck, child of Presbyterian missionaries in China who had lived through the Civil War, saw her parents' calm in time of danger "the result of their childhoods in a wartime." *My Several Worlds,* p. 39. The mother of a missionary felt that "missionary literature makes missionaries." *CHA* 20 (August 1896):145. Also, Lynda Carver to Lois Boyd, 4 March 1977.

49. "The Medical Missionary and Her Work," *WWW* 12 (October 1897):261-62 candidly described the qualifications of women doctors interested in missions.

50. Welter, "She Hath Done What She Could," 636.

51. *The Presbyterian,* 24 June 1876:14; 6 January 1872:8; *Congregational Quarterly,* 16 April 1874:279. A male Presbyterian supporter of women speaking nevertheless concluded that "the fears of some, lest the modern "woman's rights' spirit and insubordination should overwhelm the church, as the result of the admission of woman's right to speak, are entirely groundless. The class of women for whom we plead are not those who take the stump at political meetings." Harmon Loomis, "May A Woman Speak in a Promiscuous Religious Assembly?" *Congregational Quarterly* (April 1874):17.

52. Nevius, "The Home Life of Missionaries," 87.

53. *GAM* 1896:130-31.

54. *WWW* 8 (June 1893):171.

55. Hyatt, *Our Ordered Lives Confess,* 70.

56. "The United Church in Mission," 201, 211; *WWW* 35 (August 1920):186, and mimeographed report of the conference, p.12.

57. "Unmarried Female Missionaries," *HFR* 17 (April 1866):82-83; Woman's Part in Foreign Missions," *Missionary Review* 1 (May/June 1878):134-35; *A Concise History of Missions* by Edwin Munsell Bliss (New York, Chicago, Toronto, 1897), p. 253.

58. "Missionary Work of Single Women," *PMR* 23 (December 1872):381.

59. As quoted in Beaver, *All Loves Excelling,* 61-62.

60. "Unmarried Female Missionaries," 83.

61. "Missionary Work of Single Women," 381.

62. Extract of letter from Miss Agnes Morgan, Osaka, Japan, 10 January 1913, RG 81-5-2.

63. Extract of letter from Miss Emma Silver, Shanghai, China, 1 January 1913, RG 81-5-2.

64. Handwritten manual for single ladies, n.d., RG 31-43-12. See esp. p. 13.

65. Ibid., 16.

66. "The United Presbyterian Church in Mission," 197.

67. Ibid., 201-2.

68. "Roll of Missionaries." This approximate figure was obtained by these writers' count. The accuracy of the notation or whether or not marriages were systematically incorporated is not known.

69. "Missionaries of the Presbyterian Board of Foreign Missions, U.S.A., Resignations 1834-1839."

70. Margaret E. Hodge to Arthur J. Brown, 24 April 1922.

71. Brown, *The Foreign Missionary*, 120. A retired UP woman missionary said she went to India without even discussing salary, amenities, or pensions. She "went out for Christ" and was "not asking for very much and didn't get very much. . . . But we always had enough." Interview, Margaret Murdoch to Lois Boyd, 4 March 1977.

72. "Are a Man and His Wife One?," 59.

73. *WWW* 18 (September 1903):199.

74. *GAM* 1885:593.

75. Handwritten manuscript on the history of organized missionary work by Mary E. Wood (Mrs. Halsey L.), p. 7A-B; Beaver, *All Loves Excelling*, 130.

76. *Woman in Missions*, 98.

77. See statistics in the appendix of Brown's *One Hundred Years*.

78. "The Medical Missionary and her Work."

79. Ibid., 261.

80. Beaver, *All Loves Excelling*, 133. See *One Hundred Years* for descriptions of medical work in the various foreign mission stations.

81. "How Shall We Missionary Women Work?" *WWW* 14 (September 1899):241-42.

82. *Board of Missionary Preparation Committee Reports: The Preparation of Missionaries Appointed to Education Service*, rev. ed. (New York, 1929), pp. 40-52. Also in this book was an essay on the preparation of the wives of foreign missionaries by Mary Schauffler Platt, pp. 52-63. A separate publication on the qualifications and preparation of medical missionaries and nurses was published in 1918.

83. Bible women were indigenous women evangelists, taught and trained by the missionaries.

84. "The Woman Missionary" published by the WBFM, 1922; also available were "The Missionary Nurse" and "The Educational Missionary."

85. "The United Presbyterian Church in Mission," 212.

86. Brown, *One Hundred Years*, 104.

87. *Re-thinking Missions: A Laymen's Inquiry After One Hundred Years*, The Commission of Appraisal (New York and London, 1932), pp. 15-16.

88. Ibid., 264.
89. Ibid., 279-80.
90. Robert E. Speer, *"Re-thinking Missions"* Examined (New York, 1933), pp. 55-56.
91. "The United Church in Mission," 266-67.
92. *GAM* (UPUSA) 1967:392-93.
93. See chapters 2 and 3.
94. See chapter 8. One area this study has not entered is the history of minority women's service to the Presbyterian church. Many young women who generally had been trained in the early mission schools were working as teachers and missionaries. See, for example, the excellent article, with photographs, "Colored Women as Christian Workers," *HMM* 17 (April 1903):131-35, 135-37. See also Inez Moore Parker, *The Rise and Decline of the Program of Education for Black Presbyterians of the United Presbyterian Church, U.S.A. 1865-1970* (San Antonio, 1977). Black missionaries were appointed in the nineteenth and early twentieth centuries, primarily to serve in Africa and India, or in the southern states of America. Presbyterian archives in Philadelphia and Montreat both have information on various individuals. One book compiled by Hallie Paxson Winsborough, *Glorious Living: Informal Sketches of Seven Women Missionaries of the Presbyterian Church, U.S.* (Atlanta, 1937) supplies a profile of Althea Brown Edmiston, missionary to the Congo. The southern church appointed several Black women early in their mission endeavor. The influence of Black, Native American, Mexican American, Oriental women, and others deserves attention. Hopefully a history of the role of minorities in the development of American Presbyterianism will be forthcoming.

Chapter 11: Women in Education and Ministry

1. *Herald and Presbyter*, 4 March 1874:4. See also Robert W. Lynn and Elliott Wright, *The Big Little School* (New York, 1971), p. 13.
2. Anne M. Boylan, "The Role of Conversion in Nineteenth-Century Sunday Schools," *American Studies* (Spring 1979):36-37.
3. Ibid., 38-40.
4. Page Putnam Miller, "Women in the Vanguard of the Sunday School Movement," *Journal of Presbyterian History* 58 (Winter 1980):312.
5. Ibid., 312-13. For a more detailed analysis, see Page Putnam Miller, "The Evolving Role of Women in the Presbyterian Church in the Early Nineteenth Century."
6. *GAM*(USA) 1900:288.
7. *GAM*(USA) 1887:102.
8. *The Presbyterian Advance*, 8 May 1930:19.
9. Verdesi, *In But Still Out*, 116.
10. *Second Annual Report of the Board of Christian Education*, 1925, p. 19.
11. Verdesi, *In But Still Out*, 118.
12. *Catalogue of the Philadelphia School for Christian Workers 1926-27*, p. 1, and Verdesi, *In But Still Out*, 118.
13. Verdesi, *In But Still Out*, 118-19, and Dorothy Bass Fraser, "Women With a Past: A New Look at the History of Theological Education," *Theological Education* 8 (Summer 1972):213-24.

14. Verdesi, *In But Still Out*, 116-17, and Interview, Rachel Henderlite to Lois A. Boyd and R. Douglas Brackenridge, 24 January 1977.

15. *GAM*(USA) 1923, I: 220-21.

16. "General Council Minutes," 6 March 1929, p. 9.

17. Robert L. Sawyier to Harold McAfee Robinson, 1 October 1935. An overture from the Presbytery of Portland in 1934 to license Christian Educators was rejected by the Board of Christian Education because of the recent defeat of a similar overture. Harold McAfee Robinson to Lewis S. Mudge, 16 November 1934.

18. *GAM*(USA) 1937, I: 28.

19. Ibid., 1938, I: 71-75.

20. "Tentative Report of the Commissioned Church Workers," 1947. Typescript, p. 5, Record Group 11, PHS.

21. Alla Belle Cropp to William Barrow Pugh, 17 November 1943, and Hewison Pollock to William Barrow Pugh, 14 December 1943.

22. *GAM*(USA) 1946, II: 1119.

23. Harold E. Meyers, "The Presbyterian Ministry Today: A Study of Supply and Demand," Report to the Council on Theological Education, November, 1947, RG 122.

24. *GAM*(USA) 1956, II: 689-92.

25. *GAM*(USA) 1949, I: 116-17. Further modifications were made in the regulations. See, *GAM*(USA) 1955, I: 50.

26. *GAM*(UPUSA) 1959, I: 63-64.

27. *GAM*(UPUSA) 1963, I: 44 and 58.

28. *GAM*(UPUSA) 1976, I: 40-41.

29. *GAM*(UPUSA) 1974, II: 924-27.

30. Verdesi, *In But Still Out*, 145-47.

31. Ibid., 149.

32. Ibid., 149-50.

33. Ibid., 158.

34. *Presbyterian Life*, 27 October 1956:18.

35. Interview, Margaret Towner to Edward Wicklein, 20 January 1978.

36. Interview, Wilmina Rowland Smith, to Lois A. Boyd and R. Douglas Brackenridge, 5-6 May 1977.

37. *Presbyterian Life*, 19 April 1958:15-16.

38. Mary Ann Gehres, "Women's Place in the Pulpit," *Presbyterian Life*, 15 September 1959:12-14.

39. Elaine Homrighouse, "A Time for Equality," *Presbyterian Life*, 1 February 1971:18.

40. Gail A. Ricciuti, et al., "Women and the Pastorate," *Theology Today*, January 1978:425.

41. *Missionscope*, June 1981:3.

42. Elisa DesPortes Wheeler, "Women in Ministry: The Case of Anne Montgomery," Hartford Seminary Foundation Research Report, 1975, pp. 3-5.

43. Ibid., 9.

44. Ibid., 29.

45. Ibid., 35. See also, Willa Roghair, "My Search for a Pulpit," *Presbyterian Life*, 15 February 1971:18-20.

46. Penelope Morgan Colman, "Couples in Ministry," *A.D.*, November 1978:28-31.

47. *Concern*, January 1978:19.

48. *Presbyterian Panel*, November 1976, pp. 1-3.

49. Penelope Morgan Colman and Ann Dubois Conrad, *Women In Ministry* (New York, 1976), p. 13.

50. Constant H. Jacquet, Jr. *Women Ministers in 1977* (New York, National Council of Churches, 1978), p. 14.

51. *A.D.*, 22 September 1976:22.

52. Mary Faith Carson and James H. Price, "The Ordination of Women and the Function of the Bible," *Journal of Presbyterian History* 59 (Summer 1981):261.

53. Colman and Conrad, *Women in Ministry*, 4-5.

54. Ibid., 50-55.

55. *Missionscope*, June 1981, p. 3. For more statistical information, see *GAM* (UPUSA) 1976, I: 630, and 1977, I: 681-85.

56. *GAM*(UPUSA) 1976, I: 631. For a recent analysis of the status of clergywomen in the UPUSA Church, see Margaret Towner, "Reflections on a Silver Anniversary," *Monday Morning*, 5 October 1981:5-6.

Chapter 12: Ministers' Wives

1. J. H. Agnew, "Woman's Offices and Influence,"*Harper's New Monthly Magazine* 3 (October 1851), 657.

2. We are discussing the parish ministry in this chapter. Missionary wives, although subject to similar standards, lived and worked under different circumstances. They were discussed in chapter 10.

3. Printed sermons and articles in the popular church press provided characteristics, definitions, and biblical bases for a general cultural portrait of a "good wife." Some random examples include: "A Good Wife," *The Presbyterian*, 20 August 1835, unsigned. It included an extract from a sermon in the *National Preacher* of January 1835, which dealt with good wives' characteristics based on Proverbs; "Marriage Relations," *The Presbyterian*, 2 February 1839, by Rev. William Neill, using Eph. 21-23; articles in the following issues of *The Presbyterian*: 9 February 1839; 3 August 1839; 14 September 1839; 30 January 1841; 26 December 1846; 10 April 1847; 23 October 1847; 11 March 1848. The marital relationship seemed particularly popular in the 1830s and 1840s. Probably one of the most extensive and influential descriptions of marriage, especially as it related to ministers, was in Samuel Miller's *Letters on Clerical Manners and Habits Addressed to A Student in Theological Seminary, at Princeton, N.J.*, rev. ed. (Philadelphia, 1852), 319-32.

4. UPUSA women could not serve as deacons until 1922, elders until 1930, ministers until 1956. PCUS women could not serve as officers or ministers until 1965.

5. "The Minister's Wife, by a Minister's Wife," *Presbyterian Journal*, 14 September 1899:9.

6. James M. Hoppin, *Pastoral Theology* (New York & London, 1885; 1844), p. 189.

7. The following quotes are drawn from this letter, which was published as

"Hints to a Minister's Wife," Dr. John H. Rice to Mrs. Jane I. White, Feb. 13th, 1828, in *Presbyterian Magazine* 5 (1855):504-06. Reprinted in William Maxwell, *A Memoir of the Rev. John H. Rice, D.D.* (Philadelphia, 1835):334-37.

8. "The Minister's Wife," 9.

9. Catherine Lyman Adams, *Daily Duties Inculcated in a Series of Letters, addressed to the wife of a clergyman* (Boston & New York, 1835), p. 1. The copy consulted in Library of Congress.

10. *The Presbyterian*, 10 January 1846.

11. *Presbyterian Banner*, 11 June 1879:3. Reprinted from Philadelphia *Times*.

12. Eleanor F. Copeland, "James Hoge, Man of God," *Journal of Presbyterian Historical Society* 36 (June 1958):257.

13. "Ministers' Wives," *The United Presbyterian*, 28 April 1898:6.

14. "Confessions of a Minister's Wife," *Atlantic Monthly* 87 (1901):210.

15. [Martha Stone Hubbell], *The Shady Side; or, Life in a Country Parsonage, by a Pastor's Wife* (Boston, 1853), p. 71. A review of this book in *The Ladies Repository* 13 (June 1853), 284-85, indicated that the book was based on actual events in Congregational parishes.

16. Hubbell, *Shady Side*, 86.

17. See description of the local groups in Chapter 1.

18. "Ministers' Wives," 6.

19. Elizabeth Prentiss, *The Life and Letters of Elizabeth Prentiss* (New York, 1882), p. 238.

20. Journal of Mrs. James A. Laurie, Sr., 2 December 1865. Unpublished. Hereafter cited as Journal.

21. "Confessions," 210-11.

22. Journal, 1 December 1865.

23. "The Minister Wanted," *The Presbyterian*, 14 February 1900:10.

24. *Presbyterian Banner*, 11 June 1879:3.

25. Timothy L. Smith, "Protestant Schooling and American Nationality, 1800-1850," *Journal of American History* 53 (March 1967):692.

26. *The Banner of Peace*, 20 October 1848.

27. "The Journal of Rev. and Mrs. Lemuel Foster," *Journal of the Presbyterian Historical Society* 2, part 1 (September-December 1921):136; part 2 (March 1922):168. Ed. by Harry Thomas Stock.

28. Rev. George L. Walker, *Congregational Quarterly* 6 (October 1864):346.

29. *Presbyterian Banner*, 11 June 1879:3.

30. "The Minister's Wife," *The Southwestern Presbyterian*, 10 September 1903:7.

31. *Presbyterian Banner*, 4 September 1878.

32. Theodore L. Cuyler, *Recollections of a Long Life* (New York, 1902), p. 292. (Italics his.)

33. Prentiss, *The Life and Letters*, 230.

34. Elizabeth Preston Allan, *The Life and Letters of Margaret Junkin Preston* (Boston & New York, 1903):290–91.

35. Edith McBane, "Another Legacy," *Concern* (February 1977):20.

36. Ibid., 20-21.

37. "Confessions," 209.

38. Ibid., 210.

39. Ibid., 203ff.

40. *The Presbyterian*, 14 February 1900:10.

41. See chapter 11.

42. Anna Garlin Spencer, *Woman's Sphere in Social Culture*, 1912, as quoted in *The Quotable Woman*, I, 1800-1900, comp. and ed. Elaine Partnow (Los Angeles, 1980, 1977), 219.

43. "The Minister's Wife," *The Southwestern Presbyterian*, 10 September 1903:7.

44. Ibid.

45. *The Presbyterian Advance*, 2 June 1921:15. Reprinted from *Christian Century*.

46. The observations in this paragraph are based upon a general survey of denominational press articles, many of which are listed in these notes, and upon a survey of articles in the popular press. For example, *Time*, 25 April 1960 and 3 October 1960; *Look*, 1 May 1956, 99-103; *Good Housekeeping*, June 1959, 88-89, and others. See also Paul Boyer, "Minister's Wife, Widow, Reluctant Feminist, Catherine Marshall in the 1950s," in *Women in American Religion*, pp. 253-71 for a perceptive case study of one wife.

47. *The Continent* 50 (29 May 1919):673.

48. Ibid.

49. Ibid.

50. "A Minister's Musing Concerning a Minister's Wife," *The Presbyterian Banner*, 8 May 1919:18-19.

51. Eloise H. Davison, "The Minister's Wife," *The Presbyterian Tribune*, part 1, 11 April 1940:6-7; pt 2, 25 April 1940:10-11.

52. See chapter 14.

53. Dorothy Scott Ballard, "A Wife's Qualifications," *Monday Morning*, 8 July 1946:5-6. Under a paragraph on *Church Responsibilities*, the recommendation was to be a leader "only when necessary: be a guide always." (p. 5)

54. "Seminary Students' Wives," *Presbyterian Life*, 25 June 1955:31-32.

55. Ibid.

56. William Douglas, *Ministers' Wives* (New York, 1965). Specific quotations are on pages 12, 13, 14, 16, 66-72, 234.

57. A good summary of such comments is in "Let's Talk About the Minister's Wife!" *Concern*, September 1967:25-30. One can find similar in various other articles from *Presbyterian Life* and *Presbyterian Survey*. See for example: Irma Thaden, "Don't Marry a Minister—Unless. . . ." *Presbyterian Life*, 27 March 1948:14-15, 24, 30; "Pastors' Wives," *Presbyterian Life*, 3 September 1949:15; Margaret Johnson Hess, "Your Pastor's Wife: Directions for the Care and Use Of," *Presbyterian Life*, 19 July 1952: 15-16; Mrs. Walter R. Hobkirk, "Who Ministers to Ministers' Wives?" *Monday Morning*, 6 May 1963:7-9; Elizabeth D. Dodds, "Don't Pity Your Pastor's Wife," *Presbyterian Life*, 11 January 1958:16-18; Esther Eaton, "So You Married a Minister . . . where's Daddy?" *Presbyterian Survey*, August 1976:46.

58. "Memo To: The Modern Churchwoman; From: Doris Douds, Wilmington Delaware; Re: Minister's Wife," *Concern*, December 1963:22.

59. *GAM*(UPUSA) 1974:104, 97-98.

60. *Presbyterian Panel*: February, 1977 Questionnaire, June 1977, pp. i-iii.

61. Ibid., i.

62. Ibid., ii.

63. "Summary of Pastors' Wives Study Report," Research Division of the Support Agency, UPUSA, October 1977, Mimeographed.

64. See also Anne Taylor, "Ministers' Wives Hold Jobs for Money, Healthier Marriage," *The Presbyterian* (Publication of the Synod of the Sun and the Synod of Red River, PCUS), December 1974:2.

65. "Findings of the Follow-Up Study of Pastors' Wives," December 1978, Mimeographed.

66. Of course, the women taught in Sunday schools, but all indications are that their approach was traditional and related to the curricula. See also Lois A. Boyd, "Presbyterian Ministers' Wives—A Nineteenth-Century Portrait," *Journal of Presbyterian History*, 59 (Spring 1981):3-17.

Chapter 13: The Evolving Role of the Southern Presbyterian Woman

1. Mary D. Irvine and Alice L. Eastwood, *Pioneer Women of the Presbyterian Church, United States* (Richmond, 1923). This book not only gives a good summary of the general development of women's work in the PCUS but also tells its history by describing local organizations by synod. Hereafter referred to as *PW*.

2. *The Texas Presbyterian*, 21 November 1879.

3 James Woodrow, "Woman's Work and Influence," *The Southern Presbyterian*, 17 July 1879:2. See also "Female College Commencements," 5 August 1880:2.

4. Robert L. Dabney, "The Public Preaching of Women," *The Southern Presbyterian Review* 30 (October 1879):689-713.

5. Robert L. Dabney, "Let Women Keep Silence in the Church," *The Christian Observer*, 7 October 1891:1.

6. *North Carolina Presbyterian*, 7 November 1879:1.

7. *GAM(US)* 1880:186; *Minutes* of the Synod of Texas (US) 1879:136.

8. *The Presbyterian Journal*, 17 March 1887:169; *The St. Louis Presbyterian*, 29 April 1887:5.

9. *GAM(US)* 1891:260. Tenney was a leader in securing equal rights for blacks in east Texas. His liberal ideas of equality, however, did not include the right of women to speak or to teach in church.

10. Ibid.

11. Julius W. Walden, "Womanism in the South," *The Presbyterian Quarterly* 8 (April 1894):261-62.

12. W. McF. Alexander, "The Southern General Assembly 1897," *The Presbyterian Quarterly* 11 (July 1897):386-87.

13. Ibid., 386.

14. *GAM(US)* 1897:16.

15. "Report on the Sphere and Rights of Women in the Church," Minutes, Synod of Virginia, 1899:121-34. See also *The Presbyterian Journal*, 23 November 1899:15, and Ernest Trice Thompson, *Presbyterians in the South*, vol. III (Richmond, 1973):388. A writer in the *Presbyterian Journal*, 23 November 1899:15, arguing against any legislation that the report might engender, claimed, "Propriety, not legislation, shapes custom in our churches. . . . Sensible women, like sensible men, know their own spheres without legislation."

16. P. D. Stephenson, "The Woman Question," *The Presbyterian Quarterly* 22 (1889):206-28 and 685-724. The comments on southern life are on pp. 723-24.

17. R. A. Lapsley, "The Old Paths," *The Presbyterian Standard* 5 (March 1902):2.

18. *GAM*(US) 1910:67.

19. Lila Ripley Barnwell, "Women in the Church," *Presbyterian of the South,* 2 June 1926:3.

20. *The Presbyterian Standard*, 19 February 1902:11-13. See also J. R. Howerton, "May Women Speak in Public Religious Assemblies?" *The Southwestern Presbyterian,* 27 July 1893:4.

21. *GAM*(US) 1910:67.

22. *The Presbyterian Standard*, 31 May 1916:2-3.

23. *GAM*(US) 1915:30. An overture from West Hanover Presbytery asking the Assembly to "affirm its belief as to the teaching of the Scripture with regard to women speaking or praying in public or in mixed religious assemblies" was the immediate cause of the committee's appointment.

24. *GAM*(US) 1916:171-79.

25. See account in *Christian Observer*, 24 May 1916:23-24.

26. *GAM*(US) 1916:80.

27. *GAM*(US) 1916:76, 80A. See also Ernest Thompson, "The General Assembly of 1916 at Orlando," *The Union Seminary Review*, July 1916:293.

28. *Presbyterian Advance*, 1 June 1916:5.

29. Walter L. Lingle, "The Lexington Assembly 1925," *The Union Seminary Review*, July 1925:387.

30. As early as 1894, the UPNA Church permitted the secretary of the Women's Missionary Board to give an address to the General Assembly. *The United Presbyterian*, 7 June 1894:372. Katharine Bennett spoke to the USA Church in 1912.

31. *The Presbyterian Standard*, 15 August 1923:1; and *GAM*(US) 1923:68-70 and 1924:33.

32. *GAM*(US) 1925:67. The committee used *Alexander's Digest* (1922 edition) for its summary of previous actions relating to women. For some reason, the 1916 resolution was not included in that edition of the *Digest* and therefore was omitted in the 1925 action.

33. Ibid.

34. *The Presbyterian Survey*, September 1925:517.

35. *Presbyterian of the South*, 2 June 1926:3.

36. *Presbyterian of the South*, 14 April 1926:3-4.

37. *Presbyterian of the South*, 5 May 1926:7.

38. *Presbyterian of the South*, 26 May 1926:9.

39. D. Sprole Lyons, "The Pensacola Assembly," *The Union Seminary Review*, July 1926:318.

40. *GAM*(US) 1926:43-52.

41. *GAM*(US) 1955:27.

42. Ibid., 27, 52, and 89.

43. *GAM*(US) 1956:138-42.

44. Ibid.

45. *GAM*(US) 1957:38.

46. Mary Faith Carson and James J. H. Price, "The Ordination of Women and the Function of the Bible," *Journal of Presbyterian History* 59 (Summer 1981):253.

47. *Presbyterian Outlook*, 11 March 1963:4.

48. *GAM(US)* 1964:110.

49. Interview, Rachel Henderlite to R. Douglas Brackenridge and Lois A. Boyd, 24 January 1977.

50. *Presbyterian Survey*, May 1980:22-23. *Matrix*, September 1982:2. According to *Matrix*, women are reported as making up 56 percent of the active members of the PCUS currently.

51. *Presbyterian Survey*, May 1980:23.

52. *Presbyterian Standard*, 8 May 1912:6.

53. Ernest Trice Thompson, *Presbyterian Missions in the Southern United States* (Richmond, 1934), p. 97.

54. Thompson, *Presbyterians in the South* III:384-85.

55. *GAM(US)* 1875:37-38.

56. *GAM(US)* 1878:619.

57. *PW:47*.

58. *PW:46*.

59. *PW:46*.

60. Hallie Paxson Winsborough, *Yesteryears*, as told to Rosa Gibbins (Atlanta, 1937), p. 60. Hereafter cited as *YY*.

61. A particularly interesting note of irony related to the Wilmington Presbyterial is described in *Yesteryears*. A Mrs. Dubose of China was scheduled to speak to the Wilmington Presbyterial but she was staying at her brother's home, one of the ministers most opposed to women's unions. In respect to his opinions, she sent him to speak in her place while she fulfilled a speaking engagement at Davidson College, an all-male school. *YY:61*.

62. *PW:47*.

63. *PW:48*.

64. *YY:21-24*; *PW:48-51*.

65. Ibid and Janie W. McGaughey, *On the Crest of the Present* (Atlanta, 1961):14-15.

66. *YY:65-66*.

67. *YY:32*.

68. *YY:35*.

69. *Presbyterian Standard*, 10 April 1912:9.

70. *Presbyterian Standard*, 24 April 1912:6. Also, *YY:27-28*.

71. *YY:28*.

72. *YY:35*.

73. *YY:36*.

74. *YY:37*.

75. *YY:39-40*.

76. *YY:38*.

77. *YY:43*.

78. Thompson, *Presbyterians in the South* III:391.

79. *YY:44*.

80. *YY:43, 46*.

81. *YY*:45-46.
82. These include Janie McGaughey's *On the Crest of the Present*, Hallie Winsborough's *Yesteryears, Pioneer Women*, and the chapter on women in the church in volume III of Thompson's *Presbyterians in the South*.
83. *Concern*, February 1977:23-24. This essay was written by Evelyn Green, former executive secretary of the Board of Women's Work, PCUS. Also, *Presbyterian Survey*, May 1980:21-23.
84. *Reflection*, Summer 1978:16-18.
85. *YY*:66.
86. *YY*:67-68.
87. *YY*:54.
88. *Christian Century*, 17-24 June 1981:660.
89. Ibid.

Chapter 14: The Contemporary Scene

1. Brackenridge, *Eugene Carson Blake: Prophet With Portfolio*, 56-146. For another perspective of this period see John R. Fry, *The Trivialization of the United Presbyterian Church* (New York, 1975).
2. *Presbyterian Life*, 1 February 1971:17-18.
3. Interview, Wilmina Rowland Smith to R. D. Brackenridge and Lois A. Boyd, 5-6 May 1977, and *Presbyterian Life*, 15 June 1967:42.
4. *Social Progress*, July-August 1967:38-41.
5. *GAM*(UPUSA) 1969, I:314-42.
6. Ibid., 317.
7. Ibid., 319.
8. Ibid., 328-35.
9. Ibid., 337.
10. Ibid., 348.
11. Ibid., 349.
12. *General Assembly Daily News*, 19 May 1969:4.
13. *GAM*(UPUSA) 1970, I:433; *Concern*, September 1971:5; *A.D.*, July 1973:46; and *GAM*(UPUSA) 1976, I:635.
14. *Presbyterian Life*, 1 July 1971:10-12.
15. *Concern*, March 1975:7-8.
16. *GAM*(UPUSA) 1972, I:252-53.
17. "Women's Task Force Newsletter," 4 March 1972.
18. Ibid., April-May, 1972.
19. *GAM*(UPUSA) 1974, Ib:814.
20. *GAM*(UPUSA) 1979, I:349-50.
21. *GAM*(UPUSA) 1971, I:302.
22. *GAM*(UPUSA) 1975, I:602, and 1979, I:416-17.
23. *A.D.*, February 1978:58-59.
24. *GAM*(UPUSA) 1970, I:891.
25. Ibid., 1971, I:119.
26. Ibid., 1979, I:419-24.
27. Ibid., 1972, I:253-54.
28. Ibid., 1974, Ib:816-17. See also, *A.D.*, November 1973:19-23.

29. *Concern*, April 1975:7-16.
30. Ibid., January 1980:28-29.
31. For a good background of UPW during the 1970s, see Jane Parker Huber, "UPW Scrapbook," July 1979, Typescript.
32. *GAM*(UPUSA) 1964, I:81-82, and 1968, I:128-30.
33. *GAM*(UPUSA) 1970, I:398, and 1972, I:162.
34. Interview, Eleanor Gregory to R. D. Brackenridge and Lois A. Boyd, 1 August 1981.
35. *Presbyterian Life*, 15 June 1970:25-26.
36. *Concern*, September 1975, 8.
37. *GAM* (UPUSA) 1975, I:615.
38. Ibid., 1979, I:429.
39. Ibid., 1971, I:171, and 1974, Ib:826-27.
40. *Concern*, June-July 1980:33.
41. *GAM*(UPUSA) 1970, I: 434, and 1975, I:361.
42. Ibid., 1971, I:305. A complete list of overtures and other General Assembly actions concerning the status of women in church life has been compiled by R. Douglas Brackenridge and is placed in the Presbyterian Historical Society.
43. *Presbyterian Outlook*, 23 December 1974:1; *GAM* (UPUSA) 1975, I:220.
44. *GAM* (UPUSA) 1977, I:747. See also *A.D.*, July-August 1977:38.
45. *GAM* (UPUSA) 1978, I:64, and 1979, I:29-30. See also *The Presbyterian Layman*, June-July 1979:3.
46. *GAM* (UPUSA) 1980, I:47.
47. Ibid., 1979, I:91.
48. *The Presbyterian Layman*, April 1980:1.
49. *GAM* (UPUSA) 1971, I:313.
50. Ibid., 1970, I:890.
51. *A.D.*, August 1974:41.
52. *GAM* (UPUSA) 1975, I:528-39, and 1979, I:318-19.
53. Ibid., 1976, I:595-96.
54. Ibid., 1978, I:140.
55. Ibid., 1979, I:195-96.
56. Ibid., 1979, I:441.
57. Ibid., 1976, I:631, and *Missionscope*, June 1981:3.
58. *The Christian Century*, 29 April 1981:493-94.
59. *Presbyterian Life*, 15 June 1970:27.

BIBLIOGRAPHY

Archival Material

A large portion of the materials used to reconstruct this history comes from unpublished documents such as correspondence, memoranda, reports, journals, memoirs, diaries, studies, interviews, and sketches. Since the items used are so extensive and usually do not show up in a cataloging system under their descriptions, we have chosen to supply bibliographical information on the Record Groups in which the documents are found. Individual documents used are cited in the Notes with the Record Group number.

The extensive collection in the Presbyterian Historical Society is indexed and arranged according to subject matter. Since it is not always obvious that some Record Groups contain material relevant to the study of women in the American Presbyterian church, researchers should consult the Record Group Guide for more detailed information about specific material contained in each group.

Record Groups 51 and 105. Correspondence and papers of the Woman's Board of Home Missions 1879-1948 (51) and 1878-1948 (105).

Record Groups 81-99. Records from the Council of Ecumenical Missions and Relations (COEMAR) and its predecessors; material on Women's Board of Foreign Missions in early twentieth century; Women's Committee of Board of Foreign Missions; letters and papers relating to reorganization in 1920s and formation of Presbyterian Women's Organization (PWO) in the 1940s; extensive collections of correspondence between New York and mission stations throughout the world.

Record Group 101. Closed schools and stations administered by the Division of Schools and Hospitals of the Board of National Missions 1878-1966; correspondence of the Women's Executive Committee and the Woman's Board of Home Missions.

Record Group 104. Board of National Missions Division of Schools and Hospitals, Department of Educational and Medical Work; information about women's relationship to this work in the twentieth century.

Record Group 107. Unit of Sunday School Missions 1887-1960; letters of women serving as missionaries in various locations.

Record Group 111. Board of National Missions reports and historical materials 1887-1960; description of early organizations, correspondence, and committee minutes.

Record Group 121. Records of Eugene Carson Blake, Stated Clerk (1951-1966); ordination of women ministers; PWO correspondence; status of women in the church during 1950s.

Record Group 122. Records of William Barrow Pugh, Stated Clerk (1938-1950); organization of PWO and Commissioned Church Workers.

Record Group 123. Task Force on Women and related materials (1964-1973).

Record Group 125. Records of Lewis Seymour Mudge, Stated Clerk (1921-1938); reorganization and status of women in the 1920s; correspondence with

Speer, Bennett, and Hodge during 1920s and 1930s; papers relating to syllabus controversy of 1930s.

Other Materials. Other record groups contain information about specific women and events. Although the material is scattered, one can find useful information. See Record Groups 20, 26, 53, 58, 97, 116. Other materials presently unarranged include 48 boxes of Board of National Missions records, 20 boxes of COEMAR materials, and 240 boxes from the Board of Foreign Missions.

Although not listed as a Record Group, the Sheldon Jackson Collection is another source of information about women in the Presbyterian church, particularly in regard to their work for home missions. The Collection includes this pioneer home missionary's correspondence and other papers and scrapbooks from the period 1856-1908.

Microfilm records of the Ladies' Board of Missions and the Woman's Board of Foreign Missions, the Woman's Board of Missions of the Southwest, and various records of regional Boards hold reports and minutes. See also Official Denominational Records, Reports, and Publications.

Official Denominational Records, Reports, and Publications

Records

"Minutes of the Executive Committee of the National Council of Women's Organizations of the Presbyterian Church in the U.S.A.," 1942-1958.

Minutes of the General Assembly of the Cumberland Presbyterian Church, 1870-1980.

Minutes of the General Assembly of the Presbyterian Church in the United States, 1861-1980.

Minutes of the General Assembly of the Presbyterian Church in the United States of America, 1789-1957.

Minutes of the General Assembly of the United Presbyterian Church in North America, 1858-1957.

Minutes of the General Assembly of the United Presbyterian Church in the United States of America, 1958-1980.

"Minutes of the General Council of the Presbyterian Church in the United States of America," 1923-1957.

"Minutes of the Presbytery of Baltimore" (USA), 1896-97.

"Minutes of the Presbytery of Brooklyn" (USA), 12 January 1874 and 26 January 1874.

"Minutes of the Presbytery of Chemung" (USA), 1912-1919.

"Minutes of the Presbytery of Dallas" (USA), 1919.

"Minutes of the Presbytery of North River" (USA), 19 April 1836 and 20 September 1836.

"Minutes of the Presbytery of Wooster" (USA), 1920-1952.

"Minutes of the Presbytery of Zanesville" (USA), 1892-1893.

"Minutes of the Session of Third Presbyterian Church, Rochester, New York" (USA), 1953.

"Minutes of the Synod of New York" (USA), 1919-1920.

"Minutes of the Synod of Texas" (US), 1879.

"Minutes of the Synod of Virginia" (US), 1899.
"Minutes of Cedar Rapids Presbytery" (UPNA), 1943-1944.
"Minutes of Nolin Presbytery" (CP), 1889-1893.

Reports

Annual Report. The Board of Christian Education of the Presbyterian Church in
the United States of America, 1923-1957.
_____. The Board of Foreign Missions (USA), esp. 1923-1957.
_____. The Board of Home Missions (USA), esp. 1870-1922.
_____. The Board of National Missions (USA), 1923-1957.
_____. Ladies' Board, later Woman's Board of Foreign Missions (USA), 1872-
1923.
_____. Woman's Executive Committee of Home Missions, later Woman's
Board of Home Missions, 1879-1918, 1919-1924. See also Record Groups
51 and 105.
_____. Woman's North Pacific Presbyterian Board of Missions, 1887-1916.
_____. Woman's Presbyterian Board of Foreign Missions of the Southwest,
1883-1920.
Board of Missions' *Annual Report* (USA), 1834.
Board of Missionary Preparation Committee Reports. *The Preparation of
Missionaries Appointed to Education Service*. Revised edition. New York,
1929.
See also Record Groups

Publications

Bennett, Katharine, and Hodge, Margaret. *Causes of Unrest Among Women of the
Church*. Philadelphia, 1927.
Bennett, Mrs. F. S. [Katharine], comp. *How It Grew: The Story of Woman's
Organization in the Presbyterian Church in the United States of America*.
Narrative and Drama presented at the Quadrennial Meeting, Atlantic
City, New Jersey, May 15, 1942.
_____. *Status of Women in the Presbyterian Church in the U.S.A. With References
to Other Denominations*. Philadelphia, 1929.
*Case of the Rev. E. R. Craven against The Rev. I. M. See, in the Presbytery of Newark
and The Synod of New Jersey*. General Assembly Study Document.
Ecumenical Missionary Conference. 2 volumes. New York, 1900.
Henderson, Mrs. S.[amuel] M.[cFarren]. *Methods and Motives for Enlarged
Activity*. Paper read at meeting of Pittsburgh and Allegheny Council on
Woman's Foreign Missions, Pittsburgh, 1876.
Herron, Mrs. Annie R. "Foreign Missions and the Women's General Missionary
Society," Foreign Missionary Jubilee Convention of the United Pres-
byterian Church of North America. Pittsburgh, December 6-8, 1904, pp.
232-35, 237.
Manual, Board of Foreign Missions of the Presbyterian Church for the Use of
Missionary Candidates, n.d. (Nineteenth Century).
Missionaries of the Presbyterian Board of Foreign Missions, USA, Resignations
1834-1839.

Nevius, Helen S. C., "The Home Life of Missionaries," in *Counsel to New Missionaries: From Older Missionaries of the Presbyterian Church*. New York, 1905.

Policy Concerning Work Among Foreign Speaking People. Adopted March 9, 1920. Typescript.

Reports Relating to the Status of Women in the Church for the Information of the Delegates to the Conference of Women, St. Paul, Minnesota, May, 1929. Philadelphia, 1929.

Re-thinking Missions: A Laymen's Inquiry After One Hundred Years, by The Commission of Appraisal. New York and London, 1932.

Roll of Missionaries, 1832-1891. Presbyterian Church in the U.S.A. Handwritten ledger.

Roys, Mrs. Charles Kirkland. *The Missionary Wife: Her Preparation, Place and Program*. Prepared under the auspices of the Committee of Missionary Preparation, 1923.

Rules adopted by Board of Home Missions, 25 February 1890. Typescript.

Rules and Recommendations for Foreign Missionaries and Candidates of The United Presbyterian Church. Philadelphia, 1861.

Standing Rules of the Woman's Board of Home Missions of the PCUSA. Adopted June 1910. Pamphlet.

Woman's Board of Home Missions. Standing Rules. Revised edition. New York, 1913.

Woman's Board of Home Missions. Act of Incorporation and Bylaws, 1915.

Woman in Missions: Papers and Addresses presented at the Woman's Congress of Missions, October 2-4, 1893, in the Hall of Columbus, Chicago. Compiled by E. M. Wherry. New York, 1893.

Books

Adams, Catherine Lyman. *Daily Duties Inculcated in a Series of Letters, addressed to the wife of a clergyman*. Boston and New York, 1835.

Ahlstrom, Sydney. *A Religious History of the American People*. New Haven and London, 1972.

Allan, Elizabeth Preston. *The Life and Letters of Margaret Junkin Preston*. Boston and New York, 1903.

American Women in Church and Society 1607-1920: A Bibliography. Dorothy Bass, compiler. Auburn Studies in Education, Publication #2, 1973. Mimeographed, paper cover.

Armstrong, Maurice W.; Loetscher, Lefferts A.; and Anderson, Charles A. *The Presbyterian Enterprise: Sources of American Presbyterian History*. Philadelphia, 1956.

Banner, Lois W. *Elizabeth Cady Stanton, A Radical for Woman's Rights*. Boston & Toronto, 1980.

Barnes, Albert. *Notes Explanatory and Practical on the Epistles of Paul to the Corinthians*. London, 1837.

Barnhart, Marjorie. *Prisoners of Hope: A Search for Mission 1815-1822*. Philadelphia, 1980.

Barrus, Ben M.; Baughn, Milton L.; and Campbell, Thomas H. *A People Called Cumberland Presbyterians: A History of the Cumberland Church*. Memphis, 1972.

Beaver, R. Pierce. *All Loves Excelling: American Protestant Women in World Mission.* Grand Rapids, 1968.

Bennett, Katharine, et al. *The Emergence of Interdenominational Organizations Among Protestant Church Women.* New York, 1944.

Benson, Mary Sumner. *Woman in Eighteenth-Century America: A Study of Opinion and Social Usage.* New York, 1935; reissued Port Washington, 1966.

Bethune, Joanna Graham. *The Power of Faith, Exemplified in the Life and Writings of the Late Mrs. Isabella Graham.* New York & Boston, 1843.

Birney, Catherine H. *Sarah and Angelina Grimke: A Biography.* Boston, 1885.

Blake, Lillie Devereux. *Woman's Place Today.* New York, 1883.

Brown, Arthur Judson. *The Foreign Missionary: An Incarnation of the World Movement.* New York, Chicago, Toronto, London and Edinburgh, 1907.

_____. *One Hundred Years: A History of the Foreign Missionary Work of the Presbyterian Church in the U.S.A.* New York, 1936.

Calvin, John. *Commentaries on the First Book of Moses Called Genesis.* Volume 1. Grand Rapids, 1948.

_____. *The First Epistle of Paul the Apostle to the Corinthians.* Grand Rapids, 1960.

Carter, Paul A. *The Spiritual Crisis of the Gilded Age.* DeKalb, Illinois, 1971.

Chafe, William Henry, *The American Woman: Her Changing Social, Economic, and Political Roles, 1920-1970.* New York, 1972.

Clark, Elizabeth and Richardson, Herbert. *Women and Religion: A Feminist Sourcebook of Christian Thought.* New York, 1977.

Colman, Penelope Morgan, and Conrad, Ann Dubois. *Women in Ministry.* New York, 1976.

Cott, Nancy F. *The Bonds of Womanhood: "Woman's Sphere" in New England, 1780-1835.* New Haven, 1977.

Cross, Whitney. *The Burned Over District: The Social and Intellectual History of Enthusiastic Religion in Western New York, 1800-1850.* New York, 1965.

Culver, Elsie Thomas. *Women in the World of Religion.* New York, 1967.

Cuyler, Theodore L. *Recollections of a Long Life: An Autobiography.* New York, 1902.

Daggett, Mrs. L. H. *Historical Sketches of Woman's Missionary Societies in America and England.* Boston, 1879.

Deen, Edith. *Great Women of the Christian Faith.* New York, 1959.

Denton, Wallace. *The Minister's Wife as a Counselor.* Philadelphia, 1965.

_____. *The Role of the Minister's Wife.* Philadelphia, 1962.

Douglas, Ann. *The Feminization of American Culture.* New York, 1977.

Douglas, William. *Ministers' Wives.* New York, 1965.

Drury, Clifford Merrill, ed. *First White Women Over the Rockies: Diaries, Letters, and Biographical Sketches of the Six Women of the Oregon Mission Who Made the Overland Journey in 1836 and 1838.* 3 volumes. Glendale, 1963, 1966.

Drury, Clifford Merrill. *Presbyterian Panorama.* Philadelphia, 1972.

Eddy, Daniel Clarke. *Heroines of the Missionary Enterprise.* Boston, 1850.

Epstein, Barbara Leslie. *The Politics of Domesticity: Women, Evangelism, and Temperance in Nineteenth-Century America.* Middletown, Connecticut, 1981.

Finney, Charles Grandison. *Revivals of Religion.* 2d ed rev. and ed. William Henry Harding. London, 1913.

Fischer, Christiane, ed. *Let Them Speak for Themselves: Women in the American West, 1849-1900.* Hamden, 1977.

Flexner, Eleanor. *Century of Struggle.* The Woman's Rights Movement in the United States. Revised edition. Cambridge, Mass., 1975.

Fuller, Margaret. *Woman in the Nineteenth Century.* New York, 1855. Norton Library edition, 1971.

Gage, Matilda Joslyn. *Woman, Church and State: A Historical Account of the Status of Woman Through the Christian Ages: With Reminiscences of the Matriarchate.* New York, 1893.

Gibson, Elsie. *When the Minister is a Woman.* New York, 1970.

Gilman, Charlotte Perkins. *His Religion and Hers: A Study of the Faith of Our Fathers and the Work of our Mothers.* New York, 1923.

Good, James Isaac. *Women of the Reformed Church.* Sunday School Board of the Reformed Church in the U.S., 1901.

Gorham, Leta Belle. *Attitudes of the Missionary Wife.* Dallas, 1960.

Green, Ashbel. *A Historical Sketch, or A Compendious View of Domestic and Foreign Missions in the Presbyterian Church of the U.S.A.* Philadelphia, 1838.

Hanaford, Phebe Ann. *Daughters of America, or Women of the Century.* Augusta, Maine, 1882.

Harkness, Georgia. *John Calvin: The Man and His Ethics.* New York, 1958.

_____. *Women in Church and Society.* New York: Abingdon Press, 1972.

Harris, Walter. *Discourse Delivered to the Members of the Female Cent Society in Bedford, New Hampshire, July 18, 1814.* Printed pamphlet.

Hayes, Florence. *Daughters of Dorcas: The Story of the Work of Women for Home Missions since 1802.* New York, 1952.

Hays, George P. *May Women Speak?* Chicago, 1889.

Heckman, George C. *An Address on Woman's Work in the Church, before the Presbytery of New Albany.* Madison, Indiana, 1875.

Hoppin, James M. *Pastoral Theology.* New York and London, 1885; 1844.

Hudson, Winthrop. *Religion in America.* New York, 1965, 1973, 1981.

Humphreys, David. *An Historical Account of the Incorporated Society for the Propagation of the Gospels in Foreign Parts Containing their Foundation, Proceedings, and the Success of Their Missionaries in the British Colonies to the Year 1728.* London, 1730.

Irvine, Mary D. and Eastwood, Alice L. *Pioneer Women of the Presbyterian Church, United States.* Richmond, 1923.

Hyatt, Erwin T., Jr. *Our Ordered Lives Confess: Three Nineteenth-Century American Missionaries in East Shantung.* Cambridge, Massachusetts and London, 1976.

James, Janet Wilson, ed. *Women in American Religion.* Philadelphia, 1980.

Jamison, Wallace Newlin. The United Presbyterian Story. Pittsburgh, 1958.

Lawrence, Edward A. *Modern Missions in the East: Their Methods, Successes, and Limitations.* New York, 1895.

Lee, Rev. Luther. *Woman's Right to Preach the Gospel. A Sermon Preached at the Ordination of Rev. Antoinette L. Brown.* Syracuse, 1853.

Leonard, D. L. [Delavan Levant]. *Missionary Annals of the Nineteenth Century.* Cleveland and New York, 1899.

Loetscher, Lefferts A. *The Broadening Church.* Philadelphia, 1954.

Logan, J. B. *History of the Cumberland Church in Illinois, Containing Sketches of the First Ministers, Churches, Presbyteries and Synods; also a History of Missions, Publication and Education.* Alton, Illinois, 1878.

Lynn, Robert W. and Wright, Elliott. *The Big Little School.* New York, 1971.

McGaughey, Janie W. *On the Crest of the Present.* Atlanta, 1961.

Montgomery, Helen Barrett. *Western Women in Eastern Lands; an Outline Study of Fifty Years of Woman's Work in Foreign Missions.* New York, 1911.

Murphy, Thomas. *Pastoral Theology: The Pastor in the Various Duties of His Office.* Philadelphia, 1877.

Notable American Women, 1607-1950; a Biographical Dictionary. 3 volumes. Cambridge, Massachusetts, 1971.

Parker, Inez Moore. *The Rise and Decline of the Program of Education for Black Presbyterians of the United Presbyterian Church, U.S.A. 1865-1970.* San Antonio, 1977.

Parker, T. H. L. *John Calvin: A Biography.* Philadelphia, 1975.

Parker, Theodore. *Sermons on womanhood; part of a series on the spiritual development of the human race.* Boston, 1853.

Perrine, Matthew La Rue. *Women Have a Work to Do in the House of God. A Discourse delivered at the first Annual Meeting of the Female Missionary Society for the Poor of the City of New York and Its Vicinity, 12 May 1817.* Printed pamphlet.

Plaskow, Judith and Romero, Joan Arnold, eds. *Women and Religion.* Revised edition. Missoula, Montana, 1974.

Platt, Mary Schauffler. *The Home with the Open Door: An Agency in Missionary Service.* New York, 1920.

Pradervand, Marcel. *A Century of Service: A History of the World Alliance of Reformed Churches 1875-1975.* Grand Rapids, 1975.

Prentiss, Elizabeth. *The Life and Letters of Elizabeth Prentiss.* New York, 1882.

Proctor, Priscilla and Proctor, William. *Women in the Pulpit: Is God An Equal Opportunity Employer?* New York, 1976.

Prohl, Russell C. *Woman in the Church: A Restudy of Woman's Place in Building the Kingdom.* Grand Rapids, 1957.

Rogers, E. P. *The Obligations and Duties of the Female Sex to Christianity. An address, delivered at the annual examination of the Washington Female Seminary, Thursday, June 14th.* Augusta, 1849.

Ruether, Rosemary Radford and Keller, Rosemary Skinner, eds. *Women and Religion in America. Volume 1: The Nineteenth Century.* San Francisco, 1981.

Ruether, Rosemary and McLaughlin, Eleanor. *Women of Spirit: Female Leadership in the Jewish and Christian Traditions.* New York, 1979.

Russell, Letty. *Ferment of Freedom.* New York, 1972.

_____. *The Liberating Word.* New York, 1976.

Scott, Anne Firor. *The Southern Lady: From Pedestal to Politics 1830-1930.* Chicago, 1970.

Shannon, Margaret. *Just Because.* Corte Madera, California, 1977.

Shepherd, Fayette. *What May Women Do? An Inquiry.* New York, 1877.

Slaton, Sidney. *Mama Was a Preacher: The Life and Work of the Reverend Mrs. Ada Slaton Bonds.* Memphis, 1971.

Smith, Florence E. *The Missionary and Work for Women*. New York, n.d. Printed pamphlet.

Smith, H. Shelton, Handy, Robert T., and Loetscher, Lefferts A. *American Christianity: An Historical Interpretation with Representative Documents 1607-1820*. New York, 1960.

Speer, Robert E. *"Re-thinking Missions" Examined*. New York, 1933. Booklet. Contents originally appeared in "The Missionary Review of the World," January 1933.

Speer, William. *The Great Revival of 1800*. Philadelphia, 1872.

Stanton, Elizabeth Cady, Anthony, Susan B., and Gage, Matilda Joslyn, eds. *History of Woman Suffrage*. Volume 1, 1848-1861. New York, 1969, facsimile; originally published New York, 1881.

Stephenson, P. D. *The Woman Question*. Charlotte, North Carolina, 1897. Printed pamphlet.

Stewart, Robert Laird. *Sheldon Jackson: Pathfinder and Prospector of the Missionary Vanguard in the Rocky Mountains and Alaska*. New York, 1908.

Thompson, Elizabeth Osborn. *Woman's Board of Home Missions: A Short History*. New York, n.d. Booklet.

Thompson, Ernest Trice. *Presbyterian Missions in the Southern United States*. Richmond, 1934.

_____. *Presbytérians in the South*. 3 volumes. Richmond, 1963 and 1973.

Tyler, Alice Felt. *Freedom's Ferment: Phases of American Social History from the Colonial Period to the Outbreak of the Civil War*. New York, 1962. Originally published in 1944 by the University of Minnesota Press.

Tyler, Helen. *The WCTU Story: 1874-1949*. Evanston, 1949.

Verdesi, Elizabeth. *In But Still Out: Women in the Church*. Philadelphia, 1973, 1976.

Washburn, George. *Woman: Her Work in the Church*. New York, 1868.

Waterbury, J. B. *Christian Women as Workers in the Church of God*. Brooklyn, 1873.

Watt, Margaret Hewit. *The History of the Parson's Wife*. London, 1943.

Welch, Claude. *Protestant Thought in the Nineteenth Century. Volume 1, 1799-1870*. New Haven and London, 1972.

Welter, Barbara. *Dimity Convictions: The American Woman in the Nineteenth Century*. Athens, Ohio, 1976.

Wheeler, Elisa DesPortes. *Women in Ministry: The Case of Anne Montgomery*. A Research Report of the Hartford Seminary Foundation, 1975.

_____. *Clergy Couple: A Case Study of One Couple's Experience in Ministry*. A Research Report of the Hartford Seminary Foundation, 1976.

Winsborough, Hallie Paxson. *Glorious Living: Informal Sketches of Seven Woman Missionaries of the Presbyterian Church, U.S.* Atlanta, 1937.

_____ (Mrs. Hallie Paxson). *The Woman's Auxiliary, PCUS, A Brief History of its Background, Organization and Development*. Atlanta, 1927.

_____. *Yesteryears*. As told to Rosa Gibbins. Atlanta, 1937.

The Woman's Bible. 2 volumes. New York, 1895-1898.

Woosley, Louisa M. *Shall Women Preach? or The Question Answered*. Caneyville, Kentucky, 1891.

Wyker, Mossie A. *Church Women in the Scheme of Things*. St. Louis, 1953.

Periodicals

Denominational Periodicals Examined (articles used appear in Notes)

A. D. Magazine 1972-1980
The Christian Century 1920-1980
The Christian Observer 1840-1930
The Church at Home and Abroad 1887-1898
Concern 1959-1980
Congregational Quarterly 1864, 1874
The Continent 1870-1926
Home Missions Monthly 1886-1924
The Interior 1870-1926
The Herald and Presbyter 1869-1925
Monday Morning Magazine 1936-1980
Our Mission Field 1871-1885
Outreach 1947-1958
Panoplist and Missionary Magazine 1809-1818
The Presbyterian 1831-1948
The Presbyterian Advance 1910-1934
The Presbyterian Banner 1852-1937
The Presbyterian Deaconess Quarterly 1905-1910
The Presbyterian Guardian 1935-1979
The Presbyterian Journal 1875-1904
The Presbyterian Layman 1968-1980
Presbyterian Life Magazine 1948-1972
The Presbyterian Magazine 1921-1933
Presbyterian of the South 1909-1944
Presbyterian Outlook 1944-1980
The Presbyterian Quarterly 1887-1904
The Presbyterian Review 1880-1889
The Presbyterian Standard 1858-1931
The Presbyterian Survey 1911-1980
The St. Louis Presbyterian 1854-1860
The Southwestern Presbyterian 1869-1908
The United Presbyterian 1854-1958.
Woman's Work for Woman 1871-1885
Women and Missions 1924-1926
The Women's Missionary Magazine 1887-1958

Articles

Anonymous. "Confessions of a Minister's Wife." *Atlantic Monthly* 87 (1901): 202-12.

Banner, Lois W. "Religious Benevolence as Social Control: A Critique of an Interpretation." *The Journal of American History* 60 (June 1973): 23-41.

Black, William Henry. "The Cumberland Presbyterian Church: Its Origins, Distinctive Features, and the Grounds for Preserving its Denominational Integrity." *Journal of the Presbyterian Historical Society* 1 (December 1901): 189-204.

Boyd, Lois A. "Presbyterian Ministers' Wives—A Nineteenth-Century Portrait." *Journal of Presbyterian History* 59 (Spring 1981): 3-17.

_____. "Shall Women Speak? Confrontation in the Church 1876." *Journal of Presbyterian History* 56 (Winter 1978): 281-94.

_____ and Brackenridge, R. Douglas. "Rachel Henderlite: Women and Church Union." *Journal of Presbyterian History* 56 (Spring 1978): 10-35.

Brackenridge, R. Douglas. "Equality for Women? A Case Study in Presbyterian Polity 1926-1930." *Journal of Presbyterian History* 58 (Summer 1980): 142-65.

_____ and Lois A. Boyd. "United Presbyterian Policy on Women and the Church—an Historical Overview." *Journal of Presbyterian History* 59 (Fall 1981): 383-407.

Brackett, William O., Jr. "The Rise and Development of the New School in the Presbyterian Church in the U.S.A. to the Reunion of 1869." *Journal of the Presbyterian Historical Society* 13 (September 1929 and December 1929): 117–40; 145–74.

Carson, Mary Faith, and Price, James J. H. "The Ordination of Women and the Function of the Bible." *Journal of Presbyterian History* 59 (Summer 1981): 245-65.

Cole, Charles C., Jr. "The New Lebanon Convention." *New York History* 31 (1950): 385-97.

Copeland, Eleanor F. "James Hoge, Man of God." *Journal of Presbyterian Historical Society* 36 (June 1958): 67-88.

Eby, Louise S. "Can Women Make Their Way Into the Ministry?" *Christian Education* 9 (June 1929): 534-38.

Fraser, Dorothy Bass. "The Feminine Mystique, 1890-1910." *Union Seminary Quarterly Review* 4 (Summer 1972): 225-39.

_____. "Woman with Past: A New Look." *Theological Education* 8 (Summer 1972): 213-14.

Griffin, Clifford S. "Religious Benevolence as Social Control, 1815-1860." *Mississippi Valley Historical Review* 44 (December 1957): 423-44.

Gripe, Elizabeth Howell. "Women, Restructuring and Unrest in the 1920s." *Journal of Presbyterian History* 52 (Summer 1974): 188-99.

Hall, Mary L. "Historic Sketch of Spencer Presbyterian Church, Spencer, New York." *Journal of Presbyterian Historical Society* 9 (September 1918): 308-24.

Handy, Robert T. "The Protestant Quest for a Christian America." *Church History* 22 (1953): 9-20.

Hogeland, Ronald W. "Charles Hodge, The Association of Gentlemen and Ornamental Womanhood: A Study of Male Conventional Wisdom 1825-1855." *Journal of Presbyterian History* 53 (Fall 1975): 239-55.

Kerr, Hugh Thomson, Jr. "The Place and Status of Women in the Reformed Tradition." *The Presbyterian World* 22 (September 1953): 101-9.

Lingle, Walter L. "The Lexington Assembly 1925." *Union Seminary Review* (July 1925): 376-88.

Lyons, D. Sprose. "The Pensacola Assembly." *Union Seminary Review* (July 1926): 317-29.

Melder, Keith. "Ladies Bountiful: Organized Women's Benevolence in Early 19th-Century America." *New York History* 48 (July 1967): 231-45.

Miller, Page Putnam. "Women in the Vanguard of the Sunday School Movement." *Journal of Presbyterian History* 58 (Winter 1980): 311-25.

Moorhead, James M. "Social Reform and the Divided Conscience of Antebellum Protestantism." *Church History* 48 (December 1979): 416-30.

O'Hara, Mary. "Awakening the Silent Majority: The Changing Role of Women in My Church, Past, Present, Future." Study guide, Auburn Studies in Education, 1975.

Penfield, Janet Harbison. "Women in the Presbyterian Church—An Historical Overview." *Journal of Presbyterian History* 55 (Summer 1977): 107-24.

Perry, Everett L. and Perry, Margaret T. "New Church Development Policies— an Historical Overview." *Journal of Presbyterian History* 57 (Fall 1979):229-71.

Roy, Andrew T. "Overseas Mission Policies—an Historical Overview." *Journal of Presbyterian History* 57 (Fall 1979): 186-228.

Ryan, Mary P. "A Women's Awakening: Evangelical Religion and the Families of Utica, New York, 1800-1840." *American Quarterly* 30 (Winter 1978):617-23.

Schlesinger, Arthur M. "Biography of a Nation of Joiners."*American Historical Review* 50 (October 1944): 1-25.

Scott, Anne Firor. "What, Then, is the American: This New Woman? *Journal of American History* 65 (December 1978): 679-703.

Smith, Elwyn A. "The Forming of a Modern American Denomination." *Church History* 31 (March 1962): 74-99.

Smith, Timothy L. "Protestant Schooling and American Nationality, 1800-1850." *Journal of American History* 53 (March 1967): 679-95.

Smylie, James H. "Notable Presbyterian Women." *Journal of Presbyterian History* 52 (Summer 1974): 99-121.

_____. "*The Woman's Bible* and the Spiritual Crisis." *Soundings* 59 (Fall 1976): 305-28.

Stock, Harry Thomas, ed. "The Journal of Rev. and Mrs. Lemuel Foster." *Journal of the Presbyterian Historical Society* 2 (September-December 1921 and March 1922): 130-44; 156-70.

Thomas, John L. "Romantic Reform in America, 1815-1865." *American Quarterly* 17 (Winter 1965): 656-81.

Thompson, Ernest. "The General Assembly of 1916 at Orlando." *Union Seminary Review* (July 1916): 287-98.

Ulrich, Laurel Thatcher. "Virtuous Women Found: New England Ministerial Literature." *American Quarterly* 28 (Spring 1976): 20-40.

Way, Peggy Ann. "Women, the Church and Liberation: A Growth-Oriented Bibliography." *Dialogue* 10 (Spring 1971): 93-139.

Welter, Barbara. "The Cult of True Womanhood, 1820-1860." *American Quarterly* 18 (Summer 1966): 151-74.

_____. "She Hath Done What She Could: Protestant Women's Missionary Careers in Nineteenth-Century America." *American Quarterly* 30 (Winter 1978): 624-38.

Dissertations

Bailey, Alvin Keith. "The Strategy of Sheldon Jackson in Opening the West for National Missions 1860-1880." Ph.D. dissertation, Yale University, 1948.

Miller, Page Putnam. "The Evolving Role of Women in the Presbyterian Church in the Early Nineteenth Century." Ph.D. dissertation, University of Maryland, 1979.

Interviews

Alexander, Lilian Hurt to R. Douglas Brackenridge (RDB), 17 June 1981.
Blake, Eugene Carson to RDB and Lois A. Boyd (LAB), 23 February 1977.
Campbell, Barbara to RDB & LAB, 18 March 1977.
Carver, Lynda to LAB, 4 March 1977.
Cunningham, Sarah to RDB & LAB, 2 March 1977.
Gregory, Eleanor to RDB & LAB, 1 August 1981.
Henderlite, Rachel to RDB and LAB, 24 January 1977.
Hinn, Alfreda to RDB and LAB, 4 March 1977.
Kuhn, Margaret E. to LAB, 23 March 1978.
Lytle, Birdie to RDB and LAB, 2 October 1979.
Lytle, William P. to RDB and LAB, 5 May 1978.
McConnell, Elizabeth to LAB and RDB, 4 March 1977.
Meyers, Margaret Shannon to RDB and LAB, 18 June 1981.
Murdoch, Margaret to LAB, 4 March 1977.
Parker, Katherine McAfee to Barbara Roche, 1972-1973.
Smith, Wilmina Rowland to LAB and RDB, 5-6 May 1977.
Thompson, William P. to RDB and LAB, 11 March 1978.
Towner, Margaret to Edward Wicklein, 20 January 1978.
Verdesi, Elizabeth to RDB and LAB, 2 March 1977.

INDEX

PRESBYTERIAN HISTORICAL SOCIETY PUBLICATIONS

1. *The Presbyterian Enterprise* by M. W. Armstrong, L. A. Loetscher and C. A. Anderson (Westminster Press, 1956; Paperback reprinted for P.H.S., 1963 & 1976)

*2. *Presbyterian Ministry in American Culture* by E. A. Smith (Westminster Press, 1962)

3. *Journals of Charles Beatty, 1762-1769,* edited by Guy S. Klett (Pennsylvania State University Press, 1962)

*4. *Hoosier Zion, The Presbyterians in Early Indiana* by L. C. Rudolph (Yale University Press, 1963)

*5. *Presbyterianism in New York State* by Robert Hastings Nichols, edited and completed by James Hastings Nichols (Westminster Press, 1963)

6. *Scots Breed and Susquehanna* by Hubertis M. Cummings (University of Pittsburgh Press, 1964)

*7. *Presbyterians and the Negro—A History* by Andrew E. Murray (Presbyterian Historical Society, 1966)

*8. *A Bibliography of American Presbyterianism During the Colonial Period* by Leonard J. Trinterud (Presbyterian Historical Society, 1968)

9. *George Bourne and "The Book and Slavery Irreconcilable"* by John W. Christie and Dwight L. Dumond (Historical Society of Delaware and Presbyterian Historical Society, 1969)

10. *The Skyline Synod: Presbyterianism in Colorado and Utah* by Andrew E. Murray (Synod of Colorado/Utah, 1977)

*11. *The Life and Writings of Francis Makemie,* edited by Boyd S. Schlenther (Presbyterian Historical Society, 1971)

12. *A Younger Church in Search of Maturity: Presbyterianism in Brazil from 1910 to 1959* by Paul Pierson (Trinity University Press, 1974)

13. *Presbyterians in the South,* Vols. II and III, by Ernest Trice Thompson (John Knox Press, 1973)

*14. *Ecumenical Testimony* by John T. McNeill and James H. Nichols (Westminster Press, 1974)

15. *Iglesia Presbiteriana: A History of Presbyterians and Mexican Americans in the Southwest* by R. Douglas Brackenridge and Francisco O. Garcia-Treto (Trinity University Press, 1974)

16. *The Rise and Decline of Education for Black Presbyterians* by Inez M. Parker (Trinity Universty Press, 1977)

17. *Minutes of the Presbyterian Church in America, 1706-1788* edited by Guy S. Klett (Presbyterian Historical Society, 1977)

18. *Eugene Carson Blake, Prophet With Portfolio* by R. Douglas Brackenridge (Seabury Press, 1978)

19. *Prisoners of Hope: A Search for Mission 1815-1822* by Marjorie Barnhart (Presbyterian Historical Society, 1980)

20. *From Colonialism to World Community: The Church's Pilgrimage* by John Coventry Smith (Geneva Press, 1982)

21. *Facing the Enlightenment and Pietism: Archibald Alexander and the Founding of Princeton Theological Seminary* by Lefferts A. Loetscher (Greenwood Press, 1983)

22. *Presbyterian Women in America: Two Centuries of a Quest for Status* by Lois A. Boyd and R. Douglas Brackenridge (Greenwood Press, 1983)

* Out of print

About The Authors

LOIS A. BOYD is Director of Trinity University Press in San Antonio, Texas, and has also served as a press editor and freelance writer. She is the author of a booklength checklist, *Religion in Contemporary Fiction: Criticism from 1945 to the Present* and several articles in the *Journal of Presbyterian History.*

R. DOUGLAS BRACKENRIDGE is Professor of Religion at Trinity University and an ordained minister. He has written extensively on religious history including *Voice in the Wilderness, Iglesia Presbiteriana, Beckoning Frontiers,* and *Eugene Carson Blake,* as well as numerous articles.